A Century of Commitment

One Hundred Years of the Rabbinical Assembly

EDITED BY

Robert E. Fierstien

THE RABBINICAL ASSEMBLY
New York
2000

Copyright © 2000 by The Rabbinical Assembly

Library of Congress Cataloging-in-Publication Data
    Fierstien, Robert E.
    A Century of Commitment: One Hundred Years of the Rabbinical Assembly
    ISBN 0-916219-17-8
    Library of Congress Catalog Card Number: 00-130590

PRINTED IN THE UNITED STATES OF AMERICA
DESIGNED BY G&H SOHO, Inc.

THE PUBLICATION OF THIS BOOK WAS MADE POSSIBLE
THROUGH THE GENEROSITY
OF

The Scheinman Family Foundation

Isidore and Shirley Scheinman
Jeffrey and Michele Scheinman
Murray and Margaret Scheinman
David and Barbara Lansing

Highland Park, Illinois

IN MEMORY OF OUR PARENTS AND GRANDPARENTS

Charles and Ruth Scheinman
Abraham and Mildred Brickman
Rae Brickman

IN HONOR OF

Rabbi Vernon H. Kurtz

ABBREVIATIONS

AH = *The American Hebrew*

AJYB = *American Jewish Year Book*

CJ = *Conservative Judaism*

CJLS = Rabbinical Assembly Committee on Jewish Law and Standards

FP = Rabbi Fishel Pearlmutter Papers, at the Ratner Center for the Study of Conservative Judaism

GDC = Chancellor Gerson D. Cohen Papers, at the Ratner Center

JE = *The Jewish Exponent*

JTS = Jewish Theological Seminary

LCR = The RA of Israel Law Committee Responsa

PRA = *Proceedings of the Rabbinical Assembly*

WK = Rabbi Wolfe Kelman Papers, at the Ratner Center

Table of Contents

FOREWORD vii
  Seymour Essrog

INTRODUCTION. ix
  Robert E. Fierstien

A NOBLE BEGINNING: THE SEMINARY ALUMNI ASSOCIATION
  1901-1918. 1
  Robert E. Fierstien

EMERGING SELF-AWARENESS: THE RABBINICAL ASSEMBLY
  IN THE 1920S AND 1930S 21
  Herbert Rosenblum

NEW AND EXPANDING HORIZONS: THE RABBINICAL ASSEMBLY
  1940-1970. 64
  Pamela S. Nadell

COMPLETING A CENTURY: THE RABBINICAL ASSEMBLY
  SINCE 1970. 99
  Michael Panitz

THE EVOLVING CONSERVATIVE RABBI 171
  Stanley Rabinowitz

A BRIEF HISTORY OF THE RABBINICAL ASSEMBLY IN ISRAEL 199
  Theodore Steinberg

THE RABBINICAL ASSEMBLY IN LATIN AMERICA. 234
  Shmuel Szteinhendler

LOOKING TO THE FUTURE 244
  Joel H. Meyers

PRESIDENTS OF THE RABBINICAL ASSEMBLY 273

CONTRIBUTORS 275

INDEX 277

Foreword

The history of the Rabbinical Assembly is, to a remarkable degree, the history of the Jewish community in America during this past century. It is indeed significant that we publish this history during our centennial year when we take stock of our achievements and consider our impact upon twentieth-century Judaism.

When the Alumni Association of the Jewish Theological Seminary of America was organized, 15 graduates and former students formed the founding membership. By 1916 the membership rolls had grown to 61 rabbis, serving both in pulpits and in organizations. The natural constituency for these Conservative rabbis was the first generation born to Jewish immigrants from Eastern Europe. As a result of our colleagues' determined leadership, the dominant style and posture of American Jewish life was established. The observances of Shabbat and *kashrut* gained renewed respectability and appeal, as did the Hebrew language. The late Friday evening service helped maintain loyalty to the synagogue at a time when immigrants and their children faced ongoing pressures of adapting to a new country.

A commitment to Zionism and the courageous effort toward the restoration of a Jewish homeland in *Eretz Yisrael* became a cornerstone of our movement, which was always supportive and never harbored an anti-Zionist wing within its camp.

We have struggled with halakhah. In an effort to respond to contemporary needs, we have given women equal status with men in virtually every significant ritual area. The Rabbinical Assembly initiated the call to ordain women, and today we are proud to count 117 female colleagues in the Rabbinical Assembly.

It has been our challenge to reconcile halakhah with modern realities. We affirm the centrality of halakhah and cannot sit idly by and rel-

vii

egate it to a subsidiary position in the constellation of our Jewish value system. Our philosophy, as always, must be to insist that halakhah can be operative in a modern setting. Some of the areas in which the Conservative movement has used its understanding of halakhah to accommodate modern-day dilemmas include: the nuances of Shabbat observance; divorce proceedings and the problem of the *agunah;* and contemporary medical and bioethical concerns.

We have marched with the late Dr. Martin Luther King on behalf of civil rights and we have protested on behalf of Soviet Jewry and other Jewish communities under duress. Our commitment to issues of social justice has been strong and ever-present.

I strongly believe that the synagogue is the cornerstone of Jewish life in every community in which our brothers and sisters dwell. It is within the walls of the synagogue that we address the "troops" in our ongoing battle for Jewish identity, Jewish community, and Jewish survival. All of our 1454 colleagues are the "generals" who direct the activities that help keep the flames of Jewish passion, Jewish commitment, and Jewish loyalty bright and everlasting.

On a personal note, I am deeply honored and privileged to serve as the president of the Rabbinical Assembly at this milestone in our glorious history. It is indeed a mark of distinction for me to be listed among the most noted luminaries of our movement. חבלים נפלו-לי בנצימים

All of us appreciate the scholarship and dedication of our eminent editor, Rabbi Robert Fierstien, as well the quality of the articles contained in this rich and informative volume. We are indebted to our colleague and my distinguished successor Rabbi Vernon Kurtz, for obtaining the generous grant from his congregants, Isidore and Shirley Scheinman, which enabled us to publish this history.

ברוך· אתה ה׳ אלהינו מלך העולם.
שהחינו וקימנו והגיענו לזמן הזה.

Seymour Essrog
President
The Rabbinical Assembly

Introduction

In the spring of 1993, Rabbi Gerald Zelizer, then president of the Rabbinical Assembly, asked me to form and chair a committee to publish a volume in honor of the RA's forthcoming centennial. After receiving hearty words of encouragement from Seminary Chancellor Dr. Ismar Schorsch, I gladly accepted the assignment. The committee that was formed included Rabbis Gerald Zelizer, Joel Meyers, Jules Harlow, David G. Dalin, Abraham J. Karp, Saul Teplitz, and Professor Pamela S. Nadell. After meeting for several sessions, the committee decided that we should produce a history of the Rabbinical Assembly from its founding in 1901 to the present time. Keenly aware of the fact that no book-length study of the RA's history existed, we decided that a chronological approach was more desirable than a thematic one, although the latter idea had its merits as well.

This book, therefore, is a pioneering attempt to trace the growth and development of the Rabbinical Assembly. It is not an attempt to deal with the entire Conservative rabbinate; and hence, areas such as the Conservative rabbinate and scholarship, the role of Conservative rabbis in their local communities, and many other themes have not been treated. Much remains to be done; and I sincerely hope that this work will serve as an impetus for future study and research.

A few thank-yous are indeed in order. First, I would like to thank all the members of the original committee and all the authors of the various articles for their contributions. Professor Pamela Nadell and Rabbis Michael Panitz, Stanley Rabinowitz, Herbert Rosenblum, Theodore Steinberg, and Shmuel Szteinhendler have all been wonderful to work with, and I am deeply grateful to them. Special thanks go to Rabbis Guillermo Bronstein, Abraham Skorka, and Alberto (Baruj) Zeilicovich, for their contributions to Rabbi Szteinhendler's article on Latin America. I would like to thank Rabbi Jonathan Waxman for his many insightful suggestions, as well as for selecting the photographs that enhance this volume. Rabbis Gerald Zelizer, Alan Silverstein, David Lieber, and Seymour Essrog, in their capacities as presidents of the RA, were all extremely encouraging and made many helpful suggestions; and I would like to thank Rabbi Essrog for contributing the foreword. Rabbi Jonathan Schnitzer served as the liaison between the project and the RA Publications Committee and was unfailing in his support. Dr. Ismar Schorsch was most gracious with his words of encouragement, as were Rabbi Joseph Brodie and Dr. Jack Wertheimer of the Seminary. I am deeply appreciative to Rabbi Joel Meyers, who wrote the concluding chapter to this volume. Rabbi Meyers served on the original committee, always made time to discuss the project with me, and even took me on a treasure hunt to the Seminary's seventh floor, looking for archival materials on the history of the RA. Amy Gottlieb of the Rabbinical Assembly enriched this book immeasurably with her skills as an editor, and I am most grateful for her great kindness and encouragement. Thanks also to Tzipora Sofare and Rabbi David J. Fine who assisted in the editing and proofreading process, and much appreciation to Annette Muffs Botnick, RA Research Librarian, who carefully and skillfully prepared the index.

Special thanks are due to Mr. and Mrs. Isidore Scheinman for generously sponsoring the publication of this volume, a sign of their tremendous dedication to Jewish life; and thanks also go to Rabbi Vernon Kurtz, vice president of the RA, who facilitated this wonderful contribution.

The members of my congregation, Temple Beth Or, Brick, New Jersey, were extremely supportive during the years it took to complete this work, and I want to express my deep appreciation to them all, and especially to the very devoted presidents who served at that time, Samuel Lubliner and Beatrice Skydell.

Aharon, aharon haviv, thank you to my wife Ruth and my son Jeremy for their help in many ways that enabled me to prepare this book.

As the Rabbinical Assembly celebrates its centennial, it can look back with deep satisfaction upon its achievements, as well as those of its individual members. Creating the multi-faceted and dynamic movement known as Conservative Judaism, the RA has been far more than a professional organization. In areas ranging from liturgy to halakhic development, community leadership, and Zionist affairs, the RA has had an impact on every aspect of modern Jewish life. From a handful of rabbis in the United States and Canada, united by their devotion to their alma mater, the RA has grown to be a truly world-wide organization, an assembly of men and women devoted to imparting the message of Conservative Judaism. In the course of one hundred years, much has surely changed, but it is that ongoing devotion to teaching a meaningful and modernized, yet traditional approach to Judaism that provides the common thread which unites all the eras and individuals highlighted in this volume. *A Century of Commitment* is dedicated to all the members of the Seminary Alumni Association and the Rabbinical Assembly, past and present, whose good works made this book possible. As we shall see, its title is truly descriptive of reality.

Robert E. Fierstien
April 1999/*Nisan* 5759

A Noble Beginning

The Seminary Alumni Association
1901–1918

Robert E. Fierstien

When the Alumni Association of the Jewish Theological Seminary was founded in June 1901, the future must have seemed uncertain for the school's eleven graduates. The Reform movement continued to attract the modernized, Americanized elements of the Jewish community, the group that should have been most receptive to the message of the Seminary. The Reform rabbinate was well organized into the Central Conference of American Rabbis, and the temptation to join that organization would ultimately prove irresistible to some of the early graduates. The Orthodox, Eastern European element of the American Jewish community was growing daily, thanks to the immigrants who continued to pour into the port cities of the United States, but this group was deeply suspicious of the traditionalism of the Seminary and of its graduates. In addition, the Seminary itself was in deep trouble, both in terms of leadership and of finances, and there was no guarantee that it would continue to exist and give strength and support to those who had studied there.

Founding the Alumni Association may have been more of an act of hope than of confidence; but within less than two decades, the Seminary Alumni Association would transform itself into the Rabbinical Assembly, achieving national and, later, international prominence as the central organization for the entire Conservative rabbinate. How the Alumni Association grew and matured is the subject of this chapter; as we shall see, it truly was a noble beginning for an organization that would contribute so much to Jewish life in the twentieth century.

Paving the Way

As Abraham Karp has shown, by the 1860s and 1870s, the tripartite division of American Jewry was beginning to be identified by knowledgeable observers.[1] By 1886, the Orthodox scholar J.D. Eisenstein could clearly state, "Judaism in America is divided into three classes or parties: Orthodox, Conservative, and Radical."[2] In terms of the rabbinical leadership, on one side of the spectrum were the rabbis who openly embraced Reform, such as Kaufmann Kohler and the more moderate Isaac Mayer Wise, who had founded the Hebrew Union College in Cincinnati in 1875. On the opposite side of the spectrum were the Eastern European Orthodox rabbis, whose unbending traditionalism and use of the Yiddish language were suited to the immigrant congregations that they led.

In the middle of the rabbinical spectrum was a third group that Moshe Davis has called the "Historical School."[3] This group, in turn, consisted of a right and left wing. On the left were Rabbis Alexander Kohut of New York, Benjamin Szold of Baltimore, and Marcus Jastrow of Philadelphia, all of whom embraced some reforms, such as a revision of the traditional prayer book and mixed seating of men and women during services, but retained a traditional respect for observances such as the Sabbath and the dietary laws. On the right wing of the Historical School were leaders such as Sabato Morais of Philadelphia and Henry Pereira Mendes of New York, who strongly emphasized traditional practices, but were willing to include modest innovations, such as English readings and sermons, and who also emphasized formality and decorum during religious services. Together, these groups had founded the Jewish Theological Seminary in 1886, in an attempt to provide a traditional alternative to Isaac Mayer Wise's Hebrew Union College.[4]

The early Seminary was a first-rate academic institution that sought to provide its students with a thorough grounding in the entire breadth of the Jewish tradition. Not only did it emphasize Talmud and codes, like a traditional yeshiva, it also taught subjects such as homiletics, pedagogy, Jewish history, philosophy, midrash, and archaeology; and it placed a strong emphasis on biblical studies. Professors Alexander

Kohut and Joshua Joffe introduced the students to modern, critical methodology, helping to lay the intellectual foundation for the fledgling movement that would later be known as Conservative Judaism. In 1894, the Seminary held its first commencement, ordaining Joseph Herman Hertz as a rabbi; and by 1900, it had graduated eleven men.

Although the Seminary functioned well as an academic institution, it suffered from a number of problems that threatened its very existence by the turn of the century. First, Sabato Morais, the Seminary's guiding spirit and president of the faculty, had died in 1897, leaving the school bereft of leadership. In addition, the Seminary never garnered adequate financial support, and even ran at a deficit in some lean years. Rejected by many of the Eastern European immigrants who did not trust the traditionalism of the Americanized, English-speaking Seminary faculty, the school never built a solid congregational base.

Thus, for the Seminary alumni, the year 1901 must have been fraught with uncertainty. Although Seminary leaders were making a concentrated effort to bring Solomon Schechter from Cambridge to head the institution, this also must have been a source of uncertainty for the early graduates: would the revitalized Seminary still give recognition to its early products, or would it seek to make a break with its past, effectively disowning them? For rabbis at the turn of the century, life was tough enough without these added concerns, as they were generally underpaid, seldom achieved tenure of office, and were often subject to the dictatorial whims of congregational presidents and other officers.[5] For Seminary graduates in those years, the temptation to join the Reform movement's Central Conference of American Rabbis must have been very great, as the CCAR would have obviously opened up a wider field of placement opportunities and may have heightened their status as well.

When the CCAR scheduled its annual meeting for Philadelphia in July 1901, the early Seminary graduates were moved to take action, as the Conference's president, Dr. Joseph Silverman, clearly indicated his willingness to welcome them as members. In his report to the convention, Silverman emphasized this theme, declaring that "the Conference is a common meeting ground for the representatives of various shades of belief and practice. It is an arena for combating heresies and testing new theories. *It is the great clearing house of Jewish thought.*" In words that were sure to strike a responsive chord with the Seminary alumni, he continued, "We stand always upon historic Judaism, not breaking abruptly with the past—but rather building the bridge by which to make possible a transition from the past to the present and the future."[6] Thus, the annual meeting of the CCAR helped bring about the establishment of the Seminary Alumni Association in much the same way that the Pittsburgh Conference of Reform rabbis had served as the impetus for the founding of the Seminary, more than fifteen years before.

The First Decade: 1901–1909

On Monday afternoon, June 17, 1901, a small group of rabbis assembled at the North Eighth Street home of Rabbi Menahem M. Eichler, in Philadelphia, and founded the Alumni Association of the Jewish Theological Seminary. Precisely who attended that meeting cannot be determined, but the group probably consisted of those rabbis who attended the second meeting two weeks later: Rabbis Henry M. Speaker, B.C. Ehrenreich, Menahem M. Eichler, Julius H. Greenstone, and Leon H. Elmaleh of Philadelphia, Michael Fried of Pittsburgh, Morris Mandel of Washington, and Morris Waldman of New Brunswick, New Jersey.[7] The group resolved to establish two committees, one to communicate with the Seminary, and the other to draw up a constitution for the organization. In addition, the Association committed itself to five goals, which were published at length in *The Jewish Exponent* of Philadelphia:

> First. 'To help in the promotion of a higher spiritual and scholarly status in the seminary.'
> Second. 'To advance the prestige of the seminary among other theological institutions.'
> Third. 'To strive earnestly for the establishment of a stronger financial basis for the seminary.'
> Fourth. 'To develop the intellectual and spiritual standing of the members.'
> Fifth. 'To foster feelings of fellowship and mutual helpfulness among the members.'[8]

At the same meeting, officers were elected for the organization: president, Henry M. Speaker; vice president, David H. Wittenberg (Jacksonville, Florida); corresponding secretary, Menahem M. Eichler; recording secretary, Michael Fried; treasurer, Leon H. Elmaleh. In addition, an Executive Council was created, consisting of the officers, plus Bernard C. Ehrenreich, Julius H. Greenstone, Bernard M. Kaplan (Montreal), David Levine (Syracuse), Morris Mandel, and Morris Waldman.[9] The organizers of the association must have had a flair for publicity, for the local *Jewish Exponent* gave full coverage to the meeting, taking the opportunity to reflect upon its larger meaning for the American Jewish community:

> It may be the nucleus of what may some day be a very powerful organization, one with which Judaism, especially in this country, will be obliged to count on as a mighty factor. On the other hand, it may be the momentary enthusiasm of a few recently graduated young men whose tender sensibilities have been touched and moved by the unhappy condition of their Alma Mater . . . yet one who saw those earnest, and for the most part scholarly, young men seriously discussing the problems of the seminary's future could not help but be impressed by the practical methods and earnest manners which they displayed in meeting assembled. Time only can show just what the Seminary Alumni Association will be. If it does nothing else it will emphasize and encourage a high standard of scholarship in the pulpit.[10]

The reporter for *The Jewish Exponent* noted that the alumni took no stand on theological or halakhic matters at the first meeting, observing that:

> The question of religious policy seems to have been left out of consideration; at any rate it has found no place in the resolutions set forth in the association's preamble. This is very significant in so far as it seems that the graduates of the seminary, as a body, have considered the question of theological [*sic*] as non-germane to its raison d'etre.[11]

Apparently recognizing that the alumni differed from one another in their approach to the tradition, the anonymous writer noted that, "even if certain freedom in the religious policy of the individual members be countenanced—and in this broad-minded and far-sighted inaction lies the strength of the newly-founded organization—the tendency of the whole body will undoubtedly be conservative in its influence."

A week later, the paper devoted an editorial to the Alumni Association, declaring that, "it will, if it prove permanent, establish a school, a school of Jewish thought, which without official declarations will nevertheless have a great and permanent influence for good."[12] These were high expectations, indeed, for an alumni association of a school that numbered only eleven graduates; but time would show just how prescient the words of *The Jewish Exponent* truly were.

Two weeks after the founding meeting, another meeting was held on July 3, at the Philadelphia home of the new president, Henry M. Speaker. Speaker (1867–1935) was a non-pulpit rabbi who served as the founding Principal of Gratz College.[13] At this second meeting, which was deliberately timed to coincide with the CCAR convention, the eight alumni present were addressed by Phineas Israeli, a Seminary student, who spoke about the current situation of their alma mater.[14] In addition, a constitution for the organization was adopted, but no copy seems to have survived.

After this well-publicized beginning, the Alumni Association appears to have settled into a pattern of inactivity that would last for almost a decade, until it became actively involved in the planning of the United Synagogue. Annual meetings were held each June or July, and, starting in 1904, were held at the Seminary so as to coincide with the JTS graduation; but for the rest of the year, the association was largely dormant. Membership was not confined to Seminary graduates alone, for anyone who had studied at the school was eligible. Thus, B.C. Ehrenreich, who had yet to receive Seminary ordination, was an active member, as was David Liknaitz, who never completed his Seminary studies.

As we have noted, the Reform CCAR was always an attraction to early Seminary graduates; and in 1903, the Alumni Association passed a resolution declaring that "it is inconsistent with the principles and aims of the Alumni Association of the Jewish Theological Seminary to approve of the affiliation of any of its members with any existing national conference."[15] Nevertheless, the 1905 CCAR Year Book lists Aaron P. Drucker (JTS, 1902) as a member;[16] and, by 1909, Alter Abelson (1903), B.C. Ehrenreich (1905), and Bernard M. Kaplan (1898) had all joined the Conference, as had David Liknaitz.[17] Speaking about these defections in his address at the founding meeting of the United Synagogue in 1913, Solomon Schechter declared:

> That some students, trained in the Seminary, have accepted Reform positions, while it is to be regretted, has happened both before and after the reorganization. But let no man who knows the conditions of most of our strictly Orthodox synagogues, the poverty prevailing there, the starvation wages which they grant to their rabbis, the constant strife within the congregation itself, the first victim of which is the rabbi, the ungenerous treatment of the young men on the part of the congregation—no man who knows these conditions will judge uncharitably those men who have not proved themselves strong enough to become martyrs of the cause. It is with the Orthodox they

broke, not with Orthodoxy. I do not justify them, I only contend that if they sinned, they were also sinned against. The majority have remained loyal at a sacrifice impossible to be appreciated . . .[18]

With the arrival of Solomon Schechter in 1902, the Seminary's enrollment expanded; and by 1909, the Alumni Association had 45 members. Honorary membership was also granted to local New York rabbis, members of the Seminary faculty, as well as to traditional Reform rabbi Bernhard Felsenthal of Chicago, and the prominent community leader, Louis M. Dembitz of Louisville.[19]

Schechter's arrival coincided with the 1902 reorganization of the Seminary; and, at the 1903 Alumni Association meeting, held in Philadelphia, Leon H. Elmaleh led a discussion on "The Alumni and the Seminary." As *The Jewish Exponent* reported it, Elmaleh "made a strong plea in advocacy of loyalty to the reorganized seminary on the part of the graduates of the older seminary . . . The relation of the old students toward the new seminary, and of the new seminary toward the old students, were also discussed by the speaker and others present."[20] As previously noted, Schechter's arrival was clearly a cause for concern to the early graduates, and the Alumni Association helped to give them a voice and served as a common meeting-ground for alumni of both eras. In 1904, Henry M. Speaker was replaced as president by Menahem M. Eichler, another graduate of the early Seminary; and it was not until 1907 when a graduate from the reorganized Seminary, Charles Isaiah Hoffman, took over the position for the first time.[21]

In addition to promoting fellowship, the annual meetings served as an intellectual forum for the alumni, with a wide range of topics discussed at each session. Thus, in 1903, the convention turned its attention to the Kishinev pogroms in Russia, and a resolution was passed commending President Theodore Roosevelt for his protests to the Russian government.[22] Seminary faculty were always welcome guests at the meetings. Thus, in 1905, Solomon Schechter spoke on Jewish theology, and Cyrus Adler and Joshua Joffe addressed the group as well.[23] The following year, Louis Ginzberg delivered a paper on "The Importance of the Halakah in the Study of Jewish Theology";[24] and in 1907, Schechter again spoke, presenting a paper on "The Second Book of Esdras."[25] Following in the footsteps of Schechter, who was a committed Zionist, Jacob Kohn addressed the 1908 meeting, speaking on "Zionism in the Pulpit";[26] and the following year, Mordecai Kaplan spoke on "Nationalism as a Religious Dogma."[27]

Jewish education was a popular topic for discussion, and just about every annual meeting featured a paper on ways of improving the religious school. Thus, in 1903, B.C. Ehrenreich spoke on "The Sunday School," placing particular emphasis on the teaching of the Hebrew language as part of the religious school curriculum.[28] Similarly, in 1907, Julius Greenstone delivered a paper on "The Purpose and Scope of the Jewish Religious School";[29] and in 1908, Rudolph Coffee spoke on "Religious Text-books."[30]

Obviously, the annual meetings of the Alumni Association required a great deal of planning, and the Executive Committee went out of its way to ensure a good attendance. The Charles I. Hoffman papers at the Seminary Library contain a remarkable printed announcement for the June 1908 meeting. After presenting the program for the meeting, the announcement continues with the following exhortation:

> It is requested that you make every effort to attend the reunion of the Alumni. The occasion warrants and calls for your presence. These meetings renew ties of friendship and form new ones, they further reciprocal co-operation in our undertakings, they strengthen the Seminary spirit, and breathe inspiration and unity into our work. The Seminary has a message for her sons and calls upon us at this time to assemble and receive it.

Most of the annual meetings featured a banquet, often given in honor of the new Seminary graduates; and the 1908 circular requests that anyone wishing to attend this function should send a check for two dollars to the treasurer, Leon H. Elmaleh.[31]

Starting in 1904, the Alumni Association voted to establish a prize to be awarded at the Seminary graduation, in recognition of an essay written on a topic selected by the faculty. In 1904, the prize was twenty dollars, and was awarded to Abram Dobrzynski for an essay on "Techinot in Jewish Literature."[32] The prize was not awarded again until 1908, when it was raised to one hundred dollars, quite a substantial sum in those days. That year, the essay was on the "Halacha of the Book of Jubilees, Compared with the Corresponding Rabbinic Halacha," and it was split between Abel Hirsch and Elias M. Rabinowitz.[33] Subsequent topics, among others, included, "The Rise of Jewish Learning in Spain," "*Masseketh Derekh Eretz Zuta*: Translation and Introduction Based on Published Texts," "The Procedure of the Courts in Civil and Criminal Cases," and "The Duties and Rights of the Minor in His Relation to the Family and the Community." Among the winners were a number of graduates who would go on to successful careers in the scholarly world: Morris Levine, Jacob S. Minkin, Abraham Neuman, and Meyer Waxman. The money for the prize generally came from the Association's dues, but in 1909, a special assessment was levied to provide the necessary funds.[34]

From the start, the Alumni Association displayed a keen sense of social responsibility, feeling itself connected not only to the Seminary but to the entire Jewish community. In 1909, it devoted part of the annual meeting to the problems of small Jewish communities that did not have rabbinic leadership, and offered to provide literature to help them.[35] That same year, a non-pulpit rabbi, Morris Waldman of the United Hebrew Charities, spoke to his colleagues on "the necessity of the Rabbi giving more of his time to charitable institutions."[36] Apparently, some of the alumni themselves were having financial problems, for the Association voted to establish a Relief Fund to aid those in need.

Despite its social concern, however, the primary function of the Alumni Association in its early years was supporting the Seminary, particularly through the fundraising work that the graduates did in their own congregations. Apparently they were successful, for in his 1905 address at the JTS commencement, Cyrus Adler noted that "the Alumni of the Seminary are showing a considerable interest in the welfare of their Alma Mater." Adler particularly praised Rabbi Charles Kauvar of Denver for keeping his congregation loyal to the Seminary.[37]

Throughout its first decade, the Alumni Association struggled valiantly to help the Seminary graduates maintain a sense of identity, as well as of unity. Being a Conservative rabbi in the early years of the twentieth century was, indeed, a difficult task. As Jack Wertheimer has noted, "from our vantage point some eighty years later it requires considerable imagination to reconstruct the daunting task faced by early graduates of 'Schechter's Seminary' as they ventured into congregational life. How did they define their goals when there were virtually no other Conservative congregations and no United Synagogue to offer models and legitimation?"[38] The early graduates were not monolithic in their approach to the Jewish tradition: as today, there were definitely a left, right, and center to the Association; yet all of them were involved in trying to create a meaningful, modernized, and decorous approach to synagogue life that often went against the grain of their congregants, many of whom had been raised in the world of Eastern European Orthodoxy. Thus, Louis Egelson ran afoul of the board of Adas Israel in Washington, DC, when he delivered a 1910 High Holiday sermon entitled, "Some Weeds of Orthodox Judaism," in which he condemned the traditional practice of selling *aliyot* on the holidays. The congregation, in a close vote, rejected his Schechter-inspired approach to Jewish life, and Egelson's contract was not renewed.[39] As Herbert Rosenblum has noted, this was "an ordinary, typical and, therefore (from the Seminary's standpoint), troubling example of the problems faced by Seminary-trained Rabbis that ventured into moderately Orthodox congregations."[40]

The Founding of the United Synagogue and the Second Decade of the Alumni Association, 1909–1918

As time went on, it became increasingly clear to almost everyone that a new organization was needed, something that would develop backing and support for the approach of the Seminary. After all, the Union of American Hebrew Congregations had preceded both the Hebrew Union College and the CCAR; but in the fledgling Conservative movement, there was no union of congregations whatsoever, a detriment to both the Seminary and the Alumni Association. The story of the founding of the United Synagogue has been fully told by Herbert Rosenblum,[41] and in this chapter we shall confine ourselves largely to the role played by the Alumni Association as a group.

In the fall of 1909, Rabbi Herman Rubenovitz of Louisville wrote to the president of the Alumni Association, Charles Isaiah Hoffman, proposing the establishment of a Conservative Union.[42] Rubenovitz also contacted other Conservative leaders, such as Solomon Schechter and Judah Magnes, with regard to his plan. Shortly thereafter, Hoffman wrote back to say that the Executive Committee of the Alumni Association had discussed Rubenovitz's proposal and had resolved to send out a circular to ascertain the feelings of the membership. In addition, Hoffman invited Rubenovitz to deliver a paper at the 1910 annual meeting of the alumni, formally proposing the new organization.

From this point on, Rubenovitz and Hoffman worked closely together to found the Conservative Union, despite the fact that Rubenovitz's religious views were far to the left of Hoffman's; and they were soon joined by another Seminary alumnus, Jacob Kohn. For the sake of unity, these men were not eager to set out a theological or halakhic platform for the Union, but they were opposed in this by both Adler and Magnes. Adler, former chairman of the Seminary's governing board, was fearful of starting a third party in American Jewish life, and he was reluctant to encourage any break with the Orthodox. As early as August 1909, Adler had written to Schechter, declaring, "I shrink from further division";[43] and all through his life, even as the subsequent head of the Seminary, this reluctance to acknowledge the reality of Conservative Judaism would characterize his actions. Magnes, on the other hand, was a prominent Conservative rabbi, although not a graduate of the Seminary; and he wanted precisely what Adler dreaded—the formal establishment of a new movement in Jewish life, with a well-defined ideology. Nevertheless, the Alumni Association leaders rejected both of these extremes, as Seminary graduates were found in both modern Orthodox and moderate Reform congregations. As Herbert Rosenblum has noted, the alumni "were certainly opposed to extreme Reform and they were repelled by ultra-Orthodoxy, but everything in between was negotiable in terms of the new union, so why specify boundaries too rigidly?"[44]

At the 1910 annual meeting, held on June 21, Rubenovitz delivered a paper entitled, "A Union of Conservative Forces in America";[45] and afterwards, the Association enacted the following resolution:

Whereas the purposes of the Jewish Theological Seminary of America as detailed in the original act of incorporation are 'The preservation in America of the knowledge and practice of historical Judaism, as contained in the Laws of Moses, and expounded by the Prophets and Sages of Israel in Biblical and Talmudical writings,' and

Whereas these are the purposes to which other institutions of learning are devoted, and

Whereas a union of all the conservative forces in Judaism is greatly to be desired;

Resolved that to further promote these purposes a committee of the Alumni of the Seminary be appointed to invite representatives of the Faculty and Trustees of the Seminary and of the Faculty and Trustees of the Gratz College and the Dropsie College, to meet prior to December 1910, for the formulation of a plan to this end.[46]

Subsequently, Rubenovitz sent a letter to the three institutions, inviting them to a meeting at Gratz College on November 27, 1910. The letter was signed by Rubenovitz as chairman of the "Committee of Conservative Union," and also by Charles I. Hoffman, as president of the Alumni Association. Other members of the committee, as appointed by Hoffman, were Jacob Kohn, Marvin Nathan, Louis Egelson, and Benjamin Lichter; and the group met with Hoffman in Newark to formulate plans for the proposed union.[47]

Although he leaned toward the left in religious matters, Rubenovitz was careful to assure the more traditional members of the Association that the new organization would not be radical in any way. Thus, in

November 1910, Rubenovitz wrote to Hoffman to assure him that the Conservative Union would be based on the same principles that induced Sabato Morais and the other founders of JTS to oppose Isaac Mayer Wise and the Hebrew Union College: "the proposed Union is to be a direct outgrowth of the movement started at that time."[48]

As scheduled, the November 27 meeting took place at Gratz College: Rubenovitz was elected chairman, and Jacob Kohn was elected secretary. Professor Louis Ginzberg represented the Seminary, Cyrus Adler represented Dropsie College, and Henry M. Speaker and Ephraim Lederer represented Gratz College. Nevertheless, at the suggestion of Adler, Gratz and Dropsie Colleges did not formally participate in the business of the meeting, inasmuch as they were not religious institutions and did not want to take a stand on religious issues.[49] Again following Adler's traditionalist position, the representatives at the meeting avoided using the term Conservative, and merely voted to found an organization based on the traditional principles enunciated in the charter of the early Seminary.[50]

Rubenovitz, Hoffman, and Kohn worked well together in planning the new Union, but one source of disagreement was the extent to which the Alumni should control the organization, and how much power the synagogues and lay leaders were to have. Rubenovitz wanted to broaden the Committee on Conservative Union to include prominent lay leaders, but Hoffman would not go along with these plans. On March 9, 1911, Hoffman wrote to Rubenovitz, "Neither Kohn nor I see why the Alumni should lose its hold upon the movement, and its future development may be properly considered as a continuation of our efforts."[51] Five days later, Rubenovitz wrote back, "I feel convinced that the Conservative Union ought not to come before the world as an offspring of our alumni or any other one institution or organization." Nevertheless, he continued, "I hope that we shall have all our alumni, for it is from the alumni that the Union will derive its strength . . . Nor do I see any cause for apprehension, with such a committee, at the helm, that the Alumni will lose its hold upon the movement."[52] When the committee met on March 29, 1911, it now included Mordecai Kaplan and Louis Ginzberg, but no lay leaders were present.[53]

At the 1911 annual meeting, held not at the Seminary but at the summer resort of Arverne, New York (near Far Rockaway), Alumni Association president Charles I. Hoffman spoke eloquently of the need for a Conservative Union: "We ourselves and the institutions whence we proceed will not have performed its [sic] full mission until it have effected a great union of Jews in America, for the clear conception and faithful performance of a true and noble Jewish life."[54] After a thor-

ough discussion, Solomon Schechter was appointed to chair a committee "to constitute themselves such an organization"; it was to consist of
eleven members, five of whom were to be from New York.[55]

One of the high points of the 1911 convention was a paper delivered
by Herman Rubenovitz on "The Continuity of Jewish Tradition."[56] The
paper is crucial to the history of the Conservative movement, for it
marks probably the first time that any Seminary-trained ideologue had
publicly sought to define the difference between Conservative and
Orthodox Judaism. Six months before, Rubenovitz had been encouraged
by Seminary Professor Israel Friedlaender, who nevertheless had warned
that "the difficulty in regard to formulating the definite theological credo
of Conservative Judaism in distinction from Orthodox Judaism, is
greatly enhanced by the fact that no such formulation has, to my knowledge, been attempted before."[57] As we have seen, up to that time, the
tendency was for Seminary leaders and alumni to gloss over the differences between Orthodoxy and Conservative Judaism, to minimize them
or pretend that they did not exist. Such, of course, was the philosophy of
Cyrus Adler and, to a lesser degree, even Solomon Schechter. Now, for
the first time, Rubenovitz was laying them out in the open, in a highly
public way. After speaking about "the law of progress, the law of cease-
less growth and change," Rubenovitz went on to state that "[W]hen
Conservative Jews speak of the continuity of Jewish Tradition, they do
not mean, as does Orthodoxy, that the status quo in matters of religion
must be maintained at all costs, because they know that such a policy
runs counter to the law of progress and must lead to the extinction of
Judaism." Curiously, Rubenovitz's speech was not reported in the press
at the time, but it certainly is of major importance for an understanding
of the development of Conservative ideology.

As could be expected, Cyrus Adler had great difficulty with these
ideas, and apparently came to be suspicious of the Alumni Association.
Writing to Solomon Schechter on January 28, 1912, Adler declared, "I
for one do not want to be drawn into any Separatist movement by these
young men and you, I think, do not want to be drawn into one either. It
would, in my opinion, be a fatal mistake at the outset."[58] Schechter
apparently immediately disagreed with Adler on the urgency of founding the Conservative Union, for on February 2, Adler wrote again: "I
am sure that I have every desire to stand by the Alumni of the Seminary
. . . I believe that if the Conservative Union is formed it will overshadow
the Alumni of the Seminary and may even detract somewhat from the
Seminary as the authoritative center of Conservative Judaism in this
country."[59] Obviously, to Adler, the term "Conservative Judaism" had a

very different meaning than it had to Rubenovitz; and, in general, Adler avoided using the expression.

Meeting at the resort of Tannersville, New York, on June 25 and 26, 1912, the Alumni Association again discussed the proposed Union and, after hearing Solomon Schechter speak decisively on the matter, decided to issue a circular soliciting support. Carefully avoiding the term "Conservative," so as not to offend Adler, the circular was sent out to all the Alumni on July 9, 1912, signed by Mordecai Kaplan as "chairman of the Propaganda Committee" and Jacob Kohn as secretary:

> We wish to be known as an organization which invites all those who would throw their influence on the side of traditional and historical Judaism to join it. We would like to represent all of Israel, and will assume the character of a party only if it will be forced upon us. For this reason we have chosen the name 'Agudath Jeshurun—A Union for promoting Traditional Judaism in America'—A Hebrew name and a title explanatory of the purpose of the organization.[60]

Finally, on Sunday, February 23, 1913, at a meeting held at the Seminary, the United Synagogue of America was born, after four long years of planning and debate. Almost all of the leading figures of the Alumni Association and the Seminary, some thirty rabbis, were present, along with representatives of approximately twenty congregations, most of whom were led by Seminary graduates.[61] Interestingly, although the leaders of the movement who organized the United Synagogue were ordained during the Schechter period, many of the early graduates chose to participate as well.[62] Although within a short time the United Synagogue would become primarily a congregational organization, it should not be forgotten that it was, to a great degree, a product of the Seminary Alumni Association. Indeed, in its early years, the United Synagogue was largely guided by Seminary alumni. Thus, in 1916, for example, the United Synagogue Committee on Propaganda was chaired by Charles I. Hoffman; Julius Greenstone headed the Committee on Education; and Elias Solomon was chairman of the Committee on Religious Observance.[63] In 1918, Solomon was elected president of the United Synagogue, a position he would hold until 1926. Also in 1918, Jacob Kohn brought up the subject of a Conservative prayer book at a meeting of the United Synagogue Executive Council, a topic that would engage Conservative leaders for many years.[64]

In a way, the preoccupation of its leaders with the founding of the United Synagogue served as a detriment to the growth of the Alumni Association. As President Charles I. Hoffman wrote to Herman Rubenovitz in March 1913, just a month after the organization of the United Synagogue, "Our Alumni Association has been terribly neglected, and we must do our best to revivify it. I don't believe in letting it go by default."[65] In addition, as we have seen, after the United Synagogue was started, many of the leading alumni continued to take an active role in it, decreasing the time that they could devote to Alumni Association affairs.

Nevertheless, it would be wrong to assume that the Alumni Association in its second decade was solely concerned with the United Synagogue, for the group continued to serve as an intellectual forum and sponsored a number of committees that dealt with vital issues. Thus, in 1911, the chairman of the Standing Committee on Jewish Law, Abraham Hershman, reported on "the consideration of an important ritual question concerning domestic relations which had been addressed to it from Pittsburg."[66] Three years later, the 1914 JTS *Students' Annual* reported that the Committee on Jewish Law, still headed by Hershman, consisted of five rabbis. There was also a Committee on Jewish Literature, with five members, headed by Julius Greenstone; and Greenstone also chaired the Relief Committee. Mordecai Kaplan chaired the Committee on Text Books, and Jacob Kohn headed the Committee on Vacancies, an early attempt to deal with rabbinic placement.[67] In 1914, the JTS board voted to include a representative of the Alumni Association;[68] and Charles I. Hoffman was the first to serve in this capacity.

With the increasing years, the membership of the Association grew substantially. In 1905, there were only 28 members, but by 1910, the number had increased to 54, and by 1917, it had reached 104.[69] The first president was Henry M. Speaker, who served from 1901 to 1904, followed by Menahem M. Eichler (1904–1907), Charles I. Hoffman (1907–1912), Jacob Kohn (1912–1914), Elias Solomon (1914–1916), and Max Klein (1916–1918, and then 1918–1922 as RA president).

As we have seen, from the beginning, the Alumni Association avoided taking a stand on theological issues; and so it was probably for this reason that, when Mordecai Kaplan and Herman Rubenovitz convened a meeting of some fifteen rabbis at Long Branch, New Jersey, in August 1914 to discuss the theology of halakhah, they did so outside of the Association. Nevertheless, the men who attended were all Seminary alumni, and some of them, such as Charles I. Hoffman and Charles Kauvar, were highly traditional.[70] Kaplan, who would later go on to found the Reconstructionist movement, took an active role in Alumni Association affairs. He served as vice president of the organization from 1910 to 1914, and would occasionally speak at annual meetings.

Throughout its second decade, the Alumni Association continued to hold its annual meeting, often at summer resorts, and the list of speakers and topics is truly impressive. Thus, in 1910, Phineas Israeli read a paper on "The Rabbinic and Prophetic Attitude Towards Ceremonies," which was subsequently commented on by Professor Israel Friedlaender.[71] At the same meeting, Elias Solomon read a paper on "The Development of Jewish Liturgy," which was discussed by Rev. Henry Pereira Mendes, one of the founders of the Seminary. The following year, the well-known educator, Dr. Samson Benderly, spoke on Jewish education, as did Elias Solomon. In 1912, Mordecai Kaplan spoke on "Tradition and the Bible";[72] and his frank discussion of biblical criticism must have aroused the audience.[73]

A fascinating discussion took place in 1914, when Samuel Margoshes spoke on "The Effect of the Jewish Immigrant Population on the Public School in New York City." The speaker contended that the public schools "create a gap between the Jewish child and Jewish life"; and among his suggestions was the idea of teaching Yiddish in the public schools, a point "warmly contested" by the audience.[74] The following year, Professor Louis Ginzberg of the Seminary spoke on "The Halakhah As a Source of Jewish History," and Abraham Hershman also spoke on Jewish law.[75] Legal issues were once again the major topic of the 1916 convention, when Seminary Professor Moses Hyamson spoke on "Parallels and Contrasts in Roman and Jewish Law."[76] Returning to the theme of Jewish education, the 1917 convention featured a symposium on that topic, led by Julius Greenstone of Gratz College; it included discussions on the teaching of Jewish history and Hebrew language, as well as on curriculum planning and the importance of the Junior Congregation.[77] Held simultaneously with the United Synagogue convention, this annual meeting featured a joint reception for the delegates, hosted by the Alumni Association.

At the Seminary in June 1918, the Association held its last annual meeting. Part of the program was devoted to a discussion of "religious problems arising from the war," and special tribute was paid to the alumni who were serving as military chaplains.[78] Featured on the program were papers presented by Louis Ginzberg and Samuel M. Cohen "on the position of women in the synagogue in the light of Jewish law and practice."[79] With many congregations debating the permissibility of mixed seating of men and women, this topic would have been of great interest and relevance to the membership.

Nevertheless, the most significant aspect of the 1918 convention was not a paper, but rather a belief resolution—to change the name of the

Alumni Association to the "Rabbinical Assembly of the Jewish Theological Seminary." As *The Jewish Exponent* explained it, "This step was taken in order to make it possible that rabbis other than alumni who are in accord with the principles of traditional Judaism and the aims of the Seminary may become members of the association."[80] For a number of years the alumni had considered opening their organization to non-Seminary rabbis who were serving in United Synagogue congregations,[81] and so the change of name was a natural result of that idea.

As the alumni voted to change the name of the association, they must surely have considered the larger implications of that act. In 1901, the Seminary itself had faced an uncertain future; now it was a thriving and world-renowned center of Torah learning. From a collegial group of eleven young Seminary graduates in 1901, the Alumni Association had grown in size to encompass almost ten times as many members by 1918. In the early years, Seminary graduates were sometimes lured away from the fledgling Conservative movement, and now others were seeking to join. The organization had matured to the point where it was now dealing on a regular basis with significant issues, such as rabbinic placement and the interpretation of Jewish law, and the name "Alumni Association" no longer seemed to fit. For seventeen years, the Association had provided a stimulating intellectual forum for its members, while at the same time offering fellowship and encouragement for the men who were involved in the often difficult task of creating Conservative Judaism. As the Rabbinical Assembly, the organization would go forth to meet new challenges and opportunities, yet at the same time it would remain loyal to the task set by its founders—to help promote the Seminary and the cause of traditional Judaism in the modern era.

NOTES

1. Abraham J. Karp, "The Conservative Rabbi—'Dissatisfied But Not Unhappy'," in *The American Rabbinate: A Century of Continuity and Change: 1883–1983*, ed. Jacob Rader Marcus and Abraham J. Peck (Hoboken, NJ: Ktav Publishing House, 1985), p. 105.
2. Judah David Eisenstein, "Yesod HaSeminar HeHadash," in *Ozar Zikronothai, Autobiography and Memoirs* (New York, 1929), p. 206, reprinted from the *New Yorker Yidishe Zeitung*, 1886.
3. Moshe Davis, *The Emergence of Conservative Judaism: The Historical School in 19th Century America* (Philadelphia: Jewish Publication Society, 1965).
4. For a thorough study of the early Seminary, see Robert E. Fierstien, *A*

Different Spirit: The Jewish Theological Seminary of America, 1886–1902 (New York: The Jewish Theological Seminary, 1990).

5. Pamela S. Nadell, *Conservative Judaism in America: A Biographical Dictionary and Sourcebook* (New York: Greenwood Press, 1988), p. 297.
6. *AH* (July 5, 1901), p. 190.
7. Ibid. (July 12, 1901), p. 3.
8. *JE* (June 21, 1901), p. 10.
9. *AH* (June 21, 1901), p. 137.
10. *JE* (June 21, 1901), p. 10.
11. Ibid. (June 21, 1901), p. 10.
12. *JE* (June 28, 1901), p. 4.
13. Nadell, p. 243.
14. *JE* (July 12, 1901), p. 3.
15. Ibid. (July 31, 1903), p. 3.
16. *CCAR Year Book* (1905), p. 274.
17. Ibid (1909), pp. 499–501.
18. Solomon Schechter, "The Work of Heaven," in *Tradition and Change: The Development of Conservative Judaism*, ed. Mordecai Waxman (New York: Burning Bush Press, 1958), p. 169.
19. For information on membership in the Alumni Association, see *Register, JTSA*, 1904–1919.
20. *JE* (July 31, 1903), p. 3.
21. *AH* (June 7, 1907), p. 133.
22. *JE* (July 31, 1903), p. 3.
23. *AH* (June 23, 1905), p. 102.
24. Ibid. (June 22, 1906), p. 42.
25. Ibid. (June 7, 1907), p. 133.
26. Ibid. (June 12, 1908), p. 131.
27. Ibid. (June 11, 1909), p. 147.
28. *JE* (July 31, 1903), p. 3.
29. *AH* (June 7, 1907), p. 133.
30. Ibid. (June 11, 1908), p. 131.
31. Circular, dated May 11, 1908, Charles I. Hoffman Papers, Library of the Jewish Theological Seminary. Apparently, the banquets were not always well attended, for in 1906, President Menaham M. Eichler wrote to Julius Greenstone, urging him and the Arrangement Committee to cancel the dinner unless "a dozen favorable replies" were received. Letter, Eichler to Greenstone, March 29, 1906, Julius H. Greenstone Papers, Philadelphia Jewish Archives Center.
32. *JTS Register* (1904), p. 23.
33. Ibid., 1908, p. 22.
34. Letter from Charles I. Hoffman to Herman H. Rubenovitz, Dec. 27, 1909, in Herman H. Rubenovitz and Mignon L. Rubenovitz, *The*

Waking Heart (Cambridge, MA: Notre Dame Press, 1967), pp. 125–126.

35. *AH* (June 11, 1909), p. 147.
36. Ibid. (June 11, 1909), p. 147.
37. Cyrus Adler, address delivered at the 1905 JTS Commencement, in *Cyrus Adler, Selected Letters,* ed. Ira Robinson (Philadelphia: Jewish Publication Society of America, 1985), Vol. 1, p. 113.
38. Jack Wertheimer, "Pioneers of the Conservative Rabbinate: Reports from the Field by Graduates of 'Schechter's Seminary,'" *Conservative Judaism* 47:3 (Spring 1995), p. 53.
39. Stanley Rabinowitz, *The Assembly: A Century in the Life of The Adas Israel Hebrew Congregation of Washington, D.C.* (Hoboken, NJ: Ktav Publishing House, 1993), p. 308.
40. Herbert Rosenblum, *The Founding of the United Synagogue of America, 1913* (Ph.D. dissertation, Brandeis University, 1970), p. 132.
41. See Rosenblum.
42. Rubenovitz and Rubenovitz, p. 35.
43. Adler, p. 167.
44. Rosenblum, p. 189.
45. *AH* (June 24, 1910), p. 185.
46. Rubenovitz and Rubenovitz, p. 31.
47. Hoffman to Rubenovitz, August 30, 1910, Herman H. Rubenovitz Papers, Library of the Jewish Theological Seminary. Subsequently it was called the "Committee *on* Conservative Union."
48. Rubenovitz to Hoffman, Nov. 7, 1910, Hoffman Papers, JTS.
49. Rubenovitz and Rubenovitz, p. 38.
50. Rosenblum, p. 160.
51. Rubenovitz and Rubenovitz, p. 132.
52. Rubenovitz to Hoffman, March 14, 1911, Hoffman Papers, JTS.
53. Rosenblum, p. 164.
54. *AH* (July 14, 1911), p. 301.
55. Ibid. (July 14, 1911), p. 308.
56. The paper is found in the Rubenovitz Papers at the Jewish Theological Seminary, with the incorrect date of July 7, 1910, and the location specified as Arverne, New York. Inasmuch as the 1910 convention was in June and was held at the Seminary, the paper must pertain to the 1911 convention.
57. Friedlaender to Rubenovitz, January 4, 1911, in Rubenovitz and Rubenovitz, p. 42.
58. Adler to Schechter, January 28, 1912, in Adler, p. 205.
59. Adler to Schechter, February 2, 1912, quoted in Rosenblum, p. 171.
60. Rubenovitz and Rubenovitz, p. 44.
61. See Jonathan Waxman, "*Mi vaMi HaHolkhim*: A Profile of the Found-

ing Congregations of the United Synagogue," in *Yakar Le'Mordecai: Jubilee Volume in Honor of Rabbi Mordecai Waxman,* ed. Zvia Ginor (Hoboken, NJ: Ktav Publishing House/Great Neck, NY: Temple Israel of Great Neck, 1998), pp. 283–326.

62. Ibid., p. 30.
63. Minutes of the 1916 United Synagogue Annual Convention, Jacob Kohn Papers, the Library of the Jewish Theological Seminary.
64. Rubenovitz and Rubenovitz, p. 139.
65. Hoffman to Rubenovitz, March 11, 1913, in Rubenovitz and Rubenovitz, p. 135.
66. *AH* (July 14, 1911), p. 308. The nature of the question was not reported.
67. *Jewish Theological Seminary Students' Annual, 1914,* pp. 29–30.
68. *AH* (March 27, 1917), p. 617.
69. *JTS Register* (1905–1918).
70. See Mordecai M. Kaplan, *Diaries,* August 23, 1914, the Library of the Jewish Theological Seminary; also Mel Scult, *Judaism Faces the Twentieth Century: A Biography of Mordecai M. Kaplan* (Detroit: Wayne State University Press, 1993), p. 179.
71. *AH* (June 24, 1910), p. 185.
72. Ibid. (July 12, 1912), p. 293.
73. Scult, p. 179.
74. *AH* (March 27, 1914), p. 617.
75. *JE* (July 23, 1915), p. 6.
76. Ibid. (July 14, 1916), p. 2.
77. Ibid. (July 6, 1917), p. 2.
78. Ibid. (June 28, 1918), p. 2.
79. Ibid.
80. Ibid.
81. See, e.g., *JTS Students' Annual, 1914,* p. 28.

Emerging Self-Awareness
The Rabbinical Assembly in the 1920s and 1930s

Herbert Rosenblum

Introduction

In the 1920s and '30s, the American Jewish community was experiment-ing with many of the features that were to become commonplace in later decades. The synagogue-center was becoming a major community institution in the inner cities of America.[1] The Federations of Jewish Philanthropies were beginning to coordinate their campaigns with the Zionist fundraising efforts. Bureaus of Jewish Education were becoming the central coordinating agencies for metropolitan Jewish school sys-tems. The Synagogue Council of America was founded in 1926 to coor-dinate Jewish ecumenical activities. Jewish Community Councils were testing the outer limits of public relations and community policy. Anti-Semitism at home and abroad remained a continuing (even growing) concern and engaged the earnest energies of the American Jewish Com-mittee, Anti-Defamation League, American Jewish Congress and the Jewish Labor Committee.

The role of the American rabbi was similarly evolving into the now-familiar image of the Jewish clergyman, becoming increasingly involved in both the religious and organizational functions of his congregation's activities and the broader responsibilities of the large community as well. He was now being called upon to counsel his congregants in times of joy and sorrow, become a prime mover in the efforts to educate the young and the old, interpret the tradition eloquently from the religious pulpit and the communal rostrum, represent the faith in the arenas of government and interfaith circles, and somehow remain a paradigm of scholarship, probity, and piety. The pressures and tensions incurred in these processes have become familiar companions (frequently unwelcome) to the modern rabbi. Israel Goldstein offered a wonderful introduction to the issues faced by the American rabbinate in the 1920s in his 1927 publication, *Problems of the Jewish Ministry*.[2]

The Rabbinical Assembly began this period as a mere sociable Alumni Association, then gradually grew and took on more responsibilities, and by the late 1930s had become a serious partner of its sister organizations both within and without the Conservative movement. By the outbreak of World War II, the Rabbinical Assembly was a vigorous fixture on the American scene, exerting considerable influence in the shaping of American Jewish public opinion, and enjoying fully equal access to organizational and governmental councils.

It would be fair to describe the Seminary Alumni during the Schechter era as being almost totally dependent on their acknowledged master and teacher for guidance professionally, theologically, and organizationally. To his graduates Schechter represented the only model on which they could visualize building their rabbinic institutions and careers. It was not only the laymen who called JTS "Schechter's Seminary." He was the Seminary, and the Seminary was the only institution that validated the professional and ideological initiatives of its graduates. Contract problems were discussed with Schechter and his assistants, religious issues were raised with Schechter and his designated officers, placement matters were cleared with Schechter and his secretaries. He was the father image, and the alumni were in many ways his children.

With the founding of the United Synagogue in 1913 and the death of Schechter two years later, the rabbinic alumni invested great energies into the functioning of the United Synagogue and saw it as the new coordinative body of the emerging Conservative movement. They looked to it during the 1913–27 period for the guidance and support that had previously come from Solomon Schechter. When it became increasingly evident that the United Synagogue would not be able (for many reasons) to become the "parent" organization of the new movement, the Rabbinical Assembly (so renamed in 1918) found itself obliged to strike out on its own in many important directions. This

chapter will deal with the personalities, issues, and ideologies that transformed the Rabbinical Assembly from its total dependency on the Seminary and United Synagogue into a fully recognized sister agency in the
Conservative movement.

By the 1920s, the RA was already being seen as a national organization of considerable significance. The report of its annual convention in
1925 was described thusly in the Anglo-Jewish press:

> The Rabbinical Assembly consists chiefly of rabbis who have been
> graduated from the Jewish Theological Seminary of America. The
> late Solomon Schechter was the founder of the Rabbinical Assembly,
> which today numbers nearly 150 rabbis throughout the country. As
> far north as Montreal, where Rabbi Herman Abramowitz is spiritual
> leader; as far south as El Paso, where Rabbi Joseph Roth is spiritual
> leader, and as far west as San Francisco where Rabbi Herman Lis-
> sauer is spiritual leader, the scope and influence of the Rabbinical
> Assembly are felt.[3]

The Search for Definition

Movement-wise, after the reorganization of the Seminary in 1902, the
arrival of Solomon Schechter, and the founding of the United Synagogue
in 1913, the Conservative movement had become a *de facto* reality in
the religious and organizational world of American Jewry. The members
of the Rabbinical Assembly could look about them and clearly see the
outlines of a fully developed three-tiered network of American Jewish
denominational structures. The Reform had their long-established
Union of American Hebrew Congregations (1873), Hebrew Union College (1875) and Central Conference of American Rabbis (1889). The
Orthodox had rallied round the Union of Orthodox Jewish Congregations (1898), Rabbi Isaac Elchanan Yeshiva (1897), and the Union of
Orthodox Rabbis (1904).

What was equally clear, however, was that the movement's titular
leadership was still resisting the tide, and was continuing to insist that
Conservative Judaism was not to be viewed as a separate and distinct
religious movement. Continuing the Schechterian rationale of a "tendency," a "school of thought," a "unifying force," and similar non-spe-
cific terminology, the major figures at the head of the Seminary's lay and
professional leadership, such as Cyrus Adler, Louis Marshall, and Rabbis Max Drob, Charles Hoffman and Louis Finkelstein, refused to

speak of Conservative Judaism as "just another" religious denomination on the American Jewish scene.

This issue had already surfaced during the 1910s, erupting in the competing ideologies of the coalition members who united to found the United Synagogue.[4] Schechter himself, finally convinced of the organizational need for a synagogue federation in support of his Seminary, preferred not to burn his bridges, and tended to call it "the Orthodox-Conservative Union." Rabbi H. P. Mendes of Shearith Israel, leader of the Orthodox factions at the founding meeting, insisted successfully on the insertion of a clause stating ". . . that the organization did not endorse innovations that may have been introduced into the services of any of the congregations."[5]

Judah Magnes, on the other hand, had wanted to see greater boldness, and a willingness to candidly proclaim "a third movement," but was outvoted, and withdrew from all further connections with the United Synagogue.[6] The young activists (Jacob Kohn, Mordecai Kaplan, and Herman Rubenovitz) were anxious to support Magnes, but deferred to the wishes of Schechter, and waited to fight another day. Cyrus Adler, recoiling from the zeal of "these young men," prodded Schechter to resist separatism, and urged him not to despair of the possibility of joint work with the Orthodox.[7] When he then succeeded Schechter in 1915, this became the institutional guideline for the next 25 years, until his death in 1940, and it continued in modified form into the early Finkelstein years as well.

The central arena of the Rabbinical Assembly's (and the movement's) activism for the next decade (1915 to 1925) shifted to the organizational initiatives of the United Synagogue. The rabbinic prime movers in its founding process, Charles Hoffman, Mordecai Kaplan, Jacob Kohn, Herman Rubenovitz, with the addition of Max Drob and Elias Solomon, now became centrally involved with the major issues confronting the United Synagogue. These energetic rabbis, along with Cyrus Adler, Louis Ginzberg and Julius Greenstone, dominated the organizational activity of the United Synagogue until 1927, when the first layman to be elected as its president was installed.

Merely to mention the above names is sufficient to indicate how fragmented the movement indeed was. The 1913 ideological debate at the founding of the United Synagogue remained unchanged throughout the 1920s, as "these young men" (Kohn, Kaplan, and Rubenovitz) continued to fight their uphill battle for a uniquely Conservative movement and ideology. But with Cyrus Adler installed as acting (then permanent) president of the Seminary, Charles Hoffman as editor and publisher of

The United Synagogue Recorder, Louis Ginzberg as chairman of the United Synagogue's Committee on Jewish Law, and Alexander Marx as chairman of the United Synagogue's Prayer Book Committee, faced a monumentally difficult task in their desired effort to liberalize the United Synagogue.

Regularly rebuffed on the floor of the United Synagogue, these activists began to consider their additional options. The first such effort was the issuance of a "call" in June 1919 for the exploration of alternative avenues to "formulate, in terms of belief and practices, the type of Judaism that we believe you profess in common with us," in the full knowledge that they:

> . . . have failed as a group to exert an influence upon Jewish life in any way commensurate with the truth and strength of our position, and that, primarily because we have never made our position clear to the rest of the world.[8]

After a series of meetings and discussions, the "Society for the Jewish Renascence" *(Tehiat Yisrael)* was established in 1919, with Mordecai Kaplan as president, Jacob Kohn as vice president, Solomon Lamport as treasurer, and Aaron Robison as secretary. The Administrative Committee included Miss Emilie Bullowa, Rabbi Solomon Goldman, Mr. Leon Kohen, Dr. W. P. Kotkow, Dr. Elias Margolis, Prof. Max Margolis, Dr. R.H. Melamed, Mr. Emanuel Neumann, and Rabbi Herman Rubenovitz. That fall, it began a series of meetings "devoted to study and discussion," and the "active interchange of thought among our members which will insure the accomplishment of the aims of our society."[9]

The progress of these deliberations left "these young men" unsatisfied and frustrated by the casualness with which their associates drifted in and out of the periodic meetings. The reaction of the official United Synagogue family to these developments was much stronger. Jacob Kohn noted that at the January 1921 Executive Council meeting of the United Synagogue, "the *Tehiat Yisrael* received a great deal of publicity and was given unofficial recognition as the *enfant terrible* of the United Synagogue. However," he added, "I feel that we must be patient with it for life is on our side, and eventually it may become our constituency."[10]

Kohn's optimism eventually was to be validated by the gradual metamorphosis of the United Synagogue and the Seminary into a self-conscious Conservative movement in the decades that followed. But Kaplan's pessimism similarly proved true, in the short term, as his relations with his congregation, the Jewish Center, were severed, and the United Synagogue remained dominated by its right-wing leadership. As a result, he spearheaded the founding of the "Society for the Advancement of Judaism" in 1922, and set in motion the institutional developments that would produce the Reconstructionist movement during the 1930s.

The sense of frustration felt by the liberally-inclined rabbis with the practical and ideological conservatism of the United Synagogue and the Seminary continued to grow. With the Law Committee and the Prayer Book Committee of the United Synagogue seemingly hopelessly mired down in traditionalist inertia, a group of activists issued a "call" for meeting and action on January 12, 1922, signed by Israel Goldstein, Herman Rubenovitz, Jacob Kohn, Max Kadushin, and Arthur Neulander.

Identifying themselves as a "group of rabbis, officiating in conservative synagogues," they stated that the purpose of their conference was "to help standardize the ritual and the ceremonial practices of these synagogues and come to some agreement on matters of general principle, especially as they apply to higher Jewish education in our adult classes." What made such a conference timely and necessary, they said, was "the chaos which now prevails in synagogues of our type."[11]

At its first meeting, on January 19, 1922, at the home of Jacob Kohn, it was decided to name the body "The Conference of Conservative Rabbis." It resolved "not to agitate within the United Synagogue, but to work out our problems within our group and to apply the recommendations of the group to the individual synagogues."[12] Present at the meeting, in addition to the conveners, were Max Arzt and Norman Salit, and Jacob Kohn was elected chairman and Max Kadushin, secretary. The conference appointed working committees to explore and report on issues involving education, the development of prayer books and the publication of a journal.

The second meeting of the Conference of Conservative Rabbis was held on March 22, 1922, at Temple B'nai Jeshurun in New York, and in attendance were Rabbis Baroway, Neulander, Rubenovitz, Goldstein, Arzt, Kohn, Klein, Fredman, Grayzel, Kadushin, and Lupo. Max Kadushin, chairman of the Education Committee, reported that "the method of Bible study favored by the committee was based on a natural historic and psychologic view point and that the study groups of adults would find this method advantageous." The Conference endorsed the report, and then approved a proposal by Herman Rubenovitz, chairman of the Publications Committee, for the Conference to launch a journal reflecting the new thrusts of the group, and "to meet with Professor Kaplan with regard to plans for a possible amalgamation with the paper he introduced [sic] to publish."[13]

Jacob Kohn then reported for the Liturgy Committee and submitted an outline for a Sabbath morning service. The "principles by which the committee was actuated" were indicated as:

> Wherever there is a glaring archaism, the Text is to be changed; wherever it is possible to reinterpret such an archaism, the reinterpretation is to be made; and at all times to reckon with the psychology of the Synagogue people and their actual attitudes towards the prayers today.

The conference requested that the committee present a full Sabbath liturgy by the next meeting for consideration by the membership. Another meeting was held several months later at the Society for the Advancement of Judaism (SAJ), and plans were laid for a monthly journal, whose editorial board would be headed by Kaplan, Kohn, and Rubenovitz, and which would include regular features on matters touching Jewish law and Hebrew literature, as well as book reviews, editorials, etc.

The Conference does not seem to have met after that date, and its members lost interest in it. Kohn continued to play an active role in the United Synagogue Prayer Book Committee, then seeking to evolve a compromise between the traditionalists and modernists, and in October he assured Rubenovitz "that I do hope to call a meeting of the Conference of Conservative Rabbis very soon." But apparently it did not meet again, and another chapter in the ferment process ended. By November 24, 1922, Kaplan wrote to Rubenovitz:

> As far as the United Synagogue is concerned, now that the forces of reaction are so strongly entrenched therein, I do not see any possibility of accomplishing anything with it, or through it.[14]

The search for definition thereafter, during the late 1920s and 1930s, was carried on largely in the circles of the RA. The Seminary itself, under Adler's presidency, was resistant to the specifically "Conservative" label, and the United Synagogue struggles were largely concerned with annual budget crises and services to its member congregations.

Relations with the United Synagogue

The Seminary Alumni members were among the most energetic participants in the ongoing activities of the United Synagogue from its very inception. The committee that had launched the United Synagogue was largely composed of Schechter's young rabbinic disciples, and they continued their involvement throughout the early period of the organization. The first non-academic and non-rabbi to be elected president of the United Synagogue, S. Herbert Golden, was not named until 1927. The presence and participation of the rabbinate at United Synagogue conventions was so striking that Rabbi Max Drob, describing the program for the 1921 convention indicated that "the program . . . was so arranged that the rabbis did not monopolize all the discussions."[15] The roster of officers and committee chairpeople throughout the period 1913–27 was heavily weighted in favor of activist rabbis.

Many of the functions of the United Synagogue during its first fifteen years bordered on matters that were of central interest to the Seminary Alumni. Prominent among these were questions of Jewish law, Sabbath observance, *kashrut* regulation, Jewish education, placement opportunities, intergroup relations and Seminary fundraising. Matters such as these frequently came up at both the United Synagogue and the Rabbinical Assembly meetings. The fact that the United Synagogue had early-on (1918) engaged an energetic professional executive officer, Rabbi Samuel Cohen, provoked occasional protests of jurisdictional priorities from the activist Rabbinical Assembly leaders.

When Professor Louis Ginzberg was called upon to render halakhic opinions in his capacity of chairman of the Committee of Jewish Law of the United Synagogue, he would be careful to present his findings on major matters to the appropriate Rabbinical Assembly conferences as well. In 1922, for example, he submitted his opinion on the permissibility of using unfermented wine for kiddush purposes (with Prohibition implications) to both the United Synagogue and RA conventions.[16] The Seminary's million-dollar fundraising campaign in 1923 was likewise an overlapping project of the United Synagogue and the Rabbinical Assembly, with Max Drob serving as general chairman and working closely with Cyrus Adler and Louis Marshall in a precedent-setting campaign.[17]

By the mid-1920s, it had become clear to both sides that the United Synagogue and the Rabbinical Assembly had their own unique functions to fulfill, and the rabbis began more and more to seek to develop the apparatus of the Rabbinical Assembly, and to meet independently of the United Synagogue. It began to publish its own annual *Proceedings* in 1927, it organized its own Law Committee and began to agitate for its own "field worker," and sought to address the central questions that uniquely affect its membership—ideology, placement, educational methodology, social activism, congregational standards, and Seminary fundraising.

Once launched into their independent organizational existences, the occasional tensions that arose between the RA and the United Synagogue became serious enough to warrant serious negotiations. Repeatedly resolutions were passed at RA conventions to appoint committees to seek better relations with the United Synagogue. On several occasions the RA launched campaigns to assist the United Synagogue to overcome budget deficits, and avoid potential bankruptcy. The knowledge, however, that they were ultimately part of the same religious universe of discourse and tied by their mutual concern for the welfare of the Seminary, kept the occasional disagreements from getting out of hand. They cooperated regularly in projects related to Jewish education, Zionist affairs, professional placement, and Seminary fundraising. The depression era affected each of them alike—congregations suffered, rabbis went unplaced or unpaid, the Seminary had to cut back programs— but they all emerged from the 1930s much expanded, more unified, and ready to face the future with confidence.

The Adler Years

There can be no question that the history of the Rabbinical Assembly in the 1920s and '30s could easily enough be characterized as the "Adler era." Despite the fact that Adler was not a member of the Rabbinical Assembly, nor an ordained rabbi, his official and unofficial positions in the United Synagogue and the Seminary, not to mention a host of other institutions and organizations, inevitably made him the decisive figure in many of the periodic developments and issues that vitally affected the Rabbinical Assembly and the emerging Conservative movement.

He came to this role quite naturally. With his Johns Hopkins and Smithsonian involvements and his intimate connections with the "our crowd" philanthropic elite, he became Solomon Schechter's major administrative ally from 1902 to 1915 and succeeded Schechter in the organizational leadership of both the United Synagogue and the Seminary itself. At the same time, Adler was the president of Dropsie College, and the sometimes president of, among others, the American Jewish Historical Society, the Jewish Publication Society, Philadelphia's Mikve Israel, and the American Jewish Committee. Clearly, he was America's best-versed communal figure, relied upon by the "high and the mighty" philanthropic establishment for guidance in the cultural and religious spheres.

With this formidable background, Adler commanded the loyalty of the Seminary's Board of Trustees, the Seminary's faculty, the emerging leadership of the United Synagogue, and the rank and file of the Seminary's rabbinic alumni. His points of view on cultural and religious issues were generally adopted by the committees and boards of the Seminary's growing constituency. There were exceptions, of course, such as the United Synagogue's 1917 vote affirming Zionism over his objections, and the "congress" disputes of 1917, which led to his resignation from the presidency of the United Synagogue,[18] but by and large, Adler's administrative control of the Seminary and its allied institutions, while benign, was quite firm.

His ability to control the destinies of "the Conservative movement" (a term he rarely used) was based on several factors. First and foremost, he had complete control of the budgetary process, by dint of his being the human link with the wealthy members of the Seminary's Board. He was able to increase the flow of resources into areas which were close to his heart (library expansion and academic research) and to decrease the flow into areas which were distant from his interests (religious innovation and modern theology). Secondly, his personal conservatism made him a natural ally to faculty members Louis Ginzberg and Alexander Marx, both of whom commanded the type of respect from Seminary alumni that made it difficult to generate organized opposition to their (and Adler's) pronouncements. Thirdly, he gradually surrounded himself with administrative assistants (Samuel Cohen in the United Synagogue and Louis Finkelstein in the Seminary administration) who vigorously mirrored his conservative points of view, and who in turn served as convenient buffers between himself and potential opponents. Fourthly (in the Rabbinical Assembly at least), was the fact that he was a major player in the placement process for rabbinic positions. Very few rabbis were willing to openly confront him and his opinions when they knew that sometime soon they might need his active assistance in the vital matter of obtaining a new rabbinic position.

The above factors constituted a virtual strangle-hold over the directions in which the Rabbinical Assembly might seek to move in shaping its public policy and active decision-making. Only the most securely-situated and independent-minded rabbis felt confident enough to articulate vigorous dissenting opinions, and were even less likely to be willing to act upon them in opposition to Adler and his formidable allies. The names that appear in opposition in the 1910s (Jacob Kohn, Judah Magnes, Mordecai Kaplan, and Herman Rubenovitz) remain virtually the same as those who frequently demanded change in the 1920s and

'30s, with the gradual addition of names like Solomon Goldman, Israel Goldstein, and Milton Steinberg.

Some of the issues that surfaced during his tenure demonstrated graphically how difficult it could be to adopt policies in opposition to his wishes. The United Synagogue Committee on the Interpretation of Jewish Law, established in 1917, was chaired by his close associate Louis Ginzberg, who made certain that only halakhically defensible decisions were rendered by his committee. Even when the Rabbinical Assembly later constituted its own Law Committee (1927), it rarely veered from the guidelines laid down by Ginzberg. When it voted in 1935 to adopt an innovative approach to the *agunah* issue (Louis Epstein's), Ginzberg's refusal to cooperate prevailed, and the Epstein proposal was ultimately shelved in 1939.

The Prayer Book Committee of the United Synagogue, headed by Alexander Marx, agonized for six years over the issues connected to the publication of the first prayer book under its auspices. Adler, supported by both Marx and Ginzberg, was only willing to issue an aesthetically upgraded traditional prayer book, but opposed any liberal modifications in the liturgy. This impasse persisted for several years, until a compromise was effected in 1926. The United Synagogue then published its Festival Prayer Book in traditional unmodified fashion in 1927, and a separate edition with some changes was also printed with the added legend on the title page: "Adapted for the use of certain Conservative congregations by Doctor Jacob Kohn."[19]

Adler presided over the major institutions of the *de facto* Conservative movement during a vitally important phase of their development. Their membership grew rapidly during his tenure, their institutions expanded and even prospered during some very adverse social and economic periods. He managed to keep a very difficult coalition intact, without losing any of the major elements of the several wings that comprised the "Orthodox-Conservative Union." Those, however, who sought to see Conservative Judaism come into its own, as a separate, self-conscious movement, found Cyrus Adler to be an immovable opponent. The best illustration of his personal orientation is the letter he wrote to a Hartford activist, Shaia Tulin, in 1923:

The Seminary conducts a small synagogue of its own. In this synagogue there is no instrumental music. It is the hope and desire of the Faculty of the Seminary that as our graduates go out they will establish services of the same general character as those they see in the

Seminary synagogue. Nevertheless, it is fair to say that the Seminary does not prohibit its graduates from going to synagogues in which the organ is used, if these men themselves have no objection to it.[20]

As Herman Rubenovitz wrote in 1927 to Jacob Kohn, "he [Adler] always dreaded our becoming known as a separate party in Israel, but this is the very thing that must happen if we are to become an influence in American Jewish life, and be of real service to Judaism."[21]

What emerges from this brief sketch of the role of Cyrus Adler in his relationship with the Rabbinical Assembly in the 1920s and '30s is the portrait of a facilitator, a referee, a listener, and clearly, a controller dedicated to seeing to it that "these young men" not be tempted to go off any deep ends (by his standards). Leadership as such he could not offer to the Rabbinical Assembly, first of all because he was not a member, but more importantly, because he did not share the organizational and institutional goals felt very deeply by the vast majority of the rabbinic practitioners in the RA. Interestingly, Max Routtenberg, in his otherwise wonderful description of the history of the RA, goes straight from the Schechter era to the Finkelstein era, without so much of a mention of the Cyrus Adler years.[22]

Herbert Parzen, writing in the 1960s, paints an even more critical picture of the role played by Adler as it affected the RA and the Conservative movement. Contrasting Adler's permissiveness toward the non-observant and secular Jews, with whom he had ongoing contacts in his various other "presidencies," with his stern and inflexible public policies in the Seminary circles, Parzen offers the following observation:

> . . . In compensation for his helplessness in maintaining traditional patterns in the institutional setup of American Jewry, he insisted on keeping the Seminary in its set framework without change or compromise. The more his religious views were flouted elsewhere, beyond his power to control, the more he determined that the Seminary serve as their haven. Thus, the Seminary became more and more isolated from and insulated against the Jewish community that violated his religious ideals.[23]

Quite a judgment! The bottom line, however, may point to a more balanced conclusion. The Rabbinical Assembly, despite its undeniable frustrations during the Adler years, many of which were caused by factors far beyond his (or anybody else's) control, emerged from the Adler era a much larger, stronger, and self-directed organization than it had been at his accession to the Seminary's leadership. The number of affiliated Conservative congregations had grown from 40 in 1917 to 275 in 1940, far outstripping the growth rate of both the Reform and the Orthodox in the same (Adler stewardship) era.[24]

Louis Ginzberg

It would be quite impossible to understand the power of Cyrus Adler over the institutions of the Conservative movement during the 1920s and '30s without reckoning with the potent presence of Professor Louis Ginzberg. As one of the first luminaries engaged by Solomon Schechter in 1902 to give academic pre-eminence to the Seminary, Ginzberg came to occupy a Gibraltar-like position in the Seminary family in regard to all matters dealing with rabbinic law and literature. During the Schechter era, Ginzberg remained "just one" of the Seminary faculty members, but upon Schechter's death Ginzberg became visibly the great talmudic scholar who gave traditional credibility to JTS as an undisputed central institution for advanced Jewish learning. For Cyrus Adler, replacing Schechter as he did in 1915, the ability to consider Ginzberg as a colleague and ally in the organizational and doctrinal matters of the Seminary proved to be one of his strongest assets.

Interestingly, when Adler resigned precipitously from the presidency of the United Synagogue in 1917 over the "Congress issue" and Zionism, it seemed most natural and logical to designate Louis Ginzberg as the new president in his stead, and the organization continued on the precise courses of action as if Adler had remained in the presidency. Tolerably few academics and rabbis were willing during the Adler years to raise divisive issues within the United Synagogue, Rabbinical Assembly or the Seminary on matters where Adler and Ginzberg stood united. The most notable items of record in this regard were the Prayer Book controversy, the *agunah* and related Law Committee matters, and requests to issue an official "Conservative" ideological statement. On these issues, Adler, Ginzberg, and later, Finkelstein, presented a solid front that proved far too formidable to confront, or even to circumvent. It would not be until the late 1940s, after Adler's death and Ginzberg's imminent retirement, that such confrontations would begin to have even a reasonable glimmer of success.

Ginzberg's presidential address to the United Synagogue in 1918, "Our Standpoint," reflecting his superb command of modern culture as well as classic sources, provides an excellent example of his general approach to "historical Judaism," and might just as well have been written by Cyrus Adler as far as the doctrinal and public policy issues were concerned. He emphasized the words of Schechter, "we do not intend to create a new party," and went on to say "we are opposed to all separatist movements in Israel, and are prepared to fight sects and still more so, sectarians without sects."[25] He then proceeded to applaud the Schechter insertion in the preamble to the United Synagogue constitution not endorsing the changes made by any of their constituent congregations. All of these doctrinal statements would have been wholeheartedly endorsed by Cyrus Adler.

As chairman of the United Synagogue's Committee on the Interpretation of Jewish Law, Ginzberg carefully avoided going beyond the domain of summarization into the realm of legislation, thus frustrating the initiatives of the liberal cadres of the Rabbinical Assembly, and essentially paralyzing their ability to produce change even after the RA formed its own Law Committee in 1927. They might have been prepared to confront Cyrus Adler alone, but not when Louis Ginzberg stood eloquently at his side. On one of the most complex and intense halakhic issues faced by the Rabbinical Assembly in the 1930s and '40s, the *agunah* (deserted wife), the vigorous efforts by many individual members of the Law Committee (most notably Louis Epstein) ultimately proved fruitless, when Ginzberg refused to support any initiatives that were not *ab initio* acceptable to the Orthodox. As described years later by his son, Eli Ginzberg:

> . . . the looked for support never was forthcoming. Since my father did not find a solution that appeared to be a clear improvement, he preferred to let others take the responsibility for modifying the law. The fact that many Orthodox rabbis refused to acknowledge the authority of the Rabbinical Assembly helps to explain Louis Ginzberg's caution. He saw little point to developing a solution that would not be acceptable beyond the confines of the Rabbinical Assembly. He wanted no part in further splintering authority.[26]

In retrospect, Ginzberg's position remained consistent throughout his life. Those who heard his occasionally liberal and flexible analyses of contemporary Jewish issues and, therefore, looked hopefully to him for leadership in the modernization of halakhah, with particular application to the conditions applicable in the American Conservative synagogue, basically misunderstood his primary commitments. As his son later wrote:

He knew, beyond any question of doubt, that it was the authority of the law which alone had made possible the survival of the Jews and Judaism, and he had no intention of helping to shrink or confine further its domain already diminished as a consequence of the inroads of emancipation and reform . . . He hesitated at change because he knew that no matter how great his own learning, he would never be able to convince the great rabbis of Eastern Europe whose life and experiences differed so greatly from his own. And he saw little point in developing new law for American Jews, most of whom had long ago denied its authority.[27]

Given the reverence in which Louis Ginzberg was held by the vast majority of his students and colleagues, there could clearly be no serious effort to tamper with his leadership in the halakhic arena during his active tenure. It would not be until after his retirement in 1951 that the Rabbinical Assembly's Law Committee would begin to undertake the type of initiatives that would ultimately lead to a uniquely Conservative interpretation of Jewish law. By that time, it was no longer the Adler/Ginzberg wall that had to be scaled; it was the Finkelstein/Lieberman defenses (of the halakhah) that needed to be penetrated. And those eventually did not prove as formidable as those of their predecessors.

Louis Finkelstein

The Finkelstein years as president and then chancellor at the Seminary may not have begun until 1940, but the 1920s and '30s witnessed the increasingly central role that he would be playing in the evolution of the institution and the Conservative movement. An early Schechter recruit, a Columbia Ph.D. in 1918, Louis Finkelstein was ordained in 1919, and served as an active pulpit rabbi in the Bronx while becoming affiliated with the Seminary faculty as a Talmud instructor. By 1931, he joined the Seminary full time, becoming assistant to the president, and then provost in 1937, and upon Adler's death, president (then chancellor) from 1940 to 1972.

Finkelstein may have become best known to the larger community after becoming president in 1940, but among the various constituencies of the Seminary itself—students, faculty, alumni, administrators, trustees—he was a growing factor to be reckoned with throughout the 1920s and '30s. Cyrus Adler early on recognized in him the brilliant scholar, the charismatic leader and the consummate administrator on whom he could increasingly lean, as he sought to discharge his own hectic responsibilities in New York and Philadelphia. Before long, it became clear that Finkelstein was not just a junior bureaucrat in the Seminary apparatus, but was increasingly involved in the serious decision-making as well.

His emergence as a leading figure in the right wing of the movement was not all that evident at the outset of his career. Interestingly, upon his ordination, he was one of the rabbis whom Mordecai Kaplan recommended to his left-wing colleagues in 1919 as a possible candidate for inclusion in their tentative movement, "The Renascence Society," and he actually attended its first meeting. As he later apologetically wrote to Kaplan:

> It was only out of respect for you and because of our relations that I joined the Renascence. You will remember how I tried to avoid join-ing it or coming to its first meeting. I never forgave myself for that act, which once done had to be followed by more compromises with myself. I do not intend to commit such an error again.[28]

Several years later, he was already recognized as a protagonist of the right wing of the movement, and (following Adler) increasingly opposed to the identification of the Seminary with a "Conservative" movement and label. Typical of his pronouncement on the subject was his 1930 statement during his RA presidential address:

> The movement usually called Conservatism (though we, its adher-ents, believing above all in the unity of Israel, dislike the name with its implication of further schismatism) . . .[29]

In functional terms, Finkelstein played a decisive role in the evolu-tion of the Seminary and its satellite organizations. Adler and Ginzberg had earlier forged a potent partnership in their effort to control the activities of the nascent Conservative movement. The addition of Finkelstein to their ranks made them quite invincible. He became the indispensable go-between with the Rabbinical Assembly and the Semi-nary and served in a variety of chairmanships of the RA, finally becom-ing its president in 1928. By the 1930s, it had become clear that if you wanted to get something done at the Seminary, the man to talk to was Louis Finkelstein. Similarly, if members of the Rabbinical Assembly desired to change positions, Louis Finkelstein could be a knowledgeable and effective advisor.

He became a major spokesman for the traditionalist groups in the Rabbinical Assembly, but was never able to achieve an official adoption of his point of view. His address to the Rabbinical Assembly in 1927 on "The Things that Unite Us," was immediately rebutted by Eugene Kohn and others on the convention floor. His continued efforts at the 1929 and 1930 conventions to forge an ideological consensus for the movement were thwarted by the growing polarization becoming evident in the RA between the right and left wing protagonists.

As a key leader of both the RA and the Seminary during the depression years, Finkelstein was privy to the extraordinary difficulties that faced congregations, rabbis, and the Seminary as well. Congregations were being foreclosed, and consigned to dissolution; rabbis were being disengaged for inability to pay even minimal salaries, and many were unemployed; the Seminary was forced to cut back in previously unthinkable ways. Finkelstein reported in his correspondence to close friends in 1931 that rabbinic placement was dead in the water, not only for new graduates who could not find entry level positions, but for experienced rabbis as well. The clamor went up at RA conventions to cut back on numbers of students graduating and being ordained. Finkelstein, with remarkable foresight, in Pamela Nadell's words:

> . . . turned the problem on its head. The solution, he perceived, was the creation of more positions, not the training of fewer rabbis. Finkelstein won the debate. Despite the difficulty of finding suitable positions for all its men, the ranks of the RA swelled to 300 members by 1938.[30]

By the end of the 1930s, the administrative needs of the Seminary were increasingly entrusted into Finkelstein's hands. Having already established himself as a foremost scholar of the rabbinic tradition, he now turned his remarkable talents to the enlargement and enhancement of the Seminary's place in modern Jewish life. He developed a fundraising apparatus that grew rapidly in effectiveness under the able direction of Max Arzt. He cultivated the sons of the "our crowd" circles with a broad array of cultural and social programming, including the Jewish Museum, the "Eternal Light," the Institute for Religious and Social Studies, and the Conference of Science, Religion, and Philosophy. He encountered considerable opposition among RA leaders who saw in these external efforts an unnecessary dilution of the limited energies available to the Seminary and the Conservative movement. Michael Greenbaum has chronicled some of the major objections raised by Milton Steinberg and Solomon Goldman to these new Seminary undertakings, as well as his ultimate vindication by the Seminary Board in the 1940s.[31]

Later Finkelstein would also be instrumental in the founding of the University of Judaism in Los Angeles, the joint degree program with Columbia's School of General Studies, and the Israel Student Center in Jerusalem. As Pamela Nadell aptly phrased it: "Finkelstein's national standing and his centralization of the forces of Conservatism at the Seminary made him more powerful than any single individual in the movement since Solomon Schechter."[32]

The Kaplan Influence

Having singled out the strong influences exerted upon the RA by Cyrus Adler, Louis Ginzberg, and Louis Finkelstein, it is only fitting that we focus briefly on the impact on the RA during the 1920s and 1930s resulting from the writing, teaching, and activism engaged in by Mordecai Kaplan. We have already referred to his central role in the founding of the United Synagogue in 1913, the Jewish Center in 1918, the Renascence Society in 1919, the Council of Conservative Rabbis in 1922, and the Society for the Advancement of Judaism (SAJ) in 1922. Throughout this period he was at the center, or near the center, of every movement designed to liberalize the emerging Conservative movement and its approach to ritual, theology, and community structure.[33]

He was a major spokesman for the liberal wing of the RA, but was respected for his sincerity, scholarship, and dedication in all quarters. Even those who disagreed with some of his ideological positions were careful to defend his right to freely express those ideas in the halls of the Seminary, United Synagogue and the RA. In his 1930 presidential message to the RA, Louis Finkelstein expressed his regret at Kaplan's absence from the convention with these words:

> I particularly regret the absence of Professor M.M. Kaplan from this convention. In American Jewish life today he is rapidly assuming a position similar to that held by Ahad Ha-Am in Russia at the beginning of the century. He carries a heavy burden of work, and at the end of the year finds it difficult to spare the energy for a trip here.[34]

Quite a *mi shebeirakh*! And it was not mere rhetoric. Finkelstein would continue for the next forty years, in his various major leadership roles, opposing most of Kaplan's philosophic opinions, yet insisting on retaining him within the Seminary hierarchy in central administrative and academic positions.

Many years later, their ideological gaps unbridged, perhaps even widened, Finkelstein, in a letter to Kaplan, sought to explain their differences in a very personal (perhaps naive) vein:

> I believe the issues, dividing us from one another now, as they have across the years, have nothing to do with either philosophy or theology, in regard to either of which I would not be willing to pit my judgment against yours. They arise rather out of historical and biographical facts. To those in your own life, you have on occasion alluded. You saw "orthodox" Judaism at its worst, and project on Maimonides, who was a very great man, the evils you could not but notice in the enemies of Rabbi Jacob Joseph, who were pygmies.
>
> My experience with pious Jews has all been delightful and positive. The most saintly people I have known have also been the most observant of the minutiae of the *Shulhan Arukh*. Thus, I have come to feel that study of Torah and observance of it are for Jews indispensable to the saintly life.[35]

The presence of Kaplan on the Seminary's faculty was frequently a lightning rod for the hostilities of the Orthodox leadership toward the Seminary. Fundraising for the Seminary was diverted after 1921 to the Yeshiva by the opponents of Kaplan at the Jewish Center.[36] Negotiations with Yeshiva leaders for possible merger with the Seminary in 1926–27 were ultimately abandoned, partly because of Kaplan's presence on the Seminary faculty.[37] His conception of "organic" Jewish community structure was quietly but vigorously opposed by most of the vested interests in the Jewish community, including the federations, defense agencies and social service organizations.

Nevertheless, his influence over the Seminary student population and its generations of graduates was a powerful one during those decades. The formal emergence of Reconstructionism in 1935 with the publication of *Judaism as a Civilization* was merely tacit testimony to the fact that some of the most creative and vigorous leaders of the RA had already allied themselves with him. Rabbis like Solomon Goldman, Herman Rubenovitz, Jacob Kohn, and Eugene Kohn had long been his intellectual brethren. Now, among the younger members, Herbert Parzen, Max Kadushin, Edward Sandrow, Milton Steinberg, Isidor Hoffman, among others, resonated deeply to his message of creativity and liberalism.

Because of his multi-faceted activism in Rabbinical Assembly affairs, in the Seminary academic programs, in the community institutions, and in his pulpit connections, Kaplan often found himself in an unusual position to observe the realities of America Jewish life. His harsh verdict on the evolving synagogue and the rabbinate was perhaps impetuously stated in a 1921 address:

> The synagogue instead of developing rabbis who are true teachers and scholars, makes them spineless, spiritless footmen, with disgust in their hearts, milk on their lips and cobwebs on their brains.[38]

Interestingly, some of Kaplan's most important contributions to the Jewish community in the 1920s and '30s have been increasingly glossed over with the passage of time and the changing of circumstances in modern Jewish life. One of these was his insistence on the role social justice should play in the Jewish community. He deplored the evolution of the synagogue in general and his own congregations into wealth-dominated organizations. Mel Scult describes it in this manner:

> On one occasion, he talked from the pulpit of Amos as "the wide-eyed preacher" and "this radical Bolshevist." He did not hesitate to attack the evils of wealth and told his followers that "power and luxury are the very antithesis of the spiritual."[39]

His frequent pulpit attacks on the capitalists and his insistence that they should be more adequately indoctrinated with the concerns of the prophetic tradition increasingly alienated him from his board members at the Jewish Center.

With the onset of the depression years, the RA established a standing Committee on Social Justice, largely under the influence of Kaplan's ideological thrusts. Under the able leadership of some of the best and the brightest, including Israel Goldstein, Milton Steinberg, Robert Gordis, and Isidor Hoffman, this committee frequently served to galvanize the RA conventions into repeated ventures of social activism during the 1930s.

The second, seemingly forgotten principle that was near and dear to Kaplan was his vision of Jewish community organization. Kaplan's commitment to the democratic process convinced him that the only way Judaism could thrive in the modern American environment was by adopting a fully participatory governance model for American Jews and organizations, and he called this the "organic community." It clearly had its roots in Kaplan's involvement in the "Kehillah" experience of 1909–1922. As he envisioned it, one's membership in the Jewish community would entitle the individual to all the services of the community, from the synagogue of his choice to any of the educational facilities made available in the community, to the social services evolved for the community. In this way, the wealthy would be subjected to the discipline of the democratically elected directors of the local community, and the Board would truly reflect the will of the people.[40]

As can be readily imagined, this was an idea that proved attractive to non-influential members of the Jewish community, but was quietly but effectively resisted by those who dominated the major (and minor) Jewish organizations. The Jewish Community Councils that sprang up in many quarters of the country during the 1930s in response to Kaplan's writings blossomed briefly, but rapidly fell into decline. Their initial promise quickly gave way to the urgency of the needs in the 1930s to provide public relations and philanthropic support to the growing battle against anti-Semitism and Nazism. World War II, the Holocaust, and the need for unprecedented philanthropy on behalf of Israel sealed the fate of these councils and their potential to serve as the governing bodies of American Jewry. By the 1950s, most of them had changed their names to "community relations councils" and had become arms of the federations.

During the 1930s, this model of community organization was much admired by many of the leaders of the RA. In his presidential message in 1936, Eugene Kohn demanded of his colleagues that they band together and collectively seek to remodel their communities into democratic, representative "organic communities."[41] Armond Cohen, in 1940, turned a discussion on "the Synagogue and the Center" into a polemic for the radical reorganization of the Jewish community into a democratic, organic community.[42]

The Law Committee

The mechanism for handling issues of Jewish law for the emerging Conservative movement did not fall into the purview of the Rabbinical Assembly until 1927. Until that time, it was the United Synagogue that had served as the clearinghouse for halakhic matters raised by congregations and their rabbis. The United Synagogue's Committee on the Interpretation of Jewish Law was established in 1917 and was chaired by Professor Louis Ginzberg who was clearly recognized in all quarters of the movement—by laypeople, rabbis, and academics—as the logical authority on matters of Jewish law.

The questions addressed to him and his committee during those early years were the familiar ones that asked for acceptance of the norms established in the new congregations—is mixed seating permitted, for example—along with questions regarding marital status and conver-

sion possibilities.[43] It soon became clear that the committee was merely
restating existing Jewish legal precedents and resisting breaking the type
of new ground that the emerging congregations of the movement were
anxious to see. Growing increasingly uncomfortable with the clamor of
the congregations and the rabbis, Ginzberg decided to step aside from
the front lines of the intensive halakhic battlefield.

By 1927, both the United Synagogue and the Seminary were agree-
able to having the RA accept the mandate of the movement to establish
its own Committee on Jewish Law. Its first chairman was Max Drob,
who undertook the assignment with great enthusiasm, and saw in the
new committee the potential for a renewed Sanhedrin and the writing of
a new and glorious chapter in the history of the Jewish legal tradition.[44]
Needless to say, he soon ran into the same objective issues that con-
fronted the predecessor United Synagogue committee, and he proved
just as reluctant to breach the walls of existing halakhic precedents,
despite the insistent demands coming from rabbis and congregations.

In 1932, Julius Greenstone was named chairman of the committee,
and it was during his tenure (1932–36) that the *agunah* issue became
the foremost test case of the effectiveness of the Law Committee, and
was to remain so for several decades. The question of the *agunah*, as
well as the myriad ritual questions that were forwarded to the committee, inevitably begged the question: were the powers of the committee
limited to interpretation of the various traditional text sources and
authorities, or could it envision itself as being authorized by the RA to
engage in legislating new approaches that had been unanticipated by
scholars of previous generations. Greenstone's annual reports to the RA
frequently included hesitant reminders of this dilemma. In 1933, he
concluded his report by saying:

> The members of this Committee are not as yet fully agreed as to
> whether this Committee should function merely as an interpretative
> body or whether it should also assume legislative prerogatives. In
> other words, we are not quite decided as to whether we have to wait
> until questions of law in a specific manner are presented to us and
> then to pass upon them in the light of Jewish tradition and of mod-
> ern requirements, or whether we may initiate questions of larger
> import and pass judgment upon them.[45]

It would be fair to say that the left/right struggles on the committee
hinged precisely on the resolution of this issue. In his 1934 report, he
was even more direct:

... It is not possible to meet the desires and expectations of all the various forms of thought in relation to Jewish law prevalent among members of the Assembly ... We beseech the patience and the cooperation of the Assembly membership in the task that is before us.[46]

The *agunah* issue was the most visible and pressing symbol of this ongoing struggle. Rabbi Louis Epstein launched his opening proposal for the resolution of the *agunah* problem at the 1930 convention, formulated a proposed halakhic remedy, circularized its text both inside and outside the RA, and refined it periodically during the next several years. He presented it to the committee in fully documented fashion, saw it accepted in 1935 by the committee and then by the full Rabbinical Assembly, only to watch it come under severe internal and external attack. Boaz Cohen, as chairman of the "Special Committee on the *Agunah* Problem," discussed these difficulties in the 1936 *Proceedings,* and outlined the delaying procedures that the Law Committee was recommending, the bottom line of which was:

> That the Rabbinical Assembly postpone putting into operation the Agunah resolution ... until such time as a fuller clarification of this complex problem shall have resulted from the responsum of Professor Ginzberg and the correspondence with the rabbinical bodies of the various countries.[47]

Needless to say, the responsum from Professor Ginzberg was not forthcoming, and the correspondence with other rabbinical bodies led to no progress. At the 1938 convention, the Law Committee report included the further statement:

> In view of the opposition within the Committee to Dr. Epstein's proposed solution of the Agunah problem and of Professor Ginzberg's refusal to express a definite opinion on the proposition, the Committee decided not to proceed for the present with the work of implementing the resolution adopted at a former Convention approving of it. Dr. Epstein was asked to ascertain the view of Rabbinic authorities in the Old World and in Palestine and present a report of his findings on his return from his travels.[48]

The results of his subsequent international interviews were predictably negative. Despite his ten years of learned and focused activism on this central issue, Louis Epstein was ultimately compelled during his years as Law Committee chairman (1936–40) to recognize the unreadiness of the RA to confront its traditionalists from within and without, and was compelled to allow his proposal to be withdrawn in 1939.

When Greenstone reported to the 1938 convention on behalf of the Law Committee, he was forced to recognize how difficult the mandate of the committee had become, and to place on the record the fact that there was much dissatisfaction in the RA with the committee:

> Whether the Committee on Jewish Law is meeting the expectations of the Assembly membership is doubtful. I do not propose to deal with the attitude of some who regard the entire matter as trivial, since for them such a Committee is neither required nor desired. The great majority of our membership, however, clinging to the concept of Jewish law and desirous of having it placed in harmony with the needs and exigencies of our present-day circumstances, have the right to demand of this Committee a courageous and intelligent interpretation of Jewish tradition that should guide them in their lives and in their work. The complaints that the committee is too conservative, too slow, too timid and too circumscribed in its scope deserve serious consideration and attention. These complaints are for the most part based on a misunderstanding of the functions of the Committee. It is not a legislative body, nor is it intended to originate and establish general principles of law. Its main duty is to reply to specific questions put before it, in the spirit of Jewish law and tradition and in harmony with the changed conditions of our time.[49]

The dilemma could not have been more clearly stated. Greenstone himself was clearly torn in two directions, and was unable to function as a decisive influence in either direction.

What had become clear during the 1930s was that the Rabbinical Assembly was not yet prepared to take initiatives that were opposed by the Orthodox rabbinate on the outside and/or resisted by its own academic and halakhic experts within the movement. Louis Ginzberg, despite his occasional references to flexibility and liberality of the halakhic process, never proved willing to countenance RA initiatives beyond the boundaries of previously established halakhic decisions. Without his support, a failure of nerve became endemic on the Law Committee as they watched with sadness the unceasing vilification that was targeted in their direction by the organs of the Orthodox rabbinate on the subject of *agunah* initiatives.

During the 1930s, in addition, the voices of Boaz Cohen and Louis Finkelstein became serious forces in the Law Committee process. Boaz

Cohen served for many years as secretary of the Law Committee and was the official respondent to inquiries made to the committee. His classic essay, "Canons of Interpretation of Jewish Law," an authoritative re-statement of Orthodox halakhic standards, published in 1935, served, by default, as a framework for many of the processes of the Law Committee.[50] Louis Finkelstein, now a central member of the Seminary administration, exercised powerful influences in all quarters of the Conservative movement. Both men, possessed of great expertise in Talmud and Codes, had themselves become strong advocates of the Ginzberg position—not to legislate away any of the halakhic standards acceptable to the Orthodox—thus strengthening the paralytic condition that had engulfed the Law Committee.[51] It would not be until the late 1940s that the RA would mount a growingly successful rebellion against the domination of the Law Committee by the Seminary and its Talmud faculty.

The inability of the RA and its Law Committee to rise to the *agunah* challenge in the 1930s was quite demoralizing to many of its younger activists. Max Routtenberg, writing two decades later, saw in this failed process the central reason for the inability of the RA to develop a healthy respect for halakhah amongst its congregations and memberships:

> . . . this situation has come about to some extent because of the failure of nerve of those who were charged with the responsibility of keeping the law alive. There was still an opportunity to meet the problems which the people faced when there was respect for the Halakhah. That was the time to instill confidence in the people that the law could be made relevant and viable, and that it could serve their legitimate needs. But our lawmakers have been timid and cautious and they have, in large measure, paralyzed the freedom and initiative which our Law Committee should have exercised. There has been fear of what the Orthodox would say and do, fear of creating schism in Jewish life, fear of irresponsible action by the extremists on the left of our movement.[52]

Ideological Motifs

The central issue in the development of Conservative Judaism has, of course, been its ambivalent approach to the articulation of its theological commitments. At the founding of the "old Seminary" in 1886, its platform postulated a loyalty to the "talmudic writings" and "positive-

historical Judaism." With the 1902 reorganization of the Seminary, and
the advent of Solomon Schechter, the platform introduced the concept
of "Catholic Israel" as a rationale for preserving the recognizable ritual
system that comprised the common denominator for much of the Jewish world of his day.[53]

The next juncture that compelled a reconsideration of ideological
commitments was the founding of the United Synagogue of America in
1913. The preparatory meetings, beginning in 1909, disclosed the reality that there were indeed differing points of view in the broad coalition
that wished to support "Schechter's Seminary." The Sephardic element
that had been so prominent in the founding of the old Seminary had
remained quite committed to its version of traditional Judaism. The pulpit rabbis that had either been ordained by the Seminary, or had been
attracted to its banner, exhibited divergent philosophical orientations.
The Seminary administration desired above all to avoid divisiveness and
forge a congregational union that would provide strong support for the
growing financial needs of the institution.

The outcome of the debate at the founding meeting of the United
Synagogue of America in February 1913 was a constitutional preamble
that avoided the blanket commitments of the old Seminary and the
assurances of the 1902 reorganization, and urged only the retention of
traditional practices, the use of Hebrew in the liturgy, the strengthening
of Jewish education, and the opening of its membership "to all elements
essentially loyal to traditional Judaism." These vague commitments
were acceptable to the liberal elements in the founding coalition, and
were balanced with a concession to the Orthodox members present, by
the addition of a caveat that the new organization was "not endorsing
the innovations introduced by any of its constituent bodies."[54]

During the next two years, Schechter sought unsuccessfully to bring
the Orthodox constituency into the United Synagogue. Rabbi H. Pereira
Mendes of New York's Shearith Israel remained sympathetic to the
Seminary he had helped bring into being, but increasingly found himself
pressured by his own congregational leadership and the other Orthodox
leaders to cast his lot with the Union of Orthodox Jewish Congregations and the Rabbi Isaac Elchanan Seminary (forerunner of Yeshiva
University).

Upon Schechter's death in 1915, Cyrus Adler assumed the leadership
of the Seminary, determined to continue what he perceived as
Schechter's position: the Seminary as an academic institution committed, in pluralistic fashion, to traditional Judaism, entitled to remain

aloof from the denominational conflicts swirling all about it. Instructive in this regard is the advice he gave Solomon Goldman in 1925, when his Cleveland congregation was caught up in a tension-filled struggle over his advocacy of mixed seating. When Goldman solicited his assistance, Adler counseled temporizing, moderation, delay; above all, to avoid the legal battle that seemed to be looming on the horizon. Goldman chose to bypass the Adler advice, pursued his case with vigor, won the right to label his congregation "Conservative," and instituted mixed seating.[55]

Recognizing that the Seminary remained the central institution of the emerging movement did not ease the ongoing need felt by the RA for ideological clarification. The "Jewish Renascence" movement of 1919 and the "Council of Conservative Rabbis" of 1922 (both described above) were graphic evidence of the essential dissatisfaction of the RA membership with the absence of ideological leadership from above. In 1927, a revived initiative by the same people involved in the earlier efforts, with some additions, took the form of a round robin of theological exchanges between Mordecai Kaplan, Herman Rubenovitz, Solomon Goldman, Max Kadushin, and Eugene Kohn. The major issues covered were whether to work within the United Synagogue or outside of it, how to mobilize the liberally inclined members of the RA, and how to best proceed in the framing of a platform for Conservative Judaism.[56]

The question of the ideology of Conservative Judaism came periodically to the fore, with Louis Finkelstein and Mordecai Kaplan as the emerging spokesmen, respectively, for the right and left wings of the movement. After repeated efforts, mostly unsuccessful, at galvanizing a consensus of the RA behind his traditionalist viewpoint, Louis Finkelstein accepted the chairmanship of a "Committee on Formulating the Attitude of the Rabbinical Assembly" that was appointed in 1931. It gave its report at the 1932 convention. The results? As summarized by Max Routtenberg:

> Its chairman, Louis Finkelstein, expressed regret that the committee found it difficult to formulate these statements in a convention report but that a publication of a series of essays, a Symposium on Conservative Judaism, dealing with all the basic issues was contemplated. The convention accepted the report and urged the committee to go ahead with its plans.[57]

Needless to say, these lofty plans were not realized, the ideology remained unresolved and additional committees were authorized. The

1930s, with the depression and the rise of Nazism, were difficult years for the movement, and much intellectual and organizational energy had to be expanded in the areas related to institutional and financial survival. Ideological pressures had to compete at conventions with such topics as "The Economic Crisis and the Spiritual Life of The American Jew," "The Rabbi and the Congregational Budget," and "A Permanent Relief Fund for the Rabbinical Assembly." It would not be until well after World War II that serious ideological initiatives would be launched effectively.

The need for ideological guidance, however, was overwhelming, and the intellectual vigor self-evidently present in many quarters of the RA could not be stifled. The appearance of Mordecai Kaplan's *Judaism as a Civilization* in 1934 provided an irresistible springboard for further consideration of the philosophic thrusts of the new movement. Interestingly, and provocatively, Kaplan's critique of the existing versions of American Judaism simply ignored the presence of Conservative Judaism, much to the chagrin of its leading spokesmen. Max Arzt addressed the 1935 convention on "Dr. Kaplan's Philosophy of Judaism" and offered a mixed blessing to this new and revolutionary work. He confessed himself to be "a disciple of Dr. Kaplan" and stated that:

> . . . the book offers a courageous, comprehensive analysis of the complex problems facing Jews and Judaism in our day and that no creative reconstruction of Jewish life will come unless we reckon with the basic issues so splendidly formulated and analysed therein. . . . In my case I find his very approach and his methodology have influenced me profoundly, and they have stimulated me even in those conclusions in which I differ from him.[58]

He then went on to criticize the Kaplanian definition of *mitzvot* as "folkways," his redefinitions of "civilization" and "religion," and the nature of Judaism's belief in God. His bottom line, however, was, that Kaplan "has helped to break the silence which reigned within our own ranks on these questions, and nothing but the highest good can come from honest, courageous and cooperative thinking on these matters."[59]

Arzt then went further and offered his own alternative approach to the understanding and enrichment of modern Jewish life:

> To my mind conservative Judaism . . . does not announce its negations. It proclaims its affirmations. It stresses Sabbath observance, the dietary laws, the retention of Hebrew in prayer and in Jewish education, and the restoration of Palestine . . . there is so much in

our law that is vital, soul-stirring and full of aesthetic possibilities that we should not be concerned about the inevitable obsolescence of a few mitzvot.[60]

The contemporaneous appearance of Milton Steinberg's *The Making of the Modern Jew,* Eugene Kohn's *The Future of Judaism in America,* along with Kaplan's *Judaism as a Civilization,* clearly set the agenda for the further debates during the 1930s and beyond. Henry Rosenthal offered a review of all three books at the RA convention in 1934, and his personal reactions were for a mixed verdict on the Steinberg book, reserving major plaudits for the Kohn and Kaplan works. The battle lines, however, had been drawn, and the further major philosophical offerings in the 1930s, such as those by Simon Greenberg, Robert Gordis, Max Arzt and others, in addition to Milton Steinberg, Mordecai Kaplan and Eugene Kohn, would have to relate to the issues raised in these pioneering works.

When Simon Greenberg undertook at the 1933 convention to share an understanding of "Jewish Nationalism," it quickly turned into a discussion of Jewish cultural, religious and communal aspirations:

The God idea enabled the prophets of Israel to rise above the chauvinistic claptrap of the military "practical" chauvinistic Jewish nationalist of his day without in any way loving their own people less or sacrificing less in their behalf. For a nationalism of the prophetic depth and breadth, the God idea is still necessary. The ideals of social justice, universal peace, and the brotherhood of man lose their vitality and driving power when dissociated from faith in God.[61]

Robert Gordis, long an admirer of Kaplan's, broke with him during the 1930s on such central issues as the "chosenness" of Israel, the nature of revelation, and the necessity for a belief in a personal God. His oft-repeated, and oft-republished, understanding of "progressive revelation" is captured in these words:

In common with Orthodoxy and in contradistinction to Reform, Conservative Judaism recognizes that the *Torah* is binding and that Jewish law may not be set aside for the sake of caprice, convenience or fashion. Unlike Orthodoxy, however, it has learned that in keeping with every other living manifestation of human culture, Jewish law must necessarily grow if it is to remain alive. These two principles are not contradictory. Exactly as American law is binding upon all Americans, though the law is perpetually being modified by leg-

islative enactment and judicial interpretation, so Jewish law is binding upon us though it is subject to change and development. In fact,
the fundamental philosophy of Conservative Judaism, validated by
the history of three thousand years, may be succinctly set forth in
two propositions: growth is the law of life, and Law is the life of
Judaism.[62]

If the search for an appropriate ideological orientation in the 1920s
had been polarized by the Finkelsteins and the Kaplans, an entire new
generation of centrists had come into its own by the late 1930s, and it
would be augmented in the 1940s by the likes of Jacob Agus, Ben Zion
Bokser, Aaron Blumenthal, Isaac Klein, Morris Adler, and a host of
other, highly trained, philosophically sophisticated, spiritually sensitive
new rabbinic leaders of Conservative Judaism.

Convention Highlights

The annual conventions of the RA have customarily been the supreme
legislative sessions of the organization. The standing committees and
even the Executive Committee traditionally submitted major items to the
full conventions for ultimate approval. As a result, the officers and membership tended to value their own personal participation and presence at
these meetings, aside from the obvious collegialities and sociabilities
offered by these annual get-togethers. The records and minutes of these
meetings would therefore provide a fascinating insight into the manner
in which major public policy decisions were taken. Unfortunately, a great
deal of this material is not available to us; the annual *Proceedings* of the
Rabbinical Assembly conventions did not become standard publications
until the 1927 convention, and for many of the later volumes, important
discussions were not included in the printed versions.

For the conventions before 1927, we have to rely upon newspaper
accounts, as for example, in *The Jewish Exponent* and *The American
Hebrew,* or, for a limited time, *The United Synagogue Recorder.*
Although many of the leaders of the Rabbinical Assembly published sermons, scholarly works, essays, and lectures, very few of them produced
autobiographical descriptions of their personal careers, with the notable
exception of Mordecai Kaplan's legendary diaries, and lamentably did
not chronicle their activities as members and leaders of the Rabbinical
Assembly. It was Moshe Davis' inspirational example that encouraged
others to begin the process of researching the annals of Conservative
Judaism. Were it not for Herbert Parzen, Herman Rubenovitz and
Abraham Karp, our historical research tasks in these regards would be

even more difficult than they currently are.

What does become clear from the newspaper accounts of the pre-1927 conventions is that the real agenda items of the RA as a professional organization—placement, pensions, professional ethics, halakhah, ideology, social action, education, community affairs, Seminary fundraising—all began to surface early on. At the 1922 convention, for instance, as described in *The United Synagogue Recorder,* various committees were established; one to draw up a constitution, another to investigate "group insurance," another to develop a code of professional ethics to guide the placement process, and another to support the Seminary's fundraising efforts. In addition, the convention considered Louis Ginzberg's proposal to declare unfermented wine acceptable for kiddush-making purposes, thus by-passing the developing scandals associated with the Prohibition era.[63]

At the 1924 convention, held in Far Rockaway at Congregation Shaaray Tefilah, the two most memorable sessions were both Seminary related. Rabbi Max Drob, vice president of the RA, presented a check for $100,000, raised by members of the RA, to Professor Ginzberg, representing the Seminary, to underwrite the creation of the Solomon Schechter Chair in Theology. The following day, a major session was held on "Some Implications of Historic Judaism," to launch clarifications in the area of Conservative movement ideology. Norman Salit, writing later that year in *The United Synagogue Recorder,* commented on this session "that the symposium on Historical Judaism was open to serious objection. It was not that the papers were not forcibly written, but they lacked balance, judgment and sound convictions . . . [and] no opportunity was given to discuss this question from the floor . . ."[64]

The convention proceedings reveal some of the major preoccupations of the Rabbinical Assembly during the 1920s and '30s. The 1927 convention focused on an evaluation of the RA's effectiveness up to that point. The featured address by Israel Goldstein touched most of the bases that concerned the rank and file of the membership, especially on the need to define Conservative Judaism more specifically:

> It is a confusing situation, which is bound to work to the detriment of the Conservative party. As Orthodoxy becomes more and more de-Ghettoized and Reform becomes more and more Conservatized, what will be left for the Conservative Jew to do? How will he be distinguished from the other two? With both his wings substantially clipped he will surely be in a precarious position.[65]

One of the most remarkable and far-reaching addresses to the RA was the report of Morris Silverman in 1932 as chairman of the Ritual Committee. He had completed a survey of the RA membership on issues related to the prayer services in Conservative congregations, and offered his summary and recommendations to the convention. Because of its long-range significance, it may be appropriate to describe his report in some detail.

He dealt with the types of prayer books in use in these Conservative congregations, the Friday night and Sabbath morning services, levels of satisfaction and dissatisfaction, suggestions/comments and the recommendations of his committee. It will escape no one's attention that Rabbi Silverman took his own report most seriously and threw himself personally into the arena of liturgical upgradings, with untold benefits accruing to the Conservative movement and Judaism in general.

Most impressive, he noted, was the fact that 110 rabbis (of a pool of 200) had responded to his questionnaire and had apparently taken considerable time and care in framing their responses and comments. On prayer books, the findings demonstrated the prevalent chaotic situation in Conservative congregations. On the Sabbath, 29 used the Bosniak *siddur*, 15 used Singer's, 14 Bloch's, 12 Silberfeld, and 17 Goldfarb/Levinthal. On the High Holidays, 56 used Adler, 18 Bloch, 5 Jastrow, and assorted usage of Philips, Leeser, and Elzas.[66]

One of his most important findings related to the question of Friday evening services:

In response to the question as to whether the Friday Night ritual was satisfactory, 40 answered yes, and 10 more stated that the ritual was satisfactory and then proceeded to offer suggestions for improving the ritual. It should be remembered that in these 50 replies, 13 congregations have no late services, and therefore no problem with the ritual of late Friday Night Services, and that 17 have introduced supplementary sheets or pamphlets which may account for their approval of the ritual. Forty replied that the service is not satisfactory. Among the reasons given are following: most of those who attend the late Friday Night Services are interested in the address only. Ten expressed a desire for more variety in congregational music and hymns. Two intend to use the Union hymnal. Twenty have complained that there is not enough variety in responsive readings and that the English readings have become monotonous and mechanical . . . 5 objected to the poor English translation, several pointed out that the service at present does not appeal to modern worshippers . . . Several have indicated that there is a growing demand in their congregations for more English. Five men stated that few read Hebrew and yet it is impossible to give their congregations an all English service.[67]

The above comments, along with a variety of additional individual comments that he cited, illustrated very graphically the state of collective unhappiness prevalent among his rabbinical colleagues via-à-vis the liturgical activities they engaged in at these Friday night services. Eighty of his respondents answered yes to the question, "would you like to see published a supplementary prayer book containing responsive readings and new prayers . . ." And he adds, "In our opinion this is the most significant reply."

As to the Shabbat morning services, he reported a broad variety of local congregational practices, relating to occasional English readings, consecutive services and occasional liberties with the Torah readings. In addition:

Twenty-seven men find the Sabbath morning service too long. As far as changes are concerned, several have stated that unfortunately they are unable to make any changes. One wants the Rabbinical Assembly to do something about it. Others plan to eliminate extra aleeyoth and the misheberach . . . Seven expect to eliminate the repetition of the Amida by the cantor and shorten the reading of the Torah . . . It is interesting to note that 42 out of 110 of our men preach every Sabbath morning in addition to preaching at the late Friday Night Services.[68]

He then reported on the "various requests made by the Ritual Committee":

Several have stated that it would be an achievement if we could eliminate the references to sacrificial services . . . Five men stated that the entire ritual must be edited and revised if it is ever to have any vitality for modern Jews . . . Ten have asked for new supplementary readings and benedictions, and these responsive readings should have a definite theme and not be a mere collection of meaningless verses, and that the prayers ought to deal with actual problems of life . . . Others have requested for transliterated material for the adult Sabbath evening services and for a uniform prayer book for the High Holidays, which is more important than a standard prayer book for the Festivals . . .[69]

He concluded his report by urging that the RA continue its earnest research into the above areas, make available innovative material pioneered by its individual members, and in addition, launch a serious effort to formulate guiding principles for liturgical and philosophical standards that would assist the rabbis and laymen to enhance the religious services for the increasing constituencies of the Conservative movement. There is not much evidence of the RA having done much more about this report at the time, but fortunately Morris Silverman himself became so obsessed by the importance of this study that he went on to produce the historic liturgical volumes through his Prayer Book Press and, in the process, transformed American Jewry. When read in tandem with his paper delivered to the RA eight years later, "Vitalizing Public Worship," complete with the type of practical examples of his liturgical creativity that have come to be of universal use in the contemporary Conservative synagogue, the enormity of his role in influencing the transformation of the prayer traditions of the American Jewish community begins to stand out in bold relief.[70]

At the 1939 convention, Simon Greenberg painted a poignant portrait in his presidential message of the unique loneliness and frustration faced by the modern Conservative rabbi:

> No group of men serving American Israel is as subject to the sense of futility and defeat, to the feeling that they are crying in the wilderness. The cause of it is not far to seek. It is found in the very nature of the goals we have set for ourselves, in the demands that are made upon us and in ourselves. Our goals are the most comprehensive and ambitious . . . We suffer, therefore, all the disappointments, all of the heartaches and all of the torturing self-analysis which all religious leaders of our generation must suffer . . . we often feel like we are a King Canute attempting to hold back the ocean's tide.[71]

His consolation and strength came, he confided, from his membership in the RA and his participation in its conventions, avowing that "because we are not Isaiahs and Jeremiahs, we need and we seek the spiritual assurance which comes from companionship with those who feel as we do."[72]

Leon Lang reported to the 1939 convention that his survey of "Adult Education Through the Synagogue," to which more than half of the RA members responded, demonstrated a remarkably broad participation of Conservative congregations in the adult education process.[73] The 109 responses received from RA members revealed that over

25,000 Jewish men and women were involved in 265 projects in adult education and that the need for greater national coordination and preparation of materials was becoming increasingly evident.

Herbert Parzen, in a timely report in 1939, described the concerted efforts being waged by the RA, in concert with the CCAR and the RCA, to provide assistance to refugee rabbis through the JDC-sponsored Committee on Refugee Jewish Ministers. With RA member Alexander Burnstein as its executive secretary, some 34 positions had been arranged for these refugee rabbis (beyond immigration quotas) during the past year. Alas, 400 applications were still pending in Europe (who can know what their ultimate fate was), as well as an additional 150 from rabbis already here and seeking employment.[74]

Max Arzt's presidential message in 1940 was delivered in the stark shadows of the global war that had already engulfed Europe and was threatening direct consequences for Europe's Jews. In what may have been the first use of the word "holocaust," he urged "tangible acts of sympathy and succor for the innocent victims of the holocaust across the seas."[75] He acknowledges with great pain that "it is a tragic, heart-breaking but stubborn fact that Jewish life in Europe is virtually liqui-dated and that the future of Judaism depends entirely on us."[76]

Professionalization

The 1920s and '30s witnessed the emergence of the American rabbinate into a recognizable professional group, alongside the clergy components of the other major religious faiths in American society. Granted that the larger congregations frequently offered better salaries, fringe benefits and working conditions, but even in the smaller congregations, with the growth of the United Synagogue, and the national impact of the Semi-nary and its programs, the rabbinate began to appear as a possibly attractive career option for young, dedicated students of Judaism. The Rabbinical Assembly, from its outset, undertook to enhance the image and practical conditions under which its members labored in the field. Negotiations were begun to launch a pension fund, at first in conjunc-tion with the Reform rabbinate, and then later, an independent one.

The placement of rabbis was always (and still is) high on the agenda of career-seeking graduate rabbis. In the Schechter era, it was handled in the intimacy of the Seminary administration; in the Adler era, the United Synagogue became a junior partner in the process, but the major recommendations would generally be made by Adler himself or, later

on, in the 1930s, in conjunction with Louis Finkelstein. Clearly, the
competition for plum positions in the large cities was a frequent source
of unhappiness for those whose aspirations could not be met. As the
Rabbinical Assembly grew, by the late 1920s, it was increasingly
demanding a central voice in the placement process. In 1925 the RA
Executive Council passed a resolution requesting that it be represented
by delegates on the Placement Committee.[77] In 1929 Reuben Weilerstein
presented a proposal for the thorough reorganization of the Placement
Committee:

> To quote from Dr. [Louis] Epstein's preliminary report: "we must
> awaken to the fact that we are dealing with the careers of one hun-
> dred and sixty men, for all of them need the Committee's work, two
> or three times as many congregations, an annual salary reaching
> close to a million—that's a business that cannot be attended to in the
> Seminary hallway between classes."[78]

Succeeding conventions continued refining the process, and began
engaging part-time administrators to handle the referrals and paper
work, under the authority of a Rabbinical Assembly standing committee. In 1931, under the influence of the deepening depression, Simon
Greenberg advocated the establishment of a permanent relief fund, for
assisting indigent rabbis. The perennial problems connected with "free-
lance" rabbis in Conservative congregations were broached by Jacob
Freedman in 1938.

The conventions began to feature innovative programs that had been
successfully administered in various congregations and that were
deemed to be replicable by other interested rabbis. Israel Levinthal discussed his favorable results with Jewish center programming at the
Brooklyn Jewish Center at the 1926 convention, and urged that the
model be emulated widely. Louis Levitzky offered guidelines for upgrad-
ing Sabbath services at the 1927 convention. Adult education programs
were agenda items in 1926, 1929, and 1938. Louis Levitzky also outlined a successful interfaith program in 1939, and David Goldstein discussed the role of the rabbi in interfaith activities in 1940.

Jewish education became an increasingly important feature at RA
conventions, as the congregation was becoming the overwhelmingly
popular choice for parents seeking to provide Jewish training to their
youngsters. In 1928 Max Arzt gave a major address on the problems of
the congregational school, and Benjamin Grossman outlined his experiences in conducting junior congregations. In 1930 Eugene Kohn spoke

about character education in Jewish religious schools. In 1931, Leon Lang discussed the relation of progressive education in regard to Jewish education and Emanuel Gamoran described the impact of the depression on Jewish education. In 1933, Eugene Kohn explored the objectives of Jewish education in America, and in 1934, Samuel Cohen advanced the possibilities for parental education. In 1936, a broad symposium on Jewish education was chaired by Leon Lang. By the end of the 1930s the stage was set for an even more impressive involvement and leadership role for the RA in the field of Jewish education.

In response to a growing need, the RA began publishing a quarterly *Bulletin of the Rabbinical Assembly,* to keep its membership better informed of the growing scope of RA activities. Louis Finkelstein, on behalf of the Seminary, congratulated the RA, and suggested that:

> . . . the Rabbinical Assembly, which is one of the youngest rabbinical organizations in the world, has now reached maturity, fully conscious of its significance and its responsibility to Judaism in America and throughout the world.[79]

This first issue, and all succeeding issues, contained a host of committee reports and Executive Council actions, along with personal news, and contributed to a sense of participatory involvement on the part of the general membership. It even listed several rabbis who were being suspended from membership for having "failed over a period of years to give any indication of their desire to remain members of the Rabbinical Assembly."[80] (At least two of them were later readmitted and went on to distinguished careers in rabbinic work.)

By virtue of the emerging nature of the synagogue as a synagogue-center, it eventually became necessary to dialogue with the executives of the Jewish Community Centers and with the federation directors, to clarify areas of cooperation and mutual concerns. In 1930, Simon Greenberg presented a personal analysis of the appropriate relationship between synagogues and community federations, with particular emphasis on his experiences in Philadelphia. In 1932, Harry Glucksman, executive director of the Jewish Welfare Board, made a convention presentation on "Community Center in its relation to the Synagogue Center." A report of a joint conference of synagogue and center workers was published in the *RA Bulletin* in June 1939, with a series of recommendations and guidelines for further explorations. In 1940, Armond Cohen conducted a convention symposium on "The Rabbi and the Center Movement."

Summary

The era of the 1920s and 1930s in the history of the Rabbinical Assembly may seem at first blush to have been a quiet interlude between the creative, turbulent Schechter period and the heady expansion activities of the Finkelstein years. In reality, however, nothing could be further from the truth. In a broad variety of ways, the Rabbinical Assembly had changed internally, and its relationships with the Seminary and United Synagogue had undergone radical transformations.

The RA in 1920 was a relatively new and small organization, which had not as yet developed a track record of its own. Starting in 1901, as the Alumni Association of the Jewish Theological Seminary, and remaining focused on the inspired leadership of Solomon Schechter, it changed its name in 1918 to the Rabbinical Assembly of the Jewish Theological Seminary. With Cyrus Adler at the helm of the Seminary for the next two decades, the RA found it quite difficult to begin the process of discovering its autonomous existence, particularly so, as Adler was reinforced by the venerable presence of Louis Ginzberg, and subsequently by the administrative talents of Louis Finkelstein. Certainly, the young activists in 1920 who wanted the RA to strike out on its own, ideologically and programmatically, independently of the Seminary and the United Synagogue, found themselves continuously running into the insurmountable opposition of Cyrus Adler and Louis Ginzberg, joined several years later by Louis Finkelstein as well.

By 1940, however, the RA had grown substantially, right along with the continued expansion of the Conservative movement. From 1920 to 1940, the RA membership had more than tripled in size, as had the United Synagogue. It was more than numerical growth, however. The RA now had a cadre of home-grown leaders, who had graduated from the Seminary, become involved in local and national affairs, and who could now be counted upon as experienced, talented and highly trained representatives of the Conservative movement in all the areas of major functioning of the American Jewish community. In many ways, the bright young stars of the RA in 1940—such as Louis Finkelstein, Milton Steinberg, Solomon Goldman, Israel Goldstein, Max Routtenberg, Robert Gordis, Max Arzt, Louis Levitsky—leave one gasping and wondering, will we ever see their likes again?

The intervening years had forced the RA to increasingly undertake leadership positions in the Conservative movement. In the Prayer Book Committee of the United Synagogue it succeeded in winning a compromise solution over the objections of Adler, Ginzberg, and Marx. In meeting the growing financial needs of the Seminary, the RA increasingly began to play a leadership role, particularly as the "our crowd" group began to be a less decisive voice in the finances of the Seminary. The RA Law Committee, organized in 1927, quickly replaced the corresponding committee of the United Synagogue as the effective halakhic voice of the movement. Its initial results were disappointing, but even its failures pointed the way to future agendas and the necessity for changing methods and directions. It was instrumental in the founding of the Synagogue Council of America in 1926 and in seeking to speak out with a unified voice together with its Orthodox and Reform counterparts.

During the depression, the RA became a serious voice for social justice. With the rise of Nazism, attention had to be increasingly directed to finding useful methods of assisting the growing numbers of victimized Jews overseas. Here at home, the organizational structure of the Jewish community became increasingly persuaded, frequently by the RA, that the religious voice needed to be injected into the "civic," "defense," and "philanthropic" organizational activities that had previously successfully disregarded it. Areas of cooperation and concern were explored in dialogues with executives of the federation and Jewish community center fields. The Rabbinical Assembly, early on, was a pioneering voice for the cultivating of intensive education under the aegis of the synagogue.

Understandably, the area of ideology was the most intractable one to face the RA. With the United Synagogue largely unconcerned with philosophic refinements, and with the Seminary actively resisting denominational formulations, it was left to the RA to agonize over this vital component of the emerging Conservative movement. However, the self-evident divisions within the assembly made consensus-building a difficult task indeed. The RA was to remain a coalition group, consisting of several different ideological orientations, united largely by professional ties, warm human bonds, and general opposition to the extremes of the right and the left. It would not be until the 1980s that the Conservative movement, having shed part of its left and right wings, would be able to develop a joint statement of a religious platform.

NOTES

1. An illustrative description of the evolution of the "synagogue-center" is portrayed by Abraham Karp in his "A Century of Conservative Judaism in the U.S.," *AJYB* 86 (1986), pp. 26–31.

2. Israel Goldstein, ed., *Problems of the Jewish Ministry* (New York: Board of Jewish Ministers, 1927).
3. *JE,* May 1, 1925, p. 7.
4. Herbert Rosenblum, *The Founding of the United Synagogue of America, 1913,* unpublished doctoral dissertation, Brandeis University, 1970.
5. *JE,* February 28, 1913.
6. Rubenovitz, Herman and Mignon, *The Waking Heart* (Cambridge, MA: Notre Dame Press, 1967), p. 40.
7. Adler, in a letter to Schechter (January 28, 1912): "I for one do not want to be drawn into any Separatist movement by these young men . . ." Schechter Archives, Jewish Theological Seminary.
8. Herman H. Rubenovitz Papers, Library of the Jewish Theological Seminary.
9. Rubenovitz and Rubenovitz, op. cit., p. 58.
10. Ibid., letter from Jacob Kohn to Herman Rubenovitz, dated February 3, 1921.
11. Rubenovitz Papers, Library of the Jewish Theological Seminary, the "call," dated Jan. 12, 1922.
12. Ibid., minutes of the meeting.
13. Ibid.
14. Ibid., Nov. 24, 1922.
15. *The United Synagogue Recorder,* 1:2 (April 1921).
16. Ibid., 2:2 (April 1922).
17. *JE* (May 16, 1924).
18. Herbert Parzen, *Architects of Conservative Judaism* (New York: Jonathan David, 1964), pp. 120–24.
19. Herbert Rosenblum, *Conservative Judaism: A Contemporary History* (New York: United Synagogue, 1983), p. 29.
20. Ira Robinson, ed., *Cyrus Adler: Selected Letters,* Vol. 2 (Philadelphia: Jewish Publication Society of America, 1985), p. 89.
21. Rubenovitz Papers, Library of the Jewish Theological Seminary, June, 14, 1927.
22. Max Routtenberg, *Decades of Decision* (New York: Bloch Publishing, 1973).
23. Parzen, p. 125.
24. Robert Gordis, "A Program for American Judaism," in Mordecai Waxman, ed., *Tradition and Change* (New York: Burning Bush Press, 1958), p. 130.
25. Mordecai Waxman, ed., *Tradition and Change* (New York: Burning Bush Press, 1958), p. 130.
26. Eli Ginzberg, *Keeper of the Law: Louis Ginzberg* (Philadelphia: Jewish Publication Society, 1967), p. 226.
27. Ibid., p. 242.

28. Mel Scult, *Judaism Faces the Twentieth Century: A Biography of Mordecai Kaplan* (Detroit: Wayne State University Press, 1990), p. 186.
29. *PRA* (1930), p. 12.
30. Pamela Nadell, *Conservative Judaism: A Biographical Dictionary and Sourcebook* (New York: Greenwood Press, 1988), p. 302.
31. Michael Greenbaum, *Mission Conflict in Religiously Affiliated Institutions of Higher Education: The Jewish Theological Seminary of America During the Presidency of Louis Finkelstein, 1940–55,* unpublished dissertation, Teachers College, Columbia University, 1994, pp. 91ff.
32. Nadell, p. 86.
33. A brief bibliographic note on Mordecai Kaplan and the Conservative movement: his impact is so universal that virtually all publications dealing with the movement during his period of active involvement mention him and his work in extensive fashion. Thus, the biographical works of Herman Rubenovitz, Judah Magnes, Solomon Goldman, Simon Greenberg, Milton Steinberg, Cyrus Adler, Louis Ginzberg and Louis Finkelstein all devote considerable attention to their interaction with him and his ideas. The issues of the *SAJ Review* and *The Reconstructionist* rarely were published without extensive literary contributions from his pen. Specific works dealing with his life and thought include: Ira Eisenstein, and Eugene Kohn, eds., *Mordecai Kaplan: An Evaluation* (New York: 1952); Max Arzt, "Dr. Kaplan's Philosophy of Judaism," *PRA* (1938), pp. 195–219; Richard Libowitz, *Mordecai M. Kaplan and the Development of Reconstructionism* (New York: E. Mellen Press, 1983); Mel Scult, *Judaism Faces the Twentieth Century: A Biography of Mordecai Kaplan* (Detroit: Wayne State University Press, 1993); Emanuel Goldsmith, Mel Scult and Robert Seltzer, eds. *The American Judaism of Mordecai Kaplan* (New York: New York University Press, 1990).
34. *PRA* (1930), p. 18.
35. Libowitz, p. 195. The letter is dated September 15, 1960, and taken from the Kaplan Archives at the Reconstructionist Rabbinical College.
36. Scult, op. cit., p. 197.
37. Arnold Rothkoff, *Bernard Revel: Builder of American Jewish Orthodoxy* (Philadelphia: Jewish Publication Society, 1972), pp. 94–115.
38. Scult, p. 206.
39. Ibid., p. 192.
40. Mordecai Kaplan, *The Future of the American Jew* (New York: Reconstructionist Press, 1958), pp. 106–122.
41. *PRA* (1933–38), p. 255.
42. Ibid. (1940), pp. 122ff.
43. "Interesting Decisions by the Committee on Interpretation of Jewish Law," *The United Synagogue Recorder,* 1:3 (July 1921), p. 7.

44. *PRA* (1928), p. 21.
45. Ibid. (1933), p. 31.
46. Ibid. (1934), p. 103.
47. Ibid. (1936), p. 335.
48. Ibid. (1938), p. 432.
49. Ibid., p. 433.
50. *PRA* (1935), pp. 170–188.
51. "Decisions in Jewish Law," by Boaz Cohen, a summary of the decisions rendered by the Law Committee by 1938, *RA Bulletin* (April 1938), p. 7.
52. Max Routtenberg, *Decades of Decision* (New York: Bloch Publishing Co., 1973), p. 74.
53. Robert Fierstien, *A Different Spirit: The Jewish Theological Seminary of America, 1886–1902* (New York: The Jewish Theological Seminary, 1990).
54. Herbert Rosenblum, "Ideology and Compromise: The Evolution of the United Synagogue's Constitutional Preamble," *Jewish Social Studies,* 35:1 (Jan. 1973).
55. *JE* (May 8, 1925), p. 2.
56. Rubenovitz, op. cit., pp. 73–84. Also Herbert Rosenblum, "The Emergence of the Reconstructionist Movement," *The Reconstructionist,* 41:4 (May 1975).
57. Routtenberg, p. 130.
58. *PRA* (1935), p. 195.
59. Ibid., p. 200.
60. Ibid., p. 217.
61. *PRA* (1933), p. 38.
62. Robert Gordis, *Conservative Judaism: A Modern Approach to Jewish Tradition* (New York: National Academy for Adult Jewish Studies, 1956), p. 28.
63. *The United Synagogue Recorder,* 2:2 (April 1922), p. 13.
64. Ibid., 4:4 (October 1924), p. 12.
65. *PRA* (1927), p. 35.
66. *PRA* (1932), pp. 322–323.
67. Ibid., pp. 326–327.
68. Ibid., p. 329.
69. Ibid., pp. 338–339.
70. *PRA* (1940), pp. 159–179.
71. *PRA* (1939), p. 27.
72. Ibid., p. 21.
73. Ibid., pp. 48ff.
74. Ibid., p. 64.
75. *PRA* (1940), p. 78.

76. Ibid., p. 79.
77. *The United Synagogue Recorder,* 5:3 (June 1925), p. 14.
78. *PRA* (1929), p. 125.
79. *The Bulletin of the Rabbinical Assembly,* 1:1 (Nov. 1937), p. 2.
80. Ibid. (March 1939), p. 8.

New and Expanding Horizons

The Rabbinical Assembly
1940–1970

Pamela S. Nadell

In 1940 the Rabbinical Assembly of the Jewish Theological Seminary of America consisted of a small fellowship of some 300 rabbis who shared loyalty to their alma mater. Its members assembled in convention once a year to renew friendships, revisit old arguments, and take the collective pulse of their ongoing battle against the irreligiosity of much of American Jewry. In 1940, few, if any, of its members could have predicted that in less than a decade the Rabbinical Assembly of America (the name change occurred in 1940) would be transformed from a narrow alumni association of limited influence into a national body of many hundreds of rabbis, collectively charged with setting the parameters of one of the fastest growing expressions of American Jewish life, the suburban synagogue. The new horizons the men of the Rabbinical Assembly unexpectedly encountered in these years led them to target an expanding agenda. Its key items—professionalization of the rabbinate, the creation of a Conservative liturgy and literature, and fashioning a halakhah viable for the contemporary world—would lead the Rabbinical Assembly, in its middle years, to play a decisive role in defining the expressions of Conservative Jewish life in the second half of twentieth-century America.

In the wake of the crisis that engulfed European Jewry, American Jewry became, by default, the major demographic, economic, intellectual and cultural center of world Jewry. As Edward Shapiro traced in *A Time for Healing,* a history of post-World War II Jewry, a major theme of those years was how American Jews moved rapidly into the nation's social, cultural and economic mainstream, so much so that the religion of the Jews, who constitute a tiny segment of U.S. citizenry—one continually declining from a high of 3.5 percent in the 1930s—became one of the nation's three major faiths.[1] As recognized spokesmen for American Judaism, rabbis as individuals and collectively in their professional associations—Reform's Central Conference of American Rabbis, Orthodoxy's Rabbinical Council of America, as well as the Rabbinical Assembly—played not inconsiderable roles in carving out the contours of those transformations.

A Thousand Rabbis Strong

But in 1940, none of these postwar transformations was yet on the horizon. In 1940, with quotas limiting the numbers of Jewish students at virtually all major American universities, restrictive covenants on housing, and want ads stipulating no Jews need apply, anti-Semitism remained a major force circumscribing Jewish life and fixing Jewish identity. Regardless, among the Jewish responses to America had been that evident in every emancipated, modern Jewish community, a "diminution of the religious element in Jewish culture [which] could not be reversed." This had led not only to a decline in the status of the rabbi but also to competition by secular Jewish agencies with the synagogue for those Jews who continued to seek formal identification with the Jewish community.[2] The events of World War II, including the experiences of Conservative rabbis in that war, would help reverse this situation, heralding an unanticipated outburst of enthusiasm among American Jewry for synagogue life.

Yet in 1940 America remained isolated from the conflict in Europe. The Seminary alumni who assembled at their annual convention that year were still reeling from the legacy of the Great Depression: too few jobs for too many rabbis. Unquestionably horrified by what was going on in Europe, they—those employed and those still in search of positions—were powerless to do more than express a collective moral outrage in the face of "the overwhelming present tragedy and its terrifying implications for the future." Calling, "to save what can be saved . . . and to protect what can be protected," to increase support for Palestine, and "to defend our country from its enemies both within and without,"[3] Conservative rabbis, as all Americans, were impotent in the face of the carnage.

The events of December 7, 1941 would change that circumstance dramatically. Just as America's entry into World War II mobilized American men and women for the war effort, so too it called upon the men of the Rabbinical Assembly, not to bear arms as soldiers but to bring spiritual sustenance to the those who would have to fight. At the beginning of 1942 three Conservative rabbis were military chaplains. By 1944 fully one-third of the RA had joined the armed forces, as Conservatism's Chaplaincy Availability Board prioritized men to serve as military chaplains.[4]

The mobilizing of the rabbis to become chaplains in the European and Pacific theaters raised immediate problems for Conservative Judaism at home. Congregations whose rabbis joined the war effort had to be restaffed somehow. In these critical times the Jewish community at home needed religious leaders more than ever—to help synagogues mobilize for the war effort, to console mothers and fathers whose sons were sacrificed to the war, and to lead American Jewry in mourning the growing mass destruction of its brethren in Europe. At the same time the call to the chaplaincy unanticipatedly raised manifold opportunities for the rabbis. Within the first year of war work, chaplains were discovering what would soon become a widespread feeling among their colleagues—the army provided a rich field for winning men back to the synagogue and to Judaism. The rabbis became convinced that through their close contacts with young soldiers far from home, they were laying the groundwork for postwar American Judaism. And RA chaplains were, in particular, optimistic about the prospects for Conservative Judaism, for, as a mean between Reform and Orthodoxy, the Conservative synagogue service had become the norm in the armed forces.[5]

If the chaplains were right—that Jewish servicemen would return both to home and the synagogue—the Conservative rabbinate would soon face a severe manpower shortage, a complete reversal of the dire employment situation of but a few years before. In fact, already there were not enough rabbis to cope with the wartime emergency. And if these chaplains succeeded in winning soldiers back to Judaism when they returned home as civilians, they promised unparalleled growth for Conservatism.

Obviously, one solution to the manpower problem was to ordain more rabbis. In the 1930s the Seminary had graduated an average of eight rabbis a year. During the war, the Seminary increased class size and accelerated the rabbinic program, so that as many as nineteen were ordained in a single class.[6]

But the Seminary proved unable to produce rabbis fast enough for what became an exploding Conservative movement. Between 1945 and 1965 one out of every three Jews left the big cities for the suburbs. There they founded new synagogues. The emergence of suburban synagogues in the 1950s and 1960s was so striking that one historian judged: "By far the most common expression of Jewishness in suburbia was membership in a synagogue."[7]

Very often these new synagogues were Conservative. In 1945 Conservatism's congregational branch, the United Synagogue of America, counted just 190 Conservative synagogues, down from 220 in 1927. By 1949 it had swelled to 365. In the single two-year period of 1956–57, it added 130 new affiliates. By 1964 there were 778 synagogues in the United Synagogue. In 1971, as its exponential growth peaked, there were 832 Conservative synagogues in America.[8]

Many of these new synagogues were in Conservatism's traditional centers in the East and Midwest, in the suburbs of New York and Newark, Philadelphia and Baltimore, Chicago and Minneapolis. But many were not. They had sprung up as postwar Jews migrated to the sunbelt—to Phoenix, Miami and Los Angeles—and pioneer Conservative rabbis had followed.[9]

Even with the Seminary graduating thirty rabbis a year in the postwar era, the Conservative movement, from within, simply could not keep up with the demand for pulpit rabbis. Of the 132 congregations seeking rabbis in 1949, nearly 100 failed to hire one, in part because of an accelerating trend within the Rabbinical Assembly. By 1949, 28 percent of its men were not congregational rabbis. While some served the Conservative movement as administrators and Seminary faculty and a dozen had retired, eighty were employed elsewhere. They were Jewish and secular educators, administrators of Jewish organizations, military and civilian chaplains. Already a handful had immigrated to the new state of Israel. The overwhelming majority of these men remained dedicated to furthering Jewish life. In fact, an astonishingly small number of rabbis—some 6 percent in 1960—were in totally unrelated areas. The men of the RA thus continued to work within the Jewish world, but a significant and growing minority preferred careers outside the synagogue. Not surprisingly, this new tendency exacerbated the already acute lack of rabbis available to lead Conservative congregations.[10]

With the manpower shortage emerging as a regular theme at RA conventions, some saw that the admission of large numbers of rabbis ordained outside the Seminary offered an expeditious solution to the problem. Back in 1918, the Rabbinical Assembly had allowed non-Seminary graduates to apply for membership. However, RA president Max Davidson guessed that by 1944 no more than fifteen or twenty Conservative rabbis had been ordained elsewhere. But the dilemma of too few rabbis for an American Jewry widely seeking—perhaps for the first time ever—this kind of religious leadership pushed the Membership Committee to streamline the lengthy proceedings that in the past had deterred non-Seminary rabbis from attempting applications. One year later seven such rabbis joined the RA, bringing its total membership to 400.[11]

By 1953, the manpower shortage had become even more critical than during the war, as Jews in the vanguard of the suburban exodus founded hundreds of new synagogues. Despite the controversy surrounding rabbinical "outsiders"—who did not share the majority's loyalty to the Seminary and who might disrupt the RA's always delicate coalition of rabbis representing the right, left, and center of Conservative ideology and practice, the rabbis voted to admit up to 25 percent of their members from beyond the Seminary walls. By 1957, 110 rabbis, 22 percent of the then 619 members of the Rabbinical Assembly, had received ordination at institutions other than the Seminary.[12]

This striking growth in membership continued throughout the 1960s. Each new class of Seminary graduates brought on the average 22 new rabbis. Non-Seminary rabbis continued to be drawn, according to RA executive vice president Wolfe Kelman, by the RA's superior placement system and by its leading role in fashioning contemporary Jewish life. In 1969, the RA admitted its 1,000th member and counted rabbis in Canada, Mexico, Venezuela, Argentina, Brazil, Peru, England, Sweden, India, Japan, and, of course, Israel. Between 1950 and 1980, 600 rabbis belonging to other groups had sought to join the RA. Yet in this same period, fewer than ten Conservative rabbis had left for other rabbinic conferences. Surely these figures reflected the new prestige and influence the Rabbinical Assembly had won in its years of growth and expansion. What had been a small fellowship of Seminary alumni on the eve of World War II had grown three decades later into a significant and powerful religious establishment.

Extraordinarily Busy Men

As the premiere historian of Conservative Judaism, Abraham J. Karp, has shown, the American rabbi had become an extraordinarily "busy man," particularly the Conservative rabbi, who felt compelled to match the activities of his colleagues, Orthodox and Reform.[13] In the years of Conservative Judaism's expansion, this remained no less a characteristic of Conservative rabbis, especially of the two-thirds of the men of the RA who continued to serve on the front lines of synagogue life. RA executive vice president Wolfe Kelman offered a partial explanation for the enormous commitment of time and energy required of the men in the rabbinate:

> Some people say that the role of the modern rabbi is entirely new. This is not entirely true. All of the things that the rabbi does today used to be done in the past, but by a number of people; and the rabbi did what a rabbi used to do. He was the *moreh horaah*—which, of course, we hope many of our rabbis still are in their congregations. He was also the final authority in all religious matters—marriage, divorce, etc. But everything else a rabbi does was done by a *maggid*. The master of ceremonies at weddings was a *badkhan;* arrangements for funerals, for unveilings, and other duties relating to death, were attended to by the *chevreh kadisha.* Education was in the hands of the *melamed,* visiting the sick—*bikkur holim. . . .* A *linat hazedek* stayed with the dying. There were *asarah batlanim* who made up the minyan, and the congregation did not have to depend on the rabbi for that. Now the rabbi is expected to do all these things.[14]

Ordained rabbis, teachers, and preachers in Israel, Conservative rabbis in the 1940s, 1950s, and 1960s quickly found that these three titles belied the reality of their lives in the congregational rabbinate. The list of a rabbi's tasks compiled by Kelman gives only a glimpse of the duties—ruling on matters of Jewish law, officiating at rites of passage, directing educational programs, visiting the sick—engaging modern rabbis. Playing leading roles in the creation of American synagogues called "for a high order of creativity" that unexpectedly left Conservative rabbis, as Abraham Karp observed, doubly burdened in their determination to retain the traditions of the past while sanctioning some of the changes of modernity:

> The Orthodox rabbi preached on Saturday morning, the Reform on Friday, the Conservative on both, for only in his congregation were

both "major" services. The Orthodox rabbi dealt with *B'nai Mitz-vah,* the Reform with Confirmands, the Conservative with both. The Conservative rabbi would meet his Orthodox colleague at meetings of the day school and the *Vaad ha-kashrut,* but not the Reform, whom he would see at meetings of the ministerial association and the committee on religion and race, both of which were outside the realm of interest of the Orthodox. The Conservative rabbi needed to work all the harder to retain his status in the institutions serving the most "parochial" Jewish interests, where the credibility of his Orthodox colleague was not in question, and had to strive all the harder for his acceptance as a significant participant in interfaith activities, in which his Reform colleague had long been the recognized spokesman for the Jewish community.[15]

Not infrequently, RA *Proceedings* would reflect the rabbis' despair of all this activity, as some dared to voice their suspicion "that their great busyness and their creative innovations to bolster attendance—breakfasts after services, Oneg Shabbat collations, and the rest—kept them from addressing the question whether all of this is advancing Judaism."[16] One such voice was that of former RA executive vice president, Max Routtenberg, who observed in his 1965 address:

> During these past decades we have grown, we have prospered, we have become a powerful religious establishment. I am, however, haunted by the fear that somewhere along the way we have become lost; our direction is not clear, and the many promises we made to ourselves and our people have not been fulfilled.[17]

Yet, the discontent, the unease, and the often harsh self-criticism evident among some in the Rabbinical Assembly, even in what were self-evidently years of expansion and prosperity, stemmed from sources other than just dismay over the busyness of Conservative synagogue life. Rabbis were legitimately discouraged as the preponderant majority of Conservative Jews continually ignored their calls to keep Shabbat and *kashrut* at the same time that these same men and women raised millions of dollars for synagogue buildings dedicated to those traditions. They lost confidence as Orthodoxy, rather than disappearing as leading sociologists had predicted in the 1950s, persisted, to the rabbis' shock, with unexpected vigor among some Jews determined both to enjoy suburban life and to insist upon observance. And finally, toward the end of these years, as Jewish youth, repudiating the anomie of the large, institutional synagogue, crafted a particularly Jewish form of the youth culture, some rabbis wondered what was the meaning of what they had spent their lives building.[18]

In the face of this sometimes aching despair, Wolfe Kelman, the rabbi of the rabbis, remained a continuous and vociferous champion of Conservative Judaism and of its many real accomplishments. From the unique perspective of his office in Seminary headquarters and his long tenure at the heart of the Conservative rabbinate, he had a clear understanding of just how successful the rabbis and the Rabbinical Assembly really were. His annual addresses to his colleagues at their conventions continually served as reminders of their achievements and were meant to forestall the pervasive public malaise sparked by those who dwelt upon the problems of the present and the on-going weaknesses of the movement. Time and again he summoned his colleagues to take pride in their not insignificant achievements. Among these he and others counted the Rabbinical Assembly's professionalization of the rabbinate, its creation of Conservative liturgy and literature, and its leading role in formulating a halakhah viable, if not for all Conservative Jews, then for the men of the RA and their synagogues.

The Rabbis and their Trade Union

One of the very real achievements of the RA was its raising for the Conservative rabbinate and, therefore, to some extent for all American rabbis, the prestige of the rabbi in America. It did this partly by winning for rabbis the material benefits accorded to members of other professional and trade organizations. As the RA evolved into a professional association, it sought the material benefits accorded those in comparable positions. The RA determined to take care of its men and their families when they were too sick or too old to do so themselves and to set standards to govern relations among rabbis, congregations, and fellow rabbis.

The RA battled long and hard to win its "trade union" benefits, hallmarks of the Americanization of the rabbinate. These included medical, disability, and life insurance; pensions; standards for salary, tenure, and severance; vacations and sabbaticals; and rules governing relations between rabbis, assistant rabbis, and rabbis emeriti. In securing material benefits for its men, the RA showed that the American environment not only influenced its interpretations of halakhah, its educational programs, and its synagogue services, but that it equally shaped the rabbinate as livelihood. Some members of the RA growled that its concern with job benefits made it "nothing more than an employment agency catering to a restricted clientele." Nevertheless, to a great extent, the men of the RA established Conservative Judaism among American Jewry. Without question, the rabbis' path was eased by their growing economic and professional security. It is no wonder then that whenever the RA invited observers to evaluate its past, they were unanimous in emphasizing its promotion of the rabbis' material welfare. What individual rabbis could not do singly, the RA as a whole accomplished.[19]

In addition to securing "trade union" benefits, the RA set out to seize control of one other crucial aspect of the professional lives of its members—job placement. The RA's determination to regulate rabbinic placements posed one of its greatest challenges. Traditionally, both in law and in theory, a Jewish community was free to choose its rabbi and to change him at will. Any rabbi could apply for any job. But as Seminary vice chancellor Simon Greenberg observed:

> The Rabbinical Assembly, in creating its Placement Commission and in instituting its present procedures, and our congregations in submitting by and large to these procedures have set new precedents in Jewish history. It had made itself an almost indispensable intermediary between the rabbi and the congregation.[20]

Until the mid-1940s, the Placement Committee, the official employment agency for the RA, was staffed by volunteers. But in 1944 the Seminary engaged rabbi and lawyer Norman Salit to direct Conservatism's Wartime Emergency Commission to manage the complex affairs of rabbis, chaplains, and their congregations in a world at war. Placement director extraordinaire, Salit oversaw the welfare of rabbis who left pulpits to enter the armed forces and of the men who replaced them for the duration. And he planned for the postwar era when chaplains would return to the congregations they had left, when their successors would have to make new arrangements, and when the men who went straight from the Seminary to the war would have to find jobs. With the end of the war, the Wartime Emergency Commission disbanded. In its stead Bernard Segal was appointed RA executive director, head of the Placement Committee, and the RA's first full-time employee.[21]

The lack of full-time personnel had long marked the RA as the junior partner in the triumvirate of national Conservative institutions. Both the Seminary and the United Synagogue employed their own staffs, while the

RA was previously led by full-time congregational rabbis who could devote only part of their energies to its affairs. And if they were to conduct any business at all, they had to live on the East Coast. Yet the growing geographic diffusion of American Jewry militated against this limitation on RA leadership. Already California beckoned Jews, and Los Angeles promised to become a major center of American Jewish life. Turning from the east to the west, Conservative leaders devised new ways to bring home to Jews "[i]n the freewheeling atmosphere of Los Angeles"[22] their vision of Judaism for the modern world. Segal's appointment—after 1947 he was RA executive vice president—raised the position of the RA in the Conservative movement and allowed for its choosing leaders beyond a limited geographic sphere. Simultaneously, Conservative leaders launched another institution, L.A.'s University of Judaism, to bridge the distance "from sea to shining sea."

Although the executive vice president was responsible for placement and administration, in reality those who held the office in this era—Bernard Segal (1945–49), Max Routtenberg (1949–51), and most importantly Wolfe Kelman (beginning in 1951)—were first and foremost placement directors. In the immediate postwar years, all wartime replacements had to leave their posts whether or not a chaplain returned to his original congregation. Becoming a joint venture of the RA and the Seminary, the Placement Commission adopted a code of procedure. When the RA, after many years of work, finally implemented a code of professional conduct (written in Hebrew, perhaps because members had rejected earlier English drafts), it included sanctions for members who violated placement regulations.[23]

In the year between the conventions of 1949 and 1950, some 225 congregations turned to the RA for rabbis, and 150 men, or more than 40 percent of the rabbis already engaged in congregational work, applied for these new posts. This was a dramatic turnaround from the dim employment situation of but a decade before, when 33 members were unemployed.[24]

Rabbinic placement required extraordinary energy in the 1950s and 1960s in the years of exponential growth. In but one twelve-month period in 1952–53, there were more than eighty placements. Wolfe Kelman, director of the Joint Placement Commission from 1951 to 1966, proved particularly adept at this time-consuming and delicate task. As a rabbinical student he had directed High Holiday student placements and designed the students' system for pooling and redistributing their earnings based on need and seniority. But his concern for his colleagues did not begin and end with their placement. He remained their consultant and confidant, the director-general of rabbi-congregational relationships. He served as watchman for rabbis negotiating to renew their contracts and as the liaison between the Placement Commission and synagogue boards in working out amicable separation and pension plans. His pioneering work in leading the Rabbinical Assembly to adhere to strict organizational discipline helped professionalize and win dignity for the entire American rabbinate.

Self-evidently, placement work was more than one person could handle. Even before Kelman began his lengthy tenure, his predecessor, Max Routtenberg, pleaded for additional personnel for the RA. That plea went unanswered for nearly a decade, even though the RA was then the only rabbinic body in America that expected its executive officer to be both the director of placement and the administrator of its affairs. The rabbis were fortunate that in the busiest years of placement some of their ablest colleagues—Max Davidson, Louis Levitsky, Edward Sandrow, David Goldstein, Armond Cohen, and Judah Nadich—took on the burden of chairing the Placement Commission. Only in 1959 did the professional staff of the RA expand, when Jules Harlow joined as Kelman's assistant, later as director of publications. In 1965 Gilbert Epstein became director of community services, relieving Kelman of many placement chores. The additional personnel enabled the RA under Kelman's strong leadership to initiate the many new projects that marked its coming of age.

By the mid-1950s there was a strong sense of growing stability and security among Conservative congregational rabbis. Clearly, the work the RA had accomplished in the past decade in establishing a pension fund and pioneering rabbi-congregational relations played an important role in enhancing their sense of security. The wanderlust that had characterized the Conservative rabbinate of earlier decades was beginning to abate, as a "decreasing number of men . . . *actually require* a change of post [original emphasis]."[25]

In the postwar era, different forces motivated rabbis to change congregations. Aware of the expanding opportunities in the Conservative Jewish world, they looked for a refreshing challenge or a larger congregation and its greater material reward. Rabbis were so eager to live near a large center of Jewish life, preferably New York City with its Jewish educational opportunities for themselves and their families, that they would even take salary cuts for pulpits there. Rabbis sought metropolitan congregations large enough to support a cantor or teacher to share the work. But the Placement Commission had to struggle to find enough rabbis willing to serve the numerous smaller congregations of a hundred families or less, remote from metropolitan centers, where the rabbi was often the only Jewish professional in town.

Nevertheless, given the sensitive task of the Placement Commission—matching rabbis with jobs—it was rarely without its critics.[26] In 1952 and again in 1970, the RA scrutinized its work. One complaint surfaced each time. The Placement Commission was accused of favoritism, especially of those rabbis closest to New York, who could more easily maintain frequent contact. Other objections were, however, more successfully addressed. Rabbis believed that the Seminary kept tabs on its graduates and that when it disapproved of a rabbi's practices or ideology, it punished him by preventing him from being recommended to a choice pulpit. Consequently, in 1953, the Placement Commission limited the authority of Seminary representatives to the most recent graduates of the Seminary—those out less than five years. Criticism of the size, scope, and geographic representation of the commission resulted in its restructuring to make it more representative of the RA, and laymen from the United Synagogue were added. A revised Code of Ethics provided graded sanctions for violating the Placement Code. As a result, in 1953, a rabbi charged with violating placement regulations resigned from the RA.[27]

Despite efforts to address the criticisms leveled against the Placement Commission, discontent with its operation did not abate. A survey of the RA's membership in 1970 found the not unusual, yet nevertheless high, figure of 30 percent of the men of the RA critical of its work. Part of the dissatisfaction stemmed from the inherent paradox in the nature of the Conservative rabbinate. Conservative rabbis, thanks in large measure to the achievements of the Rabbinical Assembly, had become relatively well-rewarded, paid professionals. Nevertheless, the rabbis continued to prefer to think of themselves not as salaried professionals but as devoted to a calling, the heirs to the traditional East European sages whose piety, learning, and otherworldliness they idealized. Consequently, the rabbis walked a fine line between their self-image as salaried professionals—an image born out of the American setting—entitled to the material rewards of their positions, and their self-image as men of calling, spiritual leaders of their congregants. With difficulty they asked—or wished the Placement Commission to ask—their congregations to provide health and disability insurance, pay the entire annual premium on their retirement funds, supply rent-free housing, repair their parsonages, reimburse them for convention expenses, and award tenure.

But as spiritual leaders this generation of Conservative rabbis felt demeaned by the process of negotiating for these worldly necessities. As Rabbi Gilbert Kollin pointedly illustrated:

> [The interview] is still very much the old-time *probeh,* in which the candidate is subjected to a detailed examination of his ritual and theological *tsitsis,* trotted through his forensic paces before a critical crowd and then put on the spot to bargain over salary. The rabbi's stature is demolished in front of the very leadership group he must work with.[28]

The impossibility of reconciling the incongruous self-images of paid professional and spiritual leader helps to explain the often vociferous dissatisfaction the rabbis expressed over the RA's "trade union" activities, despite the fact that these were essential to enhancing the status and security of the Conservative rabbinate. Without the confidence they engendered, the RA's other major projects in its era of growth and prosperity, its shaping of Conservative literature and law, would have been inconceivable.

Disseminating Conservative Judaism: The Publications Program of the Rabbinical Assembly

The years of expansion also promised increased prosperity for Conservative Judaism and concomitantly for the RA. In 1940 the RA's annual budget was only $2,500. That covered the erratic publication of its convention *Proceedings,* the activities of its Committee on Jewish Law, and some secretarial assistance. But with the Joint Campaign for the Seminary, United Synagogue, and Rabbinical Assembly underway in the early 1940s to raise funds for Conservative Judaism, the RA's economic prospects brightened. By 1946 its budget had increased six-fold to $15,000, and an additional $10,000 in personnel expenses came from the Seminary.[29]

RA president Robert Gordis (1944–46) understood that the movement's expanding revenues permitted expanding ambitions. He called for the Conservative movement to strengthen its organizational structure, ameliorate its comparative failure in the field of education, and develop a philosophy and literature. And he summoned the RA to lead the way.[30]

Even prior to his presidential challenge, many of Gordis's colleagues had vociferously criticized their alma mater for deliberately failing to develop a strong ideological base for Conservative Judaism. Now they expected the RA to begin to fill that vacuum by creating a literature reflective of Conservative Jewish thought.

As World War II drew to a close, the RA launched this endeavor by regularizing its existing publications. The *Proceedings* of its annual conventions, with their addresses, resolutions, memorials, and committee reports, erratically published in the past, began to appear annually.

Major themes and addresses of each convention reveal the men of the RA wrestling, just as American Jews did at large, with the major themes of contemporary Jewish life: "The Returning Veteran and His Religion" (1945), "The Unity of the Jewish People Throughout the World" (1952), Zionism and the State of Israel (1956), the emerging Jewish day school (1962), Jews and Blacks (1969), Soviet Jewry (1970), and what to do with rabbis morally opposed to the Vietnam War who refused to serve as chaplains (1970). In 1963, a group of rabbis rushed from the annual meeting to Birmingham, Alabama to join the Civil Rights marchers. Five years later, less than two weeks before his tragic assassination, Dr. Martin Luther King appeared before the RA.

The *Proceedings* also demonstrate the shifting directions of RA leaders in these years when its presidency rotated among rabbis representing the right, left, and center of Conservative Jewish thought. Only later, when the more powerful center recognized the undue influence this gave the less influential wings, would this arrangement end. Rabbinical Assembly presidents in the years of expansion—Leon Lang (1940–42), Louis Levitsky (1942–44), Robert Gordis (1944–46), Israel Goldman (1946–48), David Aronson (1948–50), Max D. Davidson (1950–52), Ira Eisenstein (1952–54), Harry Halpern (1954–56), Aaron H. Blumenthal (1956–58), Isaac Klein (1958–60), Edward Sandrow (1960–62), Theodore Friedman (1962–64), Max J. Routtenberg (1964–66), Eli A. Bohnen (1966–68), and Ralph Simon (1968–1970)—would use their platforms to promote particular halakhic reforms or advocate their specific ideological and political agendas. For example, as RA president, David Aronson called both for the abolition of the second day of Festivals to symbolize unity with the new State of Israel and for a movement of Conservative Zionists to give Conservatism a voice in the new state. The prominent Reconstructionist Ira Eisenstein coordinated the first meeting ever held among the presidents of the three major rabbinical associations. But while he persuaded the rabbis to meet, he could not convince them to cooperate. And Max Routtenberg and Ralph Simon both found themselves working assiduously to smooth the often tense relations among the triumvirate of national Conservative institutions.

The committee reports presented at these meetings reveal the wide-ranging interests of the men of the RA in all aspects of Jewish life. For example, the 1947 convention heard seventeen reports, reflective of the rabbis' concern for youth (College Youth, Leadership Training Fellowship, Scouting, and Jewish Education), professional affairs (Rabbinic Ethics, Relief Fund, and Rabbinic Placement), Zionism (Hebrew Culture and Zionist Actions), and the transplantation of traditional Jewish values to America (Jewish Law, *Siyyum Hashas,* and Social Justice).

But the affairs of Conservative, American, and international Jewry, the nation and the world were not the only topics of the annual meetings. Always, the work of the practical rabbinate, helping rabbis find new and creative ways to respond to the many challenges of their work, found a place on convention programs. Educating rabbis to do their jobs better and offering them fresh ways of being preachers, communal leaders, and educators were critical components of these conclaves.

Yet regular publication of the *Proceedings* was just the beginning of what became a much larger publications program. After all, convention proceedings were read, if at all, chiefly by those who received them, the members of the RA. Other projects, however, were designed to reach wider audiences and to clarify to Conservative Jews, as well as to the rabbis themselves, the philosophy of Conservative Judaism.

In January 1945 the RA launched a journal, *Conservative Judaism,* as "clear-cut evidence of the serious desire of our most creative spirits to produce a forum of discussion and research for the crystallization of our philosophy."[31] Its editors promised that all aspects of Jewish life and thought—religious ideas, Jewish law, the changing social and economic scene, Zionism, Jewish education, and especially contemporary Jewish reality—would occupy its pages. The journal, generally a quarterly publication, had a rocky early history under its first editor, Leon Lang (1945–52). With too few submissions, poor circulation, and high expenses, the project was temporarily abandoned in 1952 to divert funds to an anthology of readings on Conservative Judaism.[32] Three years later under a new editor, Samuel Dresner (1955–64), *Conservative Judaism* reappeared. He was followed in the era of expansion by editors Jack Riemer (1964–65), S. Gershon Levi (1964–69) and Mordecai Waxman (1969–74). But it was the appointment of Jules Harlow as associate editor (1964–80; managing editor, 1962–64) that helped stabilize the journal's publication schedule. *Conservative Judaism* viewed itself as a journal of "serious, critical inquiry of Jewish texts and traditions, legacy, and law; further[ing] the quest for a Conservative theology and ideology; and explor[ing] today's changing Jewish community." Its scholarly articles on Jewish law and literature, educational curricula, and the state of the fields of Jewish research—generally, but not exclusively, written by Conservative rabbis and Seminary professors—continued to explore the key themes articulated at its founding. Although the RA sensed the need for a popular magazine for Conservative laity, *Conservative Judaism* was never that forum. Instead it was destined for the elite—Conservative leaders and readers learned in Judaica. With some three-quarters of its subscription list comprised of the rabbis of the RA, it remained influential chiefly among Conservative leadership.

Rather, what the RA first envisioned for the broad mass of Conservative Jews was a prayer book. In 1940, RA president Leon Lang called for publication of a prayer book to reflect Conservative practice. The fact that Conservative synagogues then employed a dozen different Sabbath prayer books had serious implications for the national unity of the movement. As worshipers moved from one synagogue to the next, they had to accommodate to different liturgies and somewhat different services. Surely, the diversity of prayer books was indicative of the disunity within the movement at large, a disunity the rabbis determined to combat.[33]

As Marshall Sklare has suggested, "Prior to the 1950s the emerging strength of Conservative Judaism on the local level was not reflected on the national scene. The only group that visualized Conservatism in national terms was the rabbis, organized as the Rabbinical Assembly of America."[34] One reflection of their national vision was the decision to create a liturgy for the movement. The publication of such a liturgy, to be used by the majority of Conservative congregations, would go a long way toward fostering the laity's identification with this "national movement which we call Conservative Judaism." The men of the RA believed it their responsibility, as "the collective rabbi of the Conservative Movement," to create prayer books reflective of Conservative Judaism that could win consensus among the movement's rabbis and congregations no matter where they fell on the spectrum of Conservative Jewish thought and practice. The ideological and theological decisions inherent in editing such prayer books rested, they felt, with experts—the luminaries of the Seminary or the RA—not with an individual or the lay leaders in the United Synagogue.

But unfortunately, the latter were the only ones who, until then, had published Conservative prayer books. In the past Seminary president Cyrus Adler had unequivocally opposed liturgical creativity. Determined not to see Conservative Judaism as a new wing within American Judaism, he refused to sanction any steps marking its separatism. The publication of a prayer book, emended to reflect a Conservative viewpoint, fell into the realm of just such interdicted projects. His administration, in the era when the Rabbinical Assembly was still very much the junior partner of the Seminary, would not be the one to sanction overthrowing what, he felt, had been preserved for four thousand years.[35]

After Adler's death in 1940, the Seminary, under its new president, Louis Finkelstein, showed no signs of departing from this stance. Meanwhile, Reconstructionist rabbis, then still the left wing of the RA, began publishing their own prayer books. In 1942 the Reconstructionist Foundation published *The New Haggadah,* and three years later the *Sabbath Prayer Book* appeared. This activity spurred their colleagues to their right to action.[36]

With Robert Gordis as chairman and Morris Silverman as editor, the Prayer Book Commission began revising Silverman's *Sabbath and Festival Services* (1936) for publication by the RA. In 1944, after three years of activity on the part of the RA's Prayer Book Commission, the United Synagogue—presumptuously in the eyes of the RA—announced plans to issue its own prayer book. Subsequently, the RA joined with the United Synagogue to see if the two could work together on the *Sabbath and Festival Prayer Book.* The RA retained effective control over its content: seven of the nine members of the Joint Prayer Book Commission had been its presidents; all were rabbis. But cooperation with the United Synagogue promised that both the leadership and the laity would accept this prayer book, unlike the reception accorded the United Synagogue *Festival Prayer Book* (1927), which was used in only 24 percent of Conservative congregations.[37]

When the *Sabbath and Festival Prayer Book* appeared in 1946, Gordis wrote: "The future chronicler of our movement will probably rank as the most significant single achievement in the direction of a philosophy for Conservative Judaism, the publication of our *Sabbath and Festival Prayer Book.*" This was, in his estimate, the first effort "to give expression to the spirit and the approach of our movement, by embodying them in a recognizable pattern of worship, identifiable with our convictions and accessible to the gaze of all, both within and without our ranks." Scholars of liturgy have debated the significance of the liturgical changes incorporated into the Conservative prayer book. What is not debatable, however, is that the *Sabbath and Festival Prayer Book* played a role in the sharp change that Sklare noted in Conservatism in the 1950s and 1960s. He saw the emergence of a sense on the part of the laity that Conservative Judaism constituted a national movement. By 1949, over 300 of the 365 congregations of the United Synagogue had adopted the *Sabbath and Festival Prayer Book,* enabling Conservative congregants to make themselves at home in almost any Conservative synagogue in America. Clearly, the publication of the *Sabbath and Festival Prayer Book* was a contributing factor in the laity's "transmut[ing] their loyalty to local congregations into attachment to a national movement."[38]

The RA's publication of a prayer book for the movement in its era of expansion ranks among its most important successes. In the overwhelming majority of Conservative synagogues in America, the use of the *Sabbath and Festival Prayer Book* symbolized that Conservative Judaism was indeed a national movement, that it had come of age. The rabbis recognized that "[a] congregation which adopts *our prayer books* is by that very act putting a distinctive stamp upon itself and forging ties of unity and cooperation with the movement as a whole" [emphasis added].[39] Moreover, its wide acceptance strengthened the professional association, for the revenue from its considerable sales returned to the RA.

The rabbis knew that Conservative congregants needed all sorts of specialized prayer books—for weekdays, for High Holidays, for the home, for houses of mourning, for joyous celebrations, for junior congregations, for summer camps, and even for Conservative synagogues in Israel. They envisioned the *Sabbath and Festival Prayer Book* as but their first step in their creation of Conservative liturgy. The next was to be the weekday prayer book.

Many—including Gordis—thought that with the basic principles and techniques already established and the bulk of the translation work already done for the *Sabbath and Festival Prayer Book,* the weekday prayer book would appear shortly after. But fifteen years passed before its publication. Several factors caused the unanticipated delay. First and foremost, the thorny issues of content—the translation and, when essential, emendation of the classical prayers to bring them into consonance with modern thought—remained difficult stumbling blocks. Although the Prayer Book Committee could have endorsed existing prayer books in the name of the RA or edited to its satisfaction someone else's text, it refused to do so. Instead, because it saw its work as a critical part of the RA's role in creating a literature and philosophy for Conservative Judaism, it determined to fashion the prayer book by committee—"a return to the noble example of cooperative thinking in our sacred literature of the past." But, with almost all committee members—including its successive chairmen, Rabbis Max Arzt, Jacob Agus, and Gershon Hadas—holding primary responsibilities elsewhere and no one in RA headquarters able to oversee the project in the era of Conservatism's rapid growth, it languished.[40] Only in 1959, when Rabbi Jules Harlow, fresh from the Seminary, joined the RA as its second executive officer, did the project move forward. Published, in 1961, solely under the imprint of the Rabbinical Assembly—the rabbis resented sharing responsibility for liturgical creativity with the movement's lay branch— the *Weekday Prayer Book* immediately sold out. By 1965 it had sold over 20,000 copies.[41]

Since then the RA has published a number of other "official" prayer books and services for the movement: a pamphlet for the midnight service, *Selichot* (1964); and *Yearnings* (1968), supplementary readings and meditations for the Days of Awe. Other landmark volumes would follow in the 1970s and 1980s. Much of this creativity has been the work of the movement's chief liturgist, Jules Harlow. As RA director of publications, he played major roles as editor and translator in nearly all its liturgical publications. His prayer books reveal a command of and sensitivity for the traditional and contemporary sources of Jewish creativity; a vision that remembrance of the Holocaust and the reality of the State of Israel belong in modern Jewish liturgy; and a concern for aesthetics that makes these volumes a delight to behold. Harlow helped put the RA on the map—along with the Reform movement's Central Conference of American Rabbis—as one of the leaders in American Jewish liturgical creativity.[42]

However, the prayer books and *Conservative Judaism* were not the only new aspects of the RA's publications program. Its third endeavor to develop and to disseminate Conservative philosophy in the years of expansion dates to the publication of *Tradition and Change* (1958). Edited and with an introductory survey of the Conservative movement by Rabbi Mordecai Waxman, *Tradition and Change* was the anthology that the RA had planned in 1952—and had been proposing since 1930— when it temporarily suspended publication of *Conservative Judaism*. When the volume appeared—again after the usual delays—it brought together scattered articles and addresses by representative figures of Conservatism—Solomon Schechter, Mordecai Kaplan, Cyrus Adler, Louis Finkelstein, Robert Gordis, Simon Greenberg—and pronouncements by its official bodies, including the RA's Committee on Jewish Law and Standards. The anthology incorporated the diversity of views within the Conservative movement under the broad rubrics of the origins of the movement, its philosophies, and its attitudes toward prayer, Jewish law, education, the community, and Zionism. Without ever explicitly acknowledging Marshall Sklare's pathbreaking and exceedingly influential sociological study, *Conservative Judaism* (1955), the rabbis believed the anthology set forth their opposing view "that there is a clearly defined Conservative movement, that it has an ideology, and that it is considerably more than the product of American sociological forces."[43]

In the era of expansion and prosperity, the RA would go no further in articulating that ideology than this collection of statements and opinions. Not until 1988 would Conservative leaders issue a *Statement of Principles of Conservative Judaism.* Instead the Rabbinical Assembly's publications program—the *Proceedings, Conservative Judaism,* the prayer books, and *Tradition and Change*—along with the crucial work of its Committee on Jewish Law and Standards would present to committed laity and especially to the rabbis themselves just what it meant, in this era of promise, to be Conservative Jews at home in America.

Halakhah: The Great and Agonizing Question

In 1965, vice chancellor of the Jewish Theological Seminary and former RA president, Simon Greenberg, told his colleagues:

> One of the primary characteristics of the Conservative movement, which perhaps more than any other makes it the authentic bearer of the mainstream of the Jewish tradition, is its . . . insistence upon the validity of the *Halakhah* and the need for taking the needs of modern American Jewish life into consideration . . .[44]

Nowhere is Conservative Judaism's grappling with contemporary realities, acquiescence to the imperative of moral law, and acceptance of diversity more sharply revealed than in the history of its leaders' striving to adapt the body of Jewish tradition and law, known as halakhah, to twentieth-century America.

In *Tradition and Change,* Mordecai Waxman advanced: "Conservative Judaism holds itself bound by the Jewish legal tradition, but asserts the right of its rabbinical body, acting as a whole, to interpret and to apply Jewish law." The men of the RA believed that if they could show that Jewish law was sufficiently flexible to meet head-on the changed conditions of life in the contemporary world, they would succeed in laying the foundations for American Jews' adherence to halakhah. Their triumphs and disappointments in adjusting halakhah led Max Routtenberg to claim: "The problem of Jewish law and its applicability to life remains the 'grand obsession' of the Rabbinical Assembly."[45]

For the men of the Rabbinical Assembly in the era of promise and expansion, the lingering symbol of that great obsession continued to be, as before, the *agunah*. The *agunah*—the deserted wife, who can never remarry because her husband's death remains unconfirmed or because he maliciously refuses to grant her a *get* (a Jewish divorce)—had long symbolized the moral injustice permitted in the name of Jewish law. Well into the 1990s observant Jews, especially Orthodox Jewish women, in Canada, the United States, and Israel, would continue to search for solutions, even considering secular intervention, to free Jewish women from these chains. But in the years before World War II and within Conservative Judaism, her plight remained the province chiefly of the rabbis.

In 1940 she came yet again to the Rabbinical Assembly. That year the Committee on Jewish Law indicated that it was still seeking two outstanding halakhic experts to join Seminary Professor Louis Ginzberg in forming a *beit din* to rule on the resolution proposed by Chairman Louis Epstein. Epstein suggested adding an instrument to the Jewish marriage contract that would provide, in advance, for the husband to authorize his wife, under the court's supervision, to write her own *get* when he could not or would not do it himself. But as Seminary luminaries displayed their customary reluctance to adjust halakhah to the contemporary scene, David Aronson called upon the men of the RA to take the initiative. He demanded that the Committee on Jewish Law circulate the Epstein proposal. Once one hundred members agreed, the Rabbinical Assembly itself would organize a *beit din* for implementation. The rabbis endorsed Aronson's motion, but the Committee on Jewish Law refused to cooperate. Although technically a body of the Rabbinical Assembly, it remained dominated by the Seminary and the most traditional spirits within the Conservative movement, those reluctant to make any but essential accommodations to ease the dilemma of rabbis determined to live personally within and to steer their congregants and congregations toward halakhah. The difficulty of the *agunah,* which raised the potentially troubling prospect of the legitimacy of her future children, was deemed too radical an issue for Conservative rabbis to tackle alone. Therefore, the Committee on Jewish Law refused to call the vote, asserting the RA lacked the power to introduce any measure potentially affecting all Jewry.[46]

As America entered World War II, the committee turned its attention briefly away from the *agunah* to consider the halakhic problems of men in the armed forces. The wartime emergency brought several pragmatic interpretations of tradition. The Committee ruled that soldiers were obliged to adhere to Jewish dietary and Sabbath laws only insofar as possible. It allowed rabbis to celebrate marriages on days interdicted by Jewish law for men about to be shipped overseas. Unfortunately, the war also raised the specter that these marriages might end suddenly, leaving young brides grief-stricken *agunot* if their husbands' deaths could not be validated according to the tests of Jewish law. The potential problem was so serious that in 1942 Louis Ginzberg drafted for the Committee a document, not dissimilar to Epstein's proposal, allowing a husband to authorize, in advance, agents to write his wife a *get* should he fail to return within two years of the end of the war. With relief the RA endorsed Ginzberg's text, obligated members to present it to every couple that came before them for marriage, and called upon chaplains to discuss it with the men in their charge who were already married. But Ginzberg and the Committee considered the proposal a temporary, wartime emergency measure, not a comprehensive solution to the *agunah* controversy. Consequently, at war's end these special arrangements lapsed.[47]

In the immediate postwar years, members of the RA became increasingly critical of the Law Committee and its reluctance to move forward. In 1947 the Committee's chairman, Boaz Cohen, retorted:

> We are not oblivious to the fact that a feeling exists among others that our Committee is inadequate to the task. This sentiment stems from a viewpoint toward Jewish Law not shared by the Committee, and originates in a difference in conception about the manner in which the Committee should exercise its office . . . We are content to measure our progress in inches for the time being.

While most in the Committee, content with "progress in inches," subscribed to Cohen's conviction that any other course would "be perilous, if not fatal to the principles of the continuity of Jewish Law," its members were no longer attuned to the will of the majority of the RA. As the association changed its name in 1940 from the Rabbinical Assembly of the Jewish Theological Seminary of America to the Rabbinical Assembly of America, it began to assert its independence from the very influential and very traditional forces of the Seminary. No longer would the RA—which was opening its ranks increasingly to non-Seminary rabbis—see itself as a subordinate alumni association. One reflection of its growing independence and influence was the dissolution of the Committee on Jewish Law and its replacement with the Committee on Jewish Law and Standards.[48]

Following Boaz Cohen's report at the 1947 convention, Rabbi Jacob Agus—who, although trained and ordained at institutions associated with American Orthodoxy, left them behind when he joined the RA in 1945—proposed the reorganization of the Committee. The next spring the RA held a special conference on "The *Halachah* and the Challenges of Modern Life." There Rabbi Michael Higger, a consultant to the Committee, who taught and lived at the Seminary, argued that although halakhic experts distinguished among the various forms of authority— interpretation, reinterpretation, legislation, and abrogation—if the RA presumed one form of authority, it had the power to exercise all. Out of this conference came a resolution to devote an entire day at the next convention to the three basic attitudes toward Jewish law within the RA. At the end of these discussions the rabbis would vote on the Law Committee's future.[49]

The 1948 convention in Chicago was a turning point. The symposium, "Towards a Philosophy of Conservative Judaism," with addresses by Rabbis Theodore Friedman, William Greenfeld, and Isaac Klein, representing the center, left and right wings of the RA, dealt with halakhah. The key question was whether or not the new Law Committee would be permitted to extend halakhah once the limits of legitimate interpretation had been reached. Would the RA empower the Committee to go beyond the boundaries of halakhah to allow for adjustments or innovations in the tradition? Would the reorganized Committee have the authority to abrogate laws which the people ignored or to amend ones—such as those mandating the inequality of women—which it viewed as ethically unjust? Could the Committee address areas which the tradition had never even contemplated, such as adoption? Could the Committee move away from halakhah—such as when dealing with the intermarried— where "a strictly halakhic solution would, if attempted, destroy rather than maintain and foster Jewish religious consciousness"? Would the RA allow the Committee to consider factors—the highest moral and ethical standards—other than halakhah in rendering its decisions?[50]

At the conclusion of the debate, the rabbis voted on resolutions, formulated by Louis Epstein, to redefine the composition, scope, and powers of the Committee on Jewish Law. The pivotal section read:

> The Committee shall be instructed to hold itself bound by the authority of Jewish law and within the frame of Jewish law to labor toward progress and growth of the Law to the end of adjusting it to present day religious needs and orientation, whether it be on the side of severity or leniency.

This meant that at all times and in all cases the new committee would be bound by halakhah. The rabbis defeated the resolution. Their new Committee on Jewish Law and Standards would go beyond halakhah.[51]

In so doing, the RA was responding to the very real sociological realities that the rabbis confronted, as it were, on the frontlines of Jewish life. Halakhic experts, isolated behind Seminary walls, could demand modern Jews to be bound by halakhah. But the rabbis out in the field knew better.

Suburban Jews, just then beginning their spate of edifice building, spent hundreds of millions of dollars on synagogues Arthur Hertzberg called "temples of Jewish togetherness." While synagogue membership may well have been the most common expression of Jewishness in the burgeoning suburbs, the rabbis understood, as did sociologists, that Jews expressed ethnicity, not piety, by such affiliation. In the era when "one nation, under God" was added to the pledge of allegiance, an openly religious manifestation of Jewish identity, i.e. joining a synagogue, proved most compatible with America. But less than a house of prayer, suburban synagogues signified to their members houses of assembly, places to congregate and, not coincidentally, to advertise that socially and economically Jews were at home in the American middle class. For at the same time that this spate of synagogue building took place, in the heyday expansion years of the 1950s and 1960s, anti-Semitism as a significant factor circumscribing Jewish life, declined. Simultaneously, the number of American Jews keeping kosher and the Sabbath, key indices of halakhic observance, also dropped precipitously.[52] While the RA exercised itself over halakhic issues, sociological reality revealed these increasingly out of touch with what mattered to Conservative laity. The creation of the Committee on Jewish Law and Standards (CJLS, 1948–70) was an effort to address that predicament, to assert that perhaps with the leavening factor of extra-halakhic powers, its interpretations would succeed in "the raising of the standards of piety, understanding, and participation in Jewish life" among Conservative Jewry.[53]

Expanding its ranks to twenty-five members to represent as far as possible the diverse views of the RA, the CJLS deliberately excluded Seminary faculty, unless they were also pulpit rabbis, serving on the frontlines in congregations bound by its decisions. Detroit rabbi Morris Adler, its first chairman (1948–51), declared the CJLS would "introduce into our thinking this revolutionary fact—the impact of an entirely changed world both outer and inner." And he assured his colleagues that no longer would the RA halt, stopped squarely in its tracks between its "fear of the Orthodox and danger to Reform."[54] While Michael Higger, secretary and research fellow, answered the plethora of questions posed by others, the larger Committee began initiating its own studies in the expectation that significant adaptations of Jewish law would help rabbis lead their congregants towards greater observance.[55]

The CJLS also promised to circulate signed minority and majority responsa. Rabbis could follow either, even if the minority opinion bore only a single signature. While the Committee wanted unanimous decisions binding on all, it knew that, under the historic concept of *mara d'atra,* each rabbi stood as the halakhic expert for his community. Therefore, it could "not apply sanctions against members who refuse[d] to accept even a unanimous decision. . . ."[56]

Although the *agunah* persisted in claiming attention, the CJLS began with what it perceived as one of the most critical problems of American Jewish religious life—the widespread violations of the commandment to honor the Sabbath day.[57] The rabbis planned to campaign among Conservative Jews to revitalize Shabbat. But first they found themselves confronted with the changed circumstances of contemporary life that in and of themselves caused Jews to violate Sabbath laws. Determined, unlike its predecessor, to grapple with modernity, its members acknowledged current conditions requiring halakhic innovation. In this instance, the migration to the suburbs and the widespread use of the automobile mandated a rethinking of the traditional prohibition against travel, in this case in automobiles, on Shabbat. In 1932 the Committee on Jewish Law had refused to lift the ban on automotive travel on Shabbat. By 1950, however, suburban sprawl made it increasingly impossible for many Jews—including their rabbis—to attend communal worship unless they drove. Realistically, the CJLS conceded all too few Conservative Jews participated in Shabbat services anyway. But the rabbis hoped to correct that. Having "learn[ed] to adjust our strategy to the realities of our time and place," the responsum, jointly authored by Morris Adler, Jacob Agus, and Theodore Friedman, sanctioned automotive travel when necessary to join in Shabbat worship.[58]

At the same time the CJLS also permitted the use of electricity, previously interdicted as a proscribed form of fire, in order to enhance Sabbath observance in the home. The rabbis tied these permissions to the Sabbath Revitalization Campaign, designed to encourage members of their congregations to recapture for themselves and their families the spirit of Shabbat as a day of rest, set apart from all others by the beauty of home rituals, reading of sacred literature, and participation in services. The RA thus conserved tradition—the prohibition on travel on the Sabbath was retained but for the exception of attending synagogue—but allowed for change, adjustments in the Sabbath laws designed to enhance observance. The responsum revealed that the rabbis viewed halakhah as a tool for enriching Jewish spiritual life. The RA planned that this would be the first of many such essential reinterpretations. As the CJLS charted out halakhic alternatives for an Americanized Jewry, the rabbis envisioned Conservative Jews voluntarily assuming ever greater standards of observance.

With the Sabbath Revitalization Campaign underway, the CJLS, under chairman Theodore Friedman (1951–54), turned to the status of women in Jewish law. Later, in the wake of the second wave of American feminism, this topic would emerge as a touchstone of the Conservative movement's ability to reconcile tradition and modernity. But here, in the 1950s and 1960s, the inequalities and disabilities women encountered in Jewish law chiefly engaged the rabbis. The men—and especially the women—of their congregations had not yet issued the call for change that would bring these issues to the forefront of the movement in the 1970s. Instead, when the men of the RA, in the era of "Father Knows Best," examined questions of Jewish women's legal status, they limited their concerns to the largely "unfinished business of the *agunah* problem" and the permissibility of granting women *aliyot,* the privilege of reciting the blessings before and after the public Torah reading.[59]

In 1951 the RA heard David Aronson elaborate upon the plan he had proposed in 1940 in reviewing Epstein's solution to the *agunah* controversy. Following a special conference convened by the CJLS to consider the Aronson plan, came a comprehensive strategy to solve her dilemma. But the Seminary quickly moved to head off what it viewed as the rabbis' rebellion. Seminary chancellor Louis Finkelstein told the RA that the laws of marriage and divorce were far too important for the rabbis to decide by themselves. Essentially, in matters of synagogue ritual the Seminary proved willing to concede to the rabbis the power to determine what would go on in their congregations. But when it came to critical issues of personal status with the potential to affect all Jews, not just Conservative Jews, the Seminary forbid its alumni to act alone.[60]

Consequently, in 1953, the Seminary and the RA established the Joint Law Conference, co-chaired by the RA's Theodore Friedman and the Seminary's Judah Goldin, as the only body within the Conservative movement empowered to rule on the laws of marriage and divorce. The conference established a national *beit din* and claimed the authority to enact *takkanot,* i.e. to legislate. Its founding paved the way for the *takkanah* formulated by Seminary professor Saul Lieberman, the movement's leading halakhic expert since Louis Ginzberg's death in 1953. The Lieberman *takkanah* made the *ketubah* (the Jewish wedding document) a civilly binding contract committing the bride and groom to abide by the recommendations of a *beit din* if their marriage ended in divorce. If the husband refused to give his wife a *get,* civil courts would presumably enforce compliance. As the national *beit din* soon discovered, in many instances, the persuasive power of the threat of a lawsuit could bring a recalcitrant husband to end the marriage Jewishly as well as civilly.[61]

Meanwhile, the CJLS turned to other matters. Chairman Arthur Neulander (1954–59) hoped that it would find new halakhic solutions to ongoing problems to enhance observance among Conservative Jewry. And Rabbi Max Davidson began indexing the records of the law committees of the past to document the progress already made.[62]

Not surprisingly, much of the Committee's time was taken up, as was true of its predecessors, with the routine answering of questions on *kashrut,* synagogue ceremonies and rituals, circumcision, conversion, mixed marriages and funeral rites. Many of these involved relatively minor matters. The CJLS prohibited construction work to continue on a synagogue on a holiday. It did not permit non-Jews to sing in synagogue choirs, a mark of difference between the Reform and Conservative movements. To aid isolated Jewish communities in following the laws of *kashrut,* it allowed for the kashering of frozen, properly slaughtered meat after defrosting. And the Committee took a step toward granting women equality, when, in 1955, Rabbi Aaron Blumenthal, one of its more liberal members, issued a responsum allowing women *aliyot.*[63]

Some decisions reveal the way the temper of the times shaped its judgments. In an era when the intermarriage rate was slowly rising, the CJLS could maintain its ruling against granting synagogue membership to those who had intermarried. Later, as the intermarriage rate soared among the children and grandchildren of those who were Conservative synagogue members in the 1950s and 1960s, such dissonance from the sociological reality would be impossible.[64]

Under Neulander's successors—CJLS chairmen Ben Zion Bokser (1959–60, 1963–65), Max Routtenberg (1960–63), and Israel Silverman (1965–66)—the CJLS remained preoccupied with the routine answering of questions. Because many Conservative Jews had interpreted the permission to travel to synagogue on the Sabbath as a blanket permission for driving on Shabbat, the CJLS clarified the 1950 responsum. But progress on other important issues was stymied by the large number of queries and insufficient personnel. Although it employed research consultants—among them, rabbis Michael Higger, Phillip Sigal, Marshall Meyer, and Edward Gershfield—lack of funds precluded hiring these men on more than a part-time basis. Yet, with more than 170 questions submitted in a single year, the Committee spent most of its time responding to specific questions. That left little time to initiate the kind of inquiry that had led to what the RA had deemed its path-breaking responsum on the Sabbath. The Committee pleaded its limitations before the RA, reminding them that its members were full-time pulpit rabbis, too busy to research responsa.

But once again criticism over the slow process of adaptation of halakhah to contemporary life surfaced. Many questions remained unresolved. What could the rabbis do about the widely ignored observance of the second day of festivals? Were sturgeon, swordfish, and gelatin kosher? What should the RA do to memorialize the Holocaust and to commemorate the birth of Israel? And with increasing urgency, how far could the Committee go in granting halakhic equality to women?[65]

Certainly, the greatest successes of the Committee on Jewish Law in the 1930s and 1940s and the CJLS in the 1950s and 1960s lay in setting standards for the synagogues and for the public gatherings of Conservative Jews. The Law Committees made decisions about synagogue membership, worship, rites and rituals that to a large extent unified Conservative congregations into a national movement. Their decisions, and in some cases refusal to render one, allowed for innovations in congregational practices, such as the use of a microphone, organ, and mixed choirs; a triennial cycle of Torah reading; abbreviated prayer services; and the introduction of English prayers. Not all rulings, however, permitted accommodation. The CJLS discountenanced the Shabbat afternoon (*minḥah*) bar mitzvah, preferred by some to facilitate Saturday night celebrations, and it set high standards for bar and bat mitzvah and confirmation.[66]

As "the collective rabbi of the Conservative movement," the Committee on Jewish Law and the CJLS responded to questions from the United Synagogue, Women's League, Federation of Jewish Men's Clubs, and United Synagogue Youth. The Law Committees accepted, without endorsement, some lenient, but customary, practices of Conservative congregations, such as mixed seating, as *de facto* innovations. But in other cases the committees set strict standards for the movement's national agencies which, at times, exceeded the more lenient rulings of the past. For example, in 1964 the CJLS asked United Synagogue Youth to make certain that the teenagers attending its conventions would not have to travel on Shabbat. Despite such public success, CJLS chairman Max Routtenberg voiced the dissatisfaction, shared by many, over the Committee's failure to extend halakhah creatively. He called for a law committee that would raise questions, not just answer them.[67]

With the appointment of Rabbi Benjamin Kreitman as chairman (1966–72), the CJLS entered an activist phase. The Committee issued new and more lenient opinions on the playing of bingo in the synagogue and the eating of fish in non-kosher restaurants. It allowed a swimming pool to become a *mikveh* (ritual bath) and permitted hitherto forbidden marriages between a *kohen* and a convert. It reopened the question of the observance of the second day of festivals, making their celebration optional. In recognition of the establishment of the state of Israel, it allowed for weddings to take place on days previously interdicted by Jewish law. And to adapt *kashrut*, it found gelatin, swordfish, and most hard cheeses kosher.[68]

Most importantly for the rabbis, after forty years of debate, the CJLS ended the *agunah* controversy. Throughout the 1960s, as earlier, the key symbol of the RA's difficulty in balancing tradition and change in its view of halakhah had remained the *agunah*. Yet, in these years, only one case of an *agunah* actually came before the RA, a reflection, once again, of Conservative laity's deliberate disregard of Jewish law. Wolfe Kelman reflected:

> Many of us feel that the problem of the *agunah* is symbolic of our relationship to *halachah*. We are married to it. Some of us don't want to live with it, but we don't want to divorce it.

Because the Lieberman *takkanah* only applied to marriages solemnized by the RA *ketubah*, it was, at best, a partial solution. Moreover, the new *ketubah* had not gained widespread acceptance among the rabbis. Some refused to use it because it was an insufficient stopgap measure. Others failed to endorse it because they questioned its enforceability or the desirability of involving secular authorities in a religious matter. A survey, conducted in 1968, found that, when necessary, 30 percent of Conservative rabbis would not require a *get* for a remarriage and that another 48 percent would advise women seeking remarriage who lacked *gittin* to have Reform rabbis solemnize their weddings. The dichotomy was evident. Nearly 80 percent of Conservative rabbis utilized alternative solutions to the problem of the *agunah,* ignoring the implications of the delegitimation of any children of such marriages. Meanwhile Conservative leaders agonized over what to do.[69]

Now the CJLS determined to act. Recognizing that the Joint Law Conference had not achieved its original purpose in the revision of Jewish marriage law, the RA allowed the arrangement with the Seminary to lapse. In 1968, it unanimously adopted a new proposal that added a conditional agreement, a *t'nai b'kiddushin,* to the marriage ceremony. This meant that the rabbis could annul the marriage, if necessary, after a civil divorce had been granted, if the husband refused to issue a *get.* The power of annulment meant the rabbis would not have to look to the civil courts for authority, as was necessary with the Lieberman *takkanah.* Still, this only applied to future marriages. In 1969 the CJLS *beit din* heard the case of a woman whose recalcitrant ex-husband had left her an *agunah* for eighteen years. Deciding in extraordinary cases to "invoke the powers of annulment inherent in rabbinic authority," the *beit din* annulled the marriage and informed her rabbi that he could officiate at her remarriage. With these two declarations, the RA settled the *agunah* controversy for Conservative Jews,[70] a feat meant to be a harbinger of other ways the Committee could act to resolve the inequities within halakhah and make it viable for modern Jewry.

Yet, this promising activity could not hide the crucial question. To what extent did the RA's reinterpretations of halakhah lead Conservative laity to live their lives in accordance with the dictates of Jewish law? In the non-hierarchical, non-coercive American Jewish community, the committees on Jewish law could not even command colleagues in the RA to follow their decisions. Obviously, the law committees exercised no coercive power whatsoever over the laity. By all accounts the 1950 Sabbath Revitalization Campaign was a failure. Writing in 1970 a new chapter to his major work, *Conservative Judaism,* the sociologist Marshall Sklare bluntly stated: "The fact is that there is not a Conservative synagogue in the country where most congregants practice the *mitzvoth* according to the Conservative regimen."[71]

If then Conservative Jews by and large do not follow halakhah, what has the RA's ongoing obsession meant? Were all these years of effort to adjust halakhah to the American environment a waste of energy and display of futility on the part of the Conservative rabbinate? Sidney Schwarz, a Reconstructionist rabbi, seemed to think so, arguing in his dissertation that although adherence to halakhah was the myth that united the Conservative movement:

> the practice of the laity belied that entire elite myth structure . . . Juxtaposing the CJLS decisions with the practice of the Conservative laity left one with the uneasy feeling that the tail had been wagging the dog all along.

But Conservative rabbi and historian Herbert Rosenblum suggested that "the large majority of Conservative leaders" took pride in the legislative accomplishments of the CJLS, seeing themselves, as the historian Salo Baron had observed, "true to the spirit of traditional Judaism," maintaining the validity of Jewish law while adapting it to the changing environment. Certainly, the movement's successes in insuring observance of the *mitzvot* in the synagogue and in the public gatherings of Conservative Jews kept Conservative laity observant at times and in certain places.[72]

Although the Conservative movement had only limited success in fostering personal observance among Conservative Jews, the RA's "grand obsession" with halakhah was key in the evolution of Conservative Judaism as an Americanized Judaism. As Will Herberg showed in his classic *Protestant—Catholic—Jew,* the immigrants were not expected to change their religion when they landed in America, but they were expected to accommodate American patterns of religious life. The RA's struggle with halakhah was part of that process of accommodation. From the past the RA thus preserved loyalty to halakhah and the maintenance of the rabbinic prerogative of reinterpretation. But true to the present, they took for their agenda the leading social and intellectual issues of the contemporary scene. That agenda in the era of expansion and promise—driving on Shabbat, *kashrut,* intermarriage, and even the *agunah*—most eloquently showed the Conservative rabbis' determination to meet head-on the changed circumstances of Jewish life in America. As leaders of American Jewry, they asserted their personal belief that, with adaptation, Judaism, in particular their vision of a Conservative Judaism balanced between tradition and change, remained a viable guide for themselves, their families, and their congregants.

NOTES

1. Edward Shapiro, *A Time for Healing: American Jewry since World War II. The Jewish People in America*, Vol. 5 (Baltimore: Johns Hopkins University Press, 1992); Henry Feingold, *A Time for Searching: Entering the Mainstream, 1920–1945. The Jewish People in America,*

Vol. 4 (Baltimore: Johns Hopkins University Press, 1992), p. 14; Will Herberg articulated the triumvirate of American religions in *Protestant—Catholic—Jew: An Essay in American Religious Sociology* (Garden City, NY: Anchor Books, 1960).

2. Henry Feingold, *A Time for Searching* (Baltimore: Johns Hopkins University Press, 1992), pp. 58, 63.
3. Cited in Abraham J. Karp, "The Conservative Rabbi—Dissatisfied But Not Unhappy," *American Jewish Archives* 35 (1983), pp. 221–22.
4. *PRA* (1942), pp. 56–60; *PRA* (1943), p. 164; *PRA* (1944), p. 282.
5. Harry Nelson, "A Chaplain's Pulpit," *PRA* (1943), pp. 200–06; Isaac Klein, *The Anguish and the Ecstasy of a Jewish Chaplain* (New York: Vantage Press, 1974), pp. 40–48.
6. Jewish Theological Seminary Rabbinical Department Lists.
7. Edward Shapiro, *A Time for Healing*, pp. 143, 147.
8. Pamela S. Nadell, *Conservative Judaism in America: A Biographical Dictionary and Sourcebook* (New York: Greenwood Press, 1988), pp. 336–38.
9. On two of these new American Jewish communities, see Deborah Dash Moore, *To the Golden Cities: Pursuing the American Jewish Dream in Miami and L.A.* (New York: Free Press, 1994). She uses the phrase "pioneer rabbis," p. 95.
10. Max Routtenberg, "Report of Executive Vice President," *PRA* (1949), pp. 27–38; Eli Ginzberg, "Manpower for Conservative Judaism," *PRA* (1960), pp. 19–30.
11. *PRA* (1945), pp. 16, 29–30.
12. *PRA* (1953), p. 87; *PRA* (1956), pp. 37–38; *PRA* (1957), pp. 29–31.
13. Abraham J. Karp, "The Conservative Rabbi—Dissatisfied But Not Unhappy," p. 239.
14. Wolfe Kelman, "Report of the Executive Vice President," *PRA* (1957), p. 22.
15. Karp, pp. 217, 239–40.
16. Ibid., p. 241.
17. Ibid., p. 241.
18. Ibid., pp. 241–42; Among the sociologists was Nathan Glazer, *American Judaism* (University of Chicago Press, 1957).
19. Aaron Blumenthal, "The Status of the Rabbinical Assembly in the Conservative Movement" *PRA* (1955), p. 126; Robert Gordis, "The Rabbinical Assembly and Conservative Judaism: Retrospect and Prospect," *PRA* (1955), 29, pp. 88–89.
20. Simon Greenberg, "The Role of the Rabbinical Assembly," *PRA* (1955), p. 146.
21. *PRA* (1945), pp. 11–13; *PRA* (1946), p. 52.
22. Deborah Dash Moore, *To the Golden Cities* (New York: Free Press, 1994), pp. 95.

23. Max Davidson, "Report of the Placement Committee," *PRA* (1946), pp. 316–17; Bernard Segal, "Report of the Executive Vice President," *PRA* (1947), p. 31; *PRA* (1937), p. 344.

24. *PRA* (1950), p. 35; *PRA* (1940), p. 26.

25. "Report of the Placement Commission," *PRA* (1954), pp. 95–97.

26. Wolfe Kelman, "Report of the Executive Director," *PRA* (1955), pp. 20–21.

27. *PRA* (1952), pp. 80–86; *PRA* (1970), pp. 216–17; Simon Greenberg, "The Jewish Theological Seminary of America," *PRA* (1960), p. 150; Ira Eisenstein, "President's Message," *PRA* (1953), p. 140.

28. Harry Gersh, "The Survey on Rabbinic Status," *Beineinu* 1,3 (March 1971), pp. 63–64; *Beineinu* 3,1 (January 1973), pp. 24–26; Gilbert Kollin, "Placement," *Beineinu* 1,2 (January 1971), pp. 3–8.

29. Max Arzt, "Our Expansion Program: A Reevaluation," *PRA* (1946), pp. 206–30.

30. Robert Gordis, "President's Address: New Vistas for Conservative Judaism," *PRA* (1946), pp. 59–60.

31. Robert Gordis, "The Tasks Before Us," *CJ* 1:1 (January 1945), pp. 5–6.

32. "An Appeal to our Colleagues and Readers," *CJ* 4:2 (Fall 1948), pp. 24–26; *PRA* (1953), pp. 145–46.

33. "Report of the Prayer Book Commission," *PRA* (1942), pp. 148–50.

34. Marshall Sklare, *Conservative Judaism* (New York: Schocken Books, 1972), p. 257.

35. Adler quoted by Herbert Parzen in *Architects of Conservative Judaism* (New York: J. David, 1964), pp. 98–100.

36. Mordecai Kaplan, Eugene Kohn, and Ira Eisenstein, eds. *The New Haggadah for the Pesach Seder* (New York: Behrman's Jewish Book House, 1942; rev. 1972); Mordecai M. Kaplan, Eugene Kohn, Ira Eisenstein, and Milton Steinberg, eds., *Sabbath Prayer Book* (New York: Jewish Reconstructionist Foundation, 1945).

37. *PRA* (1941), pp. 4–25; *PRA* (1942), pp. 155–56; *PRA* (1944), pp. 278–87; Robert Gordis, "Introduction to the Sabbath and Festival Prayer Book," (New York, 1946), rpt. in Mordecai Waxman, ed., *Tradition and Change* (New York: Burning Bush Press, 1958), p. 335.

38. Robert Gordis, "New Vistas," *PRA* (1946), p. 63; Robert Gordis, "Reinterpretation—Its Canons and Limits," *CJ* 13:4 (Summer 1959), p. 21; *CJ* 5:1–2 (October–January, 1948–49), back cover; Sklare, *Conservative Judaism*, p. 260.

39. Aaron Blumenthal, "Presidential Address," *PRA* (1958), pp. 49–50.

40. Robert Gordis, "Message," *PRA* (1945), p. 48; Jacob Agus, "Report of the Prayer Book Committee," *PRA* (1953), p. 98; *PRA* (1959), p. 125.

41. *Weekday Prayer Book* (New York: Rabbinical Assembly, 1961; 2d ed., 1962, 3rd ed., 1974); *PRA* (1965), p. 15.

42. *Selichot* (New York: Rabbinical Assembly, 1964); Jules Harlow, ed. and trans., *Yearnings* (New York: Rabbinical Assembly, 1968).
43. Mordecai Waxman, ed., *Tradition and Change*, pp. 3–4; *PRA* (1930), pp. 10–11.
44. Simon Greenberg, "In Honor of Louis Finkelstein," *PRA* (1965), pp. 80–81.
45. Mordecai Waxman, ed., *Tradition and Change*, p. 20; Max Routtenberg, "The Conservative Rabbinate," in *Decades of Decision* (New York: Bloch Publishing, 1973), p. 149.
46. Louis Epstein, *Li-Shealat Ha-Agunah* (New York, 1940): David Aronson, "Dr. Louis M. Epstein's 'The Agunah Question,'" *PRA* (1940), pp. 301–11; "Report of the Committee on Jewish Law," *PRA* (1941), p. 33.
47. "Report of the Committee on Jewish Law," *PRA* (1942), pp. 143–45.
48. "Report of the Committee on Jewish Law," *PRA* (1947), pp. 54–55.
49. *PRA* (1947), p. 66; *PRA* (1948), pp. 88–89; Michael Higger, "Authority to Interpret Jewish Laws," *CJ* 5:4 (June 1949), pp. 20–22.
50. "Towards a Philosophy of Conservative Judaism," *PRA* (1948), pp. 110–92.
51. "Statement and Resolutions Proposed by Rabbi Louis M. Epstein," *PRA* (1948), pp. 167–74.
52. Edward Shapiro, *A Time for Healing*, pp. 28–59, 147–50; Hertzberg term cited there, p. 149; Will Herberg, *Protestant—Catholic—Jew*, esp. pp. 31, 191–92.
53. David Aronson, "President's Message: The Demands of the New Diaspora," *PRA* (1949), pp. 136–38.
54. "Report of the Committee on Jewish Law and Standards," *PRA* (1949), pp. 46–57; David Aronson, "President's Message: At Fifty for Counsel," *PRA* (1950), pp. 98–99.
55. David Aronson, "President's Message: The Demands of the New Diaspora," *PRA* (1949), pp. 136–38.
56. "Report of the Committee on Jewish Law and Standards," *PRA* (1949), pp. 46–57.
57. *PRA* (1949), p. 86.
58. *PRA* (1932), p. 236; "Responsum on the Sabbath," *PRA* (1950), pp. 119–34.
59. "Report of the Committee on Jewish Law and Standards," *PRA* (1951), pp. 40–42.
60. David Aronson, "*Kedat Moshe Ve'Yisrael*," *PRA* (1951), pp. 120–40; "Report of the Committee on Jewish Law and Standards," *PRA* (1952), pp. 48–53.
61. "Report of the Steering Committee of the Joint Law Conference, 1953–54," *PRA* (1954), pp. 62–68.

62. "Report of the Committee on Jewish Law and Standards," *PRA* (1957), pp. 27–28.
63. For a summary of the major decisions of the CJLS, see Benjamin Kreitman, "The First Ten Years of the Committee on Law and Standards," *PRA* (1958), pp. 68–80.
64. Ibid.
65. "Report of the Committee on Jewish Law and Standards," *PRA* (1960), pp. 286–91; *PRA* (1961), pp. 188–94; *PRA* (1962), pp. 233–38.
66. "Report of the Committee on Jewish Law and Standards," *PRA* (1963), pp. 221–29.
67. *PRA* (1964), pp. 240–41.
68. "Report of the Committee on Jewish Law and Standards," *PRA* (1967), pp. 189–94; *PRA* (1968), pp. 206–28; *PRA* (1969), p. 200.
69. *PRA* (1960), p. 70; *PRA* (1961), p. 191; William Greenfeld, "Future Prospects of the Bet Din," *PRA* (1957), pp. 175–81; *PRA* (1957), pp. 58–59; "Report of the Committee on Jewish Law and Standards," *PRA* (1968), p. 215.
70. "*T'nai B'kiddushin*," *PRA* (1968), pp. 229–40; *PRA* (1969), p. 200.
71. Marshall Sklare, *Conservative Judaism*, p. 274.
72. Sidney Schwarz, "Law and Legitimacy: An Intellectual History of Conservative Judaism, 1902–1973," (Ph.D. diss., Temple University, 1982), p. 369; Baron quoted in Herbert Rosenblum, *Conservative Judaism*, (New York: United Synagogue of America, 1983), pp. 126–27.

Completing a Century
The Rabbinical Assembly Since 1970

Michael Panitz

The Rabbinical Assembly is more than a professional association. By including nearly everyone ordained as a Conservative rabbi, as well as rabbis ordained in other denominational and non-denominational seminaries who have chosen to join the Conservative movement, the RA has become virtually coterminous with the Conservative Jewish rabbinate. Therefore, the history of the RA has both institutional and cultural aspects. Institutionally, it is the record of continuity and change within the professional organization of Conservative rabbis. Culturally, it is the history of what it has meant to be a Conservative rabbi, over a period of several generations. These two histories are intertwined, and this chapter will examine both of them for the period of 1970 until the present, with emphasis on the broader dimension.

After the Expansion: Stagnation or Consolidation?

Along with Conservative Judaism itself, the RA enjoyed an enormous generation of growth in the postwar period. Its membership more than tripled, to just over 1,000 rabbis, in the quarter century following 1945. Despite the existence of strong tensions between rabbis who emphasized traditionalist stances and those advocating more and speedier adaptations to the realities of mid-century American life, the RA claimed to represent the broad center of American Jewry. Its own internal governance procedure, rotating leaders from among the different ideological branches of the denomination, seemed sufficient to mediate the tensions inherent in the coalition nature of the Conservative movement. Even the defection of the Reconstructionists in the late 1960s did not seriously erode the self-image of the Conservative movement as the denomination of choice for American Jewry.

By 1970, however, the period of expansion was largely over. No Conservative synagogues were founded between 1965 and 1971. Instead, with aging and declining memberships, Conservative synogogues were merging and closing throughout that decade.[1]

Nor was the lack of new congregations the most worrisome development. With their attention no longer diverted by the issues of hectic growth, rabbis focused increasingly on the degree to which their existing congregations were suffering an erosion of vitality.

To a large degree, the problems facing the movement began with demographic changes. The "baby bust" since 1960 reduced the pool of families with young children looking to join the Conservative synagogue. Instead of the "easy and automatic growth" of the previous generation, the Conservative movement would now have to fight just to avoid shrinking. Its suburban congregations, the mainstay of the movement, fell into decline as a result of the spread of urban problems to the inner ring of suburbs.[2]

Nor were demographics the sole problem. Beyond the dearth of young families, the Conservative movement was losing ground in the face of intertwined ideological challenges. Even in the boom years of their movement, Conservative rabbis lamented that they were not succeeding in staving off assimilation. Despite their intense efforts, they criticized themselves for the persistent shallowness of their congregants' Jewish practices. Too often, the piety of the post-war generation seemed to be confined to little more than building and joining synagogues. Twenty years of halakhic rulings designed to ease the way to observance of Jewish law did not seem to be bearing fruit. The most famous mid-century halakhic innovation of the RA Committee on Jewish Law and Standards (CLJS), allowing Jews to drive to the synagogue, did bring some Jews who would have otherwise stayed away—but, to cite a contemporary witticism, its principal effect was to allow those Jews driving anyway to park in front of the synagogue, not three blocks away. It certainly fell far short of its authors' hope, to revitalize Sabbath observance among the movement's laity. Most alarmingly, levels of intermarriage were beginning to rise.

The social upheavals of the 1960s, featuring high levels of alienation between the youth of the day and its elders, exacerbated the effects of assimilation. Although it maintained an active high school youth group (United Synagogue Youth), the movement was losing its appeal among college-age youth. As a centrist movement in an age more receptive to radicalism, Conservative Judaism was losing out both to the political and religious Left and to a resurgent Orthodoxy.[3]

The growth of Orthodoxy in North America was particularly destabilizing to Conservative observers. For decades, they had assumed that Orthodoxy was vanishing with the immigrant generation, and that Conservative Judaism represented the traditional option within the Jewish community. But by 1970, this assumption was no longer plausible. In 1972, the sociologist Marshall Sklare gave a scientific confirmation to the worries of Conservative rabbis in the field. Sklare concluded that Conservative Judaism was losing its morale, in large part due to the resurgence of Orthodoxy. The revitalization of Orthodoxy, especially the inner-Jewish missionizing of Ḥabad Hasidim, and the increased stridency of Orthodoxy's claims to being the only legitimate expression of Judaism, simultaneously impressed, frightened, and offended Conservative observers. Denominational ideologues called again and again for Conservative Jews not to lose their sense of self-esteem in the face of Orthodox triumphalism,[4] but could not succeed in providing reassurance.

As the realization sank in that Conservative Judaism had ended its era of natural growth and would henceforth have to contend with increasingly powerful rival denominations, RA members debated how to respond to the new realities of the day. Their prescriptions echoed the familiar "Right-Left" splits that have been a constant in the history of the denomination. Traditionalists argued that the movement needed to emphasize its commitment to halakhah, both in practical rulings and in founding new educational programs, so as not to lose its "best and brightest" to reinvigorated Orthodoxy.[5] Religious liberals drew the opposite conclusion. They decried the growing resistance to halakhic change, and called for the fortitude to "break through the psychological barriers to creativity in halakhah." The Conservative movement needed to find its authenticity not by following the Orthodox ever more to the Right, they argued. It had to respond to urgent issues of the day in a way that secured the loyalties of its adherents, vigorously establishing norms of distinctively Conservative practice.[6]

What both sides implicitly agreed upon was that the movement could no longer simply exist; it would have to redefine for itself what it meant to be a Conservative Jew. Mordecai Waxman, respected historian and theoretician of the movement, summed up this new direction: "Jewish life in America, which for the past quarter of a century has been concerned with the problem of creating an organizational structure, now seems desperately engaged in a search for meaning."[7]

The perennial tension between those in the Rabbinical Assembly who emphasized traditionalism and those who advocated greater accommodation was at a high point at the start of the 1970s. As at so many other times, the forum for the expression of this tension was the CJLS. Procedural difficulties, specifically the need for unanimity in order to make certain decisions, occasioned the resignations of sixteen rabbis, the large majority of the committee's members, at its December 2, 1970 meeting. The position of the majority was that traditionalists on the Seminary faculty could exploit their contacts with individual members of the CJLS to exercise a veto on any halakhic changes that they deemed too radical. In fact, although staunch advocates of halakhic change such as Seymour Siegel served on its faculty, the Seminary did embody the traditionalist branch of the movement. The preeminence of the Seminary's senior talmudists as halakhic experts, coupled with what may most charitably be described as their European-style assessment of the relative worth of rabbinic academicians as opposed to rabbis working in the field, led them to regard the proposed halakhic innovations of the religious liberals on the CJLS as not-always serious Jewish positions.

The Rabbinical Assembly president, S. Gershon Levi, responded to the coordinated set of resignations by appointing a special committee to make recommendations to the RA Executive Council about reorganizing the CJLS, and by convening a *kallah* in August 1971, to discuss the issue. The position papers and discussions of that episode reveal that, for all the participants involved, the procedural issues were really only the proverbial tip of the iceberg, the substance of which was the question of the parameters of change within the movement.[8] Ultimately, the committee resumed its work, with a procedural change requiring that a position receive a minimum of six votes in order to be registered as an official opinion of the movement. The net effect of this reorganization was to concede to the demands of the majority of the CJLS that the movement could move forward even without a total consensus of opinion. This was not to be the last issue of the generation in which the RA forced its erstwhile mentors at the Jewish Theological Seminary to accept both substantive changes and new operating rules.

The Defining Question: The Role of Women within Conservative Judaism

The CJLS, now chaired by Seymour Siegel, was back in operation in time to deal with the issue of the day that served as a principal lens for the debate on the proper direction to be taken by the movement, namely, the question of the role of women within the religious life of Conservative Judaism. The question was not new, nor was the basic willingness of the movement to take initiatives to ameliorate the status of women. Conservative rabbis had promoted the bat mitzvah ceremony in the 1930s and 1940s and had authorized granting *aliyot* to women in 1955.[9] The rabbis had twice acted to protect women against the disability of being prevented from remarrying after divorce by husbands unwilling to grant a *get*. First, in the 1950s, they adopted the "Lieberman clause" in the *ketubah*. More radically, in 1968, the CJLS granted authority to rabbinic courts to undo the religious marriage, even in the absence of a *get,* by means of *hafka'at kiddushin*.

Nonetheless, the development of feminism in America in the 1960s and 1970s brought the issue of women's rights to the fore with new urgency. From 1972, when *Ezrat Nashim,* a group of feminist protesters, demonstrated at the Rabbinical Assembly convention, until 1985, when the RA accepted its first women members, questions about gender roles in Judaism were consistently the leading ones facing the rabbis. Both proponents and opponents of changes in the status quo rightly considered the issue to be one that would define the contours of the movement.

Feminism re-emerged as a leading cause among reform-minded Americans at a time when the civil rights focus of the 1950s and early 1960s was beginning to fade. Women's rights advocates adapted the rhetoric of justice for the minority, already familiar to the American public, to press for equalization of pay for women and men in comparable jobs, for expansion of professional and business opportunities for women, and generally, for the recognition that women's societal roles need not be restricted to the domestic sphere, but could span as wide a range as men's. Politically, feminism enjoyed some signal successes in the 1970s. Although its most coveted goal, the Equal Rights Amendment to the United States constitution, failed to win ratification by a sufficient number of states, the economic objectives of feminism were furthered by the extension of affirmative action preferences to women as well as racial minorities.[10] High-profile professions as diverse as astronaut, news anchor and even Supreme Court justice opened to women in the 1970s and '80s. Even in blue-collar areas, essentially closed to women since the return of G.I.s after World War II, women made a reappearance. On road construction crews, "Men Working" signs were replaced by "People Working," to accommodate the presence of women. Furthermore, social gains accompanied the economic ones. With the entrance of women into jobs formerly held exclusively by men, the broader feminist vision of gender equality became more a part of the American consensus.

Closer to home, Reconstructionist congregations had adopted egalitarian changes and the Hebrew Union College ordained its first woman rabbi in 1972. Conservative Jewish education was co-educational, and girls at Camp Ramah, the premier informal educational program of the movement, had experimented with women wearing *tefillin* at least as early as 1958.[11] The stage was set for the encounter of feminism and Conservative Judaism.

As a replacement, of sorts, for civil rights activism, feminism did not enjoy a wide resonance among Conservative rabbis prior to 1972. The early women's movement had a counter-cultural provenance. Secular opponents of feminism connected it to the sexual libertinism of the 1960s and dismissed the women activists as "bra-burners." This made it more difficult for rabbis, struggling to guide their congregants through the rapidly shifting moral landscape of the 1960s, to identify with feminimism. Even among rabbinic liberals who supported the reform in race relations envisioned by Dr. Martin Luther King, Jr., there was also no automatic embrace of feminism. Some of these rabbis, unpersuaded that the discrimination against women was of an order comparable to that suffered by American Blacks, were uncomfortable with what seemed to them to be the dilution of the quest for justice for victims of discrimination. More pointedly, traditionalists such as David Feldman denied that the women's movement was a genuine parallel to the civil rights movement. The rabbis at the 1972 convention, as a whole, showed the demonstrators good will, but the convention organizers did not give them time on the official program. The early feminist protesters had to work hard to convince the rabbis that they were not "a few misguided malcontents," but were loyal, educated Jews, looking to change Judaism from within, and that their goal was to strengthen Jewish observance.[12]

Nonetheless, by staging their 1972 protest, feminists succeeded, to use the contemporary phrase, in "consciousness raising." At the Concord Hotel, they attracted 130 rabbis' wives "and a few curious men" to their unofficial presentation.[13] Once having put their agenda squarely in focus for the Conservative rabbinate, "egalitarianism" (in a new sense, equalizing gender roles, rather than in its older connotation of non-hierarchical socio-economic relations) seized the full attention of the rabbis. The CJLS took up the question of equalizing the status of lay men and women in the synagogue in September, 1973, and in a widely reported action, issued a *takkanah* permitting the counting of women along with men to the *minyan*.[14]

The debate over counting women to the *minyan* brought back into focus a broad theoretical question that had engaged Conservative rabbis for decades, up through the late 1960s, during their deliberations on the question of the *agunah*. Then, they had agreed that it was unethical to allow the civilly-divorced woman to languish, without permission to remarry. As long as they were unable to secure a halakhic redress of the just grievances of "anchored women," it seemed as if there was a conflict between the Jewish commitment to ethics, on the one hand, and fidelity to the legal pathways of the halakhah, on the other. But in the minds of those who authorized the remedy of *hafka'at kiddushin*, the *takkanah* resolved the conflict smoothly. As Simon Greenberg, a senior statesman of the Rabbinical Assembly and a vice-chancellor of the Seminary, explained the decision, this was not a triumph of extra-halakhic ethics over the halakhah, but rather an instance of ethics being part of the "organically sound growth and development" of the halakhah.[15] However, in this instance, Seymour Siegel's statement that counting women to the minyan could not be defended on strict halakhic grounds, but that it was an ethical imperative, and thus part of a "higher halakhah," recharged the tension between ethics and halakhah. The CJLS decision to change Jewish law on the strength of considerations allegedly extrinsic to halakhah brought traditionalists to contend that, under the pressure of feminism, Conservative Judaism was assimilating into Reform.[16] The adversarial positions of liberals, that traditionalists were ignoring the ethical dimension internal to halakah, and of traditionalists, that liberals were unjustly imposing external ethical doctrines upon the halakhah, were to remain a fixture of debates in this generation, continuing to agitate Conservative rabbis first in confrontations over feminism, and then, over homosexuality.

After the CJLS decision, the RA convened a conference of psychiatrists, rabbis and scholars to explore "Women and Change in Jewish Law." The psychiatrists present urged great caution in adopting feminist-inspired reforms. The response from religious liberals, lay, medical and rabbinic, was highly charged. These liberal critics of the psychiatrists revealed a sense of outrage at betrayal—they had always assumed that the secular disciplines were on the side of their interpretation of religion, and the counterarguments of the psychiatrists struck at that assumption.[17] Clearly, here was an issue that, once having been taken up, touched a deep chord among contemporary Conservative Jews.

Feminists had several items on the agenda of redefining the role of women within the Conservative movement. In his 1974 Presidential Address to the RA, Judah Nadich detailed the ritual changes that, in support of feminist claims, he had already recommended, as well as those he urged the CJLS to consider: the equalization of the bat mitzvah with the bar mitzvah ceremonies so that the young woman would be called to the Torah, the inclusion of women in *hakafot* (synagogue processionals in which congregants carry the Torah), using the mother's as well as the father's name in calling people up to the Torah, and reaffirming the rights of women to full participation in Conservative congregations.[18] From the standpoint of the synagogue, the CJLS decision in 1973 to allow rabbis to count adult women toward the *minyan* was the single change affecting the most Conservative women. Nonetheless, it was the struggle over the ordination of women as Conservative rabbis that most caught the attention of the movement, as well as the broader public. This struggle led to a decisive turning point in Conservative Jewish history.

While the history of the acceptance of women as rabbis within the Conservative movement has been told from the perspective of the Seminary,[19] it is important to note that the Rabbinical Assembly was the significant arena of this debate. The eventual emergence of a clear majority of Conservative rabbis favoring women's ordination was the critical change leading to the Seminary's decision. Additionally, the Rabbinical Assembly's willingness to push the Seminary on this issue, to the point of threatening to break its mother school's monopoly on producing Conservative rabbis by establishing its own ordaining body or by accepting as members large numbers of women ordained by other schools, decisively changed the balance in the relationship of those institutions.

By the mid-1970s, a few member rabbis had begun lobbying for the RA to accept ordained women rabbis as members and for the Seminary to accept women into its rabbinical training program. (These two planks are not identical, and the difference between them was to become quite important before the debate was resolved.) While few in initial number, proponents of women's ordination were not marginal within the Conservative rabbinate. They included past and current Rabbinical Assembly officers. The leader who emerged within this group was Fishel Pearlmutter. He had first raised the question of women being admitted to the RA in 1969.[20] From 1976 until his untimely death seven years later, he repeatedly raised the question of the Seminary's ordination of women as rabbis at the resolutions sessions of the annual RA conventions. In between conventions, he campaigned assiduously on behalf of women's ordination, lobbying among his fellow rabbis and crafting various parliamentary tactics to advance the cause within the RA and, if possible, at the Seminary.

In the first year of his campaign, Pearlmutter sent a circular letter to the members of the Rabbinical Assembly, and received 82 signatures in favor of a tripartite resolution, first, that the RA admit ordained women as members, second, that the Seminary admit qualified candidates to rabbinical school, and third, that the United Synagogue move to full equality regardless of gender. The Resolutions Committee for the 1976 convention asked him to remove the last two parts, apparently because of its sensitivity to a tradition that the RA not pass resolutions on matters within JTS jurisdiction,[21] but Pearlmutter refused, and included those planks as his personal amendment to the resolution. His supporters recognized the resolution was not likely to persuade the Seminary to change its position, but warmed to the struggle, and hoped that the Rabbinical Assembly itself would move faster than its parent school on the issue. Pearlmutter himself, writing to a young woman Reconstructionist Rabbinical College student who had hoped to become a Conservative rabbi, acknowledged that he did not believe that the Seminary faculty would allow Chancellor Gerson Cohen to acquiesce, but felt that within a year or two, the RA would publicly announce its willingness to accept women as members, whereupon women graduates of the Reconstructionist Rabbinical College would be prime candidates. "It is not the front door, but it is a way in."[22]

As expected, Pearlmutter's resolution did not carry in 1976. After the convention, rabbinic proponents of women's ordination debated tactics. Some despaired of change at the Seminary, and moved to have the Rabbinical Assembly outflank the school by accepting women rabbis unilaterally. Many rabbis still entertained a considerable reticence about dictating policy to their alma mater, and others, without sharing that diffidence personally, understood that it was a factor to be reckoned with in any lobbying campaign. One of Pearlmutter's allies, Jack Rosoff, wrote to him that it was a tactical mistake to "muddy the entire issue" by urging change upon the Seminary, rather than concentrating on the RA internal policy. The executive vice president of the RA, Wolfe Kelman, a high-profile supporter of women's ordination and a master bureaucrat, thought it most effective to work through the Rabbinical Assembly Constitution Committee. He did, in fact, engineer the subsitution of gender-neutral language for masculine pronouns in the RA constitution.[23] Pearlmutter nonetheless persisted in resubmitting his entire resolution, including the plank about the Seminary.

At the 1977 convention's resolutions session, rabbinic opinion on women's ordination was more or less evenly divided. Ultimately, the resolutions session produced a compromise, whereby the resolution was tabled and Pearlmutter offered a substitute resolution calling for Chancellor Cohen to form a commission that would study women's ordination and report to the Rabbinical Assembly by 1979. Some of the rabbinic proponents of women's ordination were outraged at the compromise, while others felt that Pearlmutter had attained as much as possible at the time, and still others hailed his statesmanship. Pearlmutter wrote that the proponents of women's ordination had achieved a significant measure of success in eliciting Cohen's promise to embark upon a study of the question. He felt that Cohen would be an ally in the campaign, and quoted the chancellor as saying that the first woman in the Rabbinical Assembly should be a JTS graduate.[24]

Pearlmutter's optimism proved to be justified. The Commission for the Study of Women in the Rabbinate was, indeed, a major departure from the way in which the Seminary had operated. In addition to Conservative lay leaders, Rabbinical Assembly members had the opportunity to affect the inner workings of the Seminary to a much greater degree than ever before.[25]

But what of the first plank of the tabled 1977 resolution, that the RA should accept ordained women? Had Kelman's amended, gender-neutral language actually pre-empted the opposition to women's ordination within the Rabbinical Assembly itself? After the convention, Pearlmutter reported to his colleagues that the Resolutions Committee's opinion was that the deletion of gender language in the RA constitution had rendered the Rabbinical Assembly plank of the women's ordination resolution moot.[26]

But the debate within the Rabbinical Assembly was, in fact, far from over. On the contrary, with the movement now committed to a serious study of the question of women's ordination, rabbis on both sides of the issue raised the volume of debate.

Opponents warned that the decision to ordain women was an unwarranted departure from Jewish tradition. It would blur the distinction between Conservative and Reform Judaism and would therefore lead to defections of the laity and even of traditionalist Conservative rabbis. I. Usher Kirshblum, a well-known leader of the traditionalist group, gained considerable publicity by his threat to resign if women were ordained.[27] Proponents of women's ordination countered that it was a mandate of justice, and therefore by definition within Conservative Jewish parameters. Ordaining women rabbis would not be an aping of the Reform movement, because the Conservative approach to Jewish feminism differed from Reform's position in that it was regulated change, remaining within the halakhic system. There was no need to go beyond halakhah because it was dynamic, not static, containing within itself sufficient warrant for change. Even within Orthodoxy, there had been a growing recognition of the need to ameliorate the status of women. In response to the threats of defections from the movement, proponents held that there was as strong a danger of defections from laity and rabbis dissatisfied with the maintenance of the status quo as from those opposed to change. Benjamin Kreitman, offering a United Synagogue perspective rather than a focus on the aspirations of the would-be woman rabbi, argued that ordination of women would increase the pool of candidates, which would be particularly helpful to smaller congregations.[28]

The ongoing debate strained relations within the RA membership, and occasioned laments over the polarization of a once-collegial group. In 1978, the Rabbinical Assembly president, Stanley Rabinowitz, acknowledged that internal relations among RA members were characterized by "strong feelings and strong counterreactions" on the question of rights of women in Conservative Judaism. Rabinowitz cautioned them that they would need to reaffirm their basic unity, the better to resist attacks from the Orthodox in conjunction with the latter's campaign in Israel to change the Law of Return. A year later, in his own presidential address to the rabbis, delivered just before the publication of the Commission report, Saul Teplitz urged the members to conduct their debate in "the spirit of love."[29]

The Commission report was in favor of women's ordination. The 11–3 vote of the Commission members reflected the considerable majority of Rabbinical Assembly members favoring women's ordination that had emerged by 1979. But the Seminary faculty did not go along with the Commission's recommendation. In the face of their opposition, Chancellor Cohen was forced to postpone the Faculty Senate discussion of the Commission report from May until December 1979. Rabbinical Assembly members complained of betrayal, and he attempted to reassure them that the delay was tactically necessary, so that the academicians would not feel that they had been "steamrollered."[30] In any case, it would not have been possible to admit women in the 1979–1980 academic year, so the seven-month delay would not much matter. Despite his assurances, Cohen was not able to prevail at the Faculty Senate meeting. In a charged meeting, the faculty members voted, 25–19, to table the motion.

The tensions between the majority of RA members and the Seminary now escalated still further. In response to the Seminary's refusal to implement the Commission recommendation, supporters of women's ordination within the Rabbinical Assembly resumed the discussions of 1976–77 about how to admit women without waiting for JTS. One tack would be to offer private ordination to women. Wolfe Kelman, who had earlier participated in the private ordination of a male student,[31] had offered to preside at the ordination of women students. At the institutional level, many of the rabbis renewed earlier calls for their organization to set up a *beit din* to confer ordination, rather than to rely on the Seminary for that function.[32] The most immediate threat wielded by the rabbis remained that they would accept women rabbis ordained by other seminaries as members of the Rabbinical Assembly, thus undermining the privileged position that the Seminary had in determining the answer to the basic question, "Who is a Conservative Rabbi."

Most fundamentally, the RA abandoned the official stance of neutrality implicit in having tabled Pearlmutter's 1977 resolution, and now passed a resolution in favor of women's ordination. It also urgently requested that the Seminary take up the tabled Commission recommendation and vote on it "with all deliberate speed."[33]

Within the RA itself, the unresolved question of women's ordination continued to be a source of friction, although the issue did not monopolize the rabbis' attention again until 1983. In that year, Beverly Magidson applied for membership. The timing of her application was designed to enhance the chances of her being accepted. After two years in which the rabbis had met first in Israel, and then in the Concord Hotel, the convention that year was in Dallas, Texas. By locating the membership debate away from the Northeast of the United States, where many traditionalist rabbis lived, supporters of women's ordination hoped to secure a more receptive group of rabbis to vote on Magidson's application.

The Membership Committee meeting of that convention featured a protracted debate on women's ordination. The rabbis present rehearsed the now-familiar arguments for and against, with some novel themes interspersed. Opponents, such as David Novak charged that some foreign notion of justice was overriding genuine Jewish sensibilities. Proponents, such as Alexander Shapiro, countered, with the heat of the debate reflected in his rhetorical excess, that "the issue . . . is not . . . feminism, it is not an issue that comes from the outside, and it is not the intrusion of secularism into our midst. Quite to the contrary, the issue is one that has to do with the unfolding of what religion means to us and what Judaism implies." Since the Commission for the Study of Women in the Rabbinate had recommended women's ordination, proponents of that step could argue now that there were no longer halakhic grounds to oppose it, and opponents had to look for broader reasons counterindicating it.[34]

The tension between the RA and the Seminary was also quite evident. Mordecai Levy attempted to have the deliberation on Magidson's application ruled out of order, because the 1980 resolution passed by the RA had spoken of a Seminary-ordained woman rabbi. Arnold Goodman ruled his point out of order. In that JTS had failed to ordain a woman, as resolved by the rabbis, the RA was correct to take further action. "The power to create is the power to destroy, and the plenum which passed one resolution can pass another one."[35]

The debate over women's ordination had the effect of eliciting competing definitions of what it meant to be a Conservative Jew. Opponents saw the pan-Jewish focus of the denomination threatened if women rabbis were accepted. In addition to its commitment to *k'lal yisrael,* they highlighted the movement's essential commitment to halakhah and its conservation of distinctive Jewish modes in contrast to the Reform posture of ready accommodation to outside pressures. Proponents contended that, precisely by admitting women as rabbis, the Conservative movement would finally achieve its self-definition.[36]

Ultimately, 210 rabbis voted for Magidson's admission and 75 against. That fell just short of the three-quarters majority needed for acceptance, under the Rabbinical Assembly's membership rules. The widespread feeling was that, within a year or two, women would be accepted as RA members. The handwriting was on the wall for the opponents of women's ordination.

The final stage of the debate began in May 1983, a month after the Rabbinical Assembly convention. Chancellor Cohen campaigned to have the Seminary faculty resume its discussion of the Commission report, tabled since 1979, and to vote to accept the Commission's recommendation.[37] This time, the Seminary was aware that it faced the choice of either acquiescing to women's ordination, or having the RA circumvent it. Cohen was quite concerned that the Seminary not lose its preeminent position within the Conservative movement, and he pushed it through. The Faculty Senate met on November 23. Unable to block Cohen's initiative, some talmudists on the faculty boycotted the meeting, a tactic that ultimately increased the majority within the Seminary faculty voting 25-19 to accept women into rabbinical school.[38]

In 1984, with women students already in the Seminary Rabbinical School, the debate within the Rabbinical Assembly over Magidson's application resumed. Some of the rabbis who had opposed women's ordination in previous years now changed their vote, as the Seminary had acknowledged that women rabbis were within the parameters of Conservative Judaism. Opponents now marshalled a new variation on the argument that women's ordination would lead Conservative Judaism to become a second Reform movement. In March 1983, the Central Conference of American Rabbis, the Reform rabbinic association, had accepted both patrilineal and matrilineal lineage in defining who is a Jew, to the consternation of the Conservative movement. If the RA accepted women rabbis, the argument now ran, it would only be a matter of time before it accepted patrilineality.[39]

The crucial factor in the 1984 round of the perennial debate was the awareness that relations between the Rabbinical Assembly and the Seminary had reached center stage, displacing the actual disagreement over women's ordination. The principal argument against accepting Magidson's application this year was that it was only fitting that the first woman rabbi in the RA should be a Seminary graduate, and that one more year was not too long to ask her to wait. Those who pushed for her immediate acceptance countered that once the Seminary had conceded on the issue, there was no longer any serious affront to the school in moving ahead immediately. The vote was 230 in favor of and 99 opposed to her admission, again, just short of the requisite three-quarters majority.

Rabbi Magidson and another woman rabbi, Jan Caryl Kaufman, were finally admitted to the Rabbinical Assembly in 1985, a few minutes after the admission of the first Seminary-ordained woman rabbi,

Amy Eilberg. The membership session that year was quite orderly, even anti-climactic. Four rabbis voted against the women applicants, and five abstained. But the momentous nature of the change was not lost on Conservative rabbis. Summing up his years as RA president, Alexander Shapiro called the decision to accept women rabbis "the most significant step taken by the Assembly" during his tenure.[40]

The emergence of a large majority within the RA in favor of women's ordination led the minority who opposed it to feel delegitimized. What was their place in their own association? In the 1983 Membership Committee debate, Gerald Sussman asked, "how would it be possible to remain a rabbi in in a traditional Conservative synagogue where women are not given *aliyot,* when down the street a woman may be the rabbi of a Conservative congregation? This step would make it very difficult to maintain the kind of pluralism that we now have." David Novak warned that the Conservative movement, being a coalition, could not survive the delegitimization of the traditionalist position. RA members now in the minority on a definitional issue questioned what they had in common with those on the other side of the aisle, and were no longer confident of a positive answer.[41]

Traditionalist critics of women's ordination formed a lobby, the Union for Traditional Conservative Judaism. While their rejection of egalitarianism was the occasion of their decision to create a lobby, the members of the Union also sought the strength of association to advocate for a serious commitment to halakhah, movement-wide. Criticizing Conservative Judaism as insufficiently committed to raising the level of ritual practice, they invested energy in creating programs to motivate the laity to observe Shabbat, *kashrut* and *taharat ha-mishpaḥah,* as well as the interpersonal commandments.

After the Seminary began ordaining women as rabbis, members of this lobby felt increasingly marginalized within Conservative Judaism. They responded negatively to the publication of the new Rabbinical Assembly prayer book, *Siddur Sim Shalom* and labelled it "antithetical to Jewish tradition."[42] As a culmination of the alienation they felt, they seceded from the denomination, renaming themselves the Union for Traditional Judaism. Over the next decade, they set up the apparatus of a movement. Ronald Price, a former assistant dean at JTS, became their executive vice president in 1985. Their Panel of Halakhic Inquiry, composed of leading scholars, served their membership as a replacement for the CJLS. Their greatest luminary was the renowned talmudist, David Weiss Halivni. With Halivni as anchor of a faculty, the Union opened a rabbinical school in 1990, the Institute of Traditional Judaism. In 1995, they appointed Richard Fagan as the first national director of their youth activities program. Their seminary's first ordained rabbi found work within a Modern Orthodox congregation, and Price began to refer to the group as an open-minded version of Orthodoxy.[43]

How did the Rabbinical Assembly majority respond to the concerns of the minority? At first, RA leadership made some conciliatory gestures, reaching out to reassert the integrity of the Conservative Jewish coalition. Immediately after the admission of women rabbis, Alexander Shapiro, the RA president, promised to respect the autonomy of the local rabbi. This was meant to reassure traditionalist rabbis that their professional organization would not undermine their rulings within their own congregations. He considered it vital for the RA to have "a healthy right wing, as well as left and center." Two years later, the new RA president, Kassel Abelson, sought to forge stronger links with those who had opposed women's ordination by calling for the RA to unite in a cooperative effort to increase traditional observance, a goal enunciated by the Union for Traditional Conservative Judaism. Pointing to the coexistence of two worship services at JTS, one egalitarian and one not, its new chancellor, Ismar Schorsch, called for a similar coexistence within the movement as a whole. Since the advocates of egalitarianism had accomplished their goal, the burden of sensitivity to the religious needs of their opponents now rested on them.[44]

On the other hand, once it became clear that conciliatory gestures had failed to prevent the defection of (at least some) right-wing critics of the movement, another response came to the fore: a new stridency about what the Conservative movement had become, largely as a result of its embrace of feminism. Shortly after his installation as chancellor, Ismar Schorsch defined his position as a militant centrism. In his 1986 presidential acceptance speech, Kassel Abelson stated that Conservative Judaism had become a "more militant middle." Movement leaders and theoreticians alike argued that Conservatives should not be too preoccupied with the criticisms on its periphery. They concluded that "the center has held," and that anxiety for the integrity of Conservative Judaism was overstated.[45]

The struggle over the status of women in Conservative Judaism and the schism that it occasioned led RA members to intensify their calls for their movement to define itself ideologically. Conservative leaders had, for a long time, resisted too-precise a definition of the denomination, essentially because the different ideological partners in the movement were not likely to agree on definitional matters. In the early part of the century, and up through the 1960s, the growth of the denomination obviated the need to articulate a precise self-understanding.[46] But during the debates over feminism, many rabbis concluded that Conservative Judaism could no longer thrive if it continued its strategy of avoiding definition. The debate over women's roles in Judaism not only elicited attempts at defining the denomination; it also exposed the dangers of lacking a consensus as to what it meant to be a Conservative Jew. The time had come for the movement to secure its base by stating more precisely what it was. If such a statement drove out a few who felt excluded, that would be more than counterbalanced by the gain of being able to convey to the public that the denomination had a concrete platform.

In 1985, Shapiro and Chancellor Cohen agreed to convene a conference on the ideology of Conservative Judaism. Shapiro framed the effort to formulate a new ideological statement as an "expression of the faith we share." It was no happenstance that this new effort coincided with the resolution of the women's ordination debate. Whether pleased or displeased with the result, Conservative rabbis recognized that the ordination decision itself constituted what Robert Gordis called "a major step toward the self-definition of our movement."[47]

In November 1987, the Committee on Conservative Ideology concluded its work of formulating a statement of principles, and in 1988, the various agencies of the movement jointly issued *Emet Ve-Emunah: Statement of Principles of Conservative Judaism.*

In describing the Ideology Commission's operating procedure, its chairman, Robert Gordis, explained that his committee strove to avoid two pitfalls: on the one hand, exacerbating existing tensions by taking too defining a position on controversial issues, and, on the other hand, writing so bland and latitudinarian a statement as to undercut the claim that Conservative Judaism was a movement that actually stood for specific propositions.[48] The principal solution to this dilemma adopted by the committee was to present more than one theological option. In describing God, revelation, halakhah and eschatology, the document consistently cites the various approaches coexisting in Conservative Judaism. The result struck many rabbis as underwhelming, especially after a build-up in which the document was advertised as a definitive statement, nine decades in the making.

Nonetheless, the work was immediately hailed as an important accomplishment.[49] Indeed, considering the difficulties in generating the will power to define itself, Conservative Judaism had crossed an important threshold simply by producing a movement-wide, definitive ideological statement. The Seminary and the Rabbinical Assembly followed it up with a study guide, and clearly envisioned that across the movement rabbis would make these documents key texts in a movement-wide adult education campaign, to instill in their congregants a new, sharper sense of Conservative Jewish identity. However successful that has been, the publication of *Emet Ve-Emunah* was itself a sign that Conservative Jewish leaders had become more comfortable with a denominational identity.

Testing and Reasserting the Limits of the Movement

The course and aftermath of the encounter with feminism, therefore, sharpened the focus on denominational definition among Conservative rabbis. Such a focus implied greater concern for boundary issues. The acceptance of egalitarianism established a clear boundary with Orthodoxy. What would serve as the equivalent boundary with the liberal branches of Judaism?

Given that Conservative Judaism's self-image involves a balance of "Tradition and Change," in that its most publicized decisions over the course of the period of 1973–1985 were a series of liberalizing changes in gender roles, it was not surprising that many Conservative rabbis looked for a reassertion of the balance. The need to regain a balance was all the greater, given the exultation of Reform leaders, and the concerns of some Conservative critics, that the egalitarian development of the movement was setting it up to follow the lead of Reform, or even to merge with it.

In the light of these concerns, the Rabbinical Assembly adopted positions that served to delineate more clearly its differences from the Reform and Reconstructionist branches of Judaism. While not retreating from egalitarianism, it reaffirmed traditional positions in two other debates over personal identity and gender roles.

The first of these stances emerged during the last stage of the debate over women's ordination. In March 1983, signalling a fundamental departure from Jewish tradition, the Reform rabbinate had altered its definition of Jewish identity to include children of at least one Jewish parent, father as well as mother. In that a father's Jewish identity would now be sufficient to establish the Jewishness of the child, the new stance was mis-named "patrilineality." The Rabbinical Assembly did not immediately reply. After they were accused of being in agreement with that change, however, Conservative rabbis began to distance themselves from it. At their 1984 gathering, the large majority of rabbis rose to signify their assent when their president, Arnold Goodman, invited them to take a stand reaffirming the matrilineal principle.[50]

That stand was a symbolic, rather than substantive act. Many remained concerned that, in the midst of its epochal change on women rabbis, the Conservative movement would also embrace patrilineality. Cohen's annual address to the Rabbinical Assembly on March 11, 1985, served to fuel this concern. Chancellor Cohen called for the movement to study patrilineality, and to not be afraid of following the conclusions reached by honest scholarship.[51] The rabbis present came away believing that Cohen was calling for change in this area. They recalled that he had strongly endorsed the role of scholarship in paving the way for changing tradition on the subject of women's ordination. Cohen's call for bold scholarship seemed like code language for a campaign to depart from matrilineality. The rabbis quickly introduced and passed a resolution reaffirming the traditional matrilineal principle.[52]

In retrospect, if one seeks a defining moment for Conservative Judaism in the last generation of the twentieth century, it would be the 1985 Rabbinical Assembly convention. In that brief gathering, the rabbis brought to its conclusion the most visible symbol of Conservative Jewish accommodation to modern Western developments when they inducted their first female members. At the same time, their rejection of patrilineality signified the domain in which they would continue to uphold traditional Jewish definitions against the demographic trends of the day.

Simple reaffirmation of matrilineality as the determinant of Jewish identity was not sufficient to convey the seriousness of this issue for the rabbis. One year later, the Rabbinical Assembly took the unusual step of elevating the matrilineal principle to a "standard of rabbinic practice." Henceforth, a rabbi who accepted as Jewish the unconverted child of a Jewish father and Gentile mother would be subject to censure and even expulsion from the organization.[53]

The strong sanctions involved in elevating a position to a standard of religious practice aroused considerable opposition. Matthew Simon charged that the motivation for the step was negative. "We are made insecure by traditionalists; we want to distance ourselves from the Reform movement." Others, like Stanley Rabinowitz, argued that it was incorrect to close off debate and inquiry. Some opponents of patrilineality, like Robert Gordis and Seymour Siegel, were nonetheless uncomfortable with the heavy-handedness of making the matrilineal principle a sanctioned standard of practice. The proposal seemed like a heresy-hunt.[54]

Nonetheless, a majority of the rabbis at that well-attended session voted for the proposed standard. They argued for the need to enunciate and enforce boundary positions. The standard would "define the limits of acceptable pluralism among us in a definitive and enforceable way." Adopting the standard would "state to the American Jewish community that we stand for something."[55]

The second stance in which the Rabbinical Assembly broke from the direction being taken by Reform and Reconstructionist Judaism was over the issue of homosexuality.

Homosexuals, long a silent minority in America, began to adopt a more confrontational attitude during the 1960s. Using the revolutionary slogan, "Gay is good," coined by Frank Kameny in 1968, homosexuals campaigned for a change in American attitudes and laws opposing homosexual orientation and behavior. In 1973, the members of the American Psychiatric Association voted by a narrow majority to remove homosexuality from its list of diseases. While homosexual advocates have had an uneven record in gaining judicial or legislative protection, they have succeeded in moving American public opinion about homosexuality away from the near-universal condemnation of earlier generations. The change happened in large measure because people began to believe that homosexual orientation is natural, albeit atypical, and is not a product of improper development or of seduction. In 1992, a New York Times/CBS News poll found Americans approximately evenly divided between those who believed that homosexuals choose their sexual orientation and those who believed it was not subject to change. Scientific findings, such as Simon LeVay's 1991 report on the differences in the brain structure between homosexual and heterosexual men, contributed to the erosion of the former Judaeo-Christian consensus that homosexuality was a choice, and an immoral one, at that.[56]

Growing in the public consciousness for a generation, the issue of homosexual rights came to the fore in the early 1990s, in America generally, and also specifically in Conservative Jewish circles. In his 1992 presidential campaign, Bill Clinton promised to normalize the status of homosexuals in the American military. After his election, the new president promulgated a pragmatic policy, dubbed "don't ask; don't tell," which essentially prohibited inquiry into the private sexual behavior of military personnel on the one hand, but which also left standing the existing military sanctions against homosexuality, on the other. This policy, despite its manifestly self-contradictory nature, was actually quite in line with the sexual ethic that had grown popular in America since the 1960s. This ethic permitted all intimate behavior between consenting adults, on the grounds that such private acts were beyond the scope of societal sanction. But the ethic fell short of proclaiming the moral equivalence of heterosexual and homosexual lifestyles, precisely because it took society out of the business of legitimizing or delegitimizing private behavior. A compromise in keeping with its times, the Clinton initiative on homosexuals in the military nevertheless sparked much public debate.

The discussion over Conservative Jewish policy regarding homosexuality had been developing for a number of years. As increasing numbers of Jewish homosexuals began to "come out of the closet" (to use the term fashionable since the 1970s), they attempted to integrate their Jewishness with their homosexuality. In 1976, the CLJS indicated that there should not be separate synagogues for homosexuals; like all Jews they should be integrated into synagogue life. Nonetheless, Jewish gays and lesbians established about a dozen such synagogues by 1978. Addressing the Rabbinical Assembly that year, Barry Dov Schwartz advocated that Conservative synagogues welcome homosexuals into their midst: "I would rather see a Jewish homosexual in a shul than in a shady bar." He reaffirmed that Judaism does not legitimize their sexuality as an alternative lifestyle, but argued that the keynote of rabbinic response should be acceptance of the individual.[57]

In 1990, a New York congregation serving homosexuals, Congregation Beth Simchat Torah, asked the Joint Placement Commission of the Conservative movement for help in finding a rabbi. The RA refused, and the 1,100-member synagogue hired a Reconstructionist rabbi in 1992. The request, and the debate within the RA that it occasioned, brought the controversy about defining the Conservative Jewish stand on homosexuality to center stage.

The controversy over serving homosexual congregations tested the Conservative Jewish response articulated by Schwartz, welcoming homosexuals and defending their civil rights, but not endorsing their lifestyle. A few RA members, such as Bradley Shavit Artson, sought to revise Jewish attitudes by limiting the traditional strictures against homosexuality to promiscuous behavior. Artson attempted to gain passage for a *teshuvah* defining faithful, "monogamous" homosexual relations as sacred relationships and proposing that Conservative rabbis officiate at commitment ceremonies for homosexuals, on the pattern of marriage ceremonies for heterosexuals. But the CJLS rejected that argument, and at its March 1992 meeting, a majority endorsed the *teshuvah* of Joel Roth, among others, that traditional Jewish strictures against homosexuality remain in force.

Even so, the lack of consensus of the rabbis on this issue was reflected in the eight votes for an alternate paper by Eliott Dorff, calling for the establishment of a commission to study human sexuality, including homosexuality. As with the 1977 resolution to study the role of women in the synagogue, and as with Cohen's 1985 call for a study of patrilineality, the call for the formation of this commission opened the possibility of fundamental change—to the relief of some, and strong disapproval of others.

While the 1992 CJLS was reasserting the traditional Jewish rejection of homosexuality, proponents of a liberalization of that policy organized to press for change. Eighty-three RA members created a group, *B'tsalmenu,* to work for the full inclusion of gay and lesbian Jews into Conservative Judaism. At the 1992 convention, the rabbis attending the resolutions session passed a statement reversing RA policy and authorizing its rabbis to serve congregations without regard to the sexual orientation of their members. They also passed a resolution establishing the study commission called for in the Dorff *teshuvah.*

The RA president, Gerald Zelizer, and its executive vice president, Joel Meyers, worked to find an ecumenical solution and prevent the issue from splitting the organization. In this respect, Meyers was in a different position than his predecessor, Wolfe Kelman, during the earlier debate over women's ordination. Kelman had been prominently identified with one side of that debate, whereas Meyers was able to use his good offices to negotiate with rabbis on both sides of this issue. He sought to protect both the integrity of the CJLS as the halakhic decisor for the movement and the principle that the rabbis as a whole, assembled in annual convention, exercise the supreme authority within the RA. Those potentially contradictory positions could only be sustained if the rabbis in convention stopped short of overturning a CJLS decision. In this respect, the stipulation in the resolution creating the 1992 study commission, that such an action was not an attempt to bypass the CJLS, helped to prevent an explosive disagreement from turning into an absolute schism.[58]

Zelizer and Meyers had hoped that the two years allotted for studying human sexuality would provide a cooling-off period. Their aim was partially successful, but not completely so, as the issue was stirred by additional events.

Unlike 1977, on this occasion, Chancellor Schorsch refused to have JTS join the Study Commission. He argued that homosexual advocacy was not a genuine concern of the Conservative movement.

In terms of movement involvement, there was a significant difference between the debate over women's ordination and the current one. The fault line in this issue was not between a large Rabbinical Assembly majority, pushing for change, and the Seminary, defending the status quo. In this issue, the debate was between RA members who backed the more traditionalist stance of the majority of the CJLS and those who favored the more liberal stance of the 1992 convention resolutions.

Opposition to the change in attitude towards homosexuality within the RA intensified after the 1992 convention. In February 1993, three dozen members circulated a "Statement of Concern for the Future of the Rabbinical Assembly." They criticized the 1992 resolution on Rabbinical Leadership in Gay Synagogues as the work of a vocal minority, passed without due notification of the rabbis registered at the convention. Substantively, the signatories to the Statement of Concern wrote, the resolution "disregarded the intent" of recent CJLS decisions.

As was the case with feminist demands for change, where the general campaign for equalization of rights became focused in a quest for the ordination of women rabbis, RA advocates for Conservative Jewish acceptance of homosexuality focused the issue on the fitness of avowed homosexuals to serve in religious leadership roles in the synagogue. In 1992, the CJLS issued a consensus statement, leaving the final decision on whether homosexuals might serve as religious school teachers, youth workers, and the like, in the hands of the local rabbi. This option was not only a course of prudence, but also a nod to the authority of the individual rabbi as *mara d'atra*, a value that traditionalists had complained was insufficiently respected in the feminist debates. The consensus statement was blandly worded, leaving room for two contradictory supplemental positions on the topic, authored by Kassel Abelson and Arnold Goodman. The first of these excluded homosexuals from religious leadership roles, in keeping with the "intent" of the consensus statement. The second, proceeding from the "silence" of the consensus statement on the subject, ruled to the contrary, that homosexuals were licit candidates for those roles.[59]

One of the exacerbating factors in the controversy over homosexuality was a much-publicized exchange at the 1993 RA convention between Harold Schulweis and Ismar Schorsch. In his keynote address to that gathering, Schulweis identified the cause of the weak commitment of Conservative Jewish laity as their perception that halakhah is isolated from the moral idealism of Judaism. In language reminiscent of the debate over gender roles in Judaism, Schulweis criticized his colleagues for having allowed a mind-set in which the ethical can be set aside by the halakhic. The movement's stand on homosexuality was the principal example he cited in support of this thesis.[60]

The next day, Schorsch replied, point by point. He defended the degree of involvement of the Conservative laity, as is evidenced by their willingness to sacrifice financially to educate their children at Solomon Schechter day schools. They are not looking for their rabbis to be halakhic revolutionaries. Schorsch again labelled homosexuality an alien issue, one that does not genuinely engage the attention of the Conservative movement. He pointed out that there had been no defections over the recent Seminary decision not to admit professing homosexuals to rabbinical school. The Rabbinical Assembly, he charged, was brewing an artifical storm, cloaking homosexual rights in the "bathos of ethical imperatives." Schorsch accused the rabbis of dereliction of their real duty, to work for Jewish continuity, if they persisted in treating homosexuality as a major issue "as if it were but a replay of the egalitrarian struggle." If they did not desist, they would "throw the RA into an ideological civil war in which there [would] be no winners."[61]

Strong words! Schorsch was correct in his appraisal of the low level of interest in homosexuality on the part of the Jewish public—it did not accord it the same high degree of interest as it had given to feminism. As of this writing, Conservative movement and rabbinic advocacy for homosexuals has waned, although support for their civil rights is undiminished. In one leading congregation, B'nai Jeshurun in New York City, the congegation's policy of acceptance of Jews living alternate sexual lifestyles and the Seminary's maintenance of traditional teachings proscribing homosexuality have come into conflict. But such conflict is not currently widely reported.

On the other hand, Schorsch's warning that the RA was about to plunge its membership into deadly internecine strife was overstated. When the Commission on Human Sexuality made its report the next year, at the 1994 convention, the high tension of the past two years had diminished somewhat, and a calm atmosphere once again prevailed. The report adhered to Conservative rabbinic precedent, while acknowledging that "tension and conflict are inevitable when, on the one hand, we advocate civil rights and antidiscrimination legislation and, on the other hand, give credence to biblical passages which clearly condemn homosexuality as . . . abomination." Zelizer hailed the report as going beyond the "don't ask; don't tell" attitude of the day, but as a statement of policy, it did not go beyond the pre-existing limits of Conservative Judaism.[62]

Ultimately, the Commission on Human Sexuality of the Rabbinical Assembly issued a pastoral letter providing guidance on intimate relations. The process of composition of this letter was marked by impassioned debate, extensive rewriting, and sensationalist news reporting. Eight drafts into the process, the pastoral letter, now renamed a rabbinic letter, reasserted the range of opinions within Conservative Judaism on homosexuality, referring to the CJLS responsa reaffirming traditional attitudes, as well as to the one, more liberal, alternative.[63] In sum, the Rabbinical Assembly debate over homosexuality had acknowledged lack of consensus, but unlike the response to feminism, in this instance, the rabbis did not overturn the traditional stance of their movement.

Since Conservative Judaism had not embraced fundamental change on this issue, it could not provide sufficient comfort to those who felt that, as homosexuals, they had no Jewish home within the denomination. Presentations at several RA conventions in the 1990s by homosexuals and by their rabbinic parents put a human face on the issue, but failed to move the rabbis from their movement policy.[64]

The most trying test of the unity of the RA in the course of its internal debate over homosexuality involved a member of the RA. After his ordination and his acceptance into the RA, this rabbi had become openly identified as a homosexual. Could he now obtain the benefits of the RA placement service? There was much heartache in the presenting case, as might be expected. The Placement Commission initially decided not to place a homosexual in Conservative congregations. Disagreeing amongst themselves over whether to uphold or appeal that decision, Meyers and Zelizer referred the decision to the RA Executive Council. That body reached a nuanced decision, voting not to override the Placement Commission's decision, but also to ask the Placement Commission to reconsider the case. The Placement Commission did so, and allowed the colleague to apply for a position, provided that he apprised prospective employers of his sexual orientation. Subsequently, the colleague did not find work as a rabbi, and ultimately changed professions, although he was allowed to retain his RA membership.

The degree of liberalization of policy with respect to homosexuals who already enjoyed RA membership proved to be the exception. Reflecting on the debate as a whole, Zelizer acknowledged that it had a definitional impact for Conservative Judaism: "In the course of the debate over the mega-issues of homosexuality, it became clear that a good part of the laity of the Conservative movement, as well as the rabbinic and Seminary community, will not accept radical innovations, for example, admission of practicing gays to the Seminary's Rabbinical School and/or sanctification of gay unions."[65]

Taken together, the patrilineal and homosexual debates occasioned a reassertion by the Rabbinical Assembly majority of the traditional component within the movement's sense of self. In part, this can be understood as the set of issues that served as a counterweight to the rabbis' epochal feminist changes. Nonetheless, it was not simply a matter of balancing "Right" and "Left," as will be seen by framing these decisions in the context of movement-wide developments.

Conservative Judaism in an Age of Ethnicity: Beyond "Right" and "Left"

In evaluating the Rabbinical Assembly's decisions on boundary issues such as the role of women, the formal definition of Jewish identity and the demarcation of licit sexual lifestyles, it is important to remember the context of religious developments within Conservative Judaism from the 1970s through the 1990s. During these decades, the movement reasserted numerous Jewish traditions, restoring many specifics of piety that the prior generation had allowed to lapse. In domains of behavior as diverse as worship, religious ceremony, and personal appearance, the typical Conservative rabbi of the last generation has moved away from the compromises of his or her elders. The significance of the high-profile decisions can only be fully appreciated as part of this "traditionalizing" trend.

Conservative worship services conducted by Rabbinical Assembly members in the last generation display a different emphasis, one that is arguably more at home in the rhythms and the *Gestalt* of traditional Jewish worship, than had been the case in the previous generation.

In the mid-century decades, the centerpiece of public worship at Conservative synagogues was the "late Friday night service." This service was scheduled at an untraditional hour, after dinner on Friday evening, rather than at dusk. This was meant to facilitate attendance by a generation that could neither hope to take off early from work on Friday nor to stay home on Saturday. The service was directed to the broad membership, not just those who equated prayer with *"davening."* The rabbi gave a formal sermon, rather than a *d'var torah,* applying Jewish insights to political, social or cultural issues of the day. The service, lasting about an hour, featured a combination of cantorial settings and English unison or responsive readings. The last named, especially, came to typify prayer in the Conservative setting, thanks to the widespread adoption of the Rabbinical Assembly prayer book in 1947. To this day, older congregants can recite by heart the iambic versification of the translation of the *hashkivenu* prayer: ". . . and shelter us beneath Thy wings, to keep us safe throughout the night . . ."

True, the Saturday morning service was more traditional. Its duration was about three hours, containing nearly the entire traditional Shabbat morning liturgy and a full Torah reading. Congregants were more likely to chant or read silently, with only a few English readings. But this service was not attended by all of the Friday night "regulars."

By the 1980s, rabbis were pushing their congregants to make the Shabbat morning service the centerpiece of the week's public worship, rather than the "late Friday evening service." Addressing the United Synagogue at its 1989 Biennial convention, Ismar Schorsch hailed the renewed emphasis on Shabbat morning worship as an example of the movement's reappropriation of traditional Jewish values. In 1990, the RA passed a resolution to make this refocus the official standard of the movement. Observers noted that this refocus was working. In his 1994 presidential address, Alan Silverstein expressed satisfaction that attendance at Shabbat morning services was on the increase.[66]

It is true that, by the 1980s, the late Friday night service was in decline, due to changes in patterns of family life. But it is illustrative that the transfer of the center of gravity of synagogue worship from Friday night to Saturday morning did not result in the importation of large numbers of English responsive readings into the latter service. With the exception of the abbreviation of the Torah reading to the triennial cycle, popularized by the 1980s, the Shabbat morning service remained essentially traditional in length and in its focus on Hebrew. The refocus on Shabbat morning meant that, for the typical synagogue-going Conservative Jew, prayer now meant a more traditional activity than had previously been the norm.

This refocus has caused one of the major intra-movement discussions of the last generation to recede from consciousness. Up through the 1960s, amidst widespread rabbinic laments over the decline of syna-

gogue attendance on holiday mornings, many rabbis sought a CJLS ruling to permit the non-observance of the holiday status of *yom tov sheni
shel galuyot* (the second day of the festival observed in the Diaspora).
Behind the rhetoric of those years about recognizing the significance of
the rebirth of the State of Israel by bringing the diasporic holiday calendar into conformity with Israel's was the reality of the rabbis' embarass-
ment at leading services in a largely empty sanctuary on such days.
Once a question that observers thought would define the boundaries of
Conservative Judaism, it has receded to the status of a footnote. Most
Conservative rabbis routinely conduct services on that day, whatever
the attendance level.[67]

Along with this shift in focus, rabbis in the last generation have evidenced a willingness to restore traditions of worship involving a departure from the Classic Reform emphasis on decorum and dignity. To foster a style of worship featuring chanting rather than singing and reading
means to re-evaluate the actual sound of traditional Ashkenazic worship, one distinguished by a constant murmur. More specifically, some
rabbis have revived the traditional recitation of the priestly benediction,
by the *kohanim* of the congregation on holidays—a form of piety that
was essentially ignored, in former days, since it seemed redolent of
Orthodoxy in its often discordant chorus of untrained or simply bad
voices.

The unconcern with a former generation's ideas of decorum com-
bines with a contemporary quest for religious authenticity in the
domain of religious garb. Rabbis who emerged in the 1970s typically
discarded the clerical robe and Protestant stole-like shawl of the previous generation, in favor of a traditional *tallit*.[68] More generally, while
previous generations seldom covered their heads other than when praying, eating or studying, most younger Conservative rabbis wear *kippot*
routinely.

The willingess to discard non-Jewish societal notions of propriety in
the name of reclaiming Jewish tradition is even more striking at the
cemetery than at the synagogue. While Jewish law requires that the burial of the dead be an actual, in-ground burial, Americans, Jews as well
as Gentiles, had fallen out of the practice of being present while the
grave was filled in. They accepted the arguments of professional funeral
directors that it was better to spare the mourners the grief of witnessing
actual burials.[69] In line with the congregants' strong feelings in this
regard a generation ago, the rabbi would routinely instruct the grave
crew to lower the coffin only to ground level, place a few symbolic

spadefuls of earth on the coffin, and then cover it over with a green artificial turf blanket. (At Reform funerals, one might witness a purely symbolic burial, with the rabbi placing a flower, or strewing a souffle cup of white sand, on the coffin, but not lowering the coffin into the grave.) In contemporary funerals, however, rabbis increasingly began having the coffin lowered all the way into the grave and instructing mourners and well-wishers to take part in the burial by shovelling earth on the coffin, sufficient to cover it completely. Given the strong aversion to this behavior in American society generally, it is not surprising that many congregants expressed surprise and disapproval. Despite forceful protests from congregants, that it was cruel to ask grief-stricken relatives to hear the sound of earth hitting the coffin, rabbis have persisted. As a compromise, they will sometimes place a little earth on the coffin, suspend the burial to recite the *kaddish*, dismiss the relatives, and invite others to remain and participate in the burial. But the rabbis have continued to argue for participation in burials, telling their congregants that it is one of the highest expressions of lovingkindess. Over time, it appears that the rabbinic persistence on this matter is reconciling lay Conservative attitudes to traditional teachings.[70]

The ideologic justification for recoveries of specific tradition is not, however, simply that traditional Jewish values are superior to those of the modern Western world, as is the constant refrain within Orthodox apologetics. Rather, traditions are tied to popular contemporary values. The reappropriation of Jewish tradition by Conservative rabbis is often in a configuration congenial to the movement's sense of itself and of its place in the world.

A case in point is the renewed interest in the *mikveh*. Very few Conservative rabbis spoke favorably of that institution at mid-century. A ritual bathhouse was quietly assumed to be a hold-over from the taboos and the hygienic arrangements of the pre-modern world. Conservative rabbis needed a place to conduct ritual immersions for conversion, but met that need without investing in the *mikveh* as a discrete physical institution. In the 1960s, the CJLS voted to allow the use of a swimming pool as a *mikveh*. But thirty years later, Conservative rabbis were routinely using *mikvaot* for conversions, and were concerned about building them in communities where the Orthodox denied access to their own ritual baths to Conservative rabbis.[71]

Even more tellingly, Conservative rabbis reported the upsurge of the use of the *mikveh* in the context of family purity, at least within their own families. This was not simply a nod to the traditionalist wing of

the movement; it was a reconceptualization. In the 1960s, few Conservative rabbis were teaching that family purity regulations were part of
the lifestyle of the Conservative Jew. Thirty years later, Susan Grossman
was publishing and lecturing before her fellow Conservative rabbis
about substituting the concept of *kedushah* for that of *tum'ah* as a
rationale for renewed observance of this ritual by Conservative feminists.[72] For late-twentieth century Jewish women, no less than for their
mothers, it was unpalatable to base a regimen of monthly ritual immersions on notions of uncleanliness. Nonetheless, the appeal of the ritual
practice had grown to the point that Conservative champions of the
mikveh felt motivated to find alternate rationales for its use. Far from
being a counterweight to the movement's changes on women's status,
the Conservative reappropriation of post-menstrual immersions
received a boost from feminist leaders and ideologues.

Likewise, the participation of American political liberals and moderates in the environmentalist movement since the late 1960s has provided a contemporary rationale for a set of traditions. "Back to nature"
resonates well within Conservative Jewry of the baby-boomer generation and younger, whose political agenda has included a concern to halt
the degradation of the natural environment. The predisposition of RA
members to endorse environmentalist positions is typified by their 1996
resolution in support of the Endangered Species Act.[73]

"Back to Nature" has specific ritual applications, as well as a general political signficance, within Conservative Judaism. Since 1970, the
Tu B'shvat holiday, no longer focused on the Zionist reclamation of the
land of Israel, has become a Jewish "Earth Day." Conservative synagogue schools observe the holiday, not simply by handing out dried
carob pods and Jewish National Fund fundraising kits, but by programming tree-planting ceremonies and the like. *Tashlikh,* the ritual of sym-
bolically casting one's sins in a body of water on Rosh Hashanah afternoon, has dramatically regained popularity over the past quarter
century. It is common for the rabbi to be joined on this occasion by congregants who seldom attend services, as well as by the "regulars." Similarly, even Conservative Jews who do not participate strongly in the
daily and weekly forms of piety endorsed by the movement are increasingly reappropriating the practice of building a *sukkah* on their own
property, rather than simply visiting the synagogue's. This is a striking
departure from the norm thirty years ago, when those specific rituals
were hallmarks of the practice of only the most strongly observant
within the denomination.

These examples inspire reflection on the spiritual power of religious deeds of piety, as well as the mere fact of their performance. What does it mean for a movement that its rabbis (let alone its laity) have taken part in the changed mores of the sexual revolution, yet are now coming back to the *mikveh?* Or for a denomination to be home to Jews who stay away from the synagogue except for the High Holidays, but who observe the relatively minor *tashlikh* ritual on Rosh Hashanah afternoon?

Part—but only part—of the reason for the rabbinic push for a return to tradition, and for the endorsement by the core of Conservative Jews of this effort, is receptivity to the rise of Orthodoxy, noted above. The success of Orthodoxy has certainly made it easier to contemplate fulfilling certain specifics of observance and has elevated the respectability of a whole host of pious practices. Among the laity, there is a palpable nostalgia for the perceived authenticity of the Orthodox interpretation of Judaism. But that does not explain the selectivity of the reappropriation of ritual observances, nor the enthusiasm for heightened standards of observance among those who object vociferously to Orthodox criticisms of the Conservative movement. As Harold Kushner observed during the debates over egalitarianism, the Conservative movement is fully modern in its mindset, in the sense that its members hold personal autonomy to be a key value. Even when they accept a particular halakhic stricture, it is not at the expense of personal autonomy, but rather because they are choosing to abide by it, in their quest for spiritual fulfillment.[74]

In addition to the rising popularity of religious conservatism in America since the 1970s, and of Orthodox Judaism in particular, the rise of ethnicity has been crucial to the religious developments within Conservative Judaism. American social developments after mid-century made it possible for ethnic minorities to assert themselves. In this changed social context, Conservative Jews, too, affirmed their identity, in part by embracing semi-discarded traditions. Thus, a proud affirmation of Jewish identity within a newly permissive American context, rather than a desire to subordinate personal autonomy to the discipline of the halakhah, became the strongest engine of renewed interest in ritual observance.

To appreciate the power of changing evaluations of ethnicity to affect religious behavior, it is worthwhile to reflect on the connection between the low level of tolerance for ethnic assertivness throughout much of American history and the muted religious self-expression of minorities. As long as "American" culture, meaning essentially an amalgam of White Anglo-Saxon Protestant cultures, was expected to supercede the culture of (Caucasian) immigrants, Catholic and Jewish minorities could express themselves only in ways that did not diverge too strikingly from the American norm. Even loyal Jews subscribed to the ideal of America as "melting pot"—a phrase lifted from the 1908 play praising assimilation written by Israel Zangwill.[75] More specifically, as is well known to students of American Jewish history, the Jewish Theological Seminary and, by extension, the Conservative movement, owe their existence in large measure to the desire to Americanize the Eastern European immigrants arriving at the turn of the century.

The success of American Jewry by mid-century, and of the Finkelstein administration of the Seminary in particular, was to gain recognition as one of the constituent elements of basic American culture. The Conservative rabbi was accepted at the local interfaith clergy council and was the functional equal of the Catholic priest and Protestant minister at civic events, offering invocations or benedictions at graduations and city council meetings.

But if the success of the synagogue was that it could be included in ecumenical discussions of "the church down the street," the concomitant limitation was that it could not afford to advertise too loudly its differences from the church. In this climate of opinion, Conservative rabbis allowed organ music at Shabbat services, favored Christian-style clerical robes, and quietly ordered tunafish or fruit salad at non-kosher civic functions.[76]

After mid-century, the assimilationist ethos of the melting pot declined. In the climate of social protest of the 1960s, the non-conformist became the cultural icon. The slogans of the day acclaimed as a hero the individual who "does his own thing" and who "marches to the beat of a different drummer."

The same climate of acceptance of individual or generational divergences from the norms of the middle-aged and White Anglo-Saxon Protestant "establishment" worked to legitimize the cultural distinctiveness of minority groups. For Americans of many ethnic backgrounds, it has become increasingly popular to define their identity in terms of a particular group. In a dramatic reversal, a "hyphenated-American" identity, once derided, came to be seen as a source of pride in the last third of the century. At century's end, the popularity of ethnic substitutes for an amalgamated American identity is unabated.

In this changed framework, many minorities, among them Jews, began to hold out for greater freedom to express themselves in line with their own cultural pathways. By the early 1960s, New York's Jews had achieved recognition as having gone "beyond the melting pot."[77] The Black Power revolts of the late 1960s, especially on college campuses, further empowered Jews to assert their own differences from the cultural mainstream. Seeing young Blacks wearing "Afro-picks" in their hair helped Jews, both Orthodox and non-Orthodox, to begin wearing their *kippot* on the street.

By the 1980s, headcovering had become a major statement within Jewish circles. A Jewish air force officer, Major Simchah Goldman, objected to being ordered to remove his *kippah,* and the case went all the way to the U.S. Supreme Court. While Goldman lost the case, the military ultimately moved to a policy more accommodating of the pious practices of its personnel. As of this writing, commanding officers seldom block Jewish subordinates from wearing unobtrusive skullcaps.[78]

As both the baby boomer children of the 1960s and their parents recognized, details of dress and grooming are cultural statements. When Conservative Jews began to wear *kippot* on the street in the late 1960s, they were stating a willingness to depart from the American norm of their parents' generation in a high-profile manner. They were willing for their Jewishness to stand out—perhaps because they were confident that it was now safe to do so.

Observing the growing attractiveness of ethnicity, some Conservative rabbis focused on the weaknesses of an ethnic expression of Judaism. Ethnicity could mean mere associationalism, even tribalism, rather than religious zeal. But other leaders of the Conservative movement understood that the turn to ethnicity made possible a reinvigoration of religious life. As early as 1971, Abraham Karp posited that "[t]he Jew's at-homeness in America and the decline of the church make it possible and desirable to restructure Jewish religious life along more traditional Jewish lines." Reflecting on developments at the end of the 1980s, Ismar Schorsch saw the renewed popularity of the *kippah* as an epitome of resurgence of tradition: "In a post-rational age with few external constraints, Jews have turned more ethnic, more feisty and above all, more receptive to a serious engagement with Judaism."[79]

It may be objected that ethnicity is not precisely relevant to an analysis of Jewish identity; as a religion open to conversion, Judaism is never simply the faith of an ethnic group. With intermarriage as a growing reality within Conservative Judaism, how appropriate are conclusions drawn from ethnicity to the history of that movement?

Despite this objection, ethnicity is relevant, and the facts of intermarriage and conversion do not minimize it. By and large, marriage patterns still reinforce the common memories of Conservative Jews. But surprisingly, ethnicity is not strictly limited to groups that retain strict endogamy. Sociologists have come to realize that ethnic identity in America is, in part, a fictitious construct, given the reality of intermarriage across all White American ethnic groups.[80] Among non-Jewish Caucasians, it is increasingly common for one to identify ethnically with any or several of one's ancestors. This demonstrates that ethnicity is only partially dependent on actual ancestry, but also involves an individual's wish to claim a particular group as his own. Analyses of attitudes toward Judaism on the part of Jews by choice, conducted with increased frequency in the past two decades, reveal that converts succeed in identifying with much of the Jewish heritage, albeit in different configurations than do native-born Jews.[81] As ethnicity in a pluralistic, open society such as North America is, to a large degree, self-chosen, it remains a relevant category for analyzing Jewish group identity, even though Jews are not completely an ethnic group in the precise sense of a people united by common descent.

As an explanation for the reappropriation of ritual traditions, the permission to depart from the mainstream that resulted from the American embrace of ethnicity does not stand alone. Heightened cultural and economic security went hand in hand to promote certain aspects of traditional piety, for example, in the case of the restored focus on Shabbat morning as the high point of Conservative Jewish public worship. Compared to their immigrant and second-generation ancestors, few third- and fourth-generation Jews today have to work on Saturdays. Likewise, the emergence of kosher consumers as a significant market force has produced a greatly expanded product line from which to choose. In 1998, the Nabisco corporation began to manufacture even that leading symbol of forbidden treats, the Oreo cookie, under kosher certification. The enhanced availability of such products, in turn, made it easier for Conservative rabbis to move from the "ingredient *kashrut*" norm of mid-century and to insist increasingly on kosher certification. Finally, Conservative rabbis and their congregants have genuinely responded to and joined in the general turn toward religious values and structures for guidance in a world that appears to them to have grown bewilderingly complex over the past quarter-century. As part of this receptivity to tradition as a spiritual compass, the rabbis of the current generation are more apt to emphasize that ritual behavior encodes the values of Judaism and is inseparable from them.

All of these factors make the history of contemporary Conservative Jewish halakhic developments a multi-layered reality. Evaluating the traditions changed and those retained or renewed by Conservative Jews since 1970 is not simply a matter of deciding whether they were left- or right-wing, whether there has been a preponderance of Reform-leaning or Orthodox-inspired decisions. When the record of halakhic decisions within the Conservative movement is viewed from a perspective that includes historical developments within late twentieth-century American society, it is possible to move beyond the helpful but limited categories of "right" and "left." Fundamentally, Rabbinical Assembly halakhic decisions since 1970 have respected the expansion of individual opportunities that is the hallmark of modern, liberal thought. At the same time, Conservative halakhah has reinforced the relevance of traditional modes of piety to the individual's quest for a meaningful and spiritually satisfying life.

In this respect, Conservative thought has continued to differ from both Reform and Orthodoxy. Unlike Reform, Conservative halakhic decisions have underscored the vital importance of remaining identifiably one with the entire Jewish community—hence the retention of matrilineality, and the dismissal of homosexual advocacy as the concern of a small minority. Unlike Orthodoxy, which posits a sharp conflict between the values of the religion and those of the host society in which Jews live, Conservative Judaism emphasizes receptivity to selected aspects of general ideas and behavioral norms. For the Rabbinical Assembly members of the present generation, then, there is scarcely any sense of internal contradiction between traveling with the mainstream of American public opinion on feminism, on the one hand, and raising the standards of ritual exactitude, on the other. Both decisions represent a selective internalization of aspects of general society that seem to the Conservative rabbis of the past thirty years to be in harmony with Judaism.

The Apparatus of a Denomination

The debates of the 1970s and 1980s over the correct course to be steered by Conservative Judaism were not the only factors leading to an increasingly well-articulated definition of the denomination. At the same time, the movement found its own liturgical voice and matured institutionally.

The synagogue remained the primary Conservative Jewish institution in this generation, and the various prayer books in the pews remained the principal Jewish texts consulted by Conservative Jews. In the 1970s and 1980s, Conservative Jewish liturgy came of age.

While Conservative Jews of mid-century had employed an ideologically self-conscious, distinctively Conservative *Sabbath and Festival Prayer Book,* as well as a High Holiday *mahzor* and a somewhat less ambitious daily prayer book, by 1970, all of these texts were due for updating or expansion. Except for the daily *siddur,* published in 1961, the standard liturgical collections of the movement had pre-dated the establishment of the State of Israel and scarcely reflected the impact of the Holocaust. The tone of their English was "high" and archaic, a choice no longer in fashion in the last third of the century.

The Rabbinical Assembly set itself the task of producing a new standard for the new generation. Despite limitations on the size of its staff, it viewed liturgical publications as central to its purpose and employed a director of publications, Jules Harlow. Under Harlow's guidance, the RA published an entire set of prayer books to replace the existing editions.

The first in this new series was *Mahzor for Rosh Hashanah and Yom Kippur: A Prayer Book for the Days of Awe,* published in 1972. This work, like the weekday *siddur* that preceded it by a decade, maintained the essentially conservative approach to the traditional text adopted by the *Sabbath and Festival Prayer Book* of the 1940s, but each successive work further expanded the range of Hebrew textual changes to the traditional liturgy. In the 1972 *mahzor,* the balance of old and new changed, and the expansion of the Hebrew text of the prayers reached a new order of magnitude. Harlow considered it appropriate to enrich the canon of the *mahzor* by an entire range of prayers, prose and poetry, drawn from a multitude of Jewish sources. He utilized the works of thinkers as diverse as the modern rationalists, Hermann Cohen and Leo Baeck, and Hasidic or neo-Hasidic masters, and quoted many passages from rabbinic and medieval Jewish classics, to assemble an anthology of prayers that felt new and fresh.[82]

The religious objective of such creativity was to deal with the problem of prayer in a secular age. Harlow's edition of the *mahzor* is most notable in its sustained attention to the task of helping contemporary Jews to find prayer meaningful, given the uncertainty about the enterprise of prayer that dogs people in a secularized era.

One of the principal resources marshalled by Harlow in this task is the thought of contemporary religious philosophers, notably Martin Buber, Will Herberg, and Abraham Joshua Heschel. Buber's religious existentialism, Herberg's reassertion of traditional beliefs as an antidote to the idolatrous deification of humanity, and Heschel's neo-Hasidic philosophy had each created a modernist framework for reasserting Jewish supernaturalist beliefs. In this framework, it was again possible to embrace prayer unapologetically as a central religious act. Heschel had personally taught many of the Conservative rabbis active in 1970; gradually, his thought had supplanted Mordecai Kaplan's naturalist interpretation of Judaism as the most influential of contemporary theological influences upon the Conservative rabbinate. Harlow presents Heschel's "depth theology," with its re-emphasis of theologizing away from cerebral speculation about God's existence and providence and toward living a meaningful religious life of response to God, at steady intervals throughout the *maḥzor*.[83]

In compiling a prayer book for a secular age, an editor must face the fact that liturgical texts do not, in and of themselves, solve the problem of prayer in such a climate. Harlow himself acknowledged the limitations on what new texts or formats can do. But having issued that modest disclaimer, he defended the value of making prayer part of the life that contemporary Jews live, both linguistically and theologically, and of paying attention to the aesthetics of liturgy and of the book-maker's craft.[84]

Reviewing the new *maḥzor*, the Reform historian of liturgy, Jacob Petuchowski, acclaimed Harlow's creation as a liturgical masterpiece, aesthetically, poetically, and in its striving for theological honesty.[85] The Conservative rabbinate has seconded Petuchowski's endorsement. As of this writing, the *maḥzor* is essentially the standard High Holiday text of the movement, limited only by the economic difficulties some congregations experience in changing liturgical editions.

Like the previous Conservative editions of the liturgy, Harlow's works included numerous supplemental readings designed to make the prayer book more comprehensive and more responsive to the needs of the worshipers utilizing it. But unlike previous editions, Harlow's texts reflect the awareness that, in the Conservative movement, a prayer book needs to speak to Jews not fully at home in the liturgical tradition, as well as to the more thoroughly educated. This awareness characterizes the prayer book issued by the RA shortly after the publication of its *maḥzor*, *The Bond of Life: A Book for Mourners* (1975). In addition to the daily prayers, edited for recitation in a house of *shivah*, this work included a guide to practice for the mourner, an essay by the psychiatrist Mortimer Ostow explaining grief and mourning from a psychological perspective, and an anthology of inspirational readings drawn from classical and modern Jewish literature. Introducing the daily service, Harlow addressed the mourner directly, reflecting the practical wisdom that, for many Conservative Jews, the onset of their mourning is their moment of introduction to formal daily worship. Harlow anticipated that the modern mourner might find the daily service strange at first, with seasoned worshipers reciting prayers quite rapidly. Harlow reassured his reader that, on the one hand, those reciting prayers speedily were not necessarily devoid of heartfelt prayerfulness, but that, on the other hand, the mourner should feel free to recite the prayers as quickly or slowly as he finds meaningful. The modernism of his approach is evident in his gentle reminder, "There are many paths, many ways. You must find the path proper for you."[86]

For all their creativity, the *mahzor* and the mourners' prayer book retained a traditional presentation. Not so the next RA liturgical text, a Passover haggadah, *The Feast of Freedom,* published experimentally in 1979 and then, in finished form, in 1982. The editor of the preliminary edition, Michael Strassfeld, infused the work with the same counter-cultural verve as had animated his enormously popular *Jewish Catalogue* series. Even in the 1982 form, the incorporation of Dan Reisinger's graphic art, featuring bright neon colors, recalled the so-called psychedelic art of the '60s and early '70s.

In their preface to this text, the members of the Haggadah Committee of the RA proclaimed that this *haggadah* differs from all previous editions "primarily because it is the first that faithfully reflects Conservative ideology" in which "conservation and innovation are counterbalanced in order to present, clearly and compellingly, the perennially and universally relevant themes of freedom and redemption."[87] The edition, like the book for mourners, reflects the rabbinic awareness that some readers will be unfamiliar with the rituals assumed by the text, and that all intended readers would appreciate supplementing the traditional text with a sampling of historical meditations and contemporary comments inspired by the *haggadah*. The centrist and modernist ideology of Conservative Judaism is often quite close to the surface of these comments. Explaining the lack of a direct answer to the Four Questions, a sidebar comment praises questioning itself as a sign of freedom, and cautions that many questions are not capable of a one-dimensional answer.[88] The temper of the times emerges in the translations as well as the comments. In speaking of the wicked child, this edition softens the injunction, "rap him in the teeth!," substituting the phrase "shake him by replying . . . ," a concession to the contemporary repudiation of corporal punishment in education.[89] The result of these emphases of translation and presentation was a work that announced its determination to engage the reader, without worrying about any sacrifice of dignity. *The Feast of Freedom,* if not an edition for the ages, strove to be highly relevant to its own age.

The admittedly small example of the translation of *hakhe et shinav* in the paragraph about the wicked son points to a larger point. The liturgical works of the RA tended to preserve the traditional Hebrew text, with additions, but few changes, and to use translations as the vehicle for greater freedom of expression. Only rarely was a modern Hebrew text suggested in lieu of the traditional text. In the 1946 *Sabbath and Festival Prayer Book,* a meditation just after the *kedushah* prayer in the *musaf* service could serve as a substitute for the (nearly-) traditional prayer that followed, if the rabbi were so minded to use it in that fashion. But the editors gave no instructions as to the use of the modern composition. In the 1961 *Siddur Liymot Haḥol,* an alternate text was placed alongside the more traditional version of the intermediate blessing of the *Amidah,* without indication as to which was which.

In the 1985 *Siddur Sim Shalom,* Harlow made more explicit the processes of abbreviation and substitution by which rabbis were shaping the services of their day. He employed the rubric "some congregations add" to indicate that the prayers so designated were not recited in synagogues across the movement. The positive phrasing of that rubric is but a euphemism for "some congregations delete"—a tacit admission that certain omissions from the traditional liturgy had become widespread among Conservative congregations.[90]

Change is not simply a process of deletion. In the years leading up to the publication of *Siddur Sim Shalom,* many Conservative congregations and other prayer groups had written and compiled creative liturgies. Harlow had commented on that phenomenon in 1973, judging most of the efforts mediocre, but welcoming the creativity and energy lavished on worship.[91] In *Siddur Sim Shalom,* Harlow included a judicious selection of newly and recently composed inspirational materials. These materials helped rabbis and congregants to incorporate contemporary concerns into the framework of public worship.

As was the case with the High Holiday prayer book, *Siddur Sim Shalom* received largely positive reviews, although it did have its critics, particularly in the right wing of the movement. Jacob Petuchowski acclaimed it as the best American Jewish *siddur* available. He hailed its theology as a "liberal, modernist affirmation of traditional Jewish teaching," enjoying both its retention of an essentially traditional text and the greater freedom and pluralism reflected in its English portion.[92] The new *siddur* joined the 1972 *mahzor* as the edition of choice for the movement.

Considering that *Siddur Sim Shalom* appeared at the climax of the feminist-inspired changes within Conservative Judaism, it is not surprising that its translation responds somewhat to feminist critiques of traditional prayer language. In translating *'avot*, Harlow substitutes "ancestors" for "patriarchs." But it is noteworthy that Harlow retained the traditional, male gender references to God. In translating passages where the *siddur* employs the third-person pronoun, "He," Harlow avoided substituting the nouns "God" or "Lord," or the second-person pronoun. Harlow also eschewed the more radical reform of traditional gender language, the device of alternating masculine and feminine references to God. Reflecting on this decision in 1997, Harlow defended his linguistic conservatism on the grounds that it was meritorious to preserve the connection of the *siddur* with the Bible and to avoid further splintering the Jewish people, as so-called "inclusive" language tends to do. Quoting Debra Cantor, one of the movement's pioneering women rabbis, Harlow dismissed feminine references to God as the slippery slope toward paganism.[93]

Nevertheless, others within the movement have continued to criticize gender-specific references to God in prayer. In 1992, the RA convened a working committee to revise *Sim Shalom*. It circulated an experimental version of the Shabbat and Festival morning service in which God is still referred to as "He," but references to God as "Lord" and "King" are replaced by the untranslated Hebrew *"Adonai"* and "sovereign":

> *Adonai* is sovereign, crowned with splendor
> *Adonai* reigns, robed in strength. (Psalm 93:1)[94]

The experimental edition presented both egalitarian and traditional versions of selected prayers, inviting comment from the movement over the inclusion of references to the matriarchs alongside the patriarchs in the *'avot* prayer.[95] Many revisions were incorporated into the new edition of *Siddur Sim Shalom for Shabbat and Festivals* that was published in 1998.

While most of the liturgical publications of the RA are intended for the use of Conservative congregants, one specialized compilation, the *Rabbi's Manual,* is specifically for the use of the rabbi. Here, too, the most recent revision of that work reflects historical developments within the movement since 1970. The new work is no longer called *Likkute Tefillah*, but *Moreh Derekh*, indicating that it aspires to be more than an anthology of prayers appropriate for selected occasions. In its presentation of the "Lieberman Clause" to the *ketubah* and the "Letter of Intent," the new manual reflects the contemporary consensus that, in conducting pre-marital counseling, rabbis cannot afford to ignore the high rate of divorce. Again, rabbis today are increasingly called upon to address ethics questions regarding medical care for the terminally ill, so the 1998 manual presents the RA-approved medical directives for health care. In its liturgical selections, too, the *Moreh Derekh* reflects the perspectives of the current generation. It expands upon tradition in its suggested services for naming a baby girl, for adoption, and for life transitions. After a generation of calls for Conservative Judaism to pay greater attention to the needs of parents who have struggled with infertility, suffered a miscarriage, or brought special-needs children into the world, the new manual presents an ample selection of prayers for those challenging circumstances.[96]

Rounding out the field of liturgical publications is the *luah*, a humble but important reference guide to services, day by day, throughout the year. It was long an anomaly that Conservative rabbis and lay leaders were using Orthodox guides, given the differences in specifics between the services as conducted by the two denominations. In 1994, the Rabbinical Assembly and the United Synagogue of Conservative Judaism published the first *luah* geared specifically for Conservative worship.[97]

The work of updating the editions of the sacred texts used in worship is not yet complete. Throughout the period since 1970, Conservative rabbis have regularly issued calls for an updated *humash* commentary, to replace the 1930s vintage commentary of Joseph Hertz. The intellectual battles waged by Hertz no longer seem relevant to the contemporary Conservative Jew's study of the Torah. In 1994, Harold Kushner and David Lieber reported that the RA was at last making progress on that project.[98] Over thirty scholars from the movement are contributing to the new commentary, with David Lieber serving as general editor, Harold Kushner and Chaim Potok as the main editors, and Jules Harlow handling the redaction. A new RA *humash* for congregational use will complete the updating of standard synagogue texts in the very beginning of the next century.

Even prior to the completion of a replacement to the Hertz commentary, it is possible to see a cumulative effect of the denomination's new publications. This effect has been both linguistic and ideologic. Linguistically, the set of new works has given Conservative liturgy an idiomatic English voice. Ideologically, these editions have presented contemporary Conservative thinking on the many issues that cross, or ought to cross, the congregant's mind when participating in the denomination's central public act, the gathering for regular prayer. The decisions regarding retention or replacement of traditional texts codified in these prayer books have helped to secure a movement-wide pattern of usage, flexible yet definable.

The other critical area in which the Rabbinical Assembly has helped forge a more secure and well-articulated sense of self for Conservative Jewry has been in the training of personnel for the educational and ritual needs of the movement, beyond the congregational rabbinate.

While RA members had always filled positions beyond the pulpit, the perception of the rabbinic vocation until 1970 was that the typical Rabbinical Assembly member was a pulpit rabbi. This perception was strengthened in the years immediately following the Second World War, when a large majority of the rabbis graduating from JTS took up congregational work. True, many rabbis had fulfilled service obligations and worked as military chaplains for a few years, prior to taking up their career focus in a congregation. That system collapsed during the 1960s, with the rise of anti-Vietnam sentiment, and the RA military chaplaincy requirement was abolished in 1968. With the end of the Vietnam War and the introduction of the all-volunteer military in the 1970s, the number of rabbis who served as chaplains for even a few years declined. A few RA members pursued careers in academia, but there, too, the overlap declined after the early 1970s, once the Jewish Theological Seminary opened up a graduate school, separate from the Rabbinical School. Few organizational or educational positions attracted RA members.

In the past quarter century, the emphasis on the non-pulpit aspect of the work open to rabbis has grown considerably. A considerable fraction of RA members have moved into careers as Jewish educators, and smaller numbers have pursued other non-pulpit options. Close to 40 percent of rabbis ordained at the Jewish Theological Seminary between 1990 and 1997 chose to work in Jewish education and other non-pulpit fields as their first position after graduation.

The trend to practice one's rabbinate in a domain other than the congregation has a variety of causes. Negatively, some graduates, partic-

ularly women, experience difficulties in securing congregational placement. A decade after the admission of women as RA members, its 117
women rabbis are still acting as pioneers in the congregational pulpit.
They are being hired, but not necessarily in the pulpit positions they
seek. Opposition to hiring a woman rabbi is much less in non-pulpit
fields.[99]

Beyond the brake on pulpit placement caused by the slow pace of
change in congregational attitudes, there is a generalized problem of
supply and demand. In the 1990s, the population of rabbinical students
rose sharply. JTS sharply increased the size of its rabbinical school student body, and the University of Judaism opened its own rabbinical
school, the Ziegler School of Rabbinic Studies, in 1995, with a class size
of 17 students admitted per year. RA leaders repeatedly expressed their
concern over the ability to place all of the rabbis who will be seeking
work by the end of the decade, and identify non-pulpit positions as the
most likely area of advancement for new rabbinic placement.[100]

Yet there are also positive factors behind the emergence of a substantial involvement of RA members in non-pulpit work. The Solomon
Schechter Day School movement has grown dramatically since its inception in the 1970s. Many rabbis view the Conservative day school, along
with informal educational programs such as Camp Ramah, as the salva-
tion of the movement. They argue that intensive investment in Jewish
education is finally mending the chronic weakness of Conservative
Judaism by producing a Jewishly informed and committed laity. The
move of RA members into positions in Jewish education is partly a
response to their vision of how best to serve the Jewish community at
the present historic juncture.[101]

Even as Conservative rabbis moved increasingly into Jewish education, it remained a source of frustration that, at critical points in the
life-cycle, they were unable to refer their congregants to Conservative
personnel and institutions. In 1989, the RA and the JTS began training
Conservative *mohalim*. The *brit kodesh* program brought certified
physicians to the Seminary to receive training in the religious dimension
of ritual circumcision. Similarly, the RA has trained *kashrut* supervisors.
Whereas it has not run the *brit kodesh* program regularly, it offers its
rav ha-makhshir course on an ongoing basis. At the other end of the
life-cycle, in the course of the current generation, Conservative rabbis
have become involved in the work of the *hevra kadisha,* training and
supervising committees to prepare the bodies of the deceased for burial.

The examples of *mohel* and *hevra kadisha* point to the role of the rabbi as Conservative denominational mentor, not just as "professional Jew." The Conservative rabbi had long lamented that he could not possibly fulfill all the roles that his position demanded. Nearing century's end, it is becoming clear that, thanks to the initiatives of the rabbis, the movement is finally creating a cadre of paraprofessionals and a substantial body of laity to complement the rabbi and to function as a well-rounded Jewish denomination.

A Worldwide Denominational Presence

The elaboration of a fuller denominational infrastructure has taken place primarily in North America, which remains the center of gravity of Conservative Judaism. But alongside developments in North America, the RA has become increasingly international since 1970. Its members reversed the relative disregard of Israel by the Seminary during the 1950s and 1960s. Efforts of Rabbinical Assembly colleagues have created a Conservative Jewish presence in Latin America and Europe. Today, thanks to the work of the RA, Conservative Judaism is becoming a world-wide reality.

Conservative Judaism scarcely had a presence in Israel prior to 1970. Only five congregations were affiliated with the movement in 1971. Although there was some individual effort and support, there was no movement-wide program to foster Conservative Judaism in Israel.[102]

In the early 1970s, Rabbinical Assembly leaders expressed self-criticism that Conservative Judaism had failed to establish anything significant in Israel. They called for the movement to strengthen the few congregations that did exist there and shake off its lethargy with regard to establishing a meaningful presence in Israel. Likewise, younger RA members such as Michael Graetz, who settled in Israel in the 1970s not to retire but to live, work and raise families, urged their fellow rabbis to make *aliyah*.[103]

In March, 1978, the RA created the organization for Mesorati (i.e., traditional) Judaism (later changed to Masorti, in keeping with contemporary Hebrew style), with Michael Graetz as its executive director. In November of that same year, MERCAZ (Movement for the Reaffirmation of Conservative Zionism) had its founding meeting. The movement soon began to grow beyond immigrant rabbis. Philip Spectre presented a panel of lay leaders of Masorti synagogues to the 1981 RA convention. But success was modest, and the lay leaders acknowledged that they were having difficulties in getting Israelis "in past the doorstep."[104]

Growth continued throughout the 1980s. In 1988, the RA met in Israel and focused on the theme of Conservative Judaism in Israel. The Bet Midrash ordained four rabbis. The denomination boasts a youth movement, a kibbutz, a moshav, and "TALI" schools (i.e., public schools with an augmented Jewish studies curriculum, an alternative to twin extremes of the Orthodoxy of the state religious school system and the thorough-going secularism of the secular schools). The focus on youth and education was helping the movement to grow beyond its immigrant roots. By the year 1988, there were 40 Conservative congregations and 12,000 Conservative Jews in Israel. The number of RA members in Israel grew to 120 by the end of the 1980s. They had begun publishing a journal, *Et La'asot,* and had formed their own Jewish Law Committee, the *va'ad halakhah.*[105]

The waves of immigration from Ethiopia and the Soviet Union and its successor states in the 1980s and 1990s gave the Conservative movement the opportunity to interact with new potential members. The ambivalent attitude, seemingly smacking of racism, that the Chief Rabbinate displayed toward the Ethiopians gave the Conservatives some opportunity to engage the immigrants.

Israeli RA members recognized that if they wanted to sink roots in Israeli society, they would have to go beyond the synagogue. Michael Graetz, in his inaugural address as president of the RA Israel region in 1992, analyzed the challenge as one of changing the function of religion to suit the specifics of the Israeli, as opposed to the Diasporic Jew. The synagogue functions differently in the Diaspora, where it is recognized as "Jewish space," than in Israel, where the reality of *Eretz Yisrael* grounds the Jew's sense of identity. Conservative Judaism can only be successful if it deals seriously with that fundamental issue.[106]

In addition to the different status of the synagogue, cultural obstacles to the growth of Conservative Judaism abounded. At their 1988 symposium, Israeli RA members drew attention to the challenges still to be met in transplanting Conservative Judaism to Israeli society. Jonathan Perlman, focusing on outreach to the Ethiopian Jews of Beersheva, pointed to their horror that a woman would receive an *aliyah* within eighty days of giving birth, a factor that few Western-raised Conservative rabbis would have thought to consider. Moshe Re'em asked how Jews raised to venerate the figure of Baba Sali, the rabbi as miracle-worker, could appreciate the message of Conservative Judaism.

Robert Harris shared frustrations closer to the experience of North American rabbis—reaching out to Israeli families, patiently overcoming their suspicions, leading them in a meaningful bar mitzvah ceremony, and then learning that they never had any notion of becoming part of the life of the congregation.[107]

Beyond cultural difficulties, the Conservative rabbis in Israel have faced a hostile political climate. The Orthodox rabbinic establishment made life generally difficult for the RA pioneers. Occasionally, the poor relations worsened still further, with campaigns to change the Law of Return to discredit conversions conducted by Conservative (and other non-Orthodox) rabbis. In 1970, 1977, 1988 and again in 1997, the government entertained such changes. The first two times, the proposals were defeated, with relatively little uproar. But by the third time, and even more so in the most recent debate, American Jews reacted with outrage. By the late 1980s, Israel was no longer the ideal and endangered child of the Jewish world, but a state strong enough to bear criticism from within the Jewish people.

In the early years of statehood, Conservative rabbis were unwilling to criticize Israeli policy in public. In 1970, asserting the right to do so was a contentious move. Gradually, it became more acceptable to express dissent on Israel. At the Resolutions session of the 1977 RA convention, the rabbis tabled a motion calling for such dissent to be muted. The 1982 invasion of Lebanon was a turning point. American Jews began to register open criticism of Israel more unabashedly. By 1983, it was acceptable for the RA to host an open debate over the pro-government and opposition positions regarding Israeli policy on the West Bank.[108]

The willingness to criticize Israel on foreign policy issues, in turn, made it easier for Conservative rabbis to register opposition to Israel's lack of religious pluralism. Israeli RA members responded to harassment and delegitimization on the part of the Orthodox establishment by calling for the abolition of the coercive powers of the official rabbinate, and for the disestablishment of the Chief Rabbinate itself. Ismar Schorsch made headlines in 1997 when he blasted the Chief Rabbinate as having "not a scintilla of moral worth,"[109] but even those RA members who shied away from such a blanket condemnation were united in their call for fundamental change in the management of religious affairs in Israel.

At present, Israeli RA members are involved in the Israeli government's Jewish study institutes established as an outgrowth of the Neeman Commission. In addition, recent High Court decisions have indicated that fair treatment in government funding is to be expected for Masorti institutions. Conservative Judaism has won some critical court battles, and has made some strides in winning public recognition. Clearly, much remains unaccomplished, but the change since 1970 has been striking.

Alongside the growing Rabbinical Assembly presence in Israel has been an emerging community of Conservative rabbis in Latin America. Addressing the RA in 1985, Marshall Meyer, recently arrived from Buenos Aires, described the importance of Conservative Judaism for the religious life of South American Jewry. The Conservative Seminary there, the Seminario Rabinico Latinoamericano, had ties with 47 congregations, serving 110,000 Jews, perhaps one-fifth of the Jewish population on that continent. With this magnitude of service, it is not surprising that by the 1980s, RA self-descriptions began regularly mentioning Latin America as an important area. By the mid-1990s, over 50 RA members were in Latin America. In its 1996 report, the RA Strategic Planning Committee called for an increased focus on Israeli and Latin American colleagues. Indeed, RA efforts could help the Latin American colleagues deal with the isolation that hinders their efforts, a problem arising from their geographic dispersion and from an absence of a tradition of sharing on common rabbinic issues. In recognition of the importance the RA ascribes to developing Conservative Judaism worldwide, the presidents of the Latin American and Israeli regions of the RA sit on the organization's Executive Council.[110]

The RA has also established a small presence in Europe. Establishing a Conservative congregation in England can be daunting, given the manifestation of both subtle and gross forms of opposition by local Orthodox leaders. Nonetheless, Conservative Rabbis in England report a receptivity on the part of British Jewry to their centrist vision.[111]

In sum, the growth of Conservative Judaism worldwide complements the intensification of the denomination's self-expression in North America. Both developments are aspects of the maturation of the movement.

Changes in the Style of the Conservative Rabbinate: Informality, Spirituality, Collegiality

A profound change in style has gone hand in hand with the ideologic, liturgic and institutional developments within Conservative Judaism since 1970. Rabbis conduct their services and interact with congregants in a different way than before, highlighting the expressive rather than the impressive, the informal rather than the formal, speaking the language of spirituality, and taking pains to appear collegial rather than hierarchical.

Worship in the Conservative synagogue of 1970 typically meant a rabbi, and often a cantor, standing on the pulpit, facing the congregation, directing the worshipers when to stand and sit, when to sing, read aloud or read silently. The service attempted to be decorous, while nonetheless involving the congregants.

Popular movements of that time, especially among the young, were challenging this model of service, and more fundamentally, the values of formality and impressiveness that nourished it. In 1970, Stephen Lerner reported to his fellow Rabbinical Assembly members about the *havurot* of the day, associations in which prayer was accomplished with informality and collegiality. The *havurot* appealed to the anti-authoritarian sentiments of their predominantly collegian members. Casualness in dress that would have offended the ushers of the Conservative synagogues of the day and seating arrangements (sometimes on pillows, rather than in pews) that emphasized the egalitarian nature of the prayer group were the norm in these gatherings.[112]

In the growing atmosphere of worry that replaced the optimism of the 1945–1965 Conservative rabbinate, some rabbis viewed the *havurot* as potential rivals to synagogues for the allegiance of Conservative Jews. Others, notably Harold Schulweis, saw the *havurot* as an opportunity for the Conservative synagogue to foster a sense of community among its members. Following his lead, many Rabbinical Assembly members created *havurot* in their congregations, organizing or supporting the formation of groups of families among their synagogue members. These groups would celebrate Shabbat and holidays together, dining, studying, and socializing. They would involve themselves in selected philanthropic projects. Throughout, they would enjoy an intimacy of association that seemed elusive in the "establishment" Conservative synagogue.

After a decade of rabbinic initiative in fostering *havurot,* it became clear that the new institution was not achieving a revolutionary impact. Only a few people used the *havurah* as a door into the synagogue. In the main, rather than functioning as a major instrument of outreach, the *havurot* attracted already-active synagogue members. Within this group, however, *havurah* affiliation served to intensify involvement and satisfaction with synagogue life. The success of the *havurot* was their ability to "provide a vehicle for intimacy and involvement within a Jewish ambience."[113]

The Conservative synagogue did not actually transmute into a collection of *ḥavurot*, but the new emphasis on informality became part of the culture of the movement. Rabbis sometimes came off the pulpit, to lessen the symbolic and psychological distance from their congregants. New and renovating synagogues lowered the height of the pulpit, to accomplish the same goal.[114]

The desire for informality relates in two complementary ways to powerful currents in contemporary American life: first, its equation of informality and expressiveness with authenticity, and second, its distrust of authority figures.

The social revolution of the 1960s bequeathed to the entire American culture its emphasis on emotion rather than structure. A popular motto of the decade, "Let it all hang out," expressed the ideal of sharing fully one's feelings. The generation coming of age in that time of protest devalued the restraints of etiquette. Formerly prized as marks of civilized behavior, these formal channels now came to be seen as impediments to genuine self-expression.

As applied to worship, this new ideal led rabbis to look for models of religious passion and emotional involvement. Abraham Joshua Heschel had criticized the postwar Conservative synagogue as being stuffy; now, that criticism became the in-house lament of increasing numbers of Conservative rabbis. Likewise, the admiration of Hasidism and its various refractions that passed from philosophers such as Buber and Heschel to the Jewish student counterculture of the late 1960s and into the *ḥavurah* movement also influenced the Conservative synagogue. Rabbis and cantors posed the full-throated participation of the congregants in worship as the ideal. Of course, the existence of this model in aspects of traditional Judaism made this a "revolution by tradition," but it was a transformation of the postwar Conservative synagogue nonetheless. The tone of the Conservative worship service had been polite, with rabbi and congregation reading responsively. Now, the more unruly sound of *davening* and the bodily involvement in prayer by means of *shuckling* informed the personal piety of the rabbi.

The term that came into vogue by the late 1970s, describing the expressive, informal, contemplative ideals of worship and religious life was "spirituality." Many rabbis initially scorned the quest for spirituality as a syncretistic abandonment of Jewish priorities. The lack of commitment for social action, for *tikkun olam*, on the part of the 1970s spiritual seekers puzzled many rabbinic observers, and led some to doubt that there was any deep connection between the concerns of those people and the historic agenda of the Jewish community. But some rabbis recognized that the hunger for transcendent meaning was real, if ill-informed, and that the rabbis themselves bore a measure of blame for having focused on bricks and mortar while ignoring the personal and the spiritual. "In the midst of a great deal of commotion, we have lost the emotion . . ."[115]

In 1980, eager to understand the increasing popularity of this quest, the RA convention committee invited Susannah Heschel to address the rabbis on "Changing Forms of Jewish Spirituality." Heschel pointed to the concern for Judaism's spiritual aspects as the common denominator linking the *havurah* movement, the Jewish aspect of feminism, the rise of Jewish studies at universities, the success of the *Jewish Catalogues,* the resurgence of interest in Jewish mysticism, and the channeling of religious creative writing into new *midrashim.* She identified the people attracted to these linked movements as those disillusioned with the apparent lack of quest for transcendent meaning in suburban synagogues.[116]

The quest for spirituality, identified by the Heschels, father and daughter, as a criticism of the Conservative Jewish status quo, resonated among Jewish Theological Seminary students in the 1980s. Rabbinical students asked their school to provide more spirituality, and to abandon the intellectualist emphasis of the *Wissenschaft des Judentums* movement. Some observers remained unimpressed, and considered the spirituality search a passing fad, influenced more by the flaws of the existing Seminary curriculum than by broadly-shared religious concerns. However, the Conservative theologian Neil Gillman defended the search for spirituality as one of several legitimate models of Jewish piety. Gillman counseled the Conservative rabbi to display an openness to all of these models. Seminary students enamored of the search for spirituality interpreted Gillman's analysis as a validation of their emphasis. As those students graduated and joined the Rabbinical Assembly, their openness to a previously counter-cultural protest became ever more integrated into the changing style of the Conservative rabbi.[117]

The loyalties given to the quest for spirituality do seem to have displaced the social activism of Conservative Judaism of the 1960s. Throughout the period since the 1970s, the Social Action Committee of the Rabbinical Assembly has called, with only sporadic success, for the members to become involved in the various causes of the day. A chairman of the committee, Charles Feinberg, saw the shift away from social activism as a corollary of the same change of religious climate as produced the focus on spirituality. Observers beyond the RA concur.

Rabbi Henry M. Speaker, first president of the Seminary Alumni Association (1901–1904). (Photo by Ruth S. Fierstien, from a painting by Henry Cooper. Courtesy of Gratz College)

Rabbi Max D. Klein, last president of the Seminary Alumni Association (1916–1918); first president of the Rabbinical Assembly (1918–1922). (Courtesy of the Philadelphia Jewish Archives Center)

Members of the Class of 1922 meeting with Dr. Louis Finkelstein, late 1940s. Left to right: front row: Rabbis Alter Landesman, Finkelstein, Max Davidson. Back row: Rabbis Herman Hailperin, Gershon Hadas, Joseph Miller, Morris Silverman, Max Zucker, Jules Schatz. (Virginia Stern, RA Archives)

37th Annual Convention of the RA at JTS, June 1937. (Empire Photographers, RA Archive

Golden Jubilee Convention of the RA at JTS, June 1950. (Empire Photographers, RA Archi

Members of the Law Committee, March 1955. Left to right, Rabbis Isaac Klein, David Panitz, Wolfe Kelman. (RA Archives)

Rabbi Mordecai
Kaplan, November 1957.
(RA Archives)

Rabbi Morris Silverman,
mid-1950s. (RA
Archives)

Rabbis Abraham Joshua Heschel and Wolfe Kelman, 1967. (Photo by John H. Popper. Courtesy of the Ratner Center for the Study of Conservative Judaism, Jewish Theological Seminary)

Dr. Martin Luther King addressing the RA with Rabbi Everett Gendler, 1968 Convention. (Courtesy of Naomi Camper Gendler)

Past presidents and officers of the Rabbinical Assembly with Seminary leaders, 1972. Left to right: front row: Rabbis Simon Greenberg, Harry Halpern, Gerson Cohen, Louis Finkelstein, Mordecai Waxman, Max Arzt, David Aronson, Israel Levinthal. Back row: Rabbis Ira Eisenstein, Eli Bohnen, Max Routtenberg, Robert Gordis, Ralph Simon, Judah Nadich, Mordecai Kaplan, Edward Sandrow. (RA Archives)

Honoring Rabbi Gilbert Epstein, RA convention, 1991. Left to right: Rabbis Jules Harlow, Joel Meyers, Saul Teplitz, Gilbert Epstein, David Jacobs, Irwin Groner. (RA Archives)

RA Convention in Los Angeles, 1993. Left to right: front row: Rabbis Ismar Schorsch, Harold Schulweis, Robert Wexler. Back row: Rabbis Joel Meyers, Gerald Zelizer, Joel Rembaum. (RA Archives)

Opening plenary at 1996 Convention. Left to right: Rabbi Seymour Essrog, Rabbi Alan Silverstein, Governor Madeleine Kunin (deputy secretary of education), and Rabbi David Lieber. (RA Archives)

Senator Edward Kennedy at 1997 Convention in Boston. Left to right: Rabbi Sam Chiel, Senator Kennedy, Rabbi Charles Feinberg. (RA Archives)

Rabbi Seymour Essrog and MK Ehud Barak (currently prime minister) at 1998 RA Convention in Jerusalem. (RA Archives)

Rabbi Shosh Dworsky (ordained 1998) leads *minḥah* at a conference celebrating tenth anniversary of the decision to admit women to the JTS Rabbinical School, October 1993. (Courtesy of the Jewish Theological Seminary)

Rabbis Jan Caryl Kaufman, Joel Meyers, and Elliot Salo Schoenberg, 1999. (Marjorie Gersten, RA Archives)

Reflecting on what motivated those Jews in their quest, Jonathan Woocher concluded, there are Jews who "are seeking in Judaism not a public cause but a guidepost and rationale for their daily lives."[118]

Like the new ideal of informality, the distrust of authority was a legacy of the 1960s that has sunk roots into the contemporary American psyche. The momentary outrage over President Eisenhower's lying to the American public during the U-2 spy plane incident of 1960 gave way to the more sustained, cynical response of the American public to the Johnson administration's statements regarding the Vietnam War. The phrase "credibility gap" entered the American lexicon, with newscasters reporting regularly on the latest poll tabulating how many Americans believed their government was lying to them. Mistrust of government only deepened with the Watergate debacle of 1972–1974 and with the scandals of the Reagan and Clinton administrations throughout the past two decades. Today, the tide of revulsion with elected political leaders runs unabated.

Nor was the growing sense that authorities have lost their standing confined to political leadership. The business elite of the 1980s, a decade marked by prosperity on Wall Street, was tarnished with a wave of high-publicity convictions. One such conviction that came close to home among Conservative Jews was that of Ivan Boesky, one of the principal benefactors of the Jewish Theological Seminary. Exposure of the failings of religious leaders, too, contributed to the growing climate of public cynicism. Fundamentalist Protestant preachers such as Jim Bakker and Jimmy Swaggart were accused of business offenses and sexual crimes. Even when the offender was not a famous televangelist, the conviction of clergy contributed to the corrosion of trust in religious authority figures. In the 1980s and 1990s, there were periodic reports of Roman Catholic priests being accused of child molestation.

Beyond the growth of distrust, the rise in the educational level of Conservative congregants has limited the rabbi's status as the community's "wise man." In most contemporary congregations, the rabbi is one professional among many, each of whom is paramount in his own field, and who regards other professionals more or less as equals. The pre-eminence of the rabbi in knowledge of the Jewish tradition, while acknowledged, is evaluated without the awe accorded by a previous generation.

In a related phenomenon, Americans have sought to become empowered as clients and consumers, in their relations with professionals. Physicians, for example, commonly speak of having had to develop a new style of exercising their profession, in order to contend with the expectations of the contemporary generation of patients. To the extent that congregants regard themselves as consumers of services provided by the rabbi, the assertiveness of the contemporary consumer colors this relationship as well. This is even evidenced by the growing penchant of younger congregants to address their rabbis on a first-name basis, a style that still offends laity of the old school, as well as many rabbis.

Rabbis since 1970 have operated, then, in a society that is less prepared to accord the same high level of trust in authority, including religious authority, than had formerly been the norm. This has effects on the way in which the rabbi operates. On the pulpit, sermons tend to be less "magisterial," more conversational in tone and less reliant on rhetorical mastery. It is more common for rabbis to facilitate discussions, at times dispensing with the sermon altogether. Off the pulpit, rabbis find themselves wondering, when being asked for halakhic guidance, whether their opinions will be accepted, or whether the questioner will shop for answers until finding the most congenial one.

Because there is even less cultural tolerance for authoritarianism in women than in men, women rabbis face an even greater difficulty than their male colleagues in asserting themselves authoritatively. Women are still conditioned to opt for a "gentle solution" rather than to court conflict by choosing a path that involves confrontation.[119]

The changed climate has also affected the self-image of the rabbi. While some rabbis, young and old, chafe at the loss of formal tokens of respect, others have embraced the collegiality of the newer social arrangements. They have enjoyed the warmth of a social network seldom available to their predecessors.[120] As products of an anti-authoritarian generation themselves, contemporary rabbis increasingly prefer to exercise their rabbinic leadership as mentors and facilitators.

The New Consumerism and the Administration of the Rabbinical Assembly

In their own attitude toward the Rabbinical Assembly as their professional organization, its members mirrored the move in American society toward empowering the consumer. The changes in the regulations regarding rabbinic placement, the heart of the activities of the Rabbinical Assembly, and the different style of organizational leadership since the 1980s are striking evidence for the transformation of the institutional culture of the Rabbinical Assembly, in line with contemporary social changes.

After the conclusion of the decades of its postwar growth, the RA continued to handle rabbinic placements by the same method it had employed earlier. The professional staff of the organization, i.e. its executive vice president, Wolfe Kelman and its director of placement, Gilbert Epstein, in conjunction with a rabbinic placement chairman appointed from among the RA membership, would recommend panels of rabbis to congregations. The panels were limited in number, to prevent the lay leadership of the congregations from driving down the value of rabbinic service. In fact, Kelman and his associates were zealous and tireless to raise the status of the Conservative rabbi, both materially and socially, and succeeded, in large measure.

Whatever the size of the RA, the limitation of the number of rabbis who could constitute a panel provided a perennial source of dissatisfaction. What accounted for one rabbi being named to a panel for a particularly attractive congregation, rather than another colleague with comparable seniority? Allegations of favoritism were a natural, if unpleasant, structural side-effect, built into the placement system.

Furthermore, the panel system worked less well when there were over 1000 rabbis to be served than when there was less than a third of that number. Since Kelman was so often a personal advocate for the rabbis, a personal relationship between him and them was obviously a desideratum; yet that became more and more difficult, as a consequence of the growth of the movement.

When the movement ceased its postwar expansion, and placement opportunities were more contested, such allegations took on greater urgency. In the 1970s, a group of Rabbinical Assembly members created "Project RA" in order to democratize the movement and to achieve what its members regarded as greater equity in placement.

In 1978, the Project RA leaders fielded a slate of rabbis, challenging the slate presented by the RA nominating committee. The tension between the supporters and the critics of the professional leadership of the organization also surfaced in the resolutions session of the convention that year, with Kelman's defenders promoting a statement in support of the executive vice president. The resolution was tabled.[121]

The Project RA leadership was proud of its ability to marshal a coalition of rabbis who had opposing positions on the then-hotly debated issue of women's ordination. When the emotions surrounding that debate grew so heated that the unity of the RA seemed imperiled, Project RA leaders attempted to preserve their coalition. They feared that, with rabbis coming to regard the question of women's ordination as central, Project RA was in danger of being sidetracked.[122]

Ultimately, the rabbis proposed by Project RA served as leaders of the organization, and put their stamp on it. In his 1982 Presidential Address, Seymour Cohen pointed to the sharp increase in rabbis voting for their RA officers as a sign that Project RA had succeeded in broadening the base of member involvement in their organization. He also took credit for the widened cross-section of membership reflected in the Nominations Committee.[123]

The new leaders worked to revise the placement system. In 1983, Arnold Goodman reported to the RA membership that the organization had implemented new placement procedures, designed "to avoid one colleague getting recommended while a second remains frustrated."[124]

The revision was completed in 1989, with the passage of a "Resolution on Rabbinic Freedom of Choice," or more popularly, the Lubow resolution, after Rabbi Akiba Lubow, who submitted it. This amendment fundamentally changed the way in which the Rabbinical Assembly professional staff handled the placement needs of the members. It did away with the panel system. Henceforth, any member could have his resume sent to a congregation, subject to seniority restrictions and certain limits on how many congregations could be contacted in particular time-periods. But the professional staff no longer had a role in deciding who could apply where.

At first, the new system occasionally confused congregations, because many more resumes would arrive than the laity had previously screened. But as the system became more familiar, the movement took it in stride. The rabbis reported that they were satisfied with the change.[125] The Rabbinical Assembly member, as a consumer of his professional association's services, had become fully empowered.

The new professional staff of the Rabbinical Assembly that came into office after the retirement of Rabbi Kelman in 1989 was fully aware of their mandate to serve a more empowered clientele. The current executive vice president, Joel Meyers, articulated his vision of the mission of the RA in his initial address to the membership in 1989. His first goal was to build a caring rabbinic community. He would respect the diversity among the rabbis, eschew labels, and embrace colleagues both in the pulpit and in other professional walks. This was quite a change from Kelman's vision of the RA, a vision focused on building the Conservative rabbinate into a power to be reckoned with. Meyers was in effect promising to be a civil servant, not a power broker.[126]

Gilbert Epstein retired in 1991, two years after Wolfe Kelman. Epstein is widely and fondly remembered for having "been there for the rabbi." His professional focus, though, was on the time of placement.

Epstein's successor, the current placement director, Elliott Salo Schoenberg, has reconceptualized the position, in line with the axiom that the rabbis of the organization are his customers, just as their own congregants are their customers. Beyond serving rabbis at the moments in their careers when they change positions, Schoenberg has initiated a series of programs designed to meet the needs of the member rabbis, psychological and educational, as well as strictly placement-related. He is concerned with their professional development and their understanding of the organizational dynamics of the professional settings in which they work. Even in helping rabbis during the placement process itself, the focus now includes the mental health issues of transition.[127]

The RA professional staff's new focus on the psychological and organizational-systems aspects of serving as a rabbi is shared by the organization's elected leadership. Reflecting on developments during the years 1992–1994, Gerald Zelizer reported that the Joint Placement Commission had stepped up from the technical task of attaching rabbis to congregations to the more general one of assuring that the attachment remains glued together. The 1996 mission statement for joint placement also reflects this tendency. It focuses on congregational dynamics, not just placement mechanics, and seeks to educate congregations about the emotional dynamics of hiring and caring for a rabbi.[128]

It is an additional sign of the times that, in 1993, the RA set up an Association of Retired Rabbis. By definition, this is a group that had not heavily engaged the attention of the organization's professionals in previous generations, since these colleagues' placement needs were behind them. The establishment of this new sub-group is consistent with Meyers and Schoenberg's vision of a "caring community," in which the RA provides support even beyond the active phase of its members' careers. The association of retired RA members has held annual conventions. As of 1998, each of its conventions has been better attended than the preceding one, the last one attracting 120 participants. It also publishes a newsletter, *Ha-Modi'a*, edited by Stanley Rabinowitz, featuring articles on subjects of interest to retired rabbis or reflecting their experiences. The newsletter is circulated to the active members of the RA, as well, and represents a contribution to intergenerational dialogue.

The Conservative Rabbi as a Person

The new directions in the governance of the RA and in its placement service, along with the contemporary rabbi's preference for informality and lessened interest in power-broker politics, are ultimately manifestations of a change in the self-image of the rabbi. This change affects the rabbi not only as a professional, but also as a person. As compared to the previous generation, the contemporary rabbi is quicker to acknowledge needs and limitations, both for his family and for himself.

Participants in the Conservative Jewish debates over the status of women in the synagogue correctly understood that the denomination's halakhic accommodation to feminist aspirations was a watershed for the movement. However, it has not been sufficiently noted that the greatest impact of feminism on the Conservative rabbinate is not the presence of growing numbers of women rabbis, although that is without doubt a significant development. The greatest impact is in the participation of Conservative rabbis, most of whom are still male, in the transformation of gender roles envisioned by feminism. Rabbis' wives today are more apt to be professionals or full-time employees in businesses than was the case in the "Ozzie and Harriet" generation. That has had a profound effect on the career trajectories of the rabbis themselves. Rabbis are no longer willing to relocate so many times during their careers, in large measure because the economic and emotional satisfaction of their families is bound up in the success of their wives' careers.

This is even more true for married women rabbis. After nearly a decade and a half of women serving in the Conservative rabbinate, a pattern is emerging of women rabbis reducing or temporarily halting their work when they focus on raising children. This has the effect of minimizing their career advancement moves and keeping the careers of the husbands of these rabbis an important factor in their planning.

A witticism popular at the Jewish Theological Seminary around 1985 spoke to a sociological reality: "If you call the wife of a rabbi a *rebbetzin,* what do you call the husband of a rabbi? Doctor." For all rabbis, both men and women, the economic parity of husband and wife envisioned by feminist critics of mid-century American society has helped to reshape rabbinic notions of a successful career.

Hand in hand with the disinclination to uproot one's spouse more than a very few times in one's career is a different definition of job satisfaction. Rabbis look at qualitative factors, not simply congregational size, in assessing their work.

These qualititative factors prominently feature the nurturing of the rabbi's family. Over the past twenty years, there has been a growing wave of concern for the emotional effect of the rabbinate upon the rabbi and the rabbinic family. Programs designed to validate the emotions of rabbinic family members and to help them cope with the stresses of their situation became fixtures at the annual Rabbinical Assembly conventions, starting in the 1980s. In 1983, the RA organized a new standing Committee on the Rabbinic Family, chaired by Ed and Bobbie Winter, and published a newsletter, *Chaverah*, edited by Ruby Eisenberg Creditor, for the wives of RA members to support each other.[129]

By the mid-1990s, the rabbinic awareness of the need to nurture family relationships, a novelty only twenty years before, had become conventional wisdom. In 1996, giving advice to newly-ordained rabbis, Randall Konigsburg counseled them to regard their family, then their synagogue, and then the general community as concentric circles, with the innermost one being inviolate.[130]

The contemporary rabbi sees himself in much the same way as he views each other member of his family—as a person with valid, pressing emotional needs. He is willing to confess or even proclaim them and eager to receive professional help in maintaining his psychological health. In 1982, when Leslie Friedman sent a questionnaire to the RA membership asking the rabbis to participate in a study of stress in the rabbinate, 65 percent took part. This high percentage was a sign of their desire for support. Friedman reported the conclusions of his study to the rabbis two years later. He found that rabbis showed considerably higher nonspecific psychological stress than did the general population sample. He called for training to help the rabbi understand his own psychological processes and the role he has assumed.[131]

Rabbis have responded positively to Friedman's call. The sessions of Dr. Peter Pitzele, a psychotherapist, at rabbinic gatherings are perennially crowded. He presents psychodramas, which are explorations of self and of outlook in the context of responses to biblical narratives. They are conducive to free and revealing self-disclosure. Others of his sessions allow the rabbis to understand the psychological realities underneath the surface in their relations with their synagogue boards.

This change in rabbinic self-disclosure has proceeded generationally, from younger to older rabbis. In a 1981 survey of the RA, younger members reported the highest amount of dissatisfaction with their work. They complained of a multitude of tasks that only minimally related to their image of what a rabbi ought to be doing.[132]

These younger rabbis are members of the famous "baby boomer" generation in America, a generation that is alternately praised and scorned for its preoccupation with its own psychological well-being.[133] The triumph of "Project RA" in the early 1980s brought this generation's perspectives to the fore within the leadership of the RA. In 1985, identifying himself with the concerns of younger colleagues, Alexander Shapiro hailed a new spirit of frankness among RA members. In the past, he claimed, members would routinely inflate the numbers of congregants they reported attending worship services. When asked how they were doing, they would reply, "fine," "although they were dying inside." Shapiro was pleased that those days were past. He pledged that his administration would be concerned with the psychological and also the physical welfare of the rabbis.[134]

The generational divide among the rabbis was for a while a source of some friction. When Pitzele's sessions were first programmed, a number of rabbis of the generation that had matured prior to 1970 remarked unfavorably on the willingness of their younger colleagues to confess inadequacy, to describe themselves as "broken healers." As one older onlooker remarked to this author, "What's the matter with those kids? Why don't they grow up?" As the sessions continued from year to year, more and more of the older colleagues joined in, having joined in the newly emerged consensus about the wisdom of a rabbi's self-revelations.

In fact, the climate of self-expression is shared by older and younger rabbis today. The editorial in the February/March 1998 issue of *Ha-Modi'a* explores the frustrations of the rabbinic calling, yet optimistically ventures that the elderly rabbi is the one best able to achieve self-mastery and thus contentment, precisely because of the older rabbi's superior experience in dealing with life's disappointments.[135]

The Nineties: Crisis and Confidence

From the foregoing analysis, it is evident that, between 1970 and 1990, the Conservative rabbinate had presided over a movement that had lost its sense of being the common Judaism of the American Jewish community, but that had in turn gained a new sense of its identity and its parameters. In the close of the 1980s, it seemed as if the movement had finished the hardest part of wrestling with the questions posed by feminism, that it had decided on a course of action that appealed to most of its constituents and cost relatively few defections, and that it was ready to speak with renewed assurance, based on its accomplishment in formulating a Conservative Jewish ideology. This was the balance sheet of having matured as a denomination.[136] The RA had also managed a generational shift in its internal governance and was looking forward to a new era as an institution.

But in the new decade, Conservative Judaism once again had its attention refocused on the question of its very survival. The 1990 National Jewish Population Survey revealed a dangerously high level of intermarriage among American Jews. The figure of 52 percent (later challenged and revised slightly down, but not fundamentally changed), meaning that over half of all marriages were out of the faith community, re-ignited a crisis mentality among Jewish leaders and concerned laity.

In truth, the concern about intermarriage antedated 1990. RA leaders were calling attention to it as early as 1970. In that year, Ralph Simon called upon the RA membership to respond to the rise of intermarriage by encouraging conversions to Judaism. Again, in 1978, Judah Nadich presented evidence to the RA chronicling the rise and growing acceptability of intermarriage among Conservative Jews. He shared his counseling techniques, including gambits intended to disuade couples from intermarrying. Nonetheless, Nadich recognized that many such marriages could not be forestalled, and he urged his colleagues to adopt a more positive attitude to conversion, on the one hand, and to do outreach to intermarried couples, on the other.[137] Simcha Kling's *Embracing Judaism,* published in 1987, was a response to the Rabbinical Assembly's initiative to create standard texts and curricula for the instruction of converts. But 1990 emerged as a watershed, because the population survey's statistics were so dire that concern for sheer survival of the Jewish people in the free society of the Western world came to the fore.

While the issues brought to a head by the 1990 survey are still, as of this writing, very much part of the unfinished business of Conservative Judaism, it is not too soon to discern at least the outlines of how the "Jewish continuity"[138] debate meshes with the heightened focus on Conservative Judaism as a denomination, a subset of the Jewish people having its own core and periphery.

Presenting the population study to the RA, the demographer Steven Bayme called upon the Conservative rabbis to define clearly its stance on intermarriage and on the policy implications of outreach to intermarried couples. He encouraged them to take advantage of the unique position of Conservative Judaism within the spectrum of the Jewish community to take the lead in encouraging endogamous marriages, but also to continue to underscore the importance of conversion as a goal of communal outreach.[139]

While the rabbinic response to the population survey statistics included a good deal of hand-wringing, RA leaders sounded a more upbeat note. Alan Silverstein, the RA president in the mid-1990s, outlined a three-pronged stategy to combat assimilation and intermarriage, promoting marriage within the faith, sincere conversion, and effective *keruv*.[140] According to this argument, the Conservative movement's approach to intermarriage is the most sound of all the denominations. It does not weaken the stress on endogamous marriage, because unlike the Reform, the Rabbinical Assembly does not permit its members to officiate at intermarriages, or even to participate in an ancillary fashion. Yet, it is realistic, because unlike the Orthodox, the Rabbinical Assembly is openly committed to receiving potential converts to Judaism who would otherwise be partners to an intermarriage.

An important consequence of the focus on intermarriage since 1990 has been an internal debate within the RA, mirroring a debate within the general North American Jewish community, over the respective merits of inreach and outreach. Despite the identification of intermarrying and intermarried couples as the population segment at risk, many RA members favored inreach over outreach. In their analysis, the committed core of Conservative laity would carry the movement through the crisis.

A prominent advocate of the emphasis on inreach has been Ismar Schorsch. In 1990, he called upon the RA to take seriously the emergence of a critical mass of serious Jews, to lead the Jewish community in supporting them, and to offer them opportunities for full participation in worship and meaningful study of classic religious texts. In this call for focusing on the already-committed laity, Schorsch found agreement among RA leaders. In his 1996 presidential address, David Lieber called attention to Conservative Jews, young and old, "who are looking for greater depth and meaning for their lives, who are willing to accept a religious discipline to control the chaos both within and without. We must not fail them."[141]

After living with the sense of crisis of viability for several years, Conservative rabbis were cheered to learn the results of a demographic survey conducted by Dr. Jack Wertheimer and the Ratner Center for the Study of Conservative Judaism.[142] This survey revealed that intermarriage among Conservative Jews was below the frightening levels of the national population survey, and that Conservative synagogues were holding their own. While these synagogues were attracting a narrower population than had been the case a generation earlier, their members were now apt to be more involved in Jewish practice and less ambivalent about Conservative Judaism. They respond positively to the message of the movement. This strengthened loyalty correlated with the exposure of the laity to day schools and Ramah camps, especially since 1970.

On the one hand, the Wertheimer survey confirmed that people were not simply affiliating with Conservative synagogues by default. It identified the task of capitalizing on the Conservative Jewish identity of non-synagogue members as a major challenge to the movement. But it counseled against preoccupation with those on its periphery. It urged instead that the movement strengthen its commitment to the beliefs and practices to which it subscribes, even at the risk of further alienating the underaffiliated.[143] Gains in denominational cohesiveness would weigh against the loss of such members. The policy of stabilizing, and then hoping to expand, the core of the movement's loyal members seemed to be bearing fruit.

While it is certainly overly optimistic to conclude that Conservative Judaism is free from serious concerns about having an adequate demographic base in the next generation, the Wertheimer survey gives empirical confirmation to the informal consensus shared by many Conservative rabbis as the 1990s draw to a close: the movement is stabilizing demographically, and if it will emerge smaller than in the growth era of 1945–1965, its members will nonetheless be more committed to Jewish life and learning. In retrospect, the Conservative Judaism of the postwar generation seems to many observers to have been "a mile wide and an inch deep," whereas the current generation, increasingly educated at Schechter or Jewish Community Day Schools and at Camp Ramah, increasingly willing to reappropriate and reinvigorate at least selected portions of Jewish tradition, is making up in quality what it may lack in quantity. This may indeed be the most significant accomplishment of the men and women of the Rabbinical Assembly, as leaders of the Jewish community, in the last thirty years of the century.

NOTES

I am grateful to many RA colleagues who sat for interviews and shared their knowledge of the history of the organization during the period from 1970 to the present. Joel Meyers provided constructive criticism of an earlier draft of this chapter.

This chapter is dedicated to the memory of my father, Rabbi David H. Panitz, an architect of the expansion of the postwar RA and one of its leaders for much of the period surveyed here.

1. Jack Wertheimer, *The American Synagogue: A Sanctuary Transformed* (New York: Cambridge University Press, 1987), pp. 132–133.

2. Mordecai Waxman, "President's Address," *PRA* (1975), p. 87; Edward Gershfield, "On the Seventieth Anniversary of the Rabbinical Assembly," *PRA* (1970), p. 87.

3. Gershfield, *PRA* (1970), pp. 87–90; see also the articles by William Lebeau and Hillel Silverman, pp. 96–121.

4. Wolfe Kelman, "Defeatism, Triumphalism or Gevurah?," *PRA* (1980), p. 14.

5. Wilfred Shuchat, "Towards a Philosophy of Conservative Judaism," *PRA* (1980), pp. 88–91.

6. Benjamin Kreitman, "Report of the CJLS," *PRA* (1970), p. 198; Robert Gordis, "Toward a Revitalization of Halakhah in Conservative Judaism," *CJ* 25:3 (Spring 1971), p. 51.

7. Mordecai Waxman, "Editorial Remarks," *CJ* 24:3 (Spring 1970), p. 1.

8. Edward Gershfield, "Rebuilding the Law Committee," *CJ* 25:2 (Winter 1971), pp. 59–62; Robert Gordis, *CJ* 25:3, "Further Thoughts on the Law Committee," *CJ* 26:2 (Winter 1972), pp. 60–84.

9. Jenna Joselit, "An Engendered Judaism," *CJ* 48:1 (Fall 1995), p. 51; Arthur Neulander, "Report of the Committee On Jewish Law and Standards," *PRA* (1955), pp. 33–41.

10. The Rabbinical Assembly passed a resolution supporting ratification of the ERA in 1978: *PRA* (1978), p. 230.

11. Fishel Pearlmutter, "Address to Commission for the Study of Women in the Rabbinate," December 1977; FP papers box 1, folder 4. The Pearlmutter papers are an invaluable unpublished source for the study of the struggle for women's ordination within the Conservative movement.

12. David Feldman, "Woman's Role and Jewish Law" and Paula Hyman, "Women and the Jewish Tradition," *CJ* 26:4 (Spring 1972), pp. 14 and 29–39; Alan Silverstein, "The Evolution of Ezrat Nashim," *CJ* 30:1 (Fall 1975).

13. Silverstein, p. 46. On what was inherited from earlier generations of feminist activism, and what was new to the 1960s and early 1970s, in "consciousness raising," see William O'Neill, *Everyone Was Brave: A History of Feminism in America* (Chicago: Quadrangle Books, 1971), p. 366.

14. Stephen C. Lerner, "The Editor's Page," *CJ* 29:1 (Fall 1974), pp. 3–4.

15. Simon Greenberg, "And He Writes Her A Bill of Divorcement," *CJ* 24:3 (Spring 1970), p. 140.

16. David Feldman, "The RA and the Development of Halakhah," *PRA* (1983), p. 86; David Novak, remarks in Membership Committee meeting, *PRA* (1983), p. 223.

17. "Women and Change in Jewish Law," *CJ* 29:1 (Fall 1974), pp. 5–24; "Responses," especially Arthur Green's essay, in *CJ* 29:3 (Spring 1975), pp. 36–56.
18. *PRA* (1974), pp. 24–25.
19. Gordon Tucker, "The Ordination of Women and the Culture of the Movement," *CJ* 48:1 (Fall 1995), pp. 88–92; Beth Wenger, "The Politics of Women's Ordination: Jewish Law, Institutional Power, and the Debate over Women in the Rabbinate," in Jack Wertheimer, ed., *Tradition Renewed: A History of the Jewish Theological Seminary of America* (New York: Jewish Theological Seminary, 1997), Vol. 2, pp. 485–523.
20. Fishel Pearlmutter to Susan W. Schneider, 1/25/80, FP, box 2, folder 4.
21. On the force of this tradition, see memorandum, Wolfe Kelman to Arnold Goodman, 3/2/77, in FP, box 1, folder 2.
22. Ira Eisenstein to Fishel Pearlmutter, and Fishel Pearlmutter to Carol Glass, 3/16/76, both in FP, box 1, folder 1.
23. Jack Rosoff to Fishel Pearlmutter, 4/6/77; Wolfe Kelman to Arnold Goodman, 3/2/77 and Wolfe Kelman to Fishel Pearlmutter, 6/7/77, FP box 1, folder 2.
24. Stephen C. Lerner to Fishel Pearlmutter, 7/11/77; Robert Gordis to Fishel Pearlmutter, 6/6/77; Morris Rubinstein to Fishel Pearlmutter, 6/9/77, Fishel Pearlmutter, circular letter to RA colleagues, 5/31/77, FP, box 1, folder 2.
25. Tucker, *CJ* 48:1 (Fall 1995), p. 88.
26. Fishel Pearlmutter, circular letter to RA colleagues, 5/31/77, FP, box 1, folder 2.
27. Albert Lewis to Fishel Pearlmutter, 11/7/78; Abraham Feffer to Fishel Pearlmutter, 9/29/78, FP, box 1, folder 5; Wayne Allen to Fishel Pearlmutter, 11/1/78, FP box 1, folder 3; George Vecsey, "Conservative Judaism Approves Two-Year Study on Ordaining Women," *New York Times,* May 4, 1977, p. 40.
28. Robert Gordis, "The Halakhah: Some Reflections on Theology and History," *PRA* (1980), pp. 337–344; Fishel Pearlmutter, notes on meeting with Stanley Rabinowitz, 3/14/78; Gordon Tucker, "Working Paper for Members of the Commission for the Study of Women in the Rabbinate," 11/12/77; Fishel Pearlmutter, address to the Commission, 12/77; Harold Schulweis, April 1978 position paper, all in FP box 1, folder 4; Wenger, p. 499; Benjamin Kreitman to Gerson Cohen, 3/9/78, FP box 2, folder 1.
29. Alexander Shapiro to Fishel Pearlmutter, 2/26/79, FP box 2, folder 2; Rabinowitz, *PRA* (1978), p. 12; Teplitz, *PRA* (1979), p. 15.
30. Wenger, p. 503.
31. The student was Jonathan Panitz, who had studied at JTS before

completing his rabbinical education at Leo Baeck College in London. After receiving his ordination in 1975, Panitz returned to America, where he received a second ordination from Kelman and other former teachers. Kelman defended private ordination as "ancient, authoritative, and more consistent with our anti-hierarchical tradition." Wolfe Kelman to Nilton Bonder, 9/9/88, WK, box 6, "RA Correspondence."

32. Morris Rubinstein to Fishel Pearlmutter, 2/6/80; Everett Gendler to Fishel Pearlmutter, 2/7/80; Aaron Blumenthal to Fishel Pearlmutter, Feb, 1980; Fishel Pearlmutter to Bernard Lipnick, 2/11/80; Harold Kushner to Fishel Pearlmutter, 3/28/80; Joel Meyers to Fishel Pearlmutter, 5/1/80, all in FP, box 2, folder 4.

33. *PRA* (1980), p. 299.

34. Ibid., pp. 222, 225, 229, 232.

35. Ibid., p. 226.

36. Ibid., Carl Klein, p. 235; Jacob Shtull, p. 240.

37. Gerson Cohen, circular letter of 8/24/83, "Rabbinical Assembly and other Circular Letters," GDC.

38. Wegner, pp. 512–513, holds that it was essentially the influence of the Rabbinical Assembly on the Seminary that accounts for the turnaround at JTS, after three years of inaction. She discounts the effect of the recent death of Saul Lieberman, "despite Seminary folklore." I agree that RA pressure was a major cause, but I would not dismiss the significance of Lieberman's passing for the specific timing of the Seminary's reversal. Abundant evidence exists for Lieberman's ability to control events and inhibit discussion at the Seminary, even in his late years. To add to the published sources: I attended a lecture given by Lieberman to the rabbinical school student body in September 1977, at the height of the agitation over women's ordination. In the question and answer period at the end of the lecture, the inevitable question arose about egalitarianism. Lieberman answered by citing his familiarity with medicine and stating that medical science corroborated the talmudic observation on the neurological weakness of women, as justification for the conclusion that women ought not to be allowed to serve as witnesses in Jewish judicial settings. No one dared to challenge the master, although it was clear from the constant ideological conversation at the Seminary in that year that many present thought his comments absurd.

39. "Membership Committee," remarks of Richard Yellin, Barry Rosen, Alan Yuter, *PRA* (1984), pp. 192–195.

40. *PRA* (1985), pp. 179–180; *PRA* (1986), p. 30.

41. *PRA* (1983), pp. 223, 240; Harold Stern, "Can We Be One?," *PRA* (1984), p. 29.

42. *PRA* (1986), "Resolutions," pp. 324–325.
43. Ronald Price, "The Orthodoxy of UTJ," *The Jewish Voice and Opinion* of Bergen County, NJ 11:7 (March 1998), pp. 49–51.
44. Alexander Shapiro, "President's Address," *PRA* (1985), p. 23; *PRA* (1986), p. 32; *PRA* (1987), p. 46; Ismar Schorsch, "The Seminary as Fountainhead," *PRA* (1987), p. 146.
45. Kassel Abelson, *PRA* (1986), p. 76; David Gordis, "Conserving our Gains," *PRA* (1987), p. 95; Abraham J. Karp, "A Century of Conservative Judaism in the United States," *AJYB* 86 (1986), p. 61.
46. Neil Gillman, "The Changing Paradigm of the Conservative Rabbi," *CJ* 43:2 (Winter 1990–91), p. 5, and Robert Gordis, introduction to *Emet ve-Emunah*, p. 8, explain, from different perspectives, the early reticence to formulate a statement of principles.
47. Shapiro, *PRA* (1985), p. 24; Gordis, "The Struggle for Self-Definition in Conservative Judaism," *CJ* 39:3 (Spring 1987), p. 17.
48. Gordis, "Introduction, *Emet ve-Emunah*" pp. 12–13.
49. Abelson, "On the State of the Rabbinical Assembly," *PRA* (1988), p. 92.
50. *PRA* (1984), pp. 37–38.
51. *PRA* (1985), pp. 29–38, contains an edited version of that speech, "Conservative Judaism in our Time," without reference to Cohen's remarks on patrilineality. Those remarks were reported in a *New York Times* article of March 12, 1985. Two days later, Cohen wrote to the rabbis to protest that the newspaper article was inaccurate and misleading. His clarification was that he was only authorizing discussion, not pushing for change. GDC, circular letters, March 14, 1985.
52. GDC, circular letters, August 24, 1983; *PRA* (1985), p. 185.
53. *PRA* (1986), pp. 313–322. The other standards of practice likewise delineate the boundaries of Conservative practice on issues of personal identity, covering areas such as intermarriage, and remarriage after a divorce.
54. *PRA* (1986), pp. 315, 318, 321.
55. *PRA* (1986), remarks of Joel Roth and James Michaels, pp. 314, 318.
56. Simon LeVay, *Queer Science: The Use and Abuse of Research into Homosexuality* (Cambridge, MA: The MIT Press, 1996), pp. 1–2, 143–147, 221–230, 251–254.
57. *PRA* (1978), pp. 108–114.
58. Communication from Joel Meyers, September 14, 1998. See also Gerald Zelizer, "Conservative Rabbis, Their Movement, and American Judaism," *Judaism* 44:3 (Summer 1995), pp. 293–298.
59. *CJLS*, Summary Index (1994), 9:10.
60. Harold Schulweis, "The Character of Halakhah Entering the Twenty-First Century," *CJ* 45:4 (Summer 1993), pp. 5–13.

61. Schorsch, "Marching to the Wrong Drummer," *CJ* 45:4 (Summer 1993), pp. 15–19.

62. Arnold Goodman, in *PRA* (1994), p. 25; Zelizer, "Conservative Rabbis," p. 297.

63. Eliott Dorff, "This is my Beloved, This is my Friend: A Rabbinic Letter on Intimate Relations." See also the critical response to draft #7 of the letter, Harlan J. Wechsler, "On the Teaching of *Arayot:* A Pastor's Guide," *CJ* 48:3 (Spring 1996), pp. 40–48.

64. Jonathan Springer, et al., "Lesbian and Gay Jews: Our Needs and Concerns in the Jewish Community" *PRA* (1994), pp. 196–206; Carol Ingall and Robert Goldfarb, "Lesbian and Gay Jews: Finding a Home in the Conservative Movement," *PRA* (1995), pp. 151–4.

65. I am indebted to Joel Meyers' letter to me, dated September 14, 1998, for this reconstruction of the deliberations, some unpublished, of the various leadership groups within the RA. See also Zelizer, pp. 296–7.

It must be acknowledged that the assertion of traditional standards in this area may well be tested in the next few years, if and when a rabbinical student at any of the seminaries whose ordained graduates automatically gain admission to the Rabbinical Assembly declares that he or she is homosexual.

66. Schorsch, "A Synagogue is not a Temple," *CJ* 43:2 (Winter 1990–91), p. 65; Silverstein, *PRA* (1994), p. 94.

67. Schorsch, "A Synagogue is not a Temple," p. 65, in sharp contrast to Kreitman, "*CJLS* [Report]," *PRA* (1970), p. 195.

68. Martin Levin, "2001: A Blueprint for the Rabbinate in the Twenty First Century," *PRA* (1979), pp. 114–6.

69. See James Farrell, *Inventing the American Way of Death, 1830–1920* (Philadelphia: Temple University Press, 1980), passim.

70. This narration of changes in Conservative Jewish burials is based on impressionistic data, especially conversations with numerous RA members and personal observation. It awaits formal sociological confirmation.

71. Albert Lewis, "Presidential Address," *PRA* (1989), p. 97.

72. Susan Grossman, "Feminism, Midrash and Mikveh," *CJ* 44:2 (Winter 1992), pp. 7–17 and *PRA* (1995), pp. 115–7. See also Dorff, "This is My Beloved . . . ," pp. 24–25.

73. *PRA* (1996), p. 294.

74. Harold Kushner, "Is the Conservative Movement Halakhic?," *PRA* (1980), pp. 364–9.

75. After Theodore Roosevelt declared his admiration for the play, Zangwill dedicated it to the American president. Arthur Schlesinger, *The Disuniting of America* (New York: W.W. Norton & Co., 1992), pp. 32–33.

76. Levin, "2001," p. 114.

77. Nathan Glazer and Patrick Moynihan, *Beyond the Melting Pot,* second edition (Cambridge, MA: The MIT Press, 1970), pp. 292–4.

78. The Navy's current policy is characteristic of all branches of the Armed Forces. Department of the Navy, SECNAV Instruction 1730.8A, "Accommodation of Religious Practices," December 31, 1997: "Department of the Navy policy is to accommodate the doctrinal or traditional observances of the religious faith practiced by individual members when these doctrines or observances will not have an adverse impact on military readiness, individual or unit readiness, unit cohesion, health, safety or discipline." I am grateful to Rabbi Seth Phillips (Chaplain, USN) and Rabbi David Greenspoon, a former Navy enlisted man, for their oral communications on the Navy's openness to religious self-expression on the part of Jewish personnel since the 1980s.

79. Stephen Lerner, "2001: Blueprint for the Rabbinate in the Twenty First Century," *PRA* (1979), p. 122; Abraham J. Karp, "Rabbi, Congregation, and the World They Live In," *CJ* 26:1 (Fall 1971), p. 39; Schorsch, "The Limits of History," *PRA* (1989), p. 112.

80. Richard D. Alba, *Ethnic Identity: The Transformation of White America* (New Haven: Yale University Press, 1990), pp. 1–3, 22–26, 174–175, 310, 318–319.

81. Egon Mayer, "Jews by Choice: Their Impact on the Contemporary American Jewish Community," *PRA* (1983), p. 61.

82. Jules Harlow, ed., *Maḥzor,* pp. 802–806, lists the impressive variety of sources incorporated, many for the first time, into a standard prayer book.

83. Ibid., pp. 299, 343, 358.

84. Jules Harlow, "On Editing a Prayerbook," *CJ* 26:1 (Fall 1971), pp. 61–69.

85. Jacob Petuchowski, "Conservative Liturgy Comes of Age," *CJ* 27:1 (Fall 1972), pp. 3–11.

86. *The Bond of Life* (New York: Rabbinical Assembly, 1975), p. 87.

87. *The Feast of Freedom* (New York: Rabbinical Assembly, 1982), p. 6.

88. Ibid., p. 33.

89. Ibid., p. 39. See also the deletions from the standard text of the *dayyenu* prayer, p. 60, omissions that seem to be inspired by a liberal, humanitarian discomfort with references to the despoiling of the Egyptians. One wonders if the substitution of the untranslated *mizrayim* for Egypt throughout the text was not simply to universalize the experience of redemption beyond its first appearance in Jewish history, as explained in p. 8, but also because of the political incorrectness of labelling Egypt the paradigmatic oppressor of the Jews in

a text appearing in the midst of the euphoria over the Camp David peace treaty between Israel and Egypt.

90. In his introduction to the edition, xxiv–xxviii, Harlow cites the various additions and deletions to the traditional text he has incorporated.

91. Jules Harlow, "New Dimensions in Liturgy," PRA 35 (1973), pp. 4–5.

92. Jacob Petuchowski, Review of *Siddur Sim Shalom*, CJ 38:2 (Winter 1985–6), pp. 82–87.

93. Jules Harlow, "Feminist Linguistics and Jewish Liturgy," CJ 49:2 (Winter 1997), pp. 7, 13.

94. The decision to transliterate "Adonai" rather than render it as "Lord" is a curious parallel to the Orthodox preference for "Hashem," as in the Artscroll series of prayer books. In this reviewer's opinion, the decision to substitute "Ha-shem" for a translation such as "God" in Orthodox usage has the unfortunate effect of misleading the reader into treating "Ha-shem" as an actual name of God, rather than a respectful title or circumlocution. While "Adonai" is a rabbinically approved title to prevent transgression of the Third Commandment, the editorial decision to transliterate it runs the same risk as that of the persistent use of "Ha-shem." On the other hand, "Lord," a translation, does not mislead in that fashion.

95. *Siddur Sim Shalom*, Preliminary Edition (The Rabbinical Assembly, 1994), pp. 54a, 54b, 62a, 62b and *Siddur Sim Shalom for Shabbat and Festivals* (The Rabbinical Assembly, 1998), pp. 123a, 123b, 166a and 166b. The 1998 version of *Siddur Sim Shalom* adheres to and extends other liturgical features of the work of the current generation. It contains additional supplemental readings, pp. 360–367, drawn from the writings of Conservative movement liturgists such as Jules Harlow and Ben Zion Bokser and poets such as Danny Siegel. It also provides a glossary, pp. 403–404, to help the worshiper establish a basic prayer literacy.

96. Perry Raphael Rank and Gordon M. Freeman, eds., *Moreh Derekh: The Rabbinical Assembly Rabbi's Manual* (The Rabbinical Assembly, 1998), sections A-6, A-9, A-11, C-31–37, F-24–29, I-3–45 and N-22–56.

97. Philip Pohl and Kenneth Goldrich, "The *Ruah* of the *Luah*," PRA (1994), pp. 211–5. Note the new, denominational title for the congregational body, updating "United Synagogue of America"—another sign of the increased denominational consciousness within Conservative Judaism.

98. PRA (1994), p. 15.

99. Aryeh Davidson, Ariela Keysar and Jack Wertheimer, "Where Have All the Rabbis Gone?," *JTS Magazine* 7:2 (Winter 1998); Joel Meyers, "Report of the Executive Vice President," PRA (1995), p. 70.

100. Alan Silverstein, "Denominational Jews," *PRA* (1994), p. 17; Joel Meyers, "Report of the Executive Vice President," *PRA* (1995), p. 99. One of the ironies of the history of the relations between JTS and the RA is that, in 1983, the Seminary acceded to the RA in admitting women for ordination, in large part so as not to lose its monopoly on producing Conservative rabbis; but within a dozen years, its own affiliate, the University of Judaism, broke that monopoly.

101. Gilbert Rosenthal, "Morale and Commitment," *CJ* 27:1 (Fall 1972), p. 19; Meyers, "Report," *PRA* (1991), p. 61; Silverstein, *PRA* (1994), p. 17. Filling one non-pulpit position with RA members remains largely a wish, albeit an oft-repeated one: In view of the great strength of the Federation movement, RA leaders have called for the placement of its members on the staff of Federations: Meyers, "Report," *PRA* (1994), p. 107.

102. "A Program for the Conservative Movement in Israel," *CJ* 25:3 (Spring 1971), p. 75.

103. Ralph Simon, "Presidential Address," *PRA* (1970), pp. 3–5; Mordecai Waxman, "Editorial Remarks," *CJ* 25:3 (Spring 1971) and "President's Address," *PRA* (1976), pp. 84–5; Michael Graetz, *PRA* (1976), p. 53.

104. Saul Teplitz, "Presidential Address," *PRA* (1979), p. 12; "The M'sorati Movement in Israel," *PRA* (1981), p. 19. The RA regularly passed resolutions in support of Conservative Judaism in Israel and MERCAZ. See the resolutions sections of *PRA* (1978, 1979, 1982, 1989, etc.).

105. Joseph Wernick, "The Masorti Movement in Israel" and Ismar Schorsch, "Conservative Judaism in Israel," *PRA* (1988), pp. 21–2, 26–7.

106. Michael Graetz, "Our Task in Israel," *CJ* 45:3 (Spring 1993), pp. 69–70.

107. "Being a Conservative Rabbi in Israel: The Agony and the Ecstasy," *PRA* (1988), pp. 28–48.

108. Joachim Prinz and Arthur Hertzberg, *PRA* (1970), pp. 15–33; *PRA* (1977), p. 139; *PRA* (1983), p. 33.

109. Ismar Schorsch, "Jewish Unity on the Threshold of the Millennium," *PRA* (1977), p. 89.

110. Marshall T. Meyer, "Thoughts on Latin America," *PRA* (1985), pp. 53–62; Arnold Goodman and David Lieber, "Strategic Planning Committee Report," *PRA* (1996), p. 276; On the problems facing Latin American RA members: oral communication from Joel Meyers, July 22, 1996.

111. Chaim Weiner, oral presentation to the RA members attending the Rabbinic Training Institute in Pawling, New York, in January 1997.

112. Stephen Lerner, "The Havurot," *CJ* 24:3 (Spring 1970), pp. 2–15. See also Everett Gendler, "The Havurah," *PRA* (1975), p. 153.

113. Gerald B. Bubis and Harry Wasserman, *Synagogue Havurot: A Comparative Study*, Center for Jewish Community Studies (Cincinnati: Hebrew Union College—Jewish Institute of Religion, School of Jewish Communal Service, 1983), pp. 94, 131. See also Sally Weber, "Beyond Havurah," *CJ* 37:2 (Winter 1983–4), pp. 24–27.

114. Carl M. Perkins, "Reflections of a Recently Ordained Rabbi," *CJ* 48:1 (Fall 1995), pp. 75–76.

115. Saul Teplitz, "Presidential Address," *PRA* (1979), pp. 12–13.

116. Susannah Heschel, "Changing Forms of Jewish Spirituality," *PRA* (1980), pp. 146–158.

117. Kenneth Katz, "Uninspired," and Pamela Hoffman, "A Rejoinder . . . by a Seminary Spiritualizer," *CJ* 38:4 (Summer 1986), pp. 15–18 and 23; Neil Gillman, "Judaism and the Search for Spirituality," *CJ* 38:2 (Winter 1985/6), pp. 5–18; Michael Klayman, response to "Entering the Second Century: From Scholarship to the Rabbinate," *PRA* (1986), pp. 50–51.

118. Oral communication from Charles Feinberg, January, 1997; Jonathan Woocher, *Sacred Survival, The Civil Religion of American Jews,* quoted by Irwin Groner, *PRA* (1991), p. 33.

119. Susan Grossman, "The Dual Nature of Rabbinic Leadership," *CJ* 48:1 (Fall 1995), pp. 43–47.

120. Even when complaining about their work, a fixture in Conservative rabbinic self-expression, younger rabbis differentiate between a spiritual loneliness, from which they continue to suffer, and a social loneliness about which their elders cautioned them, but which they do not personally experience. See, for example, Shalom Lewis, "The Rabbi is a Lonely Person," *CJ* 37:2 (Winter 1983–1984), pp. 40–41.

121. *PRA* (1978) Nominations Committee Report and Election," p. 221, "Resolutions," p. 232.

122. Arnold Goodman to Fishel Pearlmutter, 1/15/80, FP, box 2, folder 3.

123. *PRA* (1982), p. 32.

124. Ibid. (1983), p. 28.

125. Vernon Kurtz, "The New Placement Procedures: How Well Do They Work?" *PRA* (1992).

126. Joel Meyers, *PRA* (1989), p. 23. Meyers' awareness of contemporary rabbinic participation in the American model of the empowered customer was reflected in his choice of metaphor when I interviewed him, July 22, 1996: "Our customers are rabbis."

127. Elliott Schoenberg and Suzanne Stier, "*Eit Ratzon Katan:* Transition to a New Rabbinic Position," *PRA* (1996), p. 188. Like Meyers, albeit independently, Schoenberg chose the analogy of the relationship

between a service provider and a consumer to describe what he does for the RA membership: "I am here because I start with the consumer." (Oral communication, July 22, 1996).

128. Gerald Zelizer, *PRA* (1994), p. 81; Gerald Zelermayer and Jacob Luski, "Report of the Joint Placement Commission," *PRA* (1996), pp. 261–263.

129. *PRA* (1983), p. 29. The newsletter ultimately survived only for a brief period of time, failing on account of a lack of institutional support. Oral communication from Ruby Eisenberg Creditor, March 7, 1998.

130. *PRA* (1996), pp. 180–181.

131. Arnold Goodman, "Presidential Address," *PRA* (1983), p. 29; Leslie Friedman, "Role-Related Stress in the Rabbinate: A Report on a Nationwide Study of Conservative and Reform Rabbis," *PRA* (1984), pp. 43–47.

132. *PRA* (1980), pp. 277–279.

133. On the baby boomer generation's focus on its mental health, see Christopher Lasch, *The Culture of Narcissism: American Life in an Age of Diminishing Expectations* (New York: W.W. Norton and Company, 1991), pp. 7–12.

134. *PRA* (1985), pp. 78–81. Shapiro made it a personal priority to needle the rabbis about losing weight, so as to preserve their health. But even before he embarked on that campaign, rabbis had begun to take part in the physical fitness movement sweeping America since the 1970s. Since 1982, RA conventions have scheduled early morning runs for its running enthusiasts.

135. *Ha-Modi'a* (February–March 1998), p. 3.

136. Alan Silverstein, "Denominational Jews: Do our Titles Really Define Us?," *PRA* (1995), pp. 14–16, has chronicled the increased denominational consciousness of Conservative Judaism. His analysis, focusing on institutional and political factors, parallels the conclusions of this study, which is more focused on the intellectual and cultural aspects of Conservative Jewish identity.

137. Ralph Simon, "Presidential Address," *PRA* (1970), pp. 8–12; Judah Nadich, "Mixed Marriage," *PRA* (1978), pp. 87–96.

138. This phrase replaced the more direct "Jewish survival," popular in the 1980s, especially in Federation circles. This change may have been due to the search for a palatable euphemism.

139. Steven Bayme, "Intermarriage and Conservative Judaism," *PRA* (1991), pp. 38–43.

140. Silverstein, "Presidential Address," *PRA* (1994), p. 89; *PRA* (1995), p. 59; "Final Presidential Report," *PRA* (1996), p. 58.

141. Schorsch, "The Modern Rabbinate—Then and Now," *CJ* 43:2 (Winter 1990–91), p. 19; Lieber, *PRA* (1996), p. 79.

142. Jack Wertheimer, ed., *Conservative Synagogues and their Members: Highlights of the North American Survey of 1995–96* and *Jewish Identity and Religious Commitment* (New York: Jewish Theological Seminary, 1996 and 1997).

143. Sidney and Alice Goldstein, "Symposium—What we Have Learned," in Jack Wertheimer, ed., *Jewish Identity and Religious Commitment*, pp. 47–49. See also Steven M. Cohen, "Deconstructing the Outreach-Inreach Debate," *CJ* 49:2 (Winter 1997), pp. 26–33.

The Evolving Conservative Rabbi

Stanley Rabinowitz

Speakers at rabbinic installations are fond of referring to the modern Conservative rabbi as the heir or at least the contemporary counterpart of the prophet, priest, and sage of classical antiquity. The inspiring oratorical flourish may be forgiven, for the image helps to project a sacred role model for the young rabbi's aspirational efforts. However attractive the equation, the distinctions outnumber the similarities.

Nor is the twentieth century Conservative rabbi a continuation of the nineteenth century European *rov;* an ocean's crossing disrupted the links between the two. Rendering decisions on religious questions, handing down halakhic opinions, and attesting to *kashrut* were central to the *rov*'s calling; the rabbi[1] had different assignments. Skill in preaching in unaccented English was far more important to the early American congregation than was talmudic erudition, although fluency in Yiddish remained a desirable asset. A more important distinction was that the *rov*, both in the United States and in Europe, was engaged by the community or at least a group of congregations to serve their combined needs while the rabbi was employed by a single congregation, a shocking extravagance to the eyes of the East European immigrant.

The immigrants who arrived in the United States at the turn of the century found a new world baffling in its tantalizing alternatives between permissiveness and conformity, tolerant of variations in religious expression, and enticing in its opportunities for deviations from communally defined ritual practice. Uncertain about how much adjustment would be permitted in the new world and how much conformity would be required, some persisted in clinging to the comforting forms they recalled from their European homes, holding fast to their familiar language, *nusaḥ* and *minhag*, and even synagogue architecture, while others tested the bounds of their newly found freedoms by "Americanizing" their names, synagogue and home ritual, and eventually even their dietary and Sabbath observances.

The American rabbi served as a mediator between the old and the new. He was new wine in an old bottle, a new form of a venerable calling that emerged to meet the needs of an ancient community transplanted to the promising shores of a new land whose culture differed markedly from that of the world left behind, a new world where identification with the community was voluntary rather than compulsory. His was a daunting challenge, virtually without precedent in Jewish experience.

The earliest Seminary graduates had difficulty laying claim to the title "rabbi."[2] The Sephardic congregations used the terms *"ḥazzan"* or *"ḥakham";* the Ashkenazic congregations, too, preferred the term *"ḥazzan,"* but more frequently "reverend," or, in sweeping deference, "reverend doctor" and, in many instances, "minister." The prestigious Congregation Kehilath Jeshurun in New York called Mordecai Kaplan, who served it from 1903 to 1909, not rabbi but "minister," a reflection of their feeling that Seminary ordination did not necessarily confer an authentic rabbinic title.[3]

The founding rabbis of the Rabbinical Assembly were either immigrants or the children of immigrants, as were the members of the congregations they served. The early graduates, coming from Orthodox homes, tended to identify with those who wanted to uphold the familiar patterns of religious behavior.

Aside from the few who went on to careers of great distinction, such as Rabbi Joseph Hertz, who would become Chief Rabbi of the British Empire,[4] most of the early Seminary graduates faced difficult and painful challenges. Salaries were low; rabbis were expected to supplement their meager wages by gifts and free-will offerings. Contracts covered brief periods, seldom more than one year, with renewal at the discretion of the congregation's board or, more accurately, the *parnass* or president. With tenure uncertain, with one's future dependent upon the good will of a few powerful leaders, and with alternatives so few, rabbis seldom strayed beyond the theological and social limits defined by the congregation. Innovation was discouraged, and those enterprising souls who tried to break new ground—by abbreviating a service, eliminating a psalm or reading a prayer in English translation—paid for their temerity with professional repudiation and personal disillusionment.

Rabbis were expected to teach in the Hebrew school every day except Friday, to conduct or at least to attend daily services morning and evening, to preach an occasional sermon and to act as *ḥazzan* (cantor) and *ba'al koreh* (Torah reader) while their remuneration maintained the accepted ecclesiastical tradition that poverty was cleansing for the soul as well as an assurance of a place in *olam ha-ba* (the world to come).

In that few could perform all the assigned functions from preaching to teaching to chanting with equal skill, and because the rabbi was invariably evaluated by his least effective talent, it was little wonder that tenure was fleeting and turnover frequent. Some capitulated, turning to other callings, and others to the Reform movement where working conditions were admittedly better.

Solomon Schechter could not ignore the defections when he spoke to the first convention of the United Synagogue in 1913, saying:

> That some students, trained in the Seminary, have accepted Reform positions is to be regretted. . . . But let no man who knows the condition of most of our strictly Orthodox synagogues, the poverty prevailing there, the starvation wages which they grant to their Rabbis, the constant strife within the congregation itself, the first victim of which is the Rabbi, the ungenerous treatment of the young men on the part of those who consider themselves the pillars of the congregation—no man who knows these conditions will judge uncharitably those men who have not proved themselves strong enough to become martyrs of the cause . . . if they sinned, they were also sinned against. The majority have remained loyal at a sacrifice. . . .[5]

The rabbis who served during the first quarter of the century endured family deprivation and painful frustration in addition to philosophical challenge; they were clearly pioneers whose ordeal eased the way for their successors. Despite their difficulties, the early rabbis, driven to transmit a sacred tradition, scored significant successes and played a vital role in mediating the search for adaptation that characterized Jewish life in the early quarter of the century.

Following World War I, as the immigrant generation prospered, the rabbi shared a corresponding improvement in security and status. When congregational membership increased along with their budgets, rabbis were enlisted in the task of raising the funds to maintain both. With the engagement of the cantor and a consequent division of responsibility between them, working conditions in the rabbinate improved.

During the first quarter of the century, with the synagogue's membership only one generation removed from Orthodoxy, the word "Conservative" had to struggle for acceptance along with the rabbi who preached it. Even the United Synagogue, founded in 1913, managed to avoid including the term in its founding charter; it termed itself "traditional."[6] Not only as an adjective, written with a small "c", but even as a capitalized noun, the word remained blurred.

Like Judaism itself, the American Jew was perceived as both an ethnic and a religious entity. The rabbi in the congregation, ever the mediator, struggled to balance the relative emphasis to be placed on the religious and on the ethnic components of the Jewish tradition. In planning the *heder* or school curriculum, rabbis strained to allocate the limited available hours between instruction in the Hebrew language of prayer and the history of the Jewish people and between the beliefs of Judaism and its customs and ceremonies. The dilemma would continue to plague succeeding generations of rabbis. Eventually the terms "peoplehood" and the definition of Judaism as "an evolving civilization with religion as its primary component" would be introduced by Mordecai M. Kaplan, but while the new insight may have clarified Jewish identity, it would not do away with the dilemma.

In the post-World War II years, the Jewish community came to be regarded as a religious community, one of America's three (at the time) faith groups. As an ethnic minority, Jews were an insignificant segment of the population. However, defined as a religious group, Jews were one-third of the United States whose clergy merited inclusion among the clerical triad called upon to deliver invocations at civic gatherings; an honor for the Jewish community, an additional responsibility for the rabbi.

Preaching on Sabbath and festivals, and speaking at community functions were soon added to the rabbi's previous roles as educator and ritual functionary. His classic role models now included that of the *maggid*.

The Nazi threat turned rabbis into fundraisers and rescuers; the war turned them into chaplains. Zionism—and anti-Zionism—became commanding concerns of the rabbi, projecting some to positions of national leadership. Solomon Goldman and Israel Goldstein were examples, as were Stephen Wise and Abba Hillel Silver among the Reform.

The war, the Holocaust, and the establishment of Israel were clearly turning-points in Jewish history; nothing in Jewish life would ever again be the same. With the mobilization of rabbis for the chaplaincy, the Seminary could not ordain enough rabbis to fill the vacant pulpits. To meet the wartime emergency, the Seminary increased its admissions and accelerated the ordination of enrolled classes. For the duration, newly ordained rabbis were assigned to synagogues whose rabbis were in uniform.

New challenges expanded the rabbi's areas of concern to include communal and philanthropic activities, both local and overseas. In traversing the perilous road from the rescue of European Jewry to the establishment of the State of Israel, the rabbi was projected into positions of communal leadership. Some rabbis turned to *aliyah*.

Demobilization and a postwar boom produced exciting increases in synagogue membership, a proliferation of new congregations, and a surge of long-delayed new construction for existing synagogues. The postwar synagogue structures were no longer built in the Byzantine or Moorish styles so beloved by the immigrant generation; the new structures proclaimed modernity. Their grandeur reflected the success that the immigrant generation had found in America's promise. As many as 150 new edifices were in various stages of construction by 1955. Suddenly the number of vacant pulpits exceeded the availability of rabbis to fill them.

The postwar shortage of rabbis led to the admission of non-Seminary graduates to membership in the RA in 1944. Fifty Seminary alumni had constituted the RA in 1910; the number grew to 200 in 1930. After the war, membership reached 400. It would be over 800 in 1970 and 1200 in 1990.

Returning chaplains and newly ordained rabbis were eager to live near large Jewish population centers, preferably New York City; they would even accept reduced salaries for the sake of remaining in the metropolitan area. Consequently, smaller congregations, far removed from the center, were hard pressed to attract rabbis. To meet the need, the RA required new graduates to serve in small cities for a specified period at the beginning of their careers.

When synagogues added adult education programs to their activities, rabbis served as faculty. Rabbis discovered the inspirational potential of weekend retreats. Sermon preparation became an even more prominent adjunct to the rabbinic week. Titles were announced in the metropolitan press as well as in bulletins. As synagogues vied for attendance, the rabbi came to be evaluated primarily by his oratorical ability.

The second half of the century had barely begun when a series of crises erupted, each eclipsing the preceding one in its import. The decade of the '60s was especially violent with war, assassinations, racial strife, sit-ins, civil rights marches, and virulent anti-Israel demonstrations. The classic prophetic tradition asserted itself in the rabbi's commitment to social justice, while each crisis added another dimension to rabbinic involvement and responsibility.

Rabbis were divided over Vietnam, united in the struggle for civil rights, appalled by the assassinations of President Kennedy, his brother Robert, and Martin Luther King, Jr., and were jarred into re-examining their alliances when they realized that what had been primary in their concerns, Israel, had been abandoned in its hour of crisis, in 1967, by those with whom they had marched side by side: liberal associations, church groups, and the Black community. Many, Abraham Joshua Heschel among them, felt cheated by their allies in the civil rights movement; it was a time for painful reassessment.

Modern Israel was established in 1948, but much of American Jewry and some rabbis discovered Israel only in 1967 when they came to realize how precious Israel was to them and how precarious was her existence. Rabbis became tour leaders and took up leadership roles in campaigns for the United Jewish Appeal-Joint Distribution Committee and Israel Bonds. Many became chairmen of communal Federation drives. *Aliyah* increased.

The sudden growth of an active counter-culture, reflecting a widespread disillusionment in the Vietnam War, disturbed the Jewish community; *havurot*,[7] small sub-groupings of like-minded participants, were their corollary. Rabbis were ambivalent toward both the counter-culture and the *havurot* but could ignore neither. Some saw the *havurot* as an ill-conceived neo-Hasidic threat to the synagogue and the rabbinate; others embraced their promise. In either case, the *havurah* movement, with its emphasis on "do-it-yourself Judaism" was destined to exert a profound influence on many synagogues.

In the last quarter of the century, as congregations grew larger and as the duties of the rabbi increased, it was inevitable that rabbis would become more and more removed, not always by choice, from what had been their traditional mandate: study of Torah. Pastoral counseling had emerged as another important rabbinic responsibility; courses in pastoral counseling were added to the Seminary curriculum in 1955 and expanded in 1964. The needs of the bedridden, the bereaved, and the betrothed seemed insatiable.

The Rabbi as Critic and Innovator

Jews shared America's mid-century prosperity. Upwardly mobile, enjoying improved living conditions, Jews were increasingly susceptible to the conditioning influence of the majority culture. The rabbi, by virtue of his training, temperament, and position resisted what he considered the unhealthy intrusions of alien practices. He became the critic of the "Americanization" of Jewish culture. Israel Levinthal in Brooklyn roundly castigated the Jewish woman's preoccupation with shopping and her "blind adherence to fashion."

In virtually every community, rabbis expressed their outrage at the "Christmasification of Hanukkah." Whether in submission or reaction, but with rabbinic approval, by the 1920s, Hanukkah had become transformed into a major Jewish holiday. Sermons extolled the festival's significance. Synagogue gift shops reinforced the Hanukkah message by offering a wide array of modern *menorot*, gifts, and decorations for the home.

Throughout the century rabbis felt impelled to struggle against the increasing vulgarization of life-cycle events. Wedding ceremonies became more elaborate as clubs and hotels became popular replacements of both home and synagogue for their setting. Rabbis criticized America's bridal culture for its ostentatious displays whose vulgarities were increasingly defined by the caterer rather than the rabbi. Rabbi David Aronson of Minneapolis observed in 1940 that brides, in their procession to the canopy, seemed to carry a copy of Emily Post rather than the Bible.

Bar mitzvah celebrations imposed a new duty upon the rabbi: preparing a speech for the child to deliver. It had to be a "learned" discourse but not too profound. Scholarly rabbis had no choice but to assume the ghost-writing role for their little charges. In American social protocol, bar mitzvah loomed larger than it had ever been in Europe. "Some Bar Mitzvah parties . . . would appeal to our sense of humor by their incongruity," observed Jacob Kohn in 1932.

Not only to cultivate new sources of income, but in attempt to reclaim a measure of control over the extravagances of weddings and bar mitzvah celebrations, postwar synagogue structures provided banquet facilities to service the festive "affairs." When the site for celebratory luncheons and dinners was returned to the synagogue, the rabbi was expected to be present; frequently he was the acting "toastmaster." He may have been trained to be a scholar, but, at festive occasions, he was evaluated as a social director, a skill for which he had not been trained. Added to his traditional roles was a new one, that of the *badkhen*.

By the mid-1930s, the confirmation ceremony for both boys and girls was accepted by over 65 percent of the rabbis; some resisted. Louis Feinberg of Cincinnati, in 1922, criticized the ceremony as a Judaized version of a Christian rite. Simon Greenberg and Israel Goldstein, Jacob Agus and David Aronson were in the vanguard of attempts to establish minimal educational standards as requirements for bar mitzvah and confirmation. Many rabbis organized "*talis* and *tefillin*" and *minyan* clubs to reinforce their efforts. Vocal cantatas, the first by Judith and Ira Eisenstein,[8] and later ones incorporating popular Israeli melodies, embellished the confirmation services, replacing the conventional stilted speeches delivered by the students, most written by their rabbis.

Time and time again, rabbis deplored the widespread violation of the Sabbath. Determined to revitalize Sabbath observance, Jacob Agus and other leaders launched the "National Sabbath Observance Effort" in 1950. Rabbis throughout the country sponsored "Sabbath Institutes."

To strengthen their movement, rabbis created new institutions where none had existed. Not Orthodox, but Conservative, rabbis were founders of today's Young Israel and the Union of Orthodox Jewish Congregations. Early Seminary graduates, Louis Finkelstein, Solomon Goldman, and Simon Greenberg had organized a movement to compel Jewish shop owners in New York's East Side to close their stores on the Sabbath. In the small communities in the south, midwest and especially the west coast, rabbis, finding a relatively arid Jewish landscape, responded to the religious vacuum by establishing Hebrew schools, *mikvaot* and kosher food facilities.[9]

Rabbis found ample cause to be concerned about the observance of the dietary laws. A 1953 survey of its leadership by the United Synagogue revealed that only slightly more than one-third of its leaders observed *kashrut*. In delicatessen and restaurant, "Kosher Style" without supervision replaced halakhic *kashrut*. In many instances, the Jewish butcher's inability to compete with the lower prices of the supermarket provided young couples with their excuse for abandoning the kosher home. Rabbis, frequently with some success, sought to control the pricing of Jewish food products. Denied a role in supervising *kashrut* by an intransigent Orthodox rabbinate, the Conservative rabbi could only offer an ecclesiastical amen to the *hekhsher* of his Orthodox colleague. He thereby escaped being tarred by the shameful scandals that compromised the kosher food industry in the first quarter century.

Rabbis searched for ways to expand the observance of *kashrut*. Levinthal's Brooklyn Jewish Center ran a full-scale kosher restaurant on its premises in the early thirties. Max Arzt, in a 1940 responsum, argued that eating cooked vegetables and broiled fish in nonkosher restaurants was both halakhically permissible and realistic. Rabbis could only regret but not prevent the migration of the Passover seder from homes to hotels and banquet halls; they even led them. Passover remained widely observed.

Few aspects of religious life troubled the rabbi more than the customs associated with death and funerals. Throughout the century, rabbis struggled to impose halakhic standards of dignity, economy, and equality of treatment in funeral practices. Encouraged by the funeral industry, Jews had abandoned the simple rites of the past, preferring expensive metal coffins and embalmed prettified bodies. Rabbis were arrayed against a powerful funeral industry whose directors barely tolerated their unavoidable presence in the funeral process. The rabbis of Minneapolis, Minnesota, were leaders in resisting the funeral industry and in mandating halakhic observances at funerals. Albert Gordon accused the industry of playing on the bereaved family's superstitious beliefs. Arnold Goodman, in a televised program entitled "A Plain Pine Box," featuring a prototype of a dignified funeral, called upon the synagogue to assume the role of the funeral director. Throughout much of the century, tensions between the funeral director and the rabbi remained a constant.

At appropriate opportunities, rabbis stressed the etiquette of *shiva*, urging that the gathering not be turned into a cocktail party. The Law Committee recognized the propriety of cutting a black ribbon as a legitimate way of observing *kriah*.

Through their sermons, rabbis assumed the role of cultural arbiters and family psychologists. For guidance in rearing their children and in domestic disputes, families frequently came to their rabbis for advice. Sermons on child-rearing were familiar themes in the sermons of the 1930s. Mordecai Kaplan lectured on "Bringing Up the Jewish Child." Jacob Kohn authored a book entitled, *Modern Problems of Jewish Parents*.

Who Is a Rabbi?

In 1943 one-third of Seminary students were the sons of rabbis or Jewish educators; in 1967, the number was 20 percent. In 1987, only 7 percent of students were children of a Jewish professional. A 1985 study revealed that of 110 students responding out of 143 queried, 66 percent came from Conservative homes, 3 percent Orthodox, and 19 percent Reform; 12 percent were unaffiliated.[10]

In 1943 four out of five Seminary students came from Orthodox homes, the remainder from Conservative. In 1955 almost half of the student body came from Conservative homes. In sum, the movement which in 1943 was largely dependent on the Orthodox group for its rabbinic candidates was producing about half its own rabbis twelve years later. In the 1955 study, 24 of 118 students questioned had been members of the Leadership Training Fellowship in their teens.[11]

The 1943 study revealed that 97 percent of the students came from homes where one or both parents were foreign born. Many had yeshiva backgrounds; most were well-grounded in their knowledge of rabbinic texts. One aspect of their backgrounds presented disturbing implications for the image of the future rabbi. While prizing knowledge of Talmud and Bible in their admission policies, the Seminary of Cyrus Adler and Louis Finkelstein favored the selection of rabbinic candidates who spoke "American English." To cope with the "foreignisms" in the speech of many of the students, classes in elocution were instituted. Many a rabbi owes his pattern of speech to the instruction of a non-Jew, Arleigh Williamson.

Struggle with accents carried over into Hebrew as the yeshiva students who were familiar with the Ashkenazic pronunciation of Hebrew learned to accommodate themselves to the widely accepted Sephardic mode.[12] It wasn't easy to undo the habits of a lifetime. In overcompensation, one student rabbi, quoting a passage from Isaiah in his sermon, while trying mightily to eliminate the telltale *"oy"* sound from his speech, intoned, *"lo yisa go el go ḥerev . . ."* in a sentence in which the *"goy"* sound belonged. ("Nation shall not lift up sword against nation . . ." (Isaiah 2:4).

In 1955, 22 percent of the students were children of American-born parents; the number increased to 75 percent in 1985. Clearly, the rabbinate was no longer dependent upon European homes for its human resources as had been the case heretofore.[13]

Unlike the pattern of the first half of the century, only one student of the class entering in 1969 came from a background that included yeshiva training. The Orthodox, obviously, had become more successful in retaining the allegiance of their young people. Solomon Schechter and other day schools now replaced the yeshiva as sources for Seminary students.

Several studies have attempted to define the emotional ingredient that attracts young men and women to the rabbinate. One study concluded, "the clergy are lonely, set-apart people."[14] A rabbi-psychologist, Jack H Bloom, hypothesized that "the men who become religious professionals, who enter a world of differentness and otherness, do so because of some strong personality determinants that may differentiate them from the rest of the population."[15]

Bloom suggested that the rabbi tends to be more dependent on others for affection and that he loves in order to be loved. "The minister has a deep inner need to help others," he concluded.[16] His observation supports the insights of Rabbis Neil Gillman and Israel Silverman, Seminary registrars, who asked candidates for admission why they wanted to become rabbis. Most responded, "Because I want to help people."[17]

In an earlier pre-World War II and pre-Israel period, candidates for the rabbinate would probably have responded, "Because I want to help the Jewish people." Under the tutelage of Mordecai Kaplan, students in their sermons frequently grappled with the proposition, "What best contributes to the meaningful survival of the Jewish people?" The travails of the Jewish people had left their mark on those who remembered when the State of Israel did not exist.

The influence of the charismatic Abraham Heschel's depth theology with its emphasis on personal spirituality was a postwar phenomenon.

Quest for a Philosophy

Throughout the century, the rabbi was the mediator between tradition and change, respecting tradition while choosing adaptation and modification where necessary, usually in the face of the opposition of the Seminary faculty. It was the Rabbinical Assembly more than either the Seminary or the United Synagogue that struggled for a cogent definition of Conservative Judaism. With the reorganization of the Law Committee in 1948, the rabbi no longer turned to his professors but to the Law Committee for guidance on matters of ritual.

Rabbis took the initiative in modifying the ritual of their synagogues, sometimes transforming them from Orthodox to Conservative, while fostering institutional allegiances to the United Synagogue. At mid-century, bitter controversies erupted between the traditionalists and the innovators as congregations began to introduce new practices: mixed pews, mixed choirs, and the organ. Again, the rabbi entered the lists as mediator between the two trends as well as between his traditional theology and the challenges of modernism as expressed by Karl Marx, Sigmund Freud, the biblical critics, and the freshly invigorated expression of secularism emerging from Horace Kallen and the Jewish labor movement.

Sensing the need to respond to the challenges of contemporary life, rabbis introduced several innovations in synagogue ritual. In the 1940s, 97 percent of rabbis conducted late Friday night services in addition to earlier *Kabbalat Shabbat* services. They composed new rituals for the celebrations of Balfour Day, Mothers Day, Thanksgiving, and confirmation. In the 1970s Adas Israel in Washington, DC, commissioned Charles Davidson to compose a musical setting to replace the traditional but frequently neglected midnight Selihot service.

Bat mitzvah was eventually added to the regimen of life-cycle celebrations, with Judith Kaplan, the daughter of Mordecai and Lena Kaplan being the first, in 1922. The innovation spread, despite considerable opposition, first, to summer camps and, mid-century, to pulpits.

Rabbis took the leadership in liturgical creativity, authorizing the preparation of new prayer books for Sabbath and High Holidays, a new *haggadah*, and manuals for rabbinic use. Responding to the seminal events of the postwar world, rabbis introduced solemn *Yom Ha-Shoah* services into their calendar of observances, drawing upon music of the Holocaust and contemporary liturgical readings, which were then utilized for community and United Jewish Appeal observances. The anniversary of Israel's establishment inspired a plethora of original compositions and programs, which also were incorporated into synagogue and communal observances. History had provided ample precedent for memorial observances but, except for Hanukkah and Purim, offered few precedents for celebrating victories.

Many rabbis struggled to accommodate themselves to the demand for non-traditional wedding forms. A 1930 survey indicated that 60 rabbis would permit the use of a wedding ring set with precious stones while 100 required the traditionally modest simple gold band. The single-ring ceremony yielded slowly to the inevitable demands of bride and groom for two rings. An area in which rabbis held fast was in the requirement of a *get* for the dissolution of a marriage. Rabbis complained that some congregants were ignoring the requirement and instead were turning to Reform rabbis.

In 1950, rabbis attempted to overcome the laity's indifference to Sabbath and *kashrut* observance by a series of permissive rulings, but the gap between the leader and the led only grew wider. A 1979 survey revealed that less than 7 percent of Conservative homes claimed to be "totally kosher."[18]

The gap weighed heavily on the rabbinic conscience as did the lack of clarity in defining a cohesive Conservative philosophy. While a 1950 Law Committee ruling permitted driving to the synagogue on Shabbat, a 1964 opinion by the same Law Committee asked the USY to refrain from permitting travel for Shabbat worship at its conventions.

Rabbis themselves were hardly uniform in their personal level of observance. While formally committed to halakhic behavior, not all agreed on which halakhic mandate they would observe. Some, while avoiding eating meat, felt free to dine at non-kosher restaurants; others refused. No survey has ever sought to ascertain how many rabbis use *tefillin* or engage punctiliously in thrice daily prayer. Choosing between respect for their parents, their professors, and the perceived needs of the congregation only added to rabbinic emotional torment. In no branch of American Judaism was the tension between tradition and modernity more keenly felt.[19]

"The Orthodox have community, the Reform go to the mall and don't worry about it. We're in the middle—a good place, a tough place," complained Neil Gillman in an interview with Paul Wilkes, a Christian observer of Judaism. "Tradition and change (is) our motto. But internally, we stopped growing. And our rabbis are out there, feeling very lonely and isolated, wondering what to do next."[20] Wilkes concludes that in the Conservative movement rabbis who set standards and demand adherence to Jewish law walk in peril.

Few issues tormented the Conservative rabbinate more than those pertaining to gender distinctions in prayer and practice. The relentless forces pressing for a gender-free formulation of prayers and role equality for women in worship carried the potential of splitting the movement.

In 1955, the RA authorized what some rabbis had already introduced: calling women to the Torah and bat mitzvah; and, in 1973, counting them in the *minyan*. Women as rabbis and cantors remained on the unfinished agenda; the debate reached a feverish pitch in the 1970s.

It was the Rabbinical Assembly that pressured the Seminary to admit women to the Rabbinical School; the faculty was formally opposed. After ten years of tormenting debate, Gerson Cohen, the Seminary's chancellor, realized that "if the JTS failed to act, the RA would soon begin admitting women, . . . usurping the role of the Seminary."[21]

The first class of women was admitted to the Seminary in 1984 and to the Rabbinical Assembly the following spring, engendering a bitter reaction from opponents and resulting in the organization of a dissident group, the Union for Traditional Judaism.

Salaries, Tenure, and Turnover

In the first decade of the century, when annual synagogue dues were as little as $12, rabbinic salaries ranged from $900 to $1200, increasing to a $2,000 to $4,000 range in the period following World War I. In 1925, the low salary scale led Cyrus Adler to propose a central fund for rabbinic subvention; the proposal failed.

Throughout most of the century rabbinic salaries were respectfully modest; rabbis, like priests of old, were expected to supplement their wages with fees from free-will offerings. In the first decade, five dollars was a typical fee for officiating at a wedding, three dollars for a funeral. In 1930 it might be fifteen dollars for either.

Prior to the depression of 1929, $6,000 was considered a generous annual salary. As the result of the stock market's collapse in October 1929, the United States was plunged into the worst and longest economic depression in its history. Synagogue boards, faced with loss of membership and driven by bottom-line concerns, sought to meet their mounting deficits by reducing the salaries of rabbis and cantors who were left with little alternative but to accept the reduction in income; other positions were not available.

It was a grim period for rabbis and cantors. Salaries, frequently in arrears, were reduced by as much as 10 to 25 percent. A large number of rabbis, some recently graduated, could not find employment. As distressing as the loss of income was the diminution in morale and self-esteem. Recovery was slow.

With the end of war, salaries gradually resumed their pre-depression levels. Graduates in 1940 could earn $2,500 in their first pulpits; seasoned rabbis, as much as $10,000. A rabbi who began his career in the 1940s with a salary of $2,500 could look forward to retiring 50 years later at a compensation level of $50,000; many did, most did not.

As the century prospered, so did the rabbis. A career guidance pamphlet published by B'nai B'rith in 1969 reported: "A graduate of one of the seminaries can expect to earn a starting salary of from $7500 to $9500 per year."[22] The same pamphlet went on to state that rabbis occupying major pulpits in cosmopolitan centers could earn $25,000. The pamphlet was not referring to Conservative pulpits alone.

The Toronto Star reported in 1964 that rabbis were the highest paid clergymen in the community with one rabbi earning $50,000 per year. The best-paid Presbyterian minister, it reported, received $11,000.

The salary range in the decade of the seventies was from $2,750 to $45,000 with a median of $15,000. Fees for services may have produced an additional $1,000. Increases in salary were seldom automatic. Rabbis discovered that it was frequently necessary to move to a new congregation in order to secure an increase in salary. A study commission concluded that the rabbi was underpaid when compared to other professionals such as doctors or lawyers and suggested adopting a minimum salary of $13,000.[23] Only within the last quarter of the century did rabbinic salaries begin to parallel those paid to other professionals.

In the last decade of the century rabbinic compensation in large centers increased far beyond the dreams of the early graduates. In a conversation in 1990 with Wolfe Kelman, Louis Finkelstein asked Kelman, "How much are rabbis earning these days?" Kelman responded, "Professor, some rabbis are earning as much as $100,000." After a moment's pause, Dr. Finkelstein observed, "Well, in my day there were rabbis who also earned 100,000 subway tokens." It should be recalled that in Dr. Finkelstein's experience, subway tokens were five cents. (100,000 subway tokens equalled $5,000. In 1990, subway tokens were $1.00.)

In the current decade, Professor Finkelstein would have equated rabbinic compensation to as much as 150,000 subway tokens, with a few approaching 200,000, at the 1990 token price.

Pensions and Tenure

Pension plans for rabbis did not exist prior to 1940. Even after their acceptance, the plans came too late for some and failed to meet the needs of older rabbis. One, who had spent 50 years in the rabbinate retired in 1958 with an annual pension of $1,200 for a total income of only $3,000. Even after their widespread adoption, most retiring rabbis required annual supplements to meet the accepted standard that a rabbi's income should approximate two-thirds of the last annual salary. Gradually, increased salaries and pensions have made supplemental payments upon retirement unnecessary.

The establishment of the Joint Retirement Board in 1945 sensitized congregations to the importance of rabbinic security. Prior to that period, rabbinic tenure was a vague concept. For almost half of the century and perhaps longer, brevity of contracts, powerless rabbis, low salaries, and generalized unhappiness were largely responsible for frequent changes of pulpits.

Standardized contracts introduced in the 1970s called for an initial agreement for three years, a second for five, with tenure requiring severance upon separation after ten years. Some contracts specified one month vacations and allowed for sabbaticals.

A survey of 80 rabbis who had retired in the fifteen-year period between 1980 and 1995 revealed that most had retired between ages of 65 and 70, had served between 40 to 50 years and had occupied 3 to 5 pulpits in their careers. Three had served only one congregation; two had served eight. It was the rare rabbi who served in only one or two pulpits during his career.[24]

According to the survey, many of the early retirees had lived in parish homes. In the last twenty-five years rabbis have tended to own their own homes (usually subsidized by loans or grants from their congregations), taking advantage of liberal tax benefits as well as a rising real estate market. In most instances, the rabbi's home was the largest single asset in his estate.

Critics of the Rabbinate

Critics of the rabbinate have not been lacking either in number or in variety. For example:

Rabbis have abandoned their traditional role as men of learning; they have become pastors and social directors; they depend on oratory rather than substance and teach less and less of the moral law or text. They are far removed from daily prayer and study. They attend meeting after meeting, function after function and attempt to influence people by warm greetings and convivial conversation in the manner of functionaries at a summer hotel.[25]

Neither have the religious services escaped:

Services are long and boring, toneless, flavorless, and flat. Modern English prayers are devoid of taste, subject matter is jumbled, frequently saccharine with sentimentality. Conducting services from a theater-like platform separates worship from the people. Some critics yearned for a return to the classical center *bimah* with members seated around it.

Rabbis themselves have been among the sharpest critics, Arthur

Hertzberg foremost among them, writing that rabbis were a cross between a pastor or a parish priest, rich in eloquence and practical achievement, low in scholarship.

Hertzberg continued, "Hardly one rabbinic figure today commands the attention of the entire Jewish community. Every major Jewish city in the United States once had at least one rabbi whom people came to hear from all over the city, Sabbath after Sabbath. Milton Steinberg in New York had the last such congregation. No single pulpit plays that role any longer."[26]

Among the harshest (and unkindest) critics were social workers: A professor of social work portrayed rabbis as *bracha* brokers,"[27] as if rabbis could reject invitations to act in their priestly capacities. The 1950s were marked by growing jurisdictional conflicts between community centers and synagogues. The sharpest conflicts were with Conservative synagogues.

Many critics have frozen their Judaism and the rabbi into a mold defined by an idealized past which they recall from childhood. Ignoring the changing social conditions that have transformed both rabbi and congregation, they reject the integrity of the rabbi who, following the beat of contemporary rhythm, dares deviate from the sentimentalized image of a glorified past recalled by the critic.

Despite his perceptive insights, Hertzberg falls into the category of those who yearn for a world gone by and who measure contemporary practice by its deviation from an idealized memory. Today's congregation respects "hands-on pastoral tenderness" more than scholarship; most congregations demand not a scholar but a "young dynamic rabbi who will serve their needs."

Indeed, those critics who yearn for a rabbi (or cantor) who would resemble the *rov* (or *ḥazzan*) of the old country would probably reject him if he were available.

Hertzberg would be among the first to acknowledge that many oratorical successors to the Steinbergs, Goldmans, and Gordises are to be found in pulpits today; he was one of them. Other rabbis who have made their mark in pulpit and publications, such as Harold Kushner, Chaim Potok or Harold Schulweis, have regularly filled the lecture hall. The landscape which once enabled orators of the past to shine forth has itself become brighter, thereby dimming the radiance of individual lights. The rabbi is no longer the only educated or even the best educated person in the community or congregation. Mass audiences today turn to television for edification and entertainment, a medium which

Steinberg would hardly recognize. The public no longer flocks to hear the Silver-tongued or the Wise, nor the cantorial Rosenblatts and Kousevitzkys of yesterday; they defy resurrection.

Self-Analysis

A repetitive thread of discontent was interwoven in the variegated pattern of the rabbinic tapestry from the beginning of the century. For many reasons, discontent and self-criticism seemed to have been an adjunct to ordination.

Rabbis were aware that their esteemed professors on the faculty scarcely masked their contempt for the congregational pulpit because they felt that its demands interfered with the rabbi's primary obligation to study and write. To the distinguished professor of Talmud, Louis Ginzberg, rabbis were wasting their time delivering invocations and preaching to "pants pressers." He was unhappy when prized students deserted the academy in favor of the pulpit.

Convention proceedings have revealed profound unhappiness. Most rabbis felt overworked. The realities of Jewish life compelled them to concern themselves with areas beyond the synagogue. They were powerless to reject invitations to serve the community or to ignore the ritualized events and social gatherings demanding their presence.

Rabbis aspired to be worthy of their ordination as "preacher and teacher"; congregations required them to be more. The congregation, having defined the rabbi as pastor and administrator, expected him to remain close at home; the rabbi, as a leader in the community, was of necessity unavailable to his congregation at times, much to the displeasure of synagogue leaders.

Congregations have not always approved of the rabbi's involvement in communal activities and have declined to bask in the glory the rabbi might bring them by virtue of his public recognition. (More than one distinguished rabbi has been dismissed because of his communal and non-congregational involvements, cf. Isaac Leeser.)

Periodically, at their conventions, rabbis submitted to *heshbon hanefesh,* confessing their inadequacies and conceding their deficiencies. Successive presidential reports criticized the movement's lack of halakhic coherence and the vagueness of its ideology. Rabbis felt pressed by a newly assertive Orthodoxy and a less radical but vigorous Reform movement, giving rise to the untested assumption that Conservative Judaism was a way station between Orthodoxy and Reform. The introspective self-studies, cathartic in content, conducted at approximately ten-year intervals, are an index of the emotional health of the rabbinate.

The classic image of the rabbi has never been reconciled to a money economy. Rabbis have felt demeaned by the negotiating posture inherent in the need to ask for an increase in salary; they are no match for the more experienced and aggressive business people with whom they deal. In negotiation, friendships become obstacles. To avoid the disadvantages of their bargaining posture, some rabbis from the 1980s onward have taken to engaging lawyers to negotiate in their behalf.

Despite the discontinuity that separates them, rabbis have never stopped comparing themselves to the European rabbi whose piety, learning, and other-worldliness they have internalized; they have walked a fine line between their self-image as salaried professionals and as spiritual leaders.

Rabbis in the seventies, caught up in the great migration from urban center to suburbs, were forced to face the question whether to move or to repair deteriorating buildings. An ongoing challenge was that of *havurah*. Was it meeting an authentic need or was it a romantic yearning for the *shtetl?*

After analyzing the extensive scope of the rabbinic profession, a professionally conducted survey by a management company in 1971, identified seventeen separate duties and services included in the typical rabbinic job description.[28] Working 54 hours per week, the rabbi's work week was more typical of the independent professional such as the physician whose salary is neither limited nor fixed. The rabbi had the worst of both worlds: uncontrollable hours and a fixed salary. The report concluded that the rabbi felt alone, that his personal problems were not accorded sufficient importance, that the myriad of services and duties he was called upon to fulfill required an extended work week, spanning morning, noon and night. The sensitive rabbi felt as though he were a pie with not enough pieces to go around.

The report noted that the highest percentage of negative replies came from the younger age group, the more recent graduates. A kind of disillusionment sets in between 15 and 20 years out of the Seminary after the relative euphoria of the period following ordination.

Ten years later, in 1980, the RA "Blue Ribbon Committee," after conducting extensive hearings of the membership over the period of one year, rendering a report that confirmed much of the earlier study, concluded once again that most rabbis were not happy with their roles and felt overworked with a multitude of tasks which contributed little to the realization of their personal and professional goals. They felt so over-whelmed by the incessant demands for their presence, punctuated by endless crises requiring their instant attention, that there was little time for calm reflection, an indispensable prelude not only for prayer, but for creativity. They were forced to steal time to study, to read enough to keep abreast of new ideas, or even to read the daily press, all of which were essential to meeting their own standards, let alone the expectations of the congregation.[29]

It was inevitable that teaching and study, once regarded as the pri-mary function of rabbis, became secondary, for which they endured more criticism. When the congregation's insatiable appetite for sermons and services demanded more of them than they could possibly produce, rabbis developed a resentment of the congregation followed by a corro-sive sense of guilt for their diminished enthusiasm.

The annual conventions struggled not only with the question "Who Is A Jew?" but "Who Am I?" as the members expressed their concern with the problem of rearing their own children in the contemporary permissive environment, which meant coping with Friday night entice-ment. Many rabbis felt that children of rabbinic families faced a heavier burden in coping with culture conflict than did the children of other families; more was expected of children of rabbis than of others.

Rabbis felt trapped; they were captives of what they could least suc-cessfully and prudently reject: the security and comfort they had achieved for themselves and their families. Yet, paradoxically, for most rabbis, the rabbinate remained a sanctuary offering fulfillment and per-sonal satisfaction to those who responded to its call.

Why do Rabbis Change Pulpits?

The most frequent pattern, with exceptions, has been for a rabbi to serve his first one or two congregations for relatively brief periods with a longer tenure in succeeding posts. Securing an increase in salary, although not the only reason, remained an important motivation for a rabbi to seek another pulpit. In some instances, the rabbi may have felt the need to seek relief from an intolerable situation.

Frequently, rabbis were attracted to a congregation in a larger city because they sought a broader sphere. Some rabbis may have felt that they were evaluated by the size of their congregation and the social sta-tus of its members. A sense of defeat sometimes corroded the soul of a rabbi who remained in the village and did not climb the placement rungs that lead to the cathedral synagogue. Occasionally, it was simply boredom or a need to feel wanted that led a rabbi to seek a change of pulpit. He may have been caught up in the zest of the quest.

In most instances, by far, contracts have been terminated at the initiative of the board or the president of the congregation because of perceived dissatisfaction. The congregation judged the rabbi by his/her projected religious persona, his/her preaching, his/her manner of conducting worship, and his/her response to their personal needs. The rabbi, on the other hand, judged the congregation by the extent of the members' religious observance, their attendance at worship services, their response to the goals and programs he/she had outlined for them, and, inevitably, the salary they paid him/her. Divergencies of perceptions were inevitable.

A frequent source of friction in many congregations, was the task of maintaining a *minyan* for daily services, especially when members ceased residing in the neighborhood of the synagogue. The usual solution was to demand more frequent participation by the rabbi and the cantor and to charge them with devising ways of rotating the responsibility for providing the necessary quorum of ten. The suggested remedies seldom worked for long, for the clergy and the board each expected the other to compensate for one's own failure.

Another reason for rabbinic conflict and "turnover" was the differing definitions of the rabbinic role as enunciated by the congregation and as defined by the Seminary. Congregations wanted a rabbinic functionary who would teach, guide, inspire, visit the sick, console the bereaved, and serve the members at life-cycle events. In other words, the congregation wanted a rabbi who would function as a *priest* rather than a prophet, the role which the rabbi frequently preferred. The congregation wanted a rabbi to be a pastor; the Seminary trained him to be a scholar. The Seminary was more successful in giving its students an understanding of the history of the prayer book than in resolving the quandary over the effectiveness of the prayers. The Seminary trained its graduates in mastery of the traditional texts; congregations were far more interested in other areas which, if pursued, would leave little time for scholarly pursuits, much less for the preparation of sermons. Always working under pressure, the rabbi had to steal time in order to study.

Schooled in the exposition of midrash, biblical and talmudic commentaries and texts, the Seminary student had little training in what came to be called "pastoral psychology" or "practical theology." Courses in pastoral skill were introduced only in 1955. For most of the century, rabbis, called to officiate at marriages and funerals or to counsel the troubled, had to turn to practicing rabbis for guidance, or else learn from experience. More than one rabbinic career has been undermined by minor blunders due to inexperience.

Cyrus Adler felt that the years a rabbi spent at the Seminary were far too few and precious to waste time learning about such "simple" matters as conducting a marriage ceremony, blessing a bar mitzvah, or consoling the bereaved, at the cost of the more important goal of mastering the sacred texts. For both Schechter and Adler, the synagogue was primarily a place for scholars to earn a living so that they could pursue their real purpose: scholarship.

During the first quarter of the century, it was the Seminary president rather than a Placement Commission that selected rabbis for specific congregations. Schechter would propose his prize student of Talmud as if that were sufficient to recommend him. The most generous evaluation that Cyrus Adler could offer a congregation was that the candidate was a fine scholar. Less thought was given to the rabbi's ability as pastor or counsellor, or even as a speaker. The differing evaluations led to tragic encounters between a rabbi's performance and the congregation's expectations.

Congregations may not have felt it was their duty to allow a rabbi to spend a great deal of time ministering to causes beyond the congregation. Their own needs were primary; they paid the salary. Congregation Mikve Israel in Philadelphia in the 1850s resented Isaac Leeser's preoccupation with national concerns. A century later, many congregations were annoyed when their rabbi was not available to them when they needed his presence. A congregational leader, an unpaid volunteer who signed the rabbi's salary check, may have been disturbed when the rabbi he "employed" was beyond immediate reach of the telephone.

Finances have been another frequent source of tension. Seminary graduates were unprepared for the realities of congregational life. They frequently assumed that the laymen would raise the funds for maintaining the synagogue while the rabbi could pursue his primary duties of ministering to the membership. The rabbi soon discovered that many congregations expected the rabbi to help meet the synagogue's budget, at least to raise the funds to cover the rabbi's salary.

Under the best of circumstances, conflict in expectations was inevitable in the rabbi-congregation relationship. Each rabbi was challenged to reconcile his or her finite hours and energy with the seemingly infinite needs and demands of the congregation, community, friends, family, and personal life. A young rabbi, in an initial burst of enthusiasm, may have been tempted to accept the premise that he or she could reconcile all of these expectations. When it became apparent that fulfilling the role was beyond one person's capacity, the rabbi, initially idealized as the spiritual leader who would fulfill the promise, soon found himself/herself abandoned by those who once held high hopes for his/her success. In failing to meet expectations, the rabbi aroused both disappointment and hostility, driving congregants to seek another spiritual leader who would not disappoint them, but in the attempt to meet their expectations, the successor rabbi fell into the same trap as the predecessor. In seeking alternatives, the congregation succeeded only in repeating the process.

Every rabbi, even as every human being, possessed areas of strength and of weakness; each rabbi could excel only in limited areas. No rabbi would be totally effective in every area of the congregation's expectations. In seeking a successor to a departing rabbi, the congregation looked for a rabbi whose abilities compensated for the deficiencies perceived in the predecessor, forgetting that the successor, along with his areas of strength, would bring to the post his or her own inadequacies, which would come to be perceived only later. Thus the congregation succeeded in trading a rabbi with certain deficiencies for another with others. In the exchange, the effective strengths of each rabbi were frequently ignored.

The Next Century: The Unfinished Agenda

"Tradition and Change," and "Unity and Diversity" are slogans that need to be examined periodically. Many feel there must be limits to our diversity. Some suggest that we have placed too much emphasis on *"puk ḥazei,"*[30] arguing that we have gone too far in assigning authority to a largely unqualified mass laity, and that the time has come to place the authority for defining "Catholic Israel" in the hands of qualified scholars.[31]

•

With the passing of the "great" Schechter-appointed professors, the influence of the Seminary faculty over the rabbi has diminished. The Rabbinical Assembly today claims the right to formulate its own philosophy of Judaism with less fear of a veto from above. Will the easing of the Seminary's control over the RA lead to greater freedom of expression for rabbis or will the loosening of centralized "authoritative" links lead to chaos?

•

Rabbis have expressed their distress at the frequent expressions of anti-clericalism that have emerged from the United Synagogue. Can rabbis combat this disturbing trend? Moreover, can rabbis play a role in bridging the gap between the Seminary, the United Synagogue and the Rabbinical Assembly?

•

Many rabbis have questioned the traditional role assigned to the classical sermon. What role will the sermon play in the next century? Will it give way to a brief *d'var Torah,* a question and answer period, or discussion session?[32]

•

The ordination of women will surely transform the rabbinate in a manner which the early graduates could not have envisioned and which we now, at this transition point, cannot readily predict. Women's ordination and sensitivity to egalitarian concerns have challenged the rabbi and the congregation to ponder other questions relating to the language of prayer, procedures of synagogue ritual, and the verbalized image of God. New prayer books and prayer pamphlets already abound with gender-free innovative variations. What will become of our familiar prayer books and their traditional formulations? Congregations may be offered the proposal of engaging a rabbinic couple, a totally new situation for both rabbis and congregations.[33]

•

In the closing years of the century, a fresh source of rabbinic talent was introduced into the Rabbinical Assembly when the University of Judaism, in 1999, ordained its first graduating class after a four-year course of study, akin in content and qualifications of admission to that of the Seminary in New York.

•

A second school for ordaining Conservative rabbis, a turn of events which Schechter and Adler would have found inconceivable and which Finkelstein probably would have resisted or vetoed, will give our rabbinate for the first time in our history two faculties, two alma maters, two graduating classes, and two class photographs, the latter a superficial but significant symbol of potential differing loyalties and conflict.

That students from both schools will follow identical curricula and spend one year studying together in Israel bodes well for the future. The addition of a West Coast site for rabbinic training can only increase the influence of the movement and bring to it the freshness inherent in a diverse student population. This is further enhanced by the other Conservative rabbinic training schools: The Schechter Institute of Judaic Studies in Jerusalem, and the Seminario Rabinico Latinamericano in Buenos Aires, Argentina.

•

The challenge of finding positions to employ the increasing number of graduates emerging from multiple sources promises to be mitigated by an increasing demand for Rabbinical Assembly rabbis to serve in non-pulpit positions such as community-sponsored adult education projects, day school instruction and administration, and the chaplaincy. Moreover, there is, in the concluding decade of the century, a growing demand for Conservative rabbis to serve in Eastern Europe, Germany, England and France, as well as in Latin America.

As the country prospers, and as congregations grow in size, larger congregations realizing that they comprise multiple constituencies of diverse temperament have taken to engaging second and third rabbis to address more effectively the diverse membership.

Conclusion

In the first half of the century, rabbis were regarded by others and themselves as ethnic leaders; they emphasized ethnic and cultural concerns in their program: history, the diaspora, Hebrew, and Zionism. American Jews looked upon Judaism as a religious structure within which they carried out essentially ethnic activities.

In the last quarter of the century the American Jewish community, having defined itself primarily as a religious grouping with a diminishing ethnic component, has placed greater emphasis on the religious dimension of Judaism. The community will shape the rabbi in its own image; young men and women, motivated to turn to the rabbinate out of religious commitment, will be inevitably conditioned to assign priority to the religious and universal components of Judaism.

Rabbis will continue to try to balance their conflicting roles as both priest and prophet. While many will prefer the latter, congregations will continue to demand the former. The effective performance of priestly and social functions will provide rabbis with the freedom to perform the prophetic functions if that is their preference.

Despite the many causes for unhappiness in the rabbinate, its haunting sense of personal insecurity, and its frustrations, idealistic young people will continue to apply for admission to the Seminary and other ordaining institutions and young rabbis will continue to be ordained in great number. Testimony indicates that rabbis still find satisfactions in the vineyard of faith.

Many of these satisfactions have been enumerated in response to the

1971 survey[34] and reiterated in the survey of retired rabbis in 1995. Appended to responses were many positive evaluations:

> The rabbinate is an opportunity to experience the joys of teaching, the ability to lead a Jewish life, to foster love of Judaism, to feel wanted and needed, to earn high status and respect, to influence a congregation, and to assure high standards of social and personal behavior.
>
> It is the only job where one is forced to study compelling ideas, do *mitzvot* and generally advance human lives.

Still more amazing, the retired rabbis surveyed in 1995, all of whom had served in their pulpits for over fifty years, in recalling their careers, affirmed that, despite frustrations and occasional feelings of being victimized, they looked back in contentment over their years of service. Few had regrets for having chosen their careers and, despite all the heartaches, if given a choice of careers, they would select the rabbinate again.

Perhaps, complaining is healthy catharsis. The rabbinate remains an eternal calling; new scholars, eager to serve in the vineyard of the Lord, will ever respond *Hineni*.

NOTES

1. The use of the word "rabbi" will hereinafter mean "Conservative rabbi" unless otherwise indicated.
2. Daniel J. Elazar, "The Development of the American Synagogue," in the *American Synagogue in Transition* (Center for Jewish Community Studies/Jerusalem Center for Public Affairs/Synagogue Council of America, undated pamphlet), p. 267.
3. ". . . (at) a meeting of the Union of Orthodox Rabbis of the United States one of the resolutions adopted at the Conventions was, that if the congregations whose rabbis were there assembled took a graduate of the Theological Seminary . . . they were requested not to denominate him rabbi, but reverend or doctor, for rabbis meant something quite other than the thing represented by the graduates of the Jewish Theological Seminary." Letter from Henrietta Szold to Louis Ginzberg, August 21, 1907, in Baila Round Shargel, *Lost Love, The Untold Story of Henrietta Szold* (Philadelphia: Jewish Publication Society, 1997), p. 122 with note, p. 364.
4. Robert E. Fierstien, *A Different Spirit* (New York: Jewish Theological Seminary, 1990), p. 97.
5. Quoted in Herbert Parzen, *Architects of Conservative Judaism* (New York: Jonathan David, 1964), p. 67.
6. Mordecai Waxman, *Tradition and Change* (New York: Burning Bush

Press, 1958), p. 173. Herbert Rosenblum, *Conservative Judaism* (New York: United Synagogue, 1983), p. 32. Pamela S. Nadell, *Conservative Judaism in America* (New York: Greenwood Press, 1988), p. 326.

7. Ḥavurot, plural, ḥavurah, singular. A fellowship of individuals and couples who meet regularly for worship and study, with emphasis on volunteer participation.

8. In the 1940s, Judith and Ira Eisenstein wrote and published five cantatas, including the popular "What is Torah?," "Seven Golden Buttons" and "Our Bialik."

9. ". . . in Pasadena, California, . . . Rabbi Vorspan . . . in a period of a short few weeks, succeeded in establishing—for the first time in the history of that community—a Kosher meat market with a *mashgiach* and a *vaad ha-kashrut*." Report of Bernard Segal, executive Vice-President of RA, *PRA* (1948), p. 27.

10. Aryeh Davidson and Jack Wertheimer, "The Next Generation of Conservative Rabbis" in Nina Beth Cardin and David Wolf Silverman, eds., *The Seminary at 100*, (New York: The Rabbinical Assembly and the Jewish Theological Seminary, 1987), pp. 33–45.

11. Arthur Hertzberg, "The Conservative Rabbinate, A Sociological Study" in Blau, Friedman, Hertzberg and Mendelson, eds., *Essays in Jewish Life and Thought* (New York: Columbia University Press, 1959), pp. 309–332.

12. "T" instead of "s" for "sav" but not for "sin." "Ah" instead of "Oh," in most cases. And never "Oy" in place of "o."

13. Hertzberg, pp. 309–332.

14. M.K. Bowers, *Conflicts of the Clergy* (New York: Thomas Nelson, 1963), quoted in Jack H Bloom, "Who Becomes Clergymen?" in *The Journal of Religion and Health*, Vol. 10:1, January 1971, p. 60.

15. Jack H Bloom, ibid., p. 53.

16. Bloom, quoting E.A. Loomis Jr., "The Religion-Psychiatry Program at Union Theological Seminary," p. 65.

17. Ibid., p. 65.

18. Edward Shapiro, *A Time for Healing* (Baltimore: Johns Hopkins University Press, 1991), p. 172.

19. Daniel J. Elazar, *Community and Polity: The Organizational Dynamics of American Jewry* (Philadelphia: Jewish Publication Society, 1995), pp. 128–9.

20. Paul Wilkes, *And They Shall Be My People* (New York: Atlantic Monthly Press, 1994), p. 207. Paul Wilkes spent a full year studying Congregation Beth Israel in Worcester, Massachusetts, and the activities of its rabbi, Jay Rosenbaum.

21. Beth S. Wenger, from a conversation with Gordon Tucker, "The Politics of Women's Ordination" in Jack Wertheimer, ed., *Tradition Renewed*, (New York: Jewish Theological Seminary, 1997), Vol. 2, p. 512.

22. "Careers in the Rabbinate," B'nai B'rith Vocational Service, Washington, DC, 1969, p. 8.

23. Harry Gersh, "The Conservative Rabbi, An Economic and Professional Profile" (New York: The Rabbinical Assembly, 1971), pp. 18, 20–26.

24. Survey conducted by the Rabbinical Assembly Association of Retired Rabbis, 1996. Unpublished, Summary report in the Rabbinical Assembly "Newsletter," Fall 1996.

25. Sholome Michael Gelber, "Does the Jewish Past Have a Future?" in Blau, Friedman, Hertzberg, and Mendelsohn, eds., *Essays on Jewish Life and Thought*, pp. 251–265.

26. Arthur Hertzberg, *Being Jewish in America* (New York: Schocken, 1979), p. 100, and *Midstream*, Vol. 12, No. 1 (January 1966).

27. Gerald B. Bubis in *The Jewish Spectator* (Spring 1975), p. 58.

28. Harry Gersh, *The Conservative Rabbi: An Economic and Professional Profile* (New York: Martin E. Segal Company, 1971).

29. "Report of Blue Ribbon Committee," 80th Convention, *PRA* (May 1980), pp. 277–287.

30. "Go see what the people are doing" (B. Berakhot 45a).

31. Daniel H. Gordis, "Positive-Historical Judaism Exhausted," *CJ* 48:1 (Fall 1994), pp. 3–19.

32. Robert Kirschner, "Is There Still a Place for the Sermon?," *CJ* 48:3 (Spring 1996), pp. 14–25.

33. For a fuller treatment of the history and role of the female rabbi, see Pamela S. Nadell, *Women Who Would Be Rabbis: A History of Women's Ordination, 1889–1985* (Boston: Beacon Press, 1998); see also, Beth S. Wenger, "The Politics of Women's Ordination: Jewish Law, Institutional Power, and the Debate Over Women in the Rabbinate," in Jack Wertheimer, ed., *Tradition Renewed: A History of the Jewish Theological Seminary* (New York: Jewish Theological Seminary, 1997), Vol. 2, pp. 483–523.

34. Gersh, pp. 86–90.

A Brief History of the Rabbinical Assembly in Israel[1]

Theodore Steinberg

Part I: Loomings and Personalities: 1929–1967

As a formal organization, with elected officers, written records and a budget, the RA of Israel is quite young, no more than twenty-five years old. In other respects, such as the presence of RA members in Israel and Mandatory Palestine, its age borders on venerability. RA rabbis started coming to Palestine during the 1930s and 1940s. The records are scanty, but we know of at least two RA men who settled in Palestine during the era of the British mandate. After the State of Israel was established, individual RA members continued coming and settling. Hardly any did what in America would be called rabbinic work, such as leading and serving congregations. Many went into education and academia, a few into business, while others came to retire in Israel. As one replied when asked why he chose to retire in Israel, "I always wanted to live in a Jewish neighborhood."

In those early days, and to a lesser extent, even into the 1980s, the RA functioned very much like a *landsmanschaft* organization. RA rabbis regarded each other as colleagues who shared a similar education and outlook. Some may have known one another at the Seminary, and all had gone through the stressful experience of becoming integrated and absorbed into the Israeli milieu. Moreover, they genuinely needed each other, not so much for business and professional matters, but for friendship and mutual support, as well as for sharing vital information such as how to manage with Israeli banks.

When does the history of the RA in Israel begin? Is it with people, or with ideas, or with the organization? Or some combination of all three? Probably the latter, but first there must be people who will supply the substance to the ideas and the organization. Thus our story begins in 1929 with the late Professor Max Kadushin's journey to Palestine.

While serving as rabbi of the Humbolt Boulevard Temple in Chicago, in 1929, Kadushin took a leave of absence in order to spend a year in Palestine. The Kadushins wanted to become a Hebrew-speaking family and the Palestinian Yishuv offered the world's only total Hebraic environment. Also, it has been conjectured that Kadushin intended to apply for an appointment to the faculty at the recently-established Hebrew University. Had he had received the appointment, Kadushin would have been the first RA member to settle in Palestine, however, nothing came of his application, if indeed he ever submitted one.

The Kadushins reached Palestine, but their stay in *Eretz Yisrael* was abbreviated because of the Arab riots and troubled conditions that had broken out between Jews and Arabs in late 1929. The experience contributed to a paper that Kadushin read before the RA at its 1931 convention. He spoke about the ties between Conservative Judaism, Zionism, and Palestine and especially stressed the potential role of the American rabbi in supporting and strengthening the Zionist consciousness.

> Eretz Yisrael will not be built by those who are merely interested in it, but by those with whom it is a symbol of their whole Jewish outlook, to whom it is not an aspect merely of Jewish life, another worthy endeavor, but to whom it is the light by which they may view Jewish ethics, religion, practices, habits.
>
> Only if the rabbi has this faith in Palestine and in Israel's creative genius will he play his part in Palestine work.[2]

It is reasonable to assume that Kadushin was not intentionally giving an *aliyah* talk; moreover, he was speaking to another world—pre-Hitler, pre-Shoah, pre-World War II, pre-State of Israel, and to a group of rabbis who were trained, not to be *halutzim,* but to serve, lead, and build American Jewry. Nevertheless, whether from Kadushin or others, individual RA members did hear and respond to the call of the return to Zion.

One of the first RA members to make his way to Palestine was the late Rabbi Simon Greenberg who attended classes in Jewish studies at the Hebrew University in 1924–25, the university's first year of operation. When the university was formally dedicated in 1925, Greenberg served as an usher at the opening ceremonies, and is remembered for having assisted university President Judah Magnes in attending to the needs of visiting dignitaries.

Rabbi Greenberg did not settle permanently in Israel until late in his life. He was already in his nineties when he and Mrs. Greenberg made *aliyah* in 1992. But throughout his long and productive life, he was an avid and important supporter of every Conservative institution in Israel. The handsome education building in Kibbutz Hanaton bears his name, and the early Conservative synagogues that were established during the 1960s honor his memory for the support he secured for their struggling adult education programs. Greenberg did not limit his energies to Conservative institutions alone. In the 1970s, he played an important role in helping Kibbutz Oranim establish its teachers' seminary that would emphasize Jewish studies in an open-minded, liberal fashion of the sort Greenberg admired.[3]

Starting in the 1930s, a trickle of RA members began to make their way to Palestine with the intention of settling permanently. The earliest pioneer of whom we have a record was Rabbi Harry Davidowitz who reached Palestine in 1934. It was the era of the British mandate, and the beginning of the fifth *aliyah* when German Jews started coming to Palestine. Davidowitz did not intend to be a rabbi or a pioneering *halutz,* but a businessman. He opened a factory for the manufacture of false teeth that eventually employed two hundred workers. In June 1946, Davidowitz addressed the RA convention. He described life in Palestine during the pre-State years, the constant security hazards and Jewish self-defense, and the multiplicity of ethnic types of Jews with their different cultural and religious styles. In closing, he focused on his view of religious life in the Yishuv, which he believed was "growing there even in those places where religion had been ruled out at first as a philosophy of life." And then he criticized the rabbis, most of whom "are a bit behind the times."

> The rabbis have not yet grasped the idea that religion in Palestine must have something to say on everyday life, not only on the question of Sabbath, . . . [but on things like proper working conditions, which] should spring from the spirit of Jewish living; that fairness and justice in industry is [also] part of the Jewish heritage. . . . I never yet heard in all of my twelve years I have been in Palestine, any statement by any Rabbi expressing a religious approach to the question of justice in the differences between employers and employees.[4]

This talk by a veteran of the pioneering generations may have been the first of its kind to be delivered by a colleague to a gathering of Conservative rabbis. Rabbi Davidowitz concluded with an invitation to RA members to come to Palestine and make their unique "approach to religion and life" available to the Yishuv.

Rabbi Abraham Goldberg was another early RA settler. He arrived in Palestine in 1946, after serving as a chaplain for four years in the U.S. Army during World War II. Helped financially by the American G.I. Bill for veterans of the war, Goldberg intended to study at the Hebrew University for a year or two, and then return to the U.S. and secure a good position as a congregational rabbi.

But destiny intervened and Goldberg never got that good, well-paying job he hoped to find in America. Life was difficult in Palestine during those days. The Mandatory government applied heavy pressure on the Jewish population, and almost all young people became involved in one underground movement or another, as did Goldberg. As a result of their deepening attachment to daily life in the Yishuv, Goldberg and his wife, Rivka, felt obliged to stay on in Palestine. He became more and more involved with the defense system, at first with the Haganah and later, after statehood was declared, with the IDF, the national army. During 1948, after the British left, came a large influx of volunteers from abroad to fight for Israel. Goldberg, having had four years of wartime experience as an officer in the American Army, was appointed head of *Machal,* as the foreign volunteers were known. This posting lasted through most of 1948 and into 1949, when the War of Independence began to lessen in intensity. When the war ended, Goldberg left the army and returned to the university. Having already decided to settle in Israel, he continued in the university, specializing in talmudic studies, and received his doctorate in 1952.

Almost immediately, Goldberg was offered a junior faculty position which he accepted, and he remained on at the university, eventually as a full professor, teaching Talmud, until his retirement in 1983. Even after retirement, he continued to teach and does so as a volunteer to this very day, fifteen years after his formal retirement.[5]

In 1958, the late Rabbi Moshe Davis and his family came to settle in Jerusalem. Davis was associated with the Jewish Theological Seminary, but had long wanted to make *aliyah.* He came to Israel with an invitation from the Hebrew University to establish the Institute of Contemporary Jewry which he founded and directed for many years. His association with the Seminary continued for several years, and in his files is a photograph of Davis standing together with Rabbi Bernard Mandel-baum and the late Moshe Sharett at the dedication in 1958 of the Pen-imiah, the JTS student center and dormitory in Jerusalem. This building, located near the Israel Museum, has since become the Schechter Institute of Jewish Studies, one of Israel's leading academic institutions.[6]

Not long afterward, Rabbi Jack Cohen resigned his position as spiritual leader of the Society for the Advancement of Judaism in Manhattan, and made *aliyah* in 1961, also settling with his family in Jerusalem. Cohen served as Director of the B'nai B'rith Hillel Foundation at the Hebrew University, a position he held from 1961 until his retirement in 1983. During those years, he helped to found *Mevakshei Derekh*, the first Reconstructionist synagogue in Jerusalem, and was a member of the editorial board of *Petachim*, a Hebrew journal that he helped to found and which specialized in modern Jewish thought.[7]

Rabbi Herzl Fishman, another RA pioneer, came to Israel as a boy with his family in the 1930s, served in the Haganah and later in the IDF with the rank of major in military intelligence. He headed a special unit called *Atudah Akadama'it*, "Academic Reservists." These were young men and women, all university students, who specialized in topics of interest to the army, such as Middle East studies, water resources, and languages. Fishman, both during and after his army service was, for a number of years, a member of Israel's Foreign Service. His stay in Israel was not continuous but he returned to settle permanently in 1971. Since 1994, Fishman has served as editor of *Avar ve'Atid*, a journal of Jewish education, culture and discourse.[8]

Although the number of RA rabbis in Israel during the 1950s was small, and even fewer were engaged in rabbinic work, these were enough to prompt Sidney Greenberg, in a talk before the 1956 RA convention, to hold forth on the possible qualifications for rabbinic service in Israel. His views were based on his experiences during a sabbatical leave he had spent in Israel. Interestingly, after urging that all rabbinical students spend a year of study in Israel, he recommended that the students should not dorm at the Hebrew University but rather live and work on a Hapoel Hamizrachi [modern Orthodox] kibbutz. "This intimate contact and sharing of life's problems would be mutually enriching. . . ." We would learn from them, and "The Kibbutz would learn at first-hand our concern with, and approach to, the problems of adjusting the tradition [to] contemporary life."[9]

As Rabbi Greenberg's engaging suggestion about JTS rabbinical students living and working on a Hapoel Hamizrachi kibbutz did not go further than his convention talk, we shall never know how Hapoel Hamizrachi would have reacted to such a proposition. Would the kibbutz have been receptive to hosting a group of future Conservative rabbis, or had the chasm between the Orthodox and the non-Orthodox already grown too wide for such an experiment?

Rabbi Greenberg was not unaware of this. In his 1956 talk, he focused on the personal qualities that would be required of the Conservative rabbi who hopes to "do missionary work" in Israel. He must not only possess the highest rabbinic and personal qualifications but, "[T]he rabbi will have to be a man of courage. For every sympathizer he will find a dozen opponents. The religious leadership had expressed itself vehemently against the introduction of either Reform or Conservative congregations." A generation after these words were spoken, the situation between the Orthodox and non-Orthodox is, sadly, in most respects, about the same or worse.[10]

Rabbi Moshe Cohen z"l is known for and esteemed as the rabbi who organized Conservative synagogues in Israel. Cohen was a JTS graduate and a professional social worker when he came on *aliyah* in 1964 together with his family. The Cohens decided to make Ashkelon their home and, almost immediately, Cohen found himself with two job offers: as a Conservative rabbi, he was invited to serve as the first director of the United Synagogue and World Council of Synagogues organization in Israel; and, based on his social work credentials, the city of Ashkelon offered him a position as a youth worker in the social services department. He accepted both because, as is well known, making a living in Israel often requires one to work at more than one job.

As a social worker, Cohen continued with the city for four years, when he was offered, and accepted, a position as Professor of Social Work at Bar Ilan University in Ramat Gan, a post he held for some thirteen years.[11] His work for the United Synagogue and World Council of Synagogues continued throughout his years of residence in Israel. In that capacity, he is best known for his travels throughout the country, searching out interested persons and groups, for thus he managed to establish more than 15–20 Conservative congregations in as many communities. Whenever possible, he volunteered his services as rabbi in order to help the congregation get started.[12]

Some RA rabbis were able to spend extended periods of time in Israel. Myron Fenster spent an entire sabbatical year serving as rabbi of Moriah congregation in Haifa. As he described it, it was a year touched by immense satisfactions and even moments of bliss, along with long hours of meditating about what it means to be a Conservative rabbi in the Promised Land. "I attended more bar mitzvah parties in Israel in one year than I had in ten years in New York City and the strange thing is that I enjoyed them all. . . . It was primarily the people of Moriah that made our stay so pleasant and a source of satisfaction."

Concerning the professional side of the rabbinate, Fenster wrote: "I must say that on the basis of my experience any of the many men in our movement could honorably serve an Israeli congregation." Not that it was easy, but "Despite some initial doubts I found that with hard work, I could be thoroughly prepared whenever I faced the congregation." If Fenster is referring to the difficulty of speaking and preaching in Hebrew, he has a point. The language one has mastered in the diaspora may be quite different in style, nuance and vocabulary from the daily language of Israel.

Fenster's assessment of religious life in Israel was both melancholy and hopeful:

> I have spoken of our inability to have made a profound impression on the Israeli scene so far. On the other hand, I am convinced that there is great potential for us and our movement there. People are very much interested. They want to talk about it and hear about it. There are prominent people throughout Israel who will describe themselves as Conservative in feeling. They may not be ready to stand up and be counted but they will say, "I agree with you."
>
> Problems of faith are not absent in Israel. The tragedy is that a whole generation has grown without the habit of going to Synagogue.
>
> Recently a young girl recorded what, in a sense, is an indictment of the religious element: "So long as you do not expend your energies in explicating the meaning of faith in our lives, your efforts will be of no avail. We should like to know the relevance of a living faith. We could not understand how it is possible for a person who has lost his faith to find it."[13]

The late Simcha Kling, who also spent a sabbatical year in Israel during the early 1960s, had similar experiences. This was his third trip to Israel and he expected to find large groups of people just waiting for the good word from a representative of American non-Orthodox Judaism. To his disappointment, there was much curiosity and interest, but barely any willingness to do anything concrete. Sometimes he would ask: "If there was a Conservative synagogue here, would you attend?" The invariable answer would be: "No, not me, but there is a need for something like this."[14]

Significantly, this sentiment has been expressed in different ways again and again over the past many years: "You people have a great idea. It's beautiful and just what Israel needs. It's not for me, but it will be good for lots of Israelis." Most recently, journalist Stuart Schoffman, an American *oleh* and acute observer of Israeli life, speaking before the 1996 RA convention, made an elegant, low-keyed call to Conservative rabbis in convention assembled. After a few paragraphs about Israel's powerful and public anti-religious sentiments, he went on to say that there are, nevertheless, perceptible and nascent, though veiled, religious longings that desperately need nurturing. And so, Conservative rabbis: "Do not despair. You have much to teach [us]. There is a willingness to learn despite all of these factors which militate against it. . . . So much of the potential for this lies right here with people like you . . ."[15]

It is a song we've heard more than once. "Rabbi, you and your colleagues are the kind of spiritual leaders we need here in Israel." The speaker always means well, and probably speaks from the heart. But the reality has been different and difficult, laden with disappointment. The message of Conservative Judaism has not made a significant impact on Israel's secular Jews. Nor, for that matter, has it touched significantly the large, so-called "traditional" element of the population, the sort of Israeli who attends the synagogue on Shabbat morning and a soccer match during the afternoon. This question of why Conservative Judaism, thus far, has been unable to make more of a spiritual impact upon Israeli Jewry obviously is extremely important and merits a full study in its own right.

Rabbi Elvin Kose *z"l*, another colleague who spent a sabbatical in Israel during the 1960s, looked at the situation from the perspective of the American-Israeli membership, and had this to say:

> [The American Jew expects from Israel] the glimmerings of a new vision, a new ideal, to behold a new Jew . . . Instead, one finds an absorption in what the Israeli terms the three basic problems: security, assimilation of refugees, and economic stability. These are readily and justifiably understandable in the face of the very real basic problems they face. However, the broad non-concern with the spiritual dimension and its dismissal as relatively unimportant measured against the demands of immediate tasks tends to place a fundamental barrier between American and Israeli.[16]

The situation described in the above comments would only become more complex and difficult in the years to come. Israel was a radically different kind of Jewish society from that experienced by most American Conservative rabbis and, for that matter, by most American Orthodox rabbis, especially those who regarded themselves as being "modern" or even "liberal" in their Orthodoxy. Israel was very much an ideological society, with most citizens taking strong positions on every sort of social, political and religious issue, and this at a time when Americans were becoming indifferent to ideological questions.

Thus a doctrinaire Israeli secularist (a category barely known in America) is not simply indifferent to religion, but probably actively despises it. He is interested in moral questions but not from a religious perspective. In fact, he may regard Jewish moral teaching as being childish and, in any case, far outweighed by its, in his view, immoral ideas. Barbara Spectre gave an apt illustration of this variety of Israeli secularism in her description of a reaction to a memorial service conducted by her husband, Rabbi Philip Spectre. The service took place on the first Memorial Day after the War of Attrition. All of the mourning families attended and it was a difficult emotional experience. After the service, a sister of one of the fallen came up to Mrs. Spectre with these harsh words:

> By what right do you desecrate my brother's memory like this? . . .
> By what right do you impose on my brother's death the concept of
> *kiddush hashem?* He was dedicated to his homeland, and to his people. I knew my brother and what he believed. He did not die with
> the *Sh'ma* on his lips. The thought of *kiddush hashem* would have
> infuriated him. He died to protect his buddies, his family, and his
> land. Don't do violence to his memory.[17]

Mrs. Spectre, at first, was stunned by this verbal attack. But upon reflection, she decided that the soldier's sister was in the right; it is inappropriate and wrong to extend a sacred language to those for whom it has no meaning and nothing to do with *"their* understanding of themselves." Although much can be said about Israeli secularism and its challenge to religionists, the above brief sketch is indicative of its high seriousness, and may help the reader to understand the Israeli situation. Moreover, although this essay is being written more than twenty years after the events in Mrs. Spectre's anecdote occurred, the state of affairs has not changed, and has, in some ways, become more acute.

On the other side, religious leadership in Israel also tends to move to extreme positions. In many ways, at the present time at least, this new Jewish society is not especially hospitable to midway, moderate positions. Moderates usually are outshouted by the ultras on all sides. Some argue, tongue in cheek perhaps, that Conservative Judaism will not make much headway until it too learns how to shout and scream.

In the meantime, notwithstanding the difficulties, and because more and more rabbis were visiting Israel and experiencing the dream first-hand in all its unalloyed actuality, the Rabbinical Assembly was beginning to see the developments in Israel more and more in the light of its realities and genuine needs. In 1965, a formal RA Israel Committee was established as a standing committee of the Rabbinical Assembly, and some years later, the RA adopted a slight but symbolic change of name, moving from the Rabbinical Assembly of America to simply the Rabbinical Assembly, as an expression of its international and especially Israeli membership.

By 1958 it was reported that five RA rabbis were permanently settled in Israel. The number rose to about ten in 1961, and gradually continued to increase. According to the 1997 Membership Directory, the number of RA members permanently settled in Israel has risen to 132, living in 31 different communities, on both sides of the Green Line, including three on kibbutzim and one resident on a moshav. The numbers represent an increase in 40 years of about 1500 percent, and represent some 10 percent of the Rabbinical Assembly membership.

Part II: Really Getting Started: 1967–1985

1967 was a watershed year in Jewish history. The Six Day War and the overwhelming victory stirred up a powerful wave of national confidence and pride in Israel and throughout the Jewish world. A people who for weeks had walked in an almost palpable darkness was suddenly enveloped by an overwhelming sense of relief and exhilaration. Needless to say, the leadership and rank-in-file of Conservative Jewry were strongly moved by the events of June 1967.

One result was a rise in Conservative *aliyah*, both lay and rabbinic. It was not a mass movement but what had barely existed prior to 1967, suddenly became a perceptive trickle that would grow even stronger in the decade to come. Slowly, often starting as a minuscule *ḥavurah* in someone's living room, Israeli Conservative congregations began to sprout up, and, with the congregations, came rabbis to lead them. Although the Conservative *aliyah* was relatively modest in size, it was, nevertheless, determined to take its place in the Israeli polity.

In those early years, the active RA consisted essentially of two congregational rabbis, Charles Siegal in Haifa, and Philip Spectre of

Ashkelon. There were no scheduled meetings or annual conventions, no officers or committees, just informal consultations with each other about ordinary and extra-ordinary rabbinic problems, along with friendship and the joys and satisfactions of working in Israel. One is tempted to call this period "the heroic age," for the demands of the times called for extraordinary rabbinic fortitude and stamina on different kinds of battlefields.[18]

Rabbi Philip Spectre arrived in Israel during early summer of 1967. He had come to serve as a rabbi-teacher-advisor in Kfar Silver, a residential, agricultural high school near Ashkelon. For religious-political reasons beyond his control, the position at Kfar Silver did not materialize. The late Wolfe Kelman, in the New York RA office, was deeply interested in helping Spectre succeed and arranged for him to go to Congregation Netzach Yisrael in Ashkelon. Netzach Yisrael was then a tiny Conservative congregation which had been organized and was being led by Moshe Cohen, who served as volunteer rabbi. At the time of Spectre's arrival, the synagogue had twelve members. When Spectre left the congregation in 1982 to become the professional head of the Masorti movement, the congregation had grown twenty-fold.

About a year after Spectre's arrival, in the early summer of 1968, Charlie Siegal made *aliyah,* and began his work with the Moriah congregation in Haifa on August 1. Thus he became the second American Conservative rabbi and RA member to serve an Israeli congregation. A third Conservative congregation, Emet Ve'emunah in Jerusalem, was being led by Alfred A. Philipp, an RA member who was trained in Europe.

Most of the Conservative rabbis who made *aliyah* during this time, as was noted above, went to Israel to retire, or took positions in education or university teaching. The time had not yet arrived for establishing a more formal Israeli branch of the RA, which historically depended upon pulpit rabbis. Spectre and Siegal, the "working" RA, were in frequent touch with each other, sharing their thoughts and ideas about all the matters that concern congregational rabbis. Both men, for example, conducted active youth programs in their respective synagogues. Outings, trips, and holiday events were scheduled during the course of the year, and Siegal and Spectre took turns planning and supervising the get-togethers. They wanted their young people to meet each other and learn that others shared their outlook. In general, the two rabbis looked upon their personal and professional relationship as being, in some degree, within the context of the RA of Israel.

What was it like to be a Conservative rabbi in those days? As Siegal put it, "Aside from the usual things, preaching and teaching, youth work and going to synagogue committee meetings, the rabbis did a little bit of everything, from personally tending to the needs of the synagogue building to being his own secretary. Custodial help was not always available or was too expensive. The rabbi may not have had to wash or sweep the floors, but he often had to arrange the prayerbooks in the racks and remember to change the *parokhet* and Torah mantles for the holidays. As for secretarial help, he often had to do his own typing, or recruit someone from his family, or seek help from a willing synagogue member." Siegal also commented on the difficulty in finding suitable and affordable housing. In part, he believed it might have been because of his being a Conservative rabbi; some landlords were reluctant to rent to the Siegal family.

Spectre agreed with Siegal's assessment. He added that Israelis especially appreciated "a rabbi who worked with his hands, worked with youth, gave bar mitzvah lessons himself, ran a day camp and taught in the local TALI school." He emphasized that "being present," being with the individual or family in a time of need was far more important than talent or charisma. "A boy falls in war, and you spend time with the family. Not being able to officiate at a wedding or a funeral did not decrease your influence with your people." On the contrary, people became incensed at the disrespect shown to their rabbi.

Around this time, the late 1960s and early 1970s, Rabbi Moshe Cohen *z"l,* executive head of the Israeli branch of the United Synagogue and World Council of Synagogues, was busy organizing congregations and serving as the professional representative of the Conservative movement in Israel. Within less than a decade, the United Synagogue and World Council of Synagogues would merge into a new entity to be known as the Masorti movement, more Hebrew-speaking and more Israeli in its style and character. For ideological as well as practical reasons, such as sharing an address and office space, the Rabbinical Assembly of Israel, while continuing to maintain its separate identity and independence, agreed to become part of the overall Masorti framework.

There had been an earlier attempt in 1972 to establish a United Synagogue organization that would be based on the three Conservative congregations, located in Haifa, Ashkelon, and Jerusalem. This move was led by Rabbi Cohen, director of the United Synagogue, along with Rabbis Siegal and Spectre, all of whom agreed on the need for a closer and more formal relationship between the Conservative synagogues.

This first venture at unifying the Israeli Conservative movement did not succeed, some say, because of negative pressures from their counterparts in New York, who were afraid of losing control.[19] Those concerns were resolved and the trend toward unity did succeed a few years later in 1979 with the establishment of the Masorti movement. The new entity became the umbrella organization that embraced all the institutions of Israeli Conservative Judaism.

The World Council Newsletter published in Spring 1976 listed fourteen Israeli Conservative synagogues headed by rabbis; a fifteenth was led by a lay chairman. In addition, five other congregations were in the process of formation. The same issue featured an article about the groundbreaking ceremony of Congregation Magen Avraham, led by Rabbi Michael Graetz, in Omer, near Beersheba.

As the number of RA rabbis serving congregations grew larger, their shared problems and interests needed a more structured forum. With the rise in numbers, a critical mass was reached, and in the mid-1970s the RA Israel region was officially established. Rabbi Charles Siegal was elected president and regular monthly meetings were scheduled, with about 10–12 rabbis attending.

During these years, the RA still tended to function as a kind of rabbinic *landsmanschaft* group. Its order of business generally focused on basic bread and butter issues: techniques of membership recruitment, sharing homiletic material and program ideas, and the overriding need to find ways of raising funds to pay for congregational needs, including the rabbis' own salaries. Conservative congregations were not part of Israel's official religious establishment and, unlike most Orthodox congregations, did not receive any public funds.

Rabbi Siegal's correspondence reveals one of the stratagems used to raise money from overseas. He wrote to scores of rabbis and congregational officials trying to establish an overseas membership relationship with synagogues and individuals. One could become an overseas member of Moriah congregation for the princely sum of $10.00 per year. A synagogue could be a sister congregation to Moriah for the more munificent sum of $100 annually. Rabbi Siegal and his synagogue did much to earn a generous response from American congregations. They were cordial hosts to visiting synagogue groups and to families who wanted to celebrate a bar/bat mitzvah in Israel, a process which, to judge from Siegal's correspondence, took considerable time and effort. In one of Siegal's letters, he tried to explain why outside, overseas, support was so vital. Writing to a New Jersey rabbi, he said:

I don't know what type of facts to write you which will be helpful in convincing our colleagues of both the importance and immediacy of our needs. Perhaps they should know that an Israeli who earns the equivalent of $10,000 a year (. . . far above the average Israeli salary) retains only $4,300 after he pays direct income, defense and national security taxes, plus compulsory long-term loans to the government. This is the unfortunate reason why all public institutions in Israel are supported by funds from abroad.[20]

Both Spectre and Siegal were anxious to elevate the quality of their adult education programs by inviting top level guest lecturers, but this was expensive and out-of-reach because of the fees that had to be paid. They explained their predicament to Rabbi Simon Greenberg, a frequent visitor to Israel, and a man who always tried to be helpful to the Israeli rabbis and the fledgling congregations in particular. Rabbi Greenberg promised to assist in this matter and, in a relatively short time, managed to raise $50,000 from a Philadelphia philanthropist. Thus, a respectable speakers' fund was established.

Another example of the vital and critical help that came from overseas sources was the funding for Magen Avraham, the Omer synagogue whose groundbreaking ceremony was cited above. A major factor in its construction was the World Council of Synagogues which granted to Magen Avraham the sum of $25,000 provided by Congregation Adath Israel of Bronx, New York.[21]

The Struggle for Recognition

Without a doubt, the major issue that concerned every Conservative rabbi in Israel and especially those working with congregations was the unceasing struggle to win recognition and legitimacy as rabbis, along with the right to function fully and freely in the Israeli community.

The official religious establishment responded to requests from Conservative rabbis with three "no's": no to officiating at weddings, no to officiating at funerals, and no to presiding over conversions. No doubt, there were even more "no's," but these three were the basic ones that concerned the issue of rabbinic status and legitimacy and especially the rabbis' day-to-day relationship with their congregations.

The recognition and legitimacy issue goes back many years, probably to the moment when the first RA rabbi applied for permission to perform a wedding ceremony or a funeral. It was then that the Orthodox establishment realized that "Conservative rabbis" were not members of the "team," the official, Orthodox rabbinic confederation, but were different theologically, halakhically, and even stylistically.

As for the matter of style, one is tempted to wonder whether Conservative rabbis would have received a more welcoming reception had they looked more like Israeli rabbis, with black hats and suits, and fringes hanging outside their trousers. Lest one think otherwise, dress is not a trivial matter as common experience and the social sciences tell us. In the Israeli community, whether religious or even secular, there are many, perhaps even a majority, to whom proper clothing is part of the rabbinic uniform, and a man who goes about tieless, jacketless, and dressed in jeans or creased khakis might not be easily accepted for what he claims to be.

Clothing aside, the fact of non-recognition by most strata of Israeli Orthodoxy is longstanding, and the vehemence with which it often is expressed sometimes seems to grow stronger with the passage of time. Rabbi Philip Spectre related that during the 1970s, at a meeting of rabbis in Ashkelon, attended by the then Chief Rabbi of Israel, Rabbi Shlomo Goren z"l, the mayor of Ashkelon, who was a member of Spectre's synagogue, in good *sabra* fashion, straightforwardly asked the Chief Rabbi if he, reputed to have liberal tendencies, would help the mayor's congregation in the matter of recognition for the congregation and their rabbi. Rabbi Goren's summary response, as reported by Spectre, was just as direct and explicit: "Don't you dare bring a new religion into the city of Ashkelon."[22]

In 1980, following the first-reading defeat of a Knesset bill that would have granted equal rights to the Conservative and Reform movements, Chief Rabbi Goren, who strongly opposed the bill, replied to criticism "that only Orthodox rabbis are real rabbis, and their Judaism alone is true Judaism. The rest—why, they don't even observe *kashrut* and Shabbat."[23]

The rhetoric of denunciation can become even hotter at times, as occurred recently when the Neeman Commission's recommendations for compromise on the conversion issue were made public. A group of prominent Orthodox rabbis published a statement saying that "anyone who lends a hand to the Reform and Conservative criminals will be counted among the ranks of those who make the Lord's name hateful."[24]

On the other hand, in the same issue of the *Jerusalem Post*, Sephardic Chief Rabbi Eliahu Bakshi Doron was reported to have said that while he is ready talk to with anyone, he has less of a problem with the Conservatives. Although this comment was taken as a tactic of "divide and conquer," Bakshi Doron is known to make a clear distinction between the Conservative and Reform movements, being sharply aware that Conservative Judaism is halakhic and, therefore, "one can work with them."[25]

Whereas in the past the public had little understanding of the differences between Reform and Conservative Judaism, the many months of media discussion of the Neeman Commission deliberations during 1997–98 raised awareness of those distinctions. Nevertheless, the struggle for recognition and equal status has a long way to go.

It must be noted that always there have been exceptions to the "no's" and some rabbis have managed to establish better working relationships with the *"rabbanut,"* the official rabbinic establishment of the locality. Rabbi Charles Siegal, for example, was able to develop a friendly relationship with Rabbi Eliahu Bakshi Doron, former Chief Rabbi of Haifa, and then with his successor, Rabbi Shaar-Yashuv Cohen, which resulted in an easement in the matter of officiating at weddings. As Siegal described it, "a pleasant Sephardic rabbi was appointed to accompany me to all weddings. He served as a witness and signed the *ketubah.* Thus, everything was official." An American rabbi, who functions in almost total freedom and independence, might regard this arrangement as condescending, but the fact is that it worked unobtrusively and no one seemed to be troubled by it.

Siegal pointed out that he was known as a "right-wing" Conservative and perhaps it was this reputation that enabled him to make his way through the maze of the official Haifa rabbinate. Had he chosen to be an outspoken, militant Masorti rabbi, he, no doubt, would have been rejected by the powerful rabbinic establishment, to the detriment of his congregation. He saw his situation as a case of *ain bererah,* no alternative, and given the circumstances prevailing in Israel, his willingness to accept the rabbinate's conditions was an honorable way to serve and lead his people.

He also noted that, in his judgment, the struggle between the Masorti rabbis and the establishment rabbinate was, to some degree, over reasons other than theology. In blunt terms, the issue was money— rabbinic income. Conservative rabbis may have been perceived as a potential monetary threat to the establishment, and were bitterly opposed on financial grounds as well as for ideological reasons. Siegal often felt that the former reason may have been stronger than the latter.

Of the many anecdotes that describe the issue, the following is typical. Philip Spectre told of an event that led to an enhancement of his personal and his congregation's status in the community, if not an improvement of his relationship with the *rabbanut:*

A community social worker asked Spectre if he would teach Judaism to bar/bat mitzvah children who were students in a school for the learning disabled. These were mostly children from poor families. Spectre asked what specifically he should teach and the answer was, "enough to warrant having a bar mitzvah party." Spectre visited the school daily for a number of weeks. He taught the children some basics: Bible stories, Shabbat and candles, *ḥallah, berakhot,* etc. In the meantime, the social worker, who wanted to arrange a large, festive celebration for the children, started visiting banks and businesses in order to elicit financial support. The community, including the City of Ashkelon, responded generously and sufficient contributions were received to have one large bar/bat mitzvah party for the sixty children and their families.

A formal invitation was prepared with a note at the bottom acknowledging the generosity and help of the various supporting organizations and contributors.

The local Chief Rabbi obtained a copy of the invitation and reacted by vigorously opposing the party and the whole program. He called Spectre a missionary who was trying to convert the children to another religion. His opposition caused the businesses and the city to withdraw their support. The social worker who started the whole process became incensed and reported the story to the press. A day or two later, *Maariv,* one of Israel's major newspapers, published a scathing article about the City of Ashkelon. The headline stated: *Harav pasul, veha'yeladim p'sulim,* "The rabbi is unfit, and so are the children!" The article inflamed the community against the rabbinate, and although the rabbinate continued to oppose the event, their battle was lost. The celebration was held; the businesses that had withdrawn their support returned. The community as a whole responded with affection and good will.

Spectre regards this event as a major turning point for his congregation. Netzach Yisrael suddenly became a respected institution that does important things for the good of the City of Ashkelon.

Some think it was unfortunate that a praiseworthy end was arrived at by humiliating the opposition. It is always better if a negotiation ends with a decision that leaves both sides satisfied. Others say that it makes little difference. At the present time, the Orthodox establishment and Chief Rabbinate do not negotiate with the Conservative movement and will not concede an inch even when pushed to the wall. This argument will not be settled in this essay, but it may be helpful to state the middle position that was held by the late Rabbi Moshe Davis, among others. He believed that the nature of Israeli Orthodoxy is such that, at the present time, they will not make concessions. It is not in their nature to do so and, given the present political line-ups, they are in a position of power and can easily afford to be intransigent. The Conservative movement's only realistic choice is to continue building up its numbers by *aliyah* from without and, internally, by continuing to develop its institutions that serve the Israeli community. Israel is an intensely political society. If and when enough votes are mustered for the Masorti movement to become a recognized force on the Israeli political scene, the battle for status and recognition will be settled in the normal way, by political negotiation.[26]

The Military

Another issue that had to be faced was the question of military service. As is well-known, every Israeli citizen, in good health, with certain exceptions, is obliged to serve in the military. A rabbi can serve as *rav tzeva'ee,* a chaplain, or as a regular soldier; as the latter, he may do his service in a rabbinic unit which attends to various religious functions, such as supervising *kashrut* or arranging prayer services. Generally, only the rabbi of a congregation can attain the status of a *rav tzeva'ee.*

Rabbi Charles Siegal served as a regular soldier. Before and during the Yom Kippur war and for some years afterward, he put in long stretches of reserve duty, averaging sixty days per year. During the war itself, he was located behind the front lines, but close enough to be in the target area of Syrian artillery bombardments. In one of his letters, he tried to explain to an American colleague how terrifying the experience of being under bombardment is, and asked his colleague not to mention the matter to his wife, lest she become unduly frightened.

Rabbi Michael Graetz also served as a regular soldier, but during the Yom Kippur War he was in a rabbinic *ḥevra kadisha* unit. One of his tasks was to identify bodies which often were in very poor condition due to severe wounds and massive burns. A year after the war, when bodies were reburied in Israeli cemeteries, Graetz conducted scores of funeral services, thus functioning almost as a *rav tzeva'ee,* although he was still only a regular soldier.[27]

Rabbi Philip Spectre made an issue of the matter of being certified and doing his service as a full-fledged military chaplain. Starting in 1969, he used all of his *protek'tzia* and connections to arrange it, but nothing happened. However, he was persistent and refused to give up or become frustrated. Finally Spectre was granted the status of *rav tzeva'ee,* a full military chaplain in the IDF, but he was never called upon to serve, not even during the Yom Kippur War. When he demanded to see his file, he saw the word "Conservative" written in large letters of red ink. He protested, but there was no response. Spectre is a *rav tzeva'ee* in the IDF, but has never served in that capacity. This is another of the unresolved issues of rabbinic status.

The issue of recognition and legitimacy is by far one of the major continuing questions on the RA-Masorti agenda. If there is light at the end of the tunnel, no one has yet seen it. There is no shortage of suggested strategies, which range from a kind of passive "watch and wait" position to a "rough and ready" activism. Almost every suggestion has been attempted at one time or another and has been found less than successful. The opposition is single-minded, stubborn, and politically powerful in the Israeli system of coalition politics.

Was the late Rabbi Moshe Davis on the right track, that the Masorti movement simply has to wait until its numbers represent enough votes to give Conservative Judaism a rung on the ladder of political power? If so, from where shall the numbers come? Conservative *aliyah* from the democratic countries of the West has dwindled to a minute trickle at the present time. The hopes that were expressed years ago, that Israeli Sephardim, because of their historically liberal outlook, would join our banner, have not been fulfilled. Nor have secular Jews been attracted to Masorti views.

During the summer of 1997, about 200 members of Masorti gathered in an obscure section of the Western Wall Plaza in Jerusalem in order to hold a Tisha b'Av service. They had a police permit for their specified area. Naturally, it was a mixed congregation with men and women participating. Within five minutes, the group was spotted by ultra-Orthodox "protectors" of the Wall who immediately started an unpleasant ruckus. The police thereupon canceled their permit and, unceremoniously, instead of chasing the illegal "protectors" away, ended the service and roughly forced the Masorti faithful outside of the Wall area. So much for demonstrative activism.

Do those who counsel a "watch and wait" policy have a point? They remind us that from the perspective of history, we are a very young movement. As we have seen, Conservative Judaism in Israel was represented by a bare handful of individuals until the late 1960s. It was not until a decade and more later that Masorti achieved sufficient numerical strength to allow for establishing an organization. The

Schechter Institute of Jewish Studies has only a brief history, of not more than about twenty years. The first Conservative Yeshiva was formed in 1997, with some 12 to 15 students. There are well over a thousand synagogues in Jerusalem, and thousands more throughout the country, as compared to Masorti's total of forty congregations.

As for history, it cannot be overlooked that ultra-Orthodoxy, at its center, has roots that reach back for generations and even centuries. Those roots win them respect even from those who reject their ideas.

Of course, venerability and numbers should not be all that important in a religious framework that values wisdom, spirit, and truth. Yet it cannot be ignored. Thus the "watch and wait" attitude holds that the Masorti movement has to "earn" its right to legitimacy in the Holy Land and this, above all, requires time, people and money, the wherewithal to keep building our institutions. Our task, therefore, is to continue encouraging our people to settle in Israel, and especially to keep building a spiritual community worthy of the name. The struggle may take a hundred years, but in the end, when we shall have "earned" our rights, we will have them.

Nevertheless, Rabbi Ehud Bandel's impassioned protest voiced at the 1994 Rabbinical Assembly Convention remains the current watchword of Masorti Judaism: "Masorti Jews in Israel have had enough! We are tired of being second-class citizens, and we are determined to demand in a very clear voice what we rightfully deserve."[28] Bandel represents the activist stance. Only time will tell if he is right.

There is also another possibility, a kind of qualified activism that has potential. It is not an activism of parades and public demonstrations, but of money and hard work, and of battles that are carefully chosen.

A possible model is the Sephardic/Oriental community that has flocked to the Shas Party political banner not so much because of its extremist religious views, but because of its excellent social and educational programs. Shas supports good schools, and nurseries and kindergartens that care for children from early morning to evening, thus providing a good and inexpensive service to families with two working parents. Thanks to these and still other services provided to its people, Shas has become a growing political power in Israel.

The Masorti way is not to become a political powerhouse, but it would be interesting to observe what sort of result would be achieved if Masorti could establish a network of affordable nursery schools and kindergartens, and dozens, not a handful, of schools such as TALI, that offer a traditional curriculum of Jewish values along with an excellent general education.

This kind of activism undoubtedly would cost millions, but it might just work. And the money would have to come from private individuals and foundations, for Masorti is not eligible, as is Shas, for government support. That is why, at this moment, this program is only a dream. But Israel is a people of dreams, and this country began as a response to an irresistible dream.

Part III: From Landsmanschaft to Maturity—1985–1998

In 1992 the RA finally was able to move into its own offices. Although its association with the Masorti movement provided it with a mailing address, the office facilities were too small to provide space for both organizations. Not having an administrative professional, a secretary, office equipment, nor the funds to acquire any of these, the RA was compelled to function administratively in more or less the same informal fashion as in past years.

In the early 1990s, however, the situation changed when funds became available from the international RA. Office space suitable for both Masorti and the RA was rented on HaRav Ashi Street, in Jerusalem's San Simeon neighborhood. Now there was room for offices, a meeting room, and an area for secretaries and office equipment. All this was in a relatively uncrowded, residential neighborhood, with plenty of parking space. The only limitation was that the location was far from the center of the city and a bit hard to reach by public transportation. But it was affordable and spacious and, for the first time in Israel, the RA Israel Region, now numbering about ten percent of the entire Rabbinical Assembly, enjoyed the luxury of a place of its own.

And along with offices came an even more important entity in the person of Rabbi Andrew Sacks who was engaged to be the RA's director. It was not a full-time position at the start, but it quickly grew into one. With Sacks as director, the RA was energized and able to become a more efficient and effective organization.

Even before these major changes, from the middle 1980s on, RA Israel had started to grapple with several new issues along with the old ones. Its four essential challenges were: achieving what was deemed appropriate recognition in the international RA; forming a Law Committee that would be responsive to the unique requirements of Israel; establishing an Institute for Converts under RA-Masorti auspices; and the fourth involved undertaking certain practical projects which will be discussed below. The major continuing problem was the issue of status and recognition by the established rabbinate, including the right to officiate at weddings, funerals, and conversions.

Practical Projects

Rabbi Michael Graetz, in a 1988 written statement, urged the RA to get involved in "all areas of religion which affect the life of the individual citizen," and which do not violate Israeli law. His examples were *kashrut* and burial, both of which were subject to laws that were sufficiently "unspecific" so as to allow Conservative *batei din* or supervisory committees to play a role. Graetz's aim was to widen the range of religious choices available to the Israeli citizen. In his words:

> Our movement has historically been loathe to get our hands dirty with the nitty-gritty, e.g., *kashrut,* burial, *milah.* We have preferred to be *"derasha"* rabbis, relying on Orthodox Jews for all our concrete religious needs. If we are serious about ourselves, and really believe that we offer a full Jewish alternative way of living, then we have no choice but to be involved in those matters.[29]

Graetz urged that the RA and the Masorti movement set up their own *kashrut* committees that would give *heksherim* and *hevrot kadisha* associations in congregations and/or communities that would attend to burial rights for persons who wanted to use our services.

Graetz's call for Conservative-Masorti action has borne fruit in at least one area, that of cemeteries. A new cemetery is being constructed in the Beer Sheva-Omer area (Graetz's home and congregation are in Omer) where a wide range of rights will be available to the non-Orthodox community, including officiating at the burials and the use of coffins. The *hevra kadisha* will be trained and supervised by Rabbi Graetz. One section of the cemetery will be available for the burial of persons who are not Jewish, or whose Jewish status is doubtful. This last provision will help to obviate the several scandalous incidents which have occurred in recent years, when Israeli soldiers of doubtful Jewish status were killed in enemy action, and were refused burial in regular cemeteries.

The Recognition Issue

The problem of powerlessness and non-recognition of RA rabbis and Conservative Judaism continued through the '90s, but a major change occurred during the spring of 1998.

During the summer of 1988, Zevulun Hammer, the Minister of Religion, announced a "world festive conference of community rabbis and leaders" in honor of Israel's fortieth anniversary. It was sponsored by the Chief Rabbinate and diaspora groups and would culminate in the signing of an appropriate document.

As one might expect, no Conservative rabbi was invited to the conference. Rabbi Reuven Hammer, then president of the RA of Israel, wrote a long and respectful letter to the minister, expressing regret "that this . . . divisive action has been taken in the name of the Government of Israel . . . and that a wonderful opportunity for promoting Jewish religious unity in the context of the reality of Israel has been missed." There was no response to Hammer's letter.[30]

Another "slap in the face" occurred during the same summer when the Jerusalem religious authorities withdrew the *kashrut* license from the Bernstein Youth Hostel, located in the Conservative Center in Jerusalem. It was eventually restored, but not until a strong public protest was registered.

In his comments about the *kashrut* license affair, Rabbi Hammer remarked that: "[a]t least until our numbers grow considerably we are going to have to face continuing problems." He urged that we respond "with the dignity of a self-respecting movement," and not go to the courts like a wounded animal pleading that our "master stop beating us." Instead, he argued that the Masorti movement should establish its own *kashrut* authority.[31]

These two incidents reflect the longstanding, seemingly intractable dispute between Masorti-Conservative Judaism and Israel's established religious authorities. But ten years later, for the first time, hints of change began to appear. This became apparent during the long months of the Neeman Commission's negotiations, which are discussed further in this essay.

Rabbi Hammer, the Masorti-RA's forthright and outspoken representative to the Commission, noted certain perceptible and positive shifts in contemporary Orthodoxy. The establishment rabbinate appears to be an inbred bureaucracy that may never change. It is afraid of losing its prerogatives and is not capable of withstanding pressures from ultra-Orthodox circles. On the other hand, a number of individual Orthodox rabbis, including some who are part of the establishment, are open and ready to talk and even cooperate with Conservative rabbis.

What is behind these barely perceptible positive changes on the part of some Orthodox rabbis? Perhaps it is because they are younger and not bound by years of lock-step resistance to any view that is not their own. Perhaps it is because their willingness to be open to others has enabled them to learn what Conservative Judaism is about, and to discover that it is halakhic and seriously Jewish. Whatever the reason, we dare to hope that it will become a continuing trend.

The RA of Israel and the International RA

Ironically, the question of status and recognition was not limited to the RA and the Orthodox establishment. A trace of it appeared to enter into the relationship between the RA of Israel and the international RA based in New York. The Israeli branch, with its one hundred plus members, represented about ten percent of the entire Rabbinical Assembly membership, as well as the largest RA region. The homebase of the RA in New York, 7,000 miles distant from Jerusalem, was perceived as being less than attentive to the needs of its Israeli members. At least, some of the Israelis felt this way. In particular, they felt left out of the decision-making machinery of the RA. Except for an occasional international RA convention or summer *kallah* held in Israel, or a visit by the officers, the Israeli RA had a sense that it was not part of the "big picture."

Although it had long been an official "region," this meant little more than the right to report on activities at Executive Council meetings and the annual convention. But as these were held in the United States, except for decennial conventions in Israel, Israeli rabbis had little opportunity to participate fully in the RA International; annual trips to the U.S. simply were too expensive for the low-paid, Israeli rabbinate; and for the congregation to pay its rabbi's expenses in order to enable him to attend the RA's annual convention was unheard of in Israel.[32] Attending the more frequent Executive Council meetings was simply out of the question.

Starting in the 1970s, the RA of Israel began to call for a change in the RA constitution that would allow for an additional, elected vice president who would speak for, and be responsible for, all RA matters having to do with Israel, such as the Israel Committee, convention resolutions, publications, funding activities in Israel, and so forth. Also, this officer would not only be invited to all appropriate meetings in the U.S., including the Executive Council, but all expenses would be underwritten by the Rabbinical Assembly.[33]

The RA in New York probably was more than mildly surprised when this issue arose. It had always assumed, as did most rank and file members, that the RA is a large brotherhood of devoted rabbis who are all for one and one for all, and especially for their Israeli brethren. And so it was, and is, in many respects. But when the *Emet Ve-Emunah* booklet came out in the '70s and expressed ideas about Israel and Zionism that were contrary to the views and experience of many Israeli members, and when a new executive vice president was chosen without any Israeli input, and other similar matters arose, the RA of Israel felt unrepresented in what was their primary professional association. This is not to say that there was an objection to the new RA executive vice president—there wasn't; nor was there any denial of the right of American RA members to express their mind in *Emet Ve-Emunah:* it was only that they, a full ten percent of the worldwide Rabbinical Assembly, had no say in the matters under consideration.

Emet Ve-Emunah is a useful case in point. It was intended to be a "Statement of Principles of Conservative Judaism." The Israelis, however, were troubled by its perceived *pareve* tone toward Israel, its failure to address the issue of Conservative *aliyah* more positively, and its repeated focus on "various important centers" of Jewish life in the world, with Israel being merely one of them. Contrast this with the statement in a pamphlet entitled *The Movement of Masorti Judaism in Israel,* which states categorically: "The Masorti Movement believes in the paramount importance of a Jewish State in the Land of Israel in order to ensure the continued physical and spiritual existence of the Jewish people. The movement views the building of the land and the nation as a primary mitzvah, and believes that Israel must be the cultural center of the Jewish nation." The difference in tone and contents will be apparent to anyone who reads both pamphlets.

Rabbi Joel Meyers, executive vice president of the Rabbinical Assembly, agreed with the above assessment of the tensions between New York and Israel. He indicated that the International RA is aware of and sensitive to the situation and that much is being done to ease the relationship and encourage an atmosphere of "collegiality and cooperation." He further stated that:

> . . . the very complexity of the Israel RA requires extreme goodwill and collegiality on everyone's part. After all, within the Israel RA are not only colleagues serving Israeli congregations and institutions within our movement in Israel, but colleagues who serve institutions and in various positions having nothing to do with the movement or with religious life whatsoever. Moreover, there is the large number of retired rabbis residing in Israel. Add to this mixture the inevitable

differences between Anglo-Saxon colleagues and Sabra colleagues. And, finally mix it all with the volatile emotions of Israeli politics . . . I give great credit to all of our colleagues who are continuing to participate in the RA . . . From our perspective here, it is very important that we all work to keep a coherent Rabbinical Assembly and that we all see ourselves as part of an international rabbinic family.[34]

The tensions were considerably eased when the RA, realizing the seriousness of the matter, decided to give the Israel region the right to appoint a representative to the Executive Council (usually the president) who would be invited to all meetings, expenses paid. Unlike other regions, which have representation on the Executive Council only every few years, this would be an exceptional and permanent arrangement, thus providing the RA of Israel with a continuous presence on the RA's main policy-making body.

Beyond this necessary arrangement, the newest developments in international communications—E-mail and fax machines at present, and who knows what fabulous equipment will be available in the future— have greatly eased the problem of keeping in touch. As this is being written, the cost of a telephone call from Israel to New York is about $.25 per minute, down from $3.00 per minute, a year or two ago. Now, the only remaining communication problem is less easy to solve; namely, the seven hour time difference between the two countries. When Israelis are enjoying *seudat eser* (10 A.M. breakfast), most Americans are fast asleep, and so are Israelis when New Yorkers are beginning to think about sitting down to dinner.

The Vaad Halakhah

Another of the new challenges facing RA Israel was in the area of halakhah. It is a truism to say that Masorti-Conservative Judaism was and continues to be an halakhic movement. The ways of Jewish observance, the discipline of the Law, the definitions of personal status in accordance with birth, marriage, divorce and conversion, and the rites and ceremonies of daily Jewish living are all part of the sacred halakhic framework of Jewish existence as perceived by Conservative Judaism.

At the same time, Conservative Judaism differs from other groups within Judaism. It stands apart from Reform Judaism which is non-halakhic, and from the Orthodox, in that Conservative Judaism's halakhic perspective is more open, liberal and responsive to the changing conditions of Jewish life. For many years, the body within Conservative Judaism that was responsible for deciding halakhic issues was the Rabbinical Assembly's Committee on Jewish Law and Standards (CJLS). The Israeli rabbis, however, had a problem with this committee. The Israelis faced different halakhic problems and questions from those being considered by the CJLS, which dealt primarily with issues that arose in the United States and Canada. Therefore, during the summer of 1985, the RA of Israel decided to establish its own Law Committee, under the chairmanship of the late Rabbi Theodore Friedman, and later, Rabbi David Golinkin.

In 1987, Rabbi Golinkin, speaking for the Israel Region, reported to the RA concerning the work of the Israel Region Law Committee. In its first year (5746), eight formal *teshuvot* were written, including these: Is it permissible to milk sheep on Shabbat? In the light of the rebirth of the State of Israel and the Six Day War victory, is it permissible to fast only until *minhah* on Tisha B'Av? How should Kibbutz Hannaton, a Conservative agricultural kibbutz, observe the *shmittah* year? Obviously, these questions were not likely to arise in the Jewish communities of North America.

The following three fuller examples are from two volumes of *The Rabbinical Assembly of Israel Law Committee Responsa:*

1. Can the scheduling of *hakafot* on Simḥat Torah be changed?
The problem is that in Israel, where only one day of Yom Tov is observed at the end of the Sukkot festival, the liturgy of Simḥat Torah and Shemini Atzeret are combined into a single morning, making for a long and complex service. Further, since the joyous Torah processions are scheduled to take place before the Torah reading, and the solemn prayers of Yizkor are recited shortly after the Torah and Haftarah are read, the serious mood of Yizkor often is disrupted. Is it permissible to adjust the service so that Yizkor is not overwhelmed by the high spirits of the *hakafot*? The answer given is that the *hakafot* may be shifted to the end of the service, thus minimizing their effect on the somber tone of Yizkor.[35]

2. Can the Purim Megillah be read early in a time of emergency?
This question came up during the Scud missile attacks on Israel in 1991, when it was illegal to hold public meetings at night when the attacks usually occurred. The *teshuvah* discussed the halakhic precedents for such situations and ruled that it was halakhically legitimate to read the Megillah during the late afternoon in order to arrive home before dark.[36]

3. A final example concerns the conscription of full-time yeshiva stu-

dents who are presently automatically exempt from serving in Israel's armed forces. Rabbi Reuven Hammer, author of the *teshuvah*, reviews the halakhic literature concerning wars of defense and rules that serving in IDF is an halakhic duty "incumbent on every Jew living in the State of Israel."[37] Clearly, each of the above *she'elot* and *teshuvot* apply most directly to conditions in Israel and help to explain why the RA of Israel decided that the Masorti movement needed its own Law Committee. While theoretically, any of the issues described above could have been dealt with by any competent *"hutz-la-aretz"* halakhist, the problem might have seemed distant and abstract, while for the Israeli it was very real and urgent.

Creating an Israeli Law Committee parallel to the long-established CJLS may have been, for a time, a source of tension and friction. Happily this soon subsided and the two Law Committees have an amicable and cooperative relationship.

Who is a Jew? The Conversion Issue

One of the major issues that involved the RA of Israel over the years was that of performing conversions. Like all questions of personal status and Jewish identity (marriage, divorce, burial), conversion, by Israeli law, was under the jurisdiction of the Chief Rabbinate, and conversions (marriages and divorces also) done by non-Orthodox rabbis were not legal. The only exception to this ruling was a conversion that took place outside of Israel. A person converted to Judaism under non-Orthodox auspices overseas would be registered as a Jew upon making *aliyah* to Israel.

In 1988, the Orthodox faction in the Knesset sought to block the above-mentioned "overseas" loophole by extending the law to exclude people who were converted outside of Israel. The proposed legislation would insert the phrase *giyur ke'halakha,* "conversion in accordance with the halakhah" into the existing legislation. By this means, the Orthodox rabbinate would be given the authority to disallow any conversion not done under their "halakhic" auspices. Conservative conversions, despite their being done in accordance with halakhah, would be invalidated.

This was the basis of the so-called "Who is a Jew?" controversy of the late 1980s. Some acute observers called it the "Who is a rabbi?" controversy, for it was not really about the halakhic requirements for conversion, but rather about the rabbi who supervised the conversion.

The law might have passed in the Knesset had it not been for a powerful backlash in the Diaspora. World Jewry, with its many hundreds of thousands of Conservative and Reform Jews, raised a massive outcry against what they regarded as an act of disenfranchisement wielded against them. The Israeli government heeded the message and the Knesset legislation was withdrawn.

All the while, both before and after the "Who is a Jew" debacle, the conversion issue was especially frustrating to Israeli congregational rabbis who were unable to serve their communities in yet another vital area. They were asked to convert non-Jewish children from overseas who were adopted by Jewish families; gentiles living and working in Israel wanted to become Jewish; thousands of Russian immigrants who were pouring into the country and whose Jewishness was in doubt, needed conversion. Yet most Conservative rabbis were not legally empowered to perform conversions. The exceptions were a handful of individual rabbis who were able to establish a relationship with the local rabbinical authorities.

During the 1980s, the RA created a Committee on Conversion *(Vaadat HaGiyur)* that would focus on searching for possible solutions. One undertaking that made some progress but ultimately failed involved working with the Rabbinical Council of America (RCA). In a "Proposal for a Joint Conversion Committee," a set of conditions was delineated, including the following: rabbis of all participating groups would be permitted to teach; conversion would require belief in God and *mitzvot,* immersion and, for males, circumcision; in the interest of Jewish unity, all candidates, if certified by the Committee, would be referred to the Chief Rabbinate for conversion; if the Chief Rabbinate did not do the conversion within a reasonable time, it could be performed by an individual rabbi. Such a conversion by an individual rabbi, however, would not carry any sort of endorsement by the Institute.[38]

For various reasons, mostly on the Orthodox side, this promising attempt at cooperation was not able to get off the ground. The result was a 1989 decision to establish a Conversion Institute *(Machon HaGiyur)* under Masorti-RA auspices. Some of the conditions stated then were that the Institute, headed by a *beit din,* would work openly even to the extent of advertising its services in the press. Candidates would be instructed by professional teachers who would be paid for their services. While the Institute could not guarantee its converts full Jewish status under Israeli law, the Masorti movement and the RA would try their best to secure these rights in court, if necessary.[39]

The process has been beset with frustrating problems. The *Machon HaGiyur* has been busy guiding its conversion candidates since its creation in 1989. These conversions are still unrecognized under Israeli law. One working solution has been to refer successful candidates to Conservative *batei din* abroad, including France, England, South America, and the United States, where the conversion can be completed, thus hoping to take advantage of the overseas loophole. Over the years, about twenty percent of the *Machon HaGiyur* candidates have followed this path with varying success. The other eighty percent have simply chosen to go about their lives without bothering to seek official Israel government status as a Jew.

In recent years, however, the overseas loophole has changed for the worse. The government offices have imposed additional requirements: the applicant's conversion must take place in the country of his/her birth; the conversion must have taken place long before the person's *aliyah;* the new convert must not have lived in Israel before the conversion, and so forth; the rules and regulations can change without notice. Recalling the old Yiddish saying that it is *shver tzu zein a Yid,* one hardly knows which is more difficult, to be a Jew, or to try to become one—under Masorti auspices in the Jewish homeland.

The Neeman Commission

In 1997–98, ten years after the establishment of the *Machon HaGiyur,* the conversion crisis arose again in the Knesset. A highly publicized event took place during 1995, when the RA *beit din* converted a number of children adopted by Israeli families. When the government refused to register these children as Jews, Masorti and the Reform movement went to court in behalf of their converts.

The religious parties responded by proposing legislation that would require all converts to be approved by the Chief Rabbinate. This legislation, if passed, would effectively not only disqualify the children, but would also close the loophole for overseas converts who, heretofore, were registered as Jews.

Again, as in 1988, a large public outcry ensued, from diaspora communities that regarded the proposed legislation as an insulting infringement on their rabbis and their status as Jews. This time, the diaspora backlash was so powerful and threatening that the government sought to find some sort of compromise that would cool the situation. Thus, the Neeman Commission was formed with the agreement of both sides, the Orthodox religious parties and the Masorti and Reform movements.

The Committee was chaired by Yaakov Neeman, the Minister of Finance in the Netanyahu government. A religious man, he was highly regarded by all sides. The committee would be composed of representatives from each group and an acceptable compromise would be sought that would obviate both the lawsuit and the legislation.

As with all things political in Israel, selecting the Masorti representatives for Neeman Commission was anything but simple. The problem was not in the RA but in the Israel government's predilection to deal with Americans rather than with the Masorti leadership in Israel. According to Joel Meyers, Prime Minister Netanyahu requested that he and Jerome Epstein of the United Synagogue serve as delegates during the preliminary negotiations which led to the formation of the Neeman Commission. Meyers and Epstein, however, insisted that they be joined by Rabbis Reuven Hammer and Gil Nativ. And so it went throughout the preliminary negotiations leading to the establishment of the commission: ". . . it was obvious that the government of Israel, the Prime Minister, Natan Sharansky and others from the Cabinet were negotiating with the American Conservative Movement and the Reform Movement leadership."[40]

The Israeli government, no doubt, was more interested in mollifying American Jews who were outraged over the conversion issues, than in negotiating with local, Israeli Masorti and Reform leaders. Rabbis Meyers and Epstein, nevertheless, held their ground, insisting that Israeli Masorti/RA delegates have the primary roles in the negotiations. Rabbis Reuven Hammer and Ehud Bandel understood this task and represented the Masorti/Conservative position throughout the Neeman Commission's deliberations.

It was a very difficult process. The committee met for many months until, finally, after a number of extensions of its mandate, a modest compromise was reached. Some would call it an almost total victory for the Orthodox establishment. Essentially it said that non-Orthodox rabbis could participate in the instructional part of a prospective conversion institute and that the Chief Rabbinate would supervise all the rest, including the curriculum and the *beit din*.

Almost immediately, the ultra-Orthodox community rejected the whole thing. They would have nothing to do with Conservative and Reform rabbis. The RA met and struggled hard over whether or not to accept the compromise. Letters and faxes flew back and forth across the ocean with advice from every side. In the end, the RA of Israel decided to accept, mostly on the grounds that every hard journey begins with a single step. In this instance, the single step was an act of positive recognition accorded the RA and its representatives for the first time ever by the rabbinic establishment, especially the Orthodox members of the Neeman Committee. This was a first and it appeared to be a foundation from which to build.

But after all this, the compromise fell apart when the Chief Rabbinate refused to accept it. The RA's position was that they had gone as far as they could in bending to the demands and limits of the compromise. If the Chief Rabbis would neither accept the compromise nor meet with the members of the committee, it was all over, at least for the time being.

And so it is as of this writing, April 1998. Some technical ideas for performing conversions have been proposed but none solve the basic dilemma; namely, the refusal of the Chief Rabbis to support non-Orthodox involvement in the conversion process.

Was it a defeat for Conservative Judaism in Israel? Some may think so, and others hope so. But Reuven Hammer, the Masorti representative on the Neeman Committee for all those many months believes otherwise. He writes:

> The position of the Masorti Movement in Israel today is so far above what it was last June [1997] as to be unimaginable. From a group that was virtually unknown in Israel, that was constantly confused with the Reform, that was not recognized in any way by the government, that was not a partner for discussions much less for projects with either Orthodox parties or Orthodox Rabbis, we have become the central topic of discussion of the government, the Knesset and the Chief Rabbinate, and a topic of importance to Mafdal and Meimad. Not only did prominent Orthodox Rabbis participate in the deliberations of the Neeman Commission but they continue to appear with our representatives on panels. Even the Chief Rabbinate—for all of its statements—has also come to know what we are and to know us for ourselves. We have not only opened up cracks in the wall of the rabbinic monopoly, we have put the rabbinate on the defensive. The *Jerusalem Post* editorial entitled "Irrelevant rabbinate" says it all.[41]

Of all the difficulties and challenges faced by RA members who have chosen to make Israel their home and the locale where they would carry out their profession and calling, none has been more trying and frustrating than the brick wall of disdain and nonrecognition. If the hopes expressed above come to some degree of realization, our efforts in behalf of Judaism and Jewish life in the Land of Israel will be even more fruitful than in the past. To paraphrase the noted historian, Salo Baron: if current trends continue, there will be a bright future for the Conservative movement in Israel.

If in the next half-century, when Israel celebrates its centennial anniversary of independence, there is a multiple of just five times the present number of Conservative rabbis, educators, Jews, synagogues, institutions of higher learning, TALI schools and yeshivot:

650 rabbis, serving as educators, teachers and synagogue leaders;
100,000 Conservative/Masorti Jews
5 institutions of higher learning;
150 TALI schools;
5 yeshivot;
200 synagogues. . .

If in fifty years there will be just five times our present numbers, of synagogues, rabbis, schools and Conservative Jews, Conservative-Masorti Judaism will have grown into its rightful place in the Jewish homeland, and will have the institutional strength and moral energy to undertake its awesome task, to labor, along with others, at elevating and sanctifying the spiritual landscape of the State of Israel.

This is only a guess and a hope, of course, but it might just work. And in a hundred years, we would be not five, but eight or ten or more times our present numbers. In that the Lord helps those who try, our work is cut out for us.

NOTES

1. It has been a joy and a challenge to research and write this brief history of the Rabbinical Assembly in Israel. The joy was twofold: the pleasures of research and discovery on the one hand, and the equal pleasure of reviewing the slow but steady and stubborn growth of Conservative Judaism in the Jewish homeland. The challenge has been the difficulty of finding reliable data and documentation that tell the story. Few written records exist. Something as ordinary as the minutes of meetings are mostly non-existent prior to the late 1980s. Much of the best information was acquired through interviews with colleagues and their spouses who have lived in Israel for many years and were gener-

ous in sharing their memories. Yet, as is common in such personal reporting, the recollections of dates, places and events are occasionally imprecise and the reader will have to be forgiving.

In preparation for this essay, I interviewed a number of people, and am grateful to each of them for their time and their willingness to share important memories. These included Rabbis Charles Siegel, Philip Spectre, Jack Cohen, Abraham Goldberg, Andrew Sacks, Reuven Hammer, Yosef Green, Michael Graetz, Prof. Moshe Greenberg, Mrs. Jackie Cohen and Mrs. Lotte Davis.

I am also grateful to Rabbi Harvey Meirovich for allowing me to read his recently completed essay, "The Shaping of Masorti Judaism in Israel" which will be published in the near future by the American Jewish Committee and Bar Ilan University.

With regret, the names of some RA members who settled in Israel during the early years before and after statehood may not have been cited. The records are sparse and I was unable to identify them. Members who had settled in Palestine-Israel during the 1930s–40s generally were identified during the course of the above-listed interviews. I apologize to any whose names should have been, but were not, cited.

2. *PRA* (1931), p. 34.
3. Telephone interview with Prof. Moshe Greenberg, April 1998.
4. *PRA* (1946), pp. 1–6.
5. Interview, March 1998.
6. Interview with Mrs. Lotte Davis, April 1998.
7. Interview with Jack Cohen, March 1998.
8. Interview with Herzl Fishman, March 1998.
9. *PRA* (1956), p. 11.
10. Ibid, pp. 118–119.
11. Bar Ilan University is the only Mizrachi-style university in Israel. Cohen's position there is interesting in light of Sidney Greenberg's suggestion that JTS rabbinical students ought to experience living on Hapoel Hamizrachi kibbutzim. Mrs. Moshe Cohen, however, told me that her husband was never addressed as "Rabbi" but always as "Mr.," during his years at Bar Ilan. She is certain that this was deliberate.
12. Telephone interview with Mrs. Moshe Cohen, March 1998.
13. *PRA* (1964), pp. 26, 27, 29.
14. Ibid., p. 41.
15. *PRA* (1996), p. 47.
16. *PRA* (1965), p. 68.
17. *PRA* (1981), p. 83.
18. Unless otherwise indicated, the material depicting the experiences of Charles Siegel and Philip Spectre is taken from interviews with them. Rabbi Siegel was interviewed on January 18, 1998, and Rabbi Spectre on January 29, 1998.

19. Meirovich, "The Shaping of Masorti Judaism in Israel," p. 2.
20. Letter to B.D. Schwartz, Perth Amboy, NJ, September 22 (no year given—probably 1972).
21. *World Council Newsletter*, Spring 1976, unpaged.
22. *PRA* (1975), pp. 47–50.
23. *Jerusalem Post* (December 26, 1980).
24. Ibid. (January 27, 1998).
25. Ibid.
26. Interview with Lotte Davis, April 1998.
27. Telephone Interview with Michael Graetz, April 1998.
28. *PRA* (1994), p. 112.
29. Statement by Michael Graetz, August 21, 1988, sent to RA members.
30. Reuven Hammer, letter to Zevulun Hammer, July 19, 1988.
31. Reuven Hammer, statement on Bernstein Youth center *kashrut* license revocation, undated.
32. In fairness, it should be noted that many American congregations do not subsidize their rabbi's expenses when the convention is in Israel, as the cost is quite high.
33. Reuven Hammer, letter to RA international president, Al Lewis, co-signed by 25 RA members.
34. Letter from Joel H. Meyers, September 14, 1998.
35. David Golinkin, *LCR* "The Timing of Hakafot on Simchat Torah," Vol. 2 5747, pp. 21–27.
36. David Golinkin, *LCR*, "Reading the Megillah Early in Time of Emergency," Vol. 4 (5750–5752), pp. 31–33.
37. Reuven Hammer, *LCR*, "Conscription of Yeshiva Students into the IDF," Vol. 2 (5747), pp. 67–71.
38. Statement found in Masorti-RA files, unsigned and undated.
39. Minutes of Giyur Committee, Rabbi Pesach Schindler, chairman, June 27, 1989.
40. Joel H. Meyers, letter, September 14, 1998.
41. For a detailed discussion of the Neeman Commission, see Reuven Hammer, "The Conversion Crisis and its Impact," in *Kehillaton* . . . ., No. 7 (March 1998), p. 5, and Harvey Meirowitz, "The Shaping of Masorti Judaism . . .", pp. 37–52 on the "Who is a Jew" question, and pp. 53–58 on the Neeman Commission.

The Rabbinical Assembly in Latin America

Shmuel Szteinhendler

Marshall T. Meyer's, *z"l*, arrival in Argentina in 1959 was the starting point for a new era of Jewish life in Latin America. A new rabbinical model was formed for the society and the community, a rabbinical model that broke with traditional patterns previously known in Latin America, sharing destinies, emotions, passions, anxieties, quests, and challenges with all congregants alike.

Up to that time, Jewish life in Argentina was based upon a transference of the European model brought by the immigrants, some of whom had arrived in the nineteenth century, others at the beginning of the twentieth century, and still more after the Second World War. Jewish life was centered around organizations such as the *hevra kadisha* (for burying the dead), the *hakhnassat kallah* (for dowering brides), the *hakhnassat orchim* (for helping poor transients) and the Jewish hospital. In addition, a large number of *landsmanschaften* brought together people from their home communities in Russia and Poland. There were also Hebrew day schools, four different Jewish community centers for social, cultural, and athletic activities, plus Zionist youth organizations such as Hashomer Hatzair, B'nai Akiva, Dror, Betar, and Habonim. Indeed, the community's links to Israel were very strong, and Zionist life in general was quite active. Unfortunately, Sephardim and Ashkenazim did not intermingle at that time, and marriage between the two groups was frowned upon, due to prejudice. Most significantly, the religious life of the community was conducted in an extremely old-fashioned way, and younger people and young couples did not participate.

In the early 1960s, when Rabbi Meyer founded the Latin American Rabbinical Seminary that today holds his name in blessed memory, he chose a quotation from the Prophet Isaiah, *"atem aydai,"* "You are My witnesses," as a motto. This motto was instilled in every one of the students who went through that house of study, enabling them to grow and develop in their rabbinic vocation. Their challenge was to be able to reach out with dignity, with authenticity, with passion, with Torah—to witness. The rabbi had to be able to encourage and motivate, to gather in the withdrawn, to respond to the younger generation, and to transform himself into a committed Jewish model. This was the approach to young rabbis arriving from different backgrounds: some were *morim* (teachers), others *madrihim* (youth counselors), and others were people who became connected with their Jewish essence through their contact with this experience and challenge.

The task was not easy. The establishment that existed at that time opposed the appearance of a new life option, one committed to a vivid experience of the Torah's teachings and that contained within itself the essential paradigm of *continuity and tradition.* Soon people learned about Conservative Judaism, whose rabbinate offered a promise of religious services where celebration was held not merely with systematic and formal prayer, but where there was also an exaltation of each religious experience, each melody, each *tefillah.* All of a sudden *Adon Olam* could be sung to a tune from a film, or to an old *niggun.* Rigidity was disappearing, formality was no longer required.

Thus, the first Conservative synagogue, Bet El, located in Buenos Aires, with two rabbis, summoned Jews of all ages who were thirsty for understanding, for learning, for searching, for questioning and finding answers. The new rabbinic model showed that Judaism was not removed from universal issues. It was expressed out loud for the first time that nothing human is foreign to Jews. Taboos were broken in areas such as conversions, poverty, human rights, and interfaith dialogue; and works of deep theologic and philosophic Jewish content were published, compiled by non-Jewish editors.

Spanish translations for the first time were included in *siddurim,* making all people present active participants in the service, not merely listening to the traditional *hazzan.* Everyone could join in and authentically live the experience of *tefillah.* Sermons broke away from the traditional format, discussing not only the *parashah*, but also relevant contemporary subjects. More and more people were attending; no advertisement was needed other than word of mouth.

A new style of celebration for b'nai mitzvah brought renewed spirit; children were learning, understanding and participating. They arrived highly motivated each Friday and Shabbat, with awakened desire for Torah learning, for sharing, helping, celebrating, living and growing.

Thus, a new rabbinic model emerged, a rabbi who could dance with young and old, cry and laugh, play ball and go bicycling, swim in the pool, and share *mahane* (camp) and *madrihim* (youth counselor) meetings. The triple meaning of *beit knesset* (house of assembly), *beit midrash* (house of study), and *beit tefillah* (house of prayer) was revitalized. Soon this model spread out, and from many different places requests appeared for this new type of rabbi. The word had gone out not only within Argentina, but to other Latin American countries as well; and their needs were hard to fulfill, as time was required for training a sufficient number of Conservative rabbis.

Theodore Friedman's help from Israel was essential, as one of the first requirements of the Seminario was that of a compulsory period of study in Israel under his supervision; and only after this and the other requirements were fulfilled, was the *smikhah* obtained. Extensive contact with Israel strengthened each future rabbi's commitment to the Zionist ideal, to Israel, and to the Hebrew language. On the other hand, the requirement of general studies resulted in a broad knowledge that allowed for widened contact with Jews and non-Jews alike.

Through the years the task of Conservative rabbis broadened. Where there was pain, rabbis were there to be seen. Where there was injustice, they were there. Where there was intolerance, they were there to raise their voices. In the same manner, wherever there was dialogue, affection, understanding, and solidarity, rabbis were there to share it. Eventually, Conservative rabbis occupied pulpits in distant cities of Argentina, where no rabbi had been present since the early years of the century, where chaos within religious life existed, and where all that was left were elderly *minyanim* and hopelessness about continuity. The task was tough, absent generations had to be attracted, reaching out to people who considered religion "out of fashion." The rabbis succeeded and a vibrant renewal occurred. Schools, institutions, even communities that had considered themselves ready to disappear soon found a new flame, a new opportunity. The fresh air of rebirth was awakening a Jewish revival. The Seminary students, future rabbis, strengthened the Conservative communities in both large and small cities, establishing a rabbinic presence for our movement in Argentina (Buenos Aires, La Plata, Mar del Plata, Tucuman, Mendoza, Cordoba, Rosario, Entre Rios, Chaco, and others), Bolivia, Brazil, Chile, Cuba, Colombia, El Salvador, Mexico, Paraguay, Peru, Puerto Rico, Santo Domingo, Uruguay, and Venezuela. Nowadays, rabbis from our movement, graduates of the Seminario, are also serving in Israel and in the United States.

Since its founding, rabbis from the Seminario have been accepted by the international Rabbinical Assembly. While celebrating the twenty-fifth anniversary of the Seminario, considering the large number of rabbis serving in our region, it was deemed necessary to establish some form of structure that would link us together. In addition, it was decided that it would be interesting to create working contacts with rabbis from other movements. Thus URAL, the Latin American Union of Rabbis, was established, with Angel Kreiman as president. Although affiliation with the RA continued, and contact was maintained with the RA central office, nevertheless, a need was perceived for a common agenda with all regional rabbis, regardless of their orientation. Unfortunately, the initiative did not work, as there was no answer from rabbis of other denominations. On the contrary, in more than one case, there were those who tried to discredit us. Later on, through the initiative of Rabbi Mordejai Levin, it was agreed that, to further the goals of the regional Conservative rabbis, an affiliate of the RA should be established, creating the Latin American Region of the International Rabbinical Assembly of Conservative Judaism.

First, a yearly regional convention was initiated. Later, Rabbi Mordejai Levin compiled information from the Committee on Jewish Law and Standards, and distributed it to colleagues. Subsequently, a regional Vaad Hakavod was established, and an exchange of information through the computer net was instituted among colleagues. Incentives were created to encourage our regional colleagues to attend international conventions, through the support of the executive vice president, Joel Meyers, and also that of the international presidents, Alan Silverstein, David Lieber, and Seymour Essrog, as well as Elliot Schoenberg. There was close contact with colleagues from the Israel region, and projects were shared with them.

Over time, a regional computer net was formed (RAVLAT), along with a bi-monthly bulletin. A Placement Committee for the region was organized, and books were sponsored for publication. Our region is often invited to participate in key events of the different communities, organizations, and institutions of the countries in which we are present. In relation to the discussions involving the *ḥok hahamara*, we had an active participation in the countries in which we serve. Rabbi Margit Baumatz serves as executive coordinator, and does an excellent job in maintaining contact with members, following up on projects and agendas. We bring colleagues and other professionals to our region to hold training sessions and classes. Together with the Latin American Rabbinical Seminary (obviously with the RA's approval), we have agreed upon a new edition of the *siddur* that will be based on *Siddur Sim Shalom*'s latest edition, and adapted to our region. Apart from conventions, in those cities where there is more than one rabbi working, meetings of the *kallot* type are held to share experiences, study, and even to celebrate.

On a personal note, being part of the RA has been highly valuable to my rabbinate, offering a sense of belonging and identity, an opportunity for sharing proposals, strategies, doubts, endeavors, searches, questions and answers with the diversity of a group. The RA has helped me grow and connect with colleagues from other places, and provides a source of inspiration to my rabbinate.

In order to widen the description of the impact of the rabbinate in our region, I would like to append this article with three statements from my colleagues which testify to the evolutionary and enriching process that our association promotes.

Reaching Out in South America

by Guillermo Bronstein

The history of the Conservative movement in South America takes us back as far as 1862, when two lonely Alsatian Jews, praying in a park in Buenos Aires, promised themselves that by the following Yom Kippur, they would daven in their own synagogue. That first congregation still exists, the Libertad Street Shul, close to the Colon Opera Theatre in downtown Buenos Aires.

Since then the aura of the Conservative movement has helped to develop and promote Jewish identity for many people, including myself and many of my colleagues who grew up distant from Jewish life.

The great milestone, both for the movement and for Latin American

Jewish communities in general, occurred when Rabbi Marshall T. Meyer arrived at the gaucho's shores in 1959. He became the young people's rabbi in the same Libertad Street Shul, established almost one hundred years before. Marshall, z"l, brought with him principles that replaced the old notions about what it means to be Jewish, and established a new rabbinic image. In our first years in Mahane Ramah, we began to hear about the World Council, JTS, and the Rabbinical Assembly. Those were for us the unknown sounds of a distant music, but in our teacher's mouth they really sounded like a mysterious tune arrived from a magic Jewish dominion. It's now so sweet to recall those great and beloved teachers who were brought by Marshall's initiative to teach in the recently established (1963) Seminario Rabinico Latinoamericano, teachers who widened our intellectual and academic knowledge of humanism, Judaism, Bible, philosophy, and other subjects: Seymour Siegel, Theodore Friedman (our dear "viejo" in Israel), Alan Letofsky, Gerry Zelizer (my bar mitzvah rabbi), Jeff Wohlberg, Jerome Epstein, Haim Avni, Istvan Veghazi, Hertzel Fishman, Shmuel Avidor Hakohen, Pinhas Peli, Moshe Tutnauer, Richard Freund, Mordejai Edery, and so many others to whom I apologize for not recalling their names.

Without Conservative Judaism, only the Holy One knows what quality of Jewish life we would have today. Without the Rabbinical Assembly, at least fifty rabbis would be lacking today in Latin America, and more than eighty communities in the region would be without Jewish ideologic and rabbinic leadership. Today, Spanish-speaking members of the Rabbinical Assembly serve from southern Argentina and Chile to Mexico, and even the United States and Israel.

Hundreds of Hebrew batei sefer (schools), sports clubs, libraries, and cultural centers have been influenced by the Seminario in Buenos Aires and by the Rabbinical Assembly rabbis elsewhere on the continent. Many of those institutions were once so heavily secular that learning about religion was forbidden inside their walls. That was true, for example, at the Hebraica in Buenos Aires until 1975, when a student of the rabbinical school was appointed to conduct religious services in the club's country place, some 30 km outside the city, where bar or bat mitzvah ceremonies have been held since that moment. The same could be said about Montevideo, Lima, Cordoba, Santiago, Bogota, Mar del Plata, Sao Paulo, Rio de Janeiro, and many other Jewish centers. It was understood that the rabbis within the Rabbinical Assembly had a message to transmit, knew how to do it, and to whom. It's true that large numbers of Orthodox circles bloomed in the '70s and '80s. Some of them belonged to the historic kehillot establishment; others bloomed and spread as a result of their reaction toward our achievements and successes. They and the people within them were never our target, but ours were surely theirs. Nevertheless, and in spite of all this, Latin American Judaism still needs dynamic answers to contemporary challenges. Our past success has been based on a foundation of halakhah and tradition, an understanding of mitzvot, a critical approach to Talmud Torah, and a constant pursuit of meaning in everyday life.

In future decades we will face very important tasks. The first is to broaden the list of communities affiliated with us, and not only nominally as is now true in many places. We must find these communities, approach them, and serve them with rabbis, resources, and programs. To some extent, this has begun. Colleagues are presently in tiny communities such as the Dominican Republic, El Salvador, and La Paz, and there was one in Quito. I believe that this is only the beginning, and that in the near future all Jews who speak Spanish will know and feel that the Rabbinical Assembly is there to serve them.

The second task is to turn our efforts to those and many other small communities that are in danger of losing congregations very soon. We have a moral commitment to them, a mitzvah to fulfill that can neither be delegated nor easily answered with sociological apology. Scholars tell us that this is the flow and direction of twentieth-century urban culture: minor entities tend to disappear and there is no strength to oppose that tendency. The colleagues in the Rabbinical Assembly cannot sit back and watch this happen. Dozens of previously active congregations seek to hand over their sifrei *Torah and to rent out their synagogues and social halls, simply because they feel abandoned by the Jewish institutional world. We should strive to use all our might and human resources, if not to save them, then at least to let them know that there is a rabbinical organization throughout the Americas to whom they matter. Permit me here to honor our colleagues who serve in distant and small synagogues in Argentina, Bolivia, Chile, the Dominican Republic, El Salvador, Puerto Rico, Cuba, Mexico, and others, for understanding and for committing themselves to this beautiful task.*

Rabbi Guillermo Bronstein, Associacion Judia de Beneficencia y Culto de 1870, Lima, Peru; vice president of the Latin American Region of the Rabbinical Assembly.

Half a *Yovel* of Rabbinical Service in Argentina

by Abraham Skorka

❧

T*he concept of* yovel *(jubilee) has been explained and utilized in a great many articles and books during the 1998 year in which we celebrated the first* yovel *of the State of Israel. This has inspired me to count the years of my own rabbinical service in Argentina in terms of half a* yovel.

Looking back on what has happened during this time, what appears before my eyes is the juxtaposition of two images. The first is that of the Yom Kippur War, which took place at the beginning of my rabbinic career, on Shabbat Bereshit 5734/1973. The bitter and bloody call to reality for our brothers in Zion marred the little dream they had after the victory of the Six Day War. The days were full with fear, anxiety and sorrow, when the possibilities of an atomic clash between East and West approached levels never reached before.

The second image is that of the social violence in Argentina which led to the terrible days of the "desaparecidos" (missing people), among whom the Jewish rate was very high, as well as the "special" treatment they received during the torture sessions.

There were years in which, after a long period of political proscriptions in Argentina—and under the influence of the terrorist movements in several places in the world—violent groups began to operate in the country in order to obtain governmental power and establish a socialistic regime.

Day after day, we heard about blasts and the terrorist attacks. The activities of these groups increased and many Jewish youth participated.

The pillar of Argentina Jewry was until then the Zionist movement, which had yielded many important fruits (kibbutzim in Israel were founded in the '40s and '50s by halutzim *trained in Argentina; one of the best networks of Hebrew schools in the world, in which Hebrew was the primary language, was established throughout Argentina. The influence of Zionism vanished and Jewish youth asked for new horizons, among them revolutionary causes. Then began the great development of the Conservative communities in Argentina (prior to then only a small number of community centers—founded by German Jews on the style of the classical "Gemeinde," with the only exception of Bet El," founded by Rabbi Marshall Meyer—were in the country). The task at that time was to show young people a modern religious way of practicing Judaism.*

Rabbi Meyer was the great leader in this turning point in Argentine Jewish history. Through his deeds, and in particular the creation of the Seminario Rabinico Latinoamericano, graduates played and are playing a significant role all over Latin America, and even in the United States and Israel.

During these years I officiated in two communities: in Lamroth Hakol (two and a half years) and in Benei Tikva, from April 1976 up to the present. Benei Tikva, founded at the end of the '30s by Jews who had escaped from Nazi Germany, saw its transformation from a German-speaking "Gemeinde" to a modern Argentine, Spanish-speaking community. Its members are of different origins (Polish, Sephardic, etc.).

At the same time I taught halakhah and Talmud in the Seminario. In 1984, I went to the Jewish Theological Seminary, and under the auspices of the Rabbinical Assembly studied "torat ha-get ve-siduro" with Rabbi Max Weine, z"l; and subsequently the Bet Din Le-Sidur Gittin was organized at the Seminario, joining the previously established Bet Din Le-Giurim.

In December 1986, I was designated Rector of the Seminario, a great challenge for the second half of Yovel.

Rabbi Dr. Abraham Skorka, rector of the Seminario Rabinico Latinoamericano, and rabbi of Congregation Benei Tikva in Buenos Aires, Argentina.

Between Life and Death

by Alberto (Baruj) Zielicovich

༒

*T*he five-year-old child looked out the window watching the group of people that had gathered at the house across the street.

"What's happening, mommy?" The mother answered that the little old lady who lived in that house had passed away. Very naturally, the child again asked:

"And who killed her?"

In the city of Medellin, Colombia, by the end of the '80s and begin-ning of the '90s, natural death was the exception. With a record of close to 120 killings a week, it was clear enough that life had no value.

I graduated as a rabbi from the Latin American Rabbinical Semi-nary in Buenos Aries, Argentina, and while in Israel at Neve Schechter, I obtained smikhah *in May 1988.*

In September of that same year, I arrived at the Israelite Union of Beneficence as rabbi of the Medellin Community. Violence had not yet exploded as it did beginning in 1989, when the government and the Drug Dealing Cartel of Medellin, with Pablo Escobar as its leader, con-fronted each other in a cruel and unmerciful war. Massacres, fire engines, abductions, and executions were daily occurrences. My wife Graciela and I decided to stand by our community, giving them emo-tional and spiritual support even though we were risking our own lives. I can today recognize the influence of the founder of the Latin Ameri-can Rabbinical Seminary, Marshall T. Meyer, who with personal exam-ple taught us to be leaders not only during the good times.

It was a very painful period. Burying a sixteen-year-old who was shot only for standing at a street corner . . .

Going to the morgue with the parents of a nineteen-year-old boy, community madrikh, *who was killed with 21 people at a restaurant . . .*

Right before Rosh Hashanah, being at the family home of a 70-year-old father, who suffered from diabetes and cardiac ailments, and who had been kidnapped. Together, we "jumped" every time the phone rang . . .

Burying a 25-year-old young man killed while leaving the university and then being in the company of the father when he received his son's posthumous medical professional degree . . .

Six years were spent surrounded by pain, and by fear, but also very much by love. I received unconditional support from my colleagues of the regional RA, as well as from the authorities at the Latin American Rabbinical Seminary. Their letters, but even more, the physical presence of those visiting Medellin during those terrible moments, gave me the courage to move ahead.

During that time I had the historical opportunity to participate in the beit din *formed in Havana, Cuba, which not only performed conversions, but also raised the first* huppah *in thirty-five years of communism.*

Today many of those converts live freely in Israel.

Rabbi Alberto (Baruj) Zeilicovich, rabbi of the Association Israelite Montefiore of Bogota, Colombia; formerly rabbi in Medellin.

Looking to the Future

Joel H. Meyers

A n historic milestone was passed at the Baltimore Convention of April 1999, as newly ordained rabbis were inducted into the Rabbinical Assembly. For the first time in the Assembly's history, rabbis from five seminaries of the Conservative movement were admitted into membership: from the Jewish Theological Seminary, from the first class of the Ziegler School of Rabbinic Studies in Los Angeles, from Machon Schechter in Jerusalem, from the Seminario Rabinico Latinoamericano in Buenos Aires, and from the Jewish Theological Seminary of Budapest in Hungary, a school with which the Rabbinical Assembly has had a long-established history. In addition, the Assembly continued its long-standing practice of admitting into its ranks rabbis ordained from non-movement seminaries who have accepted a commitment to its ideology and halakhic practice. Thus, close to sixty new rabbis entered the Rabbinical Assembly, all of whom would ultimately have positions in settings throughout the Jewish community and the Jewish world.

Could the eight rabbis, gathered in Philadelphia 100 years ago trying to establish a Conservative rabbinical partnership have imagined that, a century later, the Rabbinical Assembly would comprise close to 1500 rabbis, men and women, ordained in different parts of the world, yet bound together in commitment and dedication to common purpose and values?

The mission of the Rabbinical Assembly from its very inception in 1901 has been to promote and enhance the well-being and the welfare of the Conservative rabbinate, and it has done so by pursuing three primary goals: (1) providing for the professional growth, development, and personal support of rabbis and their families; (2) utilizing the strength of the Rabbinical Assembly to promote the growth and well-being of the Conservative movement; and (3) calling upon the abilities of our colleagues to influence the larger arena of Jewish life by taking leadership roles in Jewish communal organizations, Jewish education, interfaith, work and other activities. Similarly, a strategic action plan completed by a study committee in 1996 concluded that the purpose of the Rabbinical Assembly was: "To kindle the passion of the Jewish people in the service of God, Torah and Klal Yisrael, to energize the Conservative movement, and to support the Conservative Rabbi." The report went on to note several specific objectives to be achieved by the Assembly: (1) to provide for the professional growth and well-being of the rabbi; (2) to provide religious leadership for the Conservative movement; (3) to provide a recognized public presence on the national and international scene; and (4) to provide adequate funding for the Assembly to effectively do its work.[1] This, no doubt, will continue to be the mission of the Assembly during its next 100 years.

The very strength of the Assembly has always emanated from the collective ability of its members to influence and impact the people with whom we have contact, with whom we teach and pray, and who seek our guidance and leadership. This is true in every area of our rabbinate and in each of the areas of the rabbinate to which we devote ourselves. It is borne out continuously by the constant desire of the leadership of the arms of our own movement, and leadership throughout Jewish organizational life, to reach members of the Rabbinical Assembly, to influence us, and to secure our participation in other organizational efforts. Hardly a day passes in which we are not asked for our mailing list, or to participate as part of a coalition, or to support a project being undertaken by another organization. Everyone knows that we as a rabbinate have been able to mobilize our people in behalf of the Jewish community as a whole, in behalf of Jewish study and learning and the building of Jewish institutions, and in support of all causes that impact our community and the greater society.

As we celebrate our centennial, there are 1454 members of the Rabbinical Assembly. Of these, 753 occupy pulpits as senior rabbis, associates, or assistants; 502 are in various rabbinic positions in the Jewish community, serving as educators in day schools and afternoon schools, serving as university faculty, camp directors, military and hospital chap-

lains, and serving various Jewish organizational positions; and 199 are
retired. In addition, there are three honorary members in the Assembly,
non-rabbis who have provided extraordinary spirit to the Jewish people. Our 117 female colleagues follow a similar pattern of rabbinic
work as their male counterparts, with approximately 60 percent occupying congregations and 40 percent in non-congregational work. The
majority of rabbis work in the United States. About 10 percent of our
membership resides in Israel; 44 colleagues are in Latin America, including Mexico; 36 are in Canada; 9 in England; 2 in France; 2 in Germany;
5 in Hungary; 2 in Sweden; 2 in Australia; and 1 in South Africa.

While these statistics may be of demographic interest, they tell us
little about the trends impacting rabbinic work as we enter the twenty-
first century. First, throughout the RA's history, except the period
immediately following the Second World War, about 60 percent of rabbis have entered congregational work. Our records indicate that this is
a long-term trend and, if anything, is today moving closer to a
fifty/fifty split between those colleagues going into pulpits and those
going into other areas of rabbinic service. Despite what the data indicate, a strong proclivity persists within our own movement, as within
the entire American Jewish community, to applaud pulpit rabbis as
"real" rabbis while those entering other areas of rabbinic work are
deemed to be involved in lesser value of service. "Where is your congregation, rabbi?" is the standard second question every rabbi hears
following the initial query, "What do you do?" In reality this is not
surprising, as it is not surprising that the Rabbinical Assembly, as well
as the arms of the Conservative movement, devote large expenditures
of time and energy to serving the needs of congregational rabbis. Without congregations, after all, there would be no movement; without
congregational rabbinic leadership, there would be no committed,
involved laity to help create the synagogues, schools, camps, and institutions of a movement, all of which had a profound, wide-ranging
impact upon Jewish communal life and society as a whole. Nevertheless, one noticeable change has been the increasing number of non-congregational positions that have become available to rabbis within this
current decade.

These alternative positions, like congregational positions, have
begun to be viewed as positions of significance by the rabbinate and
are carrying status and good financial compensation, as well as interesting rabbinic work satisfaction. Thus, these areas of rabbinic calling
have become competitive with pulpit positions. For example, many

large Jewish community centers have created the position of rabbinic educator on the center staff, enabling a rabbi to teach and reach individuals in a creative and far-reaching way. The increasing numbers of Jewish day schools and day high schools have resulted in a call for rabbis to fill key educational and administrative posts. Hospital chaplaincy has become highly professionalized today, with the rabbi as chaplain being viewed as a unique specialist within the rabbinic family. Also, an increasing number of major private Jewish foundations have sought rabbis as their directors or as leading members of their staffs in order to help direct funding opportunities and help create unique programs in Jewish education, family education, and in Jewish social service.

While pulpits have continued to draw the majority of rabbis to service, the nature of congregational work itself is undergoing a change. Congregational leadership realizes that most congregations are composed of multiple constituencies, and a single rabbi cannot possibly fully serve all constituencies within a congregational community. Therefore, many more congregations are engaging second and third rabbis today. Notably, two congregations in our movement have four rabbis each on their congregational staff. Clearly, this not only brings immense benefit to the congregation, but it also means that the rabbis must negotiate areas of individual and cooperative work and together plan how to best benefit the congregational community that they serve.

In actuality, the daily work of the congregational rabbi has not really changed much during the past one hundred years: teacher, pastor, preacher, counselor, halakhic interpreter, community organizer, fundraiser, youth worker—the religious professional generalist, *par excellence.* What does change from decade to decade is the emphasis placed on one area of rabbinic work over others—preaching in one decade, programming in another, creative liturgy in a third. And, of course, the methods rabbis need and use to lead their people change each decade as rabbis are called upon to respond to new challenges of societal and cultural changes. As the century changes, rabbis are being called upon more and more to teach texts to their congregants and to help nurture their spiritual growth and deepening commitment to observance. At the same time, they are approached for religious guidance to the very complex and difficult issues raised by industrial and technological advances concerning the very nature of life itself.

A noticeable change has also occurred in the self-definition of success among rabbis, which is a reflection of issues impacting the larger society as we come to the close of the twentieth century. In the '50s and '60s, rabbinic success usually meant moving from a smaller to a larger pulpit in a major metropolitan area. Today, success may very well be measured by a rabbi feeling he or she is making an impact on the congregation and community, and choosing to remain in place rather than seeking to move to a larger congregation or a different community. Rabbis tend to remain in place longer today, especially in congregations of mid-size. Also, rabbis often consider first the well-being of their families and will choose to remain in place because their family is content, enjoying the community, friends, and their style of life. In addition, often both members of the rabbinic couple today are professionals and the rabbi's spouse must have a satisfactory work experience, as does the rabbi. Therefore, any move will involve not only a search for a rabbinic position, but usually consideration of availability of professional positions for the spouse. Finally, there is today a push to build a greater Conservative movement, one outside of North America. It is desired by many European communities, in England, for example, or Germany, or Australia, that Conservative rabbis lead congregational communities. The Rabbinical Assembly has been urging both rabbinical schools, as well as colleagues to consider service outside of North America in a major effort to increase the Conservative movement's presence throughout the world.

Among the more crucial changes affecting the rabbinate during this century has been the ordination of women and the participation of our female colleagues in the Rabbinical Assembly. The impact of the decision to ordain women made in the mid-'80s (and examined more fully elsewhere) is still evolving. The current 117 female colleagues in the Assembly represent less than 1 percent of the membership. Yet, despite their few numbers, they have had a profound effect upon the Assembly and the Conservative movement during these past 15 years, positively impacting our approach to prayer and our understanding of Torah, and helping us gain an ideal perspective on life issues. Female colleagues seeking pulpits continue to have a more difficult time than their male counterparts in terms of placement, but fare far better today than a decade ago, and placement is becoming much more equalized as our Conservative community changes. However, a pattern has emerged in which our female colleagues begin their employment in either pulpit or non-pulpit settings and then change their work settings early on (e.g., shifting from pulpit to education, or from education to chaplaincy, etc.) and/or working part-time as they begin to raise families. This is of special consideration and requires further exploration.

Great credit is due to Elliot Schoenberg, associate executive director of the Rabbinical Assembly, whose primary responsibility is placement director, and who has developed, together with the Placement Commission, an entirely new approach to the placement process. Most important has been that rabbinic placement is not solely in the congregational realm, but rather in terms of the entire arena of placement possibilities. Although, for reasons articulated above, congregational placement still must be the most important concern of the Assembly, there is also an absolute recognition of the requirement to help rabbis find positions most appropriate to their desires and abilities.

Emphases are thus placed in two directions today. For rabbis entering the pulpit, new sets of materials have been prepared. A descriptive booklet has been written for congregational search committees, describing the placement process, including material which should be covered by a congregational board and its search committee before an application for rabbinic leadership is submitted to the Placement Commission, including exercises for the search committee to do as a group to better enable them to interview rabbinic candidates. Special emphasis is placed on helping all candidates receive an objective reception for their resumes and interviews, especially female candidates. Rabbis are helped to define more clearly their own goals in searching for a congregational community. Help is given to determine whether a rabbi wishes to accept his or her own pulpit, or serve as an assistant or associate rabbi in a larger congregation. Once the process has been completed and a match made between rabbi and congregation, every new rabbi and congregation is asked to attend a transition seminar led by both an organizational consultant who has served as a congregational president and Rabbi Schoenberg. Moreover, the entire process for both congregation and rabbi is viewed not as placement alone, but as part of a dynamic process of transition, of moving from one congregation to another or from one rabbinic position to another on the part of the rabbi, and of accepting new rabbinic leadership and integrating new rabbinic leadership into the community on the part of the congregation.

For those rabbis seeking other than congregational positions, a tremendous effort has been made to explore opportunities with Jewish communal agencies and organizations, as well as with educational institutions. This has resulted in some of these institutions rethinking their educational programs and their integration of rabbinic expertise into their agency work or program. New positions have been created where none existed in the past, such as rabbi in charge of education at Jewish community centers or rabbi as spiritual guide and mentor within a day school. In addition, a special training program has been developed with the Federation Guidance Service to train counselors to work specifically with rabbis seeking help in changing rabbinic career directions and in sorting out options available. The Rabbinical Assembly has provided subventions for rabbis to participate in this very helpful program.

No matter what our rabbinic work setting, the central role of the rabbi remains constant, that of being an exemplar of Torah and its values in the broadest use of that term, and of being a teacher of that Torah and its values in all that we do. That, after all, is precisely what keeps the rabbi in the special role of religious leader and guide for our people. What we come to appreciate as well is that while fulfilling this mission, every rabbi's work undergoes evolutionary change depending on the rabbi's work setting, the rabbi's age and years of service, and the ever-changing nature of our Jewish communities and society as a whole.

We recognize, therefore, how important it is to view the life and work of the rabbi on a continuum from the time of entering rabbinical school through the many, many years of service and into retirement. This has led to the development of an entire series of seminars, workshops, kallot, rabbinic practicums and forums for rabbis to learn and to explore various aspects of the rabbinate and the dynamics of personal and communal growth and change. Thus, continuing study courses have been offered in Tanakh and Gemara, in halakhic development, in addition to seminars on practical halakhic decision-making with faculty from the Seminary and members of our Committee on Jewish Law and Standards, and practicum on kashrut supervision, counseling in specific situations, and other subjects. Two- and three-day workshops have been offered, focusing on developing strategies for change within communal structures, developing better adult education programs, helping to create more effective participation in aspects of synagogue and Jewish communal life. There have been special workshops involving lay leadership of congregations and rabbis in understanding how to build stronger partnerships between the synagogue staff and lay leadership, as well as workshops for rabbis according to specific areas of work, such as rabbis who are in mid-size congregations, or rabbis who are primarily engaged in education. Each summer the RA, together with the Seminary and Machon Schechter, presents a week-long study seminar in Jerusalem on a specific theme; and this past summer, for the first time, a week-long summer kallah was held in New York, consisting of serious text study, practical seminars on managing synagogue change and building adult education programs, and wonderful opportunities for fun, relaxation, and camaraderie.

Just as a great amount of time is spent with rabbinical school seniors who are entering the rabbinate, we have also begun to spend similar time with our colleagues who are contemplating retirement. Retirement seminars have been developed and RA senior staff has been available to consult with colleagues and congregations about issues surrounding this life transition. In addition, we have keenly supported the Retired Rabbis Association, which began five years ago, and meets annually for a major gathering usually in Miami Beach, Florida.

As part of efforts to create a more effective rabbinate and to build a more coherent Rabbinical Assembly, both Elliot Schoenberg and Joel Meyers spend time with rabbinical school students in the United States, in Latin America, and in Israel. They meet with each rabbinical school class in a series of seminars to introduce the work of the Rabbinical Assembly and practical issues in the rabbinate to rabbinical students. This is done in New York and Los Angeles. The executive vice president has met with rabbinical students in Buenos Aires, and every year there is a meeting in Jerusalem with all the rabbinical students studying at Machon Schechter. All of these are attempts to connect students to the rabbinate, to the Rabbinical Assembly, and to future prospects of serving the Jewish community as members of the Conservative rabbinate. To complete this area of work, a very important seminar, *Eit Machar,* is held each June with rabbis who have been ordained a year or two maximally. This special seminar is both an occasion for reflection and examination of that which was exciting and that which was unnerving during the first year of work as a rabbi, and an opportunity to look forward and ask what each of the new rabbis will be doing in the future, based on what they have learned during their first year or two as rabbis.

In addition, the Rabbinical Assembly has been the motivating force to bring other seminaries and synagogue bodies together with our sister rabbinical associations every other year to examine key issues pertaining to the rabbinate and Jewish life. To help in all of our efforts, we have utilized consultants and specialists within the Jewish and non-Jewish world. We have been fortunate in finding individuals who are willing to help the Rabbinical Assembly in many different ways, whether it is with the salary survey, strategic planning, or retirement consulting. Moreover, we continue to offer support and guidance for our colleagues throughout their rabbinic careers.

In addition to a very successful program with Jewish vocational service, which we developed in order to help colleagues who wish to think through various options of rabbinic service, the RA continues to maintain a "care line," enabling any rabbi or a member of the rabbi's family to talk with an experienced colleague, 24 hours a day, 7 days a week. And of course, the Rabbinical Assembly, through the good support of colleagues and other contributors, maintains an assistance fund for emergency financial support when needed, and continues to benefit from an endowed fund established by an early benefactor of our movement, Jacob H. Schiff, who provided a fund for rabbinic help. This fund also has provided financial loans and support in very difficult situations for colleagues and their families.

One of our greatest challenges is to ensure a balance on the committees and within the leadership structures of the Assembly that is representative of the membership of the Assembly, both in terms of halakhic practice and philosophy. While the RA is a rather broad umbrella, it represents a movement with an ideology and a unique approach to the study and interpretation of Torah. It is crucial that we maintain our shared vision, while respecting our differences. We expect much of each other as colleagues, especially understanding and tolerance, as well as a respect for our own diversity. One of the great challenges, therefore, is to integrate our membership well, to find ways in which we can meet one another and share views, as well as develop an appreciation for the different approaches we take in our rabbinate.

One cannot stress enough the importance of the willingness of our colleagues to serve the needs of the Rabbinical Assembly. Little could be accomplished without the voluntary efforts of the members of the Assembly. It is the energy, creativity and constancy of effort of so many that has enabled the Rabbinical Assembly to publish works of major importance, to provide leadership for the Conservative movement in North America and throughout world, and to provide organizational leadership within the movement and within Jewish communal life. The presidents of the Rabbinical Assembly have each brought not only a particular leadership style to the Assembly, but have served as spokespersons for the entire movement. They have given unceasingly of their time and energies while in office to serve both the individual members and the Assembly as a whole. Members of the Assembly have responded and volunteered to participate on committees and in projects, requiring great effort, and even financial cost, to bring benefit to colleagues and to the movement as a whole. The support for much of the volunteer work falls to the staff of the Rabbinical Assembly at its offices at 3080 Broadway. It is interesting to note that the first employee of the Rabbinical Assembly was Bernard Segal, who was engaged as executive director of the Placement Committee and was then appointed the first executive vice president in 1947. At that time the RA had a membership of approximately 400 members, and it was felt that full-time professional leadership was needed to serve along with the elected officers of the Assembly. The membership realized that there was a serious lack of continuity among administrations and that the increasing geographic spread of colleagues necessitated a central office and centralized functions, along with a consistent hand at the helm of the Placement Committee. Max Routtenberg succeeded Bernard Segal, serving as executive vice president from 1949–1951, and he in turn was succeeded by Wolfe Kelman, who served the Assembly from 1951–1989. Initially, each of the executive vice presidents also served as director of placement for the Joint Placement Commission.

In 1965 the Rabbinical Assembly engaged Gilbert Epstein as director of community services, freeing Rabbi Kelman of day-to-day responsibility in the area of placement. In 1959, Jules Harlow joined the RA initially as assistant to Kelman, and then was promoted to director of publications. As described in prior chapters, the period under the stewardship of Wolfe Kelman, Gilbert Epstein, and Jules Harlow was the period of great development and expansion of the Rabbinical Assembly and the entire Conservative movement. It was a time when the Rabbinical Assembly exerted tremendous creative force on the American Jewish scene, creating the Solomon Schechter Day School movement and Camp Ramah, and influencing much of the development of American Jewish life. As the key executive, serving nearly four decades, Wolfe Kelman exerted a powerful influence upon the development of Assembly activities and the direction of the movement as a whole. Through his constant concern and efforts, the welfare and status of the congregational rabbi improved significantly, not only for Rabbinical Assembly members, but for the entire American rabbinate. His was a constant voice raised in behalf of those less fortunate, in strong support of a developing halakhah, in urging constant cooperation between movements and organizations, based upon respectful reciprocity. He was a powerful force in shaping the postwar rabbinate and the Conservative movement.

Beginning in 1989 and extending over the next few years, the entire professional staff of the Rabbinical Assembly changed. Joel

Meyers succeeded Wolfe Kelman in 1989, first holding the title of executive director for two years to enable Rabbi Kelman to complete a full 40 years with the title of executive vice president, and then assuming the title of executive vice president to continue that tradition. He was joined by Elliot Salo Schoenberg as director of placement, and several years later the staff was augmented by Jan Caryl Kaufman as director of programming. During the prior decades, the RA had grown tremendously. It had also undergone several internal stresses. It was now necessary to consolidate the administrative structure of the Assembly, to lay the groundwork for absolute responsiveness to the membership on the part of the Rabbinical Assembly leadership, and to provide a deeper level of caring and support for the RA membership. Thus, the committee structure of the Rabbinical Assembly was strengthened and made more representative. The entire placement process was reviewed and the Placement Commission renewed. Seminars and workshops were developed to provide both text learning as well as programs of professional growth and development. Members of the professional staff and senior officers visit all the regions of the Assembly and there have been ongoing efforts to enhance connections between Assembly rabbis. The advances of technology have been utilized to help speed responsiveness to internal RA affairs and to reach out to colleagues in multiple ways. Several internal discussion groups have even established. Committees communicate via e-mail. The RA has developed a website for members and the general public. Support for the work of the major committees of the Rabbinical Assembly has been divided among the Assembly's professional staff.

With the increasing pace of communication, technological change, and enhanced, individualized work with rabbis, congregations and communal organizations, coordinating RA activities has become even more intense and time-bound. This has necessitated a constant flexibility and willingness to learn new skills on the part of all members of the Assembly staff. We take note in this volume of their efforts and commitment to the members and work of the Assembly: Arnold Marans, who has served with distinction and has been an indispensable asset as RA comptroller; Hoa Browne, who has served as assistant to the executive vice president for a decade; Helen Besofsky, secretary to both Gil Epstein and Elliot Schoenberg for more than 25 years; Amy Gottlieb, editor for the RA and managing editor of *Conservative Judaism;* Sara Gunther, our bookkeeper; Lori Brooks-Hislop who has been our receptionist for more than 14 years; and two part-time staff members, Annette Muffs Botnick, our research librarian, and Rabbi David Fine, who manages several projects for the RA. In addition to our permanent staff, the RA has had the good fortune of part-time help from a dedicated corps of rabbinic students over the years, who have served as secretaries to the Law Committee and as assistants to Elliot Schoenberg and Joel Meyers. Lastly, we wish to remember the long-time service of Laura Schwab who retired from the RA after 28 years as bookkeeper.

During this past decade, three major Rabbinical Assembly committees focused their work in directions which have had a direct impact upon the work and thought of the entire movement. The Placement Commission, functioning in a spirit of good cooperation, focused its energies on developing placement policies that encompassed the totality of the congregational setting for rabbis as they moved from rabbinical school, through decades of service, until retirement. For the first time the Placement Commission began to take an active role within the United Synagogue regional structures and began to hold seminars and workshops regionally, at United Synagogue biennial conventions and with United Synagogue regional staff. At the same time, the Commission strengthened its hand over the governance of congregations that violated placement procedures, yet showed itself quite willing to permit waivers to its regulations when doing so was in the best interest of the congregation and rabbi. After years of tension between the United Synagogue and the Rabbinical Assembly around the control of the Placement Commission and issues surrounding the placement of rabbis, in 1998 and 1999 the United Synagogue leadership was openly praising the work of the Placement Commission and its director, and applauding the efforts of the Commission to meet the complex work of helping congregations and rabbis match well.

Likewise, during this past decade, the Rabbinical Assembly's Committee on Jewish Law and Standards underwent a transformation in the way the Committee approached questions placed before it. The committee began to take an activist role in exploring issues impacting Jewish life and the life of general culture. To do so, the chairman of the committee, Kassel Abelson, and co-chairman, Elliot Dorff, established several working sub-committees that focused on bio-medical issues, family life issues, *kashrut,* and human sexuality. The committee issued medical directives to be utilized by all, advocated the *mitzvah* of organ donation, and grappled with many of the newly emerging issues of bio-genetic engineering. With the proliferation of organizations offering *kashrut* supervision and a variety of symbols being utilized by supervisory services, the committee tried to bring some order to the complex subject of *kashrut* supervision in order to provide rabbis with greater guidance and a greater comfort level.

Lastly, the Publications Committee has taken on a creative role in driving the Rabbinical Assembly and, by extension, the Conservative movement, in new directions. In addition to promoting publications internal to the well-being of the movement, such as the revision of *Siddur Sim Shalom,* the publication of the new *Rabbi's Manual,* and the work being done to revise the *Maḥzor,* the committee has determined that the Rabbinical Assembly should begin a new publications imprint and begin to publish popular works by movement authors. In addition, *Conservative Judaism* has been renewed with articles offering fresh perspectives on Jewish texts, issues concerning the Conservative movement, and the Jewish world at large.

It is interesting to note that as the 1990s draw to a close, the Rabbinical Assembly has produced a flurry of publications of major importance. In short order, there was the publication of a revised *Siddur Sim Shalom for Shabbat and Festivals* under a committee chaired by Leonard Cahan, which was widely received, and a follow-up volume containing the weekday *tefillot* is being readied for publication under the guidance of Avram Reisner. A new two-volume *Rabbi's Manual,* edited by Perry Rank and Gordon Freeman, made its debut in both hardcover and looseleaf format. A *Maḥzor* committee has been hard at work under the chairmanship of Edward Feld. New volumes of Law Committee responsa have been published by David Golinkin in Israel and by Kassel Abelson in the United States. Simcha Kling's *Embracing Judaism* has been revised by his son-in-law, Carl Perkins. The Publications Committee has several exceptional manuscripts slated for publication. In addition, one of the largest and most important undertakings has been the writing of a new *Ḥumash* commentary for synagogue use reflecting our Conservative approach to Torah. This volume, under the general editorship of David Lieber, with primary editorship in the hands of Harold Kushner and Chaim Potok, and with Jules Harlow as literary editor, is scheduled to be published in the spring of 2001. All of these efforts, added to the quarterly *Conservative Judaism* which continues to grow in leadership and in stature, mark a full publication program for the Rabbinical Assembly.

Beginning with the presidency of Gerald Zelizer, the Social Action Committee of the RA also began to develop a renewed program. First, President Zelizer urged the publication of a series of short pamphlets on contemporary issues. After the appearance of several of these, such as,

Are You Considering Conversion to Judaism? by Alan Silverstein, and *After Life* by Jack Reimer, the Social Action Committee began to produce an annual position paper on contemporary issues: immigration, health care, welfare reform, and the environment. This led to two rabbinic "letters," major essays, written by Elliot Dorff, for the Assembly: "This Is My Beloved, This Is My Friend: A Rabbinic Letter on Intimate Relations" and "You Shall Strengthen Them: A Rabbinic Letter on the Poor."

In addition to these efforts to disseminate the Assembly's position on contemporary issues, both as educator and advocate, the Social Action Committee has established an annual advocacy day in Washington, DC, which enables colleagues to meet with key congressional leaders and to press the RA's social justice agenda. In this regard, an excellent working relationship has been enjoyed with the Religious Action Center in Washington, through which cooperative efforts are organized.

In 1995, the RA attempted to establish a committee on contemporary Jewish values to parallel that of the work of the Committee on Jewish Law and Standards. This new committee would focus its discussions and ultimately its papers on Jewish thought rather than on halakhic matters. However, after several meetings, the committee failed to develop a focused agenda and its work ceased. It became apparent to RA leadership that they needed to find a way to maintain such exploration and discussion of theological questions. Committed to this idea, David Lieber was able to secure a grant to hold a Conference on Theology. This conference, convened at Camp Ramah in the Berkshires in 1997, brought together Conservative rabbis and academics from several countries for serious discussion of prepared papers. Papers and responses were subsequently published in a special edition of *Conservative Judaism* (Winter 1999), which received wide review and praise.

Perhaps one of the most important but controversial events of this past decade which has continuing implications for the rabbinate and the movement was the inauguration of the Ziegler School of Rabbinic Studies at the University of Judaism in Los Angeles. For many years, rabbinical students were able to begin their studies at the University of Judaism before moving to the Jewish Theological Seminary for their second and subsequent years of rabbinic studies. This served both institutions and the movement well, as it provided a group of serious students and role models for the University of Judaism and its undergraduate and graduate students, and at the same time, it enabled students on the west coast who might not otherwise have initially been able to spend their years in New York to begin their rabbinical studies. However, relationships between the parent institutions, the Jewish Theological Seminary and the University of Judaism, were not always the most cordial. There were constant signs of tension between both institutions concerning the relationship of governance and the funding of programs. The tension on the part of senior level leaders filtered down to the administrators of the rabbinical school program at the University of Judaism and the rabbinical school at the Seminary. A certain level of tension existed between these layers of the institutions, as well, concerning such matters as admission standards, admissions testing, and academic requirements. In 1994 the University and the Seminary announced their parting of the ways, and the University declared its independence as an institution, indicating that it would no longer be considered a member of the Conservative family of academic institutions. However, the rabbinical school training program, by agreement, continued in place. After two further years of increasing strain, the new president of the University of Judaism, Robert Wexler, who had succeeded David Lieber, announced that the University was beginning a full-time rabbinics program which would be independent of the University and which he hoped would continue to be part of the Conservative movement and its institutions.

The announcement of the formation of the Ziegler School of Rabbinic Studies sent reverberations throughout the Conservative movement and the Jewish world. The Seminary reacted with anger, feeling betrayed by its own alumni who headed the University and the new Ziegler School, and feeling that the Seminary, which had begun the University of Judaism, would in fact now be forced to compete with a new rabbinical school.

It was at that moment that the Rabbinical Assembly played a key role in not only maintaining equilibrium within the movement, but in moving both rabbinical schools and their leadership toward reconciliation. Alan Silverstein, who was president of the RA at the time, and Joel Meyers flew to Los Angeles just two days before Rosh Hashanah for a meeting with Robert Wexler, David Lieber and several other University leaders. In a frank discussion they indicated that they would support the new rabbinical school but that there must be respect and cooperation between both institutions. Rabbis Silverstein and Meyers indicated that the Rabbinical Assembly would establish a procedure to work with the Ziegler School to review curriculum and standards and would seek to have the rabbinical school graduates meet the requirements for admission into the Rabbinical Assembly. Rabbi Wexler and his colleagues pledged their support and help and expressed a desire to cooperate with the Seminary. When Rabbi Meyers returned to New York he met with Chancellor Schorsch and urged acceptance and cooperation. Meanwhile, the Rabbinical Assembly's Administrative Committee asked the Membership Committee to establish a curriculum sub-committee and begin to examine the curricula of all of the seminaries in the movement, but to especially focus on the curriculum of the new Ziegler School of Rabbinic Studies. The Seminary and the movement were concerned that the Ziegler School academic program, as proposed, was not strong enough and omitted a year of study in Israel from its curriculum. But here, too, the RA leadership urged patience and indicated that the initial curriculum that was proposed by the Ziegler School would no doubt undergo revision once the school began to admit students and to train them.

Now that the first graduates of the Ziegler School have been admitted into the Rabbinical Assembly, it has become apparent that the Rabbinical School is succeeding. Students from the west coast opt to study in New York, and students from the east coast opt to study in California. Newly ordained rabbis from both institutions are working in all parts of the country, not locating themselves either on one coast or the other. The curriculum of the Ziegler School has, in fact, undergone revision and extension from the four-year program to a five-year program, with a year in Israel. The deans of both institutions are in regular consultation. The senior students from both institutions spend a week together each winter in New York in practical seminars and at interviews for rabbinic positions, all sponsored by the RA. Obviously, the culture and the education at both institutions are different, but the students from both institutions are well prepared to be rabbis.

Meanwhile, the Membership Committee, under the guidance of its chairman, Alvin Berkun, began an extensive review of the curricula at the other movement seminaries. As a result of the review at the Seminario Rabinico in Latin America and the other rabbinical schools of our movement, it became apparent that the Rabbinical Assembly would have to play an increasing role in drawing all of the schools closer together and in unifying certain aspects of rabbinic training. Precisely because rabbis who work in all parts of the world and in all areas of Jewish life look to the Rabbinical Assembly for placement, for support and guidance, for collegiality, and for a common sense of mission and direction as a part of a worldwide Conservative presence, the Assembly must continue to assume a strong coordinating and cooperative role in the education and training of rabbis. The long-term health and strength of the Conservative movement depend upon it.

The Rabbinical Assembly has always been an active force within the Jewish organizational structure of the United States and an active participant with other major organizations and coalitions seeking to promote the welfare of society as a whole. Whether in relation to other Jewish religious movements or to major Jewish organizations, the RA has pursued a consistent course of action. On the one hand it has been an advocate for positions articulated by the Assembly and by the movement, whether they be religious, social or political, and at the same time the RA has been a strong advocate for finding a common ground, with a willingness to participate in coalitions and programs of other movements and organizations, rather than seeking to create its own or duplicate what currently exists. The Assembly leadership has steadfastly refused to be drawn into negative debates and campaigns and has consistently sought out positive avenues for cooperative engagement and development of common programs which would benefit the Jewish community as a whole, while maintaining the integrity of the RA's positions. This has led to the Rabbinical Assembly being a sought-after participant in crucial areas of Jewish communal organizational work.

For example, the president and the executive vice president of the RA are active participants in the Conference of Presidents of Major Jewish Organizations, where the Rabbinical Assembly is a voting member. Both RA representatives have served on Conference committees and have been active presences at Conference meetings. Because of its independent stance, as well as its commitment to the openness and diversity of Jewish life, the RA has often been one of the organizations to whom all parties have turned for serious discussion and consultation and has served as a bridge between organizations espousing opposite agendas. In 1998 and 1999 the Conference of Presidents was under attack with claims that it was no longer an effective representative voice in Jewish life and that it was not responsive enough to the peace initiatives being proffered by Israel. In addition, strong criticism was raised concerning the selection of Conference chairmen and the role of the executive vice chairman of the Conference. The RA took a strong position in defense of the Conference, its leadership and its work, and pointed out that were the Conference to be destroyed it would be impossible to recreate such a meeting ground for the entire Jewish organizational community. The RA's position was consistently voiced within Conference discussions, as well as publicly, when questioned by other organizations or the press. Overcoming organizational self-interest enough to build cooperative associations and programs is very difficult in Jewish life; it is quite easy to destroy coalitions and cooperative ventures, and much more difficult to rebuild them.

This was evidenced as well in the demise of the Synagogue Council of America, which, during decades of rather shaky history, managed to bring together the three major religious streams in the United States for common planning, especially for high-level dialogue with the Catholic and Protestant churches. None of the religious streams had developed independent interfaith committees, but together, through the Synagogue Council, a strong interfaith program was developed with annual meetings of the Synagogue Council and the National Conference of Catholic Bishops, meetings at the Vatican and high-level discussions with the National Council of Churches. With the demise of the Synagogue Council, the RA, as well as the other components of Jewish religious movements in the United States, were bereft of a vehicle through which to conduct such dialogue. Under the leadership of the Rabbinical Assembly, especially that of Mordecai Waxman who has been the leading Rabbinical Assembly presence at high-level dialogues and who had served as a past president of the Synagogue Council of America, the RA took the lead in trying to reestablish the Synagogue Council. The Orthodox declined to participate, but the Reform movement (consisting of the CCAR and the UAHC), the RA, and the United Synagogue established the National Council of Synagogues to serve as interfaith dialogue representatives of both movements.

A similar pattern of near demise occurred when the International Jewish Committee on Interreligious Consultations (IJCIC), the international coalition for interfaith dialogue consisting not only of the religious streams, but also of the American Jewish Committee, the World Jewish Congress and B'nai B'rith International, nearly went out of existence due to internal strife and lack of adequate funding and representation. The Rabbinical Assembly again took a strong position, insisting that it was crucial to maintain such an umbrella organization because here, too, was a meeting ground for both religious and secular organizations engaged in high-level interfaith dialogue. The RA even offered office space and staff support. The work accomplished by the IJCIC had been crucial in helping to promote better cooperation and understanding. Its demise would not only create a vacuum in interfaith dialogue, but would, in fact, replace orderly consultation and representation from within the mainstream Jewish community with a series of independent and conflicting meetings and discussions. In the spring of 1999, a reformulated and recommitted IJCIC began to function.

The power of the members of the Assembly working in consort on a particular issue was clearly demonstrated during the Knesset debates surrounding a conversion law in 1996. The Masorti movement in Israel had gone to court in order to allow children converted by its *beit din* to be registered as members of the Jewish community. The Orthodox Knesset parties submitted legislation that would ban conversions by any religious authority not recognized by the Chief Rabbinate. The proposed law and the debates surrounding the law were couched in language that would not only deny religious rights to Conservative rabbis, but were reminiscent of prior debates on the very subject of Jewishness which cast aspersions upon the rabbis and members of the Conservative and Reform movements worldwide. Discussions concerning the conversion bill began in the Knesset during the fall of 1995, and within Israel, RA colleagues strongly protested the Knesset proposals and sought to galvanize support among the Israeli public. By the time of the Rabbinical Assembly annual convention in Boston in April 1996, there was growing mobilization and anger on the part of the American Conservative and Reform communities in protest to what was seen as a divisive and destructive pending move within the Knesset to pass this bill. During that period of the convention, Prime Minister Netanyahu was in Washington, DC, meeting with the president of the United States and other government officials. United States officials asked about the conversion bill and the ensuing dispute in the American and Israeli Jewish communities. The prime minister hastily asked for a meeting with leaders of the Conservative and Reform movements. On the Monday afternoon of the convention, the executive vice president of the Rabbinical Assembly, the executive vice president and president of the United Synagogue, and the chancellor of the Seminary flew from Boston to Washington, DC. They were joined there by the president of the UAHC, the executive vice president of the CCAR, the president of ARZA, the president of MERCAZ, and presidents and executives of the UJA and CJF. There ensued a forthright and heated discussion with the prime minister of Israel and Israeli officials concerning the lack of equal rights for the

Conservative and Reform movements in Israel and the disastrous effects the passage of the conversion bill would have on Israel/Diaspora relations. The prime minister asked representatives of the Conservative and Reform movements to meet with representatives of his office that week in order to possibly avoid a Knesset battle on the conversion bill and a split between the American and Israeli Jewish communities. Joel Meyers and Jerome Epstein were asked to serve as representatives of the Conservative movement, Eric Yoffie and Ami Hirsch were given the task by the Reform movement, and on that Friday morning a meeting was to be held at the Israel Consulate in New York with Bobby Brown, advisor to the prime minister for Diaspora Affairs, members of the foreign ministry and prime minister's office, as well as the consulate, to try to find a workable solution to the divisive issues at hand.

Meanwhile, when Rabbis Meyers and Epstein returned from Washington close to midnight, the entire convention reassembled to hear what had happened and to determine actions that would be taken. It was decided to mount a protest at the Boston Israeli Consulate and present a petition to the consul general in Boston, expressing the convention's outrage at what was taking place in Israel and demanding that legislation be withdrawn and that our rabbis be accorded equal privileges with all members of the Israeli rabbinate. Such a protest rally was held and a meeting took place between the consul general and David Lieber, president of the RA, and other RA leaders in the consulate offices. The next day, Bobby Brown, advisor to the prime minister, and Gideon Meir, advisor to the foreign minister, came to the convention and addressed the plenum. It is difficult to describe the mix of feelings among RA members at that time. Every RA member had a deep love for and commitment to Israel, and many colleagues at the convention were Israelis. This began a year of strong protest mounted by every member of the Assembly around the world. Delegations of rabbis and congregants visited with every Israeli consul; letter-writing campaigns were held in synagogues, and rabbis were outspoken in their local Jewish press. Rabbis in Santiago, Chile, refused to participate in a community-wide meeting at which a member of the Knesset was to speak, as that MK had voiced support of the conversion bill. This caused a crisis within the Chilean Jewish community, and the Israeli ambassador held a meeting with rabbis and communal leaders, attempting to convince the rabbis not to mount such a protest. The rabbis maintained their positions strongly, and maintained that the events in Israel were an insult to them and to their communities.

The continuing level of leadership effort on this issue would ultimately lead the government of Israel to create the Neeman Commission, which would work out a way to permit participation of Conservative and Reform rabbis in conversions and remove the conversion bill from the Knesset table. Following the lead of Israeli colleagues, RA members have continued to press for equality and fair treatment for all religious streams in Israel.

Moreover, the strong influences of the Assembly's rabbis and their Reform colleagues raised the issue of greater Federation funding for the Conservative and Reform movements in Israel. Rabbis argued that within Israel the Orthodox religious establishment was supported by governmental funding, and Diaspora communities should increase the level of support for religious pluralism in Israel. Concerned with outspoken criticism on the part of rabbis in the United States, the UJA president asked for a meeting with the Conservative and Reform leadership, which resulted in the formation of the Federation's Unity Campaign, designed to raise $10 million each for Reform and Conservative movement projects and programs in Israel. Again, the power of the collective rabbinate was apparent.

The relationship between the religious movements and the Federations in North America has been an area of ongoing concern for some time, alternating between strong cooperation and difficult tension. When a planned merger between UJA and CJF was announced, the RA, the United Synagogue, the UAHC and the CCAR, at times joined by the RCA and the OU, met with CJF and UJA leadership to insist that the religious streams have a voice and a role in the planning of the new Federation structure. While the religious streams were in discussion and lobbying Federation leadership, the struggles for religious diversity in Israel came to the fore. The RA took an active role within the Conservative movement, and together with the Reform movement, advocated for increased Federation funding for religious pluralism in Israel. A separate Federation campaign for pluralism was then conducted and has been helpful. On the other hand, all the attempts to encourage the religious streams to participate in the restructuring process of the Federation in the United States failed. The religious streams were kept out of all serious discussions and are, at this writing, determining whether or not they will participate in even a minor way in the new entity, the United Jewish Communities. Despite disappointment at what occurred, here, too, the RA has taken a strong position of continuing support for Federation and its activities. Care must be taken lest a communal structure built over 100 years be destroyed. We live at a time when individual desires tend to outstrip commitments to community so that each person, whether of extreme wealth or of minimal gift-giving, wishes to designate funds for specific projects. This has brought benefit to Jewish education, to areas of social welfare that otherwise would not have been served, and to Jewish institutions that would have otherwise not been funded. At the same time, there exists the danger of destroying communal structures which benefit the entire community as a whole, even if individuals do not participate fully in those activities. Without such structures it would be difficult to raise funds for emergency relief, to support a family service agency, for example, or to benefit programs which serve the international Jewish community. Therefore, the RA has been strong in its support of the United Jewish Communities, while continuing to advocate for those concerns that are important to the Assembly and to the Conservative movement and for direct involvement in key areas which impact the quality of Jewish life. Community level support has become important, and the Assembly strongly urges rabbis to participate more fully in local communal life and to assume greater leadership roles at the leadership tables of local Federations and communal agencies.

Relationships between the Rabbinical Assembly and the other rabbinical associations, the CCAR, the RCA and the RRA, are always good. There is a keen recognition that we must be supportive of each other's efforts in congregational and communal life, and that despite differences, even at times public disagreements, the care and well-being of rabbis is our foremost mission and task. The executive vice presidents have a long history of meeting often and consulting with one another concerning issues affecting the rabbinate and the movements. Each association focuses primarily on the well-being of rabbis, and they work well together to support rabbis across religious streams. In addition, presidents and vice presidents of the associations regularly meet to discuss areas of mutual concern to rabbis to the life of the broader Jewish community. It is sometimes difficult for the organizations to hold joint sessions, but this issue is under discussion as the year 1999 ends.

During the '90s, an area of concern most talked about by the leadership of the Conservative movement, especially by members of the Assembly, has been the lack of significant development of new congregational communities. While the number of congregations in North

America, currently at 780, has decreased slightly from the significant boom in congregational membership in the United Synagogue during the late '60s and early '70s, there has been relatively little done to create new congregations in areas of developing Jewish populations.

A constantly expressed disappointment has been the United Synagogue's failure to adequately and aggressively nurture synagogue development in the United States and Canada, while at the same demanding that other arms of the movement not enter this arena. Both RA and Seminary leadership have strongly advocated a change in United Synagogue priorities, and as the century draws to a close, it would not be surprising for new synagogues to be nurtured directly by the RA and the two seminaries in the United States. Most recently, the RA and the United Synagogue have agreed to jointly fund a program to create new congregations.

At the same time, the World Council, originally created by the major arms of the movement to develop the movement outside the United States, has been inadequately funded and unable to pursue its mission. Hence, until the late 1990s, overseas development of the movement had been moribund. The presence of dynamic rabbinic leadership at key moments and a committed core group of lay leaders intent on creating a Conservative presence are the factors that enabled the movement to develop outside of the United States and Canada. Even in Israel, the building of the movement began in haphazard fashion rather than with clear planning. Happenstance determined where communities would emerge and who among our rabbis would be available to go on *aliyah* to help build congregational communities, serve as teachers, or provide faculty for Machon Schechter. If it were not for the unceasing and committed efforts of members of the Rabbinical Assembly to build a movement in Israel, there in fact would be no movement there today. In Argentina, the charismatic Marshall Meyer and a series of assistant rabbis from the United States helped lay the groundwork for the Conservative movement's presence in Latin America and for the building of a seminary and a camping system. In England, the leadership and courage of Louis Jacobs and his break with the Orthodox Chief Rabbinate laid the foundation for what has become the Assembly of Masorti Synagogues. In France, a group of dedicated laity committed themselves to building a Conservative congregation, which today is spearheading the growth of a Conservative movement in France. The movement has been unable to provide a significant number of rabbis and teachers to serve in the states of the former Soviet Union; has been unable to respond to the call for building congregations in Western Europe, especially in Germany; and has been unable to respond to the call of laity to create Conservative congregations in countries such as Australia and South Africa. An international presence and connectedness between Conservative communities around the world is due to the tremendous efforts of Benjamin Kreitman, who, following his retirement as executive vice president of the United Synagogue, was asked to serve as executive vice president of the World Council. Rabbi Kreitman has gathered a lay board to work for the World Council and has unceasingly maintained contact with Conservative communities throughout the world, speaking to leadership on the phone, visiting, writing, and seeking out sources of funding. He has also contributed funds of his own in order to help cement the international ties of a worldwide Conservative movement.

In 1998, a group of fourteen rabbis, all of whom had a direct relation to, or strong interest in countries outside the United States, gathered at the Seminary in New York for a very special meeting chaired by Joel Meyers. This meeting grew out of a discussion of the Rabbinical Assembly's Administrative Committee concerning the inability of the movement to develop new congregational communities outside the United States and within the United States. The group invited Roy Clements, president of Mercaz Olami, to join them, as Mercaz Olami served as an international coordinating body for Conservative Zionist Groups around the world. At the table were also Rabbis Kreitman, Joseph Wernik, who chaired the board of the Masorti movement in Israel, and colleagues from Latin America. As a result of this and several follow-up meetings, the group determined that it would serve as a steering committee to promote the coherent development of a worldwide movement and set in motion a plan to grow the Conservative movement outside of North America. To do this, the members of the steering committee agreed to serve as area coordinators, striving to learn both the make-up of the overseas areas for which they were responsible, as well as current status of the Conservative movement in those areas and the resources available to grow the movement. As a direct result, several immediate new ventures developed. Under guidance of Charles Simon, rabbinical students from the United States began to serve as weekend rabbis in small communities in England and France. Funds were solicited to help develop new congregations both inside and outside of Paris. Through the efforts of Carl Wolkin, further funds were received to help fund a rabbinic position in a growing community north of London. This enabled the congregation to engage a new graduate of Machon Schechter. In February 1999, under the guidance of Joe Wernik, Roy Clements, and Harry Freedman, the executive director of the movement in England, the European Conservative Congregations and the European Association of Masorti Communities were formed, agreeing to hold a conference for European Conservative educators, which would be coordinated through the London offices of the Assembly of Masorti Synagogues.

As the century drew to a close, Gordon Freeman became the chair of the Steering Committee, Alan Silverstein was elected incoming president of the World Council, and discussions were underway for a one-, two- and three-year plan to coordinate worldwide activities and fundraising efforts in order to build the Conservative movement overseas, country by country, while maintaining the central goal of strengthening the movement in Israel. In addition to discussing structure and opportunities for growth, the committee decided to establish a fund for rabbinic development within the RA to help communities engage a rabbi, which in every instance is the key element to continuing growth and development.

The Rabbinical Assembly spearheaded this effort because time and again it has proven to be the only arm of the movement able to take a broader and longer view of movement developments and to garner the support of both professional and lay leadership for projects beneficial to the movement as a whole. Moreover, as the only international arm of the movement, and the one providing key leadership, the Assembly increasingly has become the integrating force of the movement, holding it together by providing a common approach to its religious values and to its organizational development and outlook.

What major trends can one predict as the Assembly enters its next one hundred years of sacred service? First and foremost must be the very nature of our ideology and program as a Conservative movement. How will we maintain this constantly dynamic and shifting balance between tradition and change, between halakhic certainty and halakhic evolution, which has been one of our key characteristics as a rabbinate? In 1990, Pamela Nadell, writing in *Judaism,* spoke of the Conservative rabbi as the great ethnic mediator being able to bridge and merge our Jewish culture in all of its aspects, with our Western culture in all of its aspects.[2] And, almost a hundred years earlier, Solomon Schechter, when speaking of the Seminary he was about to head, said:

> [Judaism] demands control over all your actions. . . . It insists upon the observance both of the spirit and the letter. . . . [However] You

must not think that our intention is to convert this school of learning into a drill ground where young men will be forced into a certain groove of thinking, or, rather not thinking, and after being equipped with a few devotional texts, and supplied with certain catch words, will be let loose upon an unsuspecting public to proclaim their own virtues and the infallibility of their masters . . . I would consider my work . . . a complete failure if this institution would not in the future produce such extremes as on the one side a raving mystic who would denounce me as a sober Philistine; on the other side, an advanced critic, who would rail at me as a narrow minded fanatic, while a third devotee of strict orthodoxy would raise protest against any critical views I may entertain.[3]

This omnipresent, inherent tension within each of us and within our ranks has energized our study, our debates, and the creative work that has emanated from the Assembly throughout its history. Thus, the Assembly, its programs, projects, and its public face are a reflection of the amalgamation of each of our positions and views. Our diversity has given us our strength, as well as provided our proverbial gray hairs in anxious moments of disarray and ferocious debate.

What will the next generation bring? What will the face of the Rabbinical Assembly be? What will be the source of its creative energy and action? How will both the processes of change within the totality of Jewish life and general culture impact us? That is one key question which none of us can foresee, but awaits a response in the decades ahead. Some predict that the forthcoming Jewish population study of the American Jewish community at the turn of the century will indicate a Conservative movement with a shrinking membership base, but at the same time a strengthening commitment to the movement, an increasing level of knowledge and observance, and a strong desire on the part of many not yet in the movement to become part of it. It is always difficult to be a centrist movement; it is easier to define onself clearly right or clearly left. Yet, I believe we will respond well, and we will keep before us always the balance that has given us our Conservative ideology: a position which favors the side of tradition, yet is willing to experiment with change, as change has enabled us to continue to prosper for these thousands of years.

A second issue impacting the RA is the constant evolution of technology and its effect upon our lives as individuals and as communities. Already, the Law Committee is asking the question of whether a *minyan* can be held on the Internet. As we all realize, technological change is just beginning to have an impact upon our lives. No doubt, a decade from now, a generation from now, there will in fact be a totally different way of approaching the acquisition of knowledge, the study of text, the understanding of the universe, the interaction of peoples and events, the manufacture of homes, the production of food, and the caring for physical life. What will our Jewish sources help us see and understand about life itself, about our relationship to God, about observance, about prayer, about caring for the universe? The technological revolution, our ability for instantaneous communication, the mobility of all peoples, and the internationalization of commerce will confront us as we strive to maintain a distinctive identity as a Jewish community, with our time-bound observances and our particular boundaries. How will we help ourselves and our community maintain our uniqueness and define our place? As Morris Allen noted, "The question is, what will it take to make the Jew of the 21st century a connected and passionate Jew, one who is able to transmit an enduring message of Judaism, and to find meaning in their own life as a Jew?"[4]

Our relationship to Israel and its impact on our Jewish identity is an issue already confronting us. We, in the Assembly, will be increasingly drawn to define our commitment to *Eretz Yisrael* as both *morasha* (legacy) and *moledet* (homeland). How do we and hence the people we lead and serve relate to land and people? And, even more importantly, how do we as a Conservative community help strengthen our presence in Israel? We cannot be a movement, existing only in the Diaspora West. A strong presence in Israel is essential. There will have to be a deliberate and movement-wide gathering of financial resources, along with *aliyah*, to strengthen our presence in Israel and to serve as a catalyst for other Israelis to join with us. The very nature of *aliyah* from Western countries may change with the availability of quicker flights and faster communication. We may well end up living in two countries, our own and Israel. But we will have to make a commitment to Israel first.

Another area of future development will be the emphasis on building a movement worldwide. The Rabbinical Assembly will be a leading force in building Jewish communal life, not only in Israel and in Latin America, but in a Jewishly-growing Europe as well. Along with this, the movement will become fully egalitarian. We have a continuing commitment to permit and encourage diversity within our movement; hence, we now have a commitment to maintain both non-egalitarian and egalitarian congregations. However, there is a natural momentum toward seeing men and women as equals, involved together religiously, as well as in all other areas of life. I believe this is inevitable and will come to pass in all movements, not only in our own.

Finally, the Rabbinical Assembly will continue to grow in numbers and will take on an increasingly international look. Regions will be restructured to enable greater participation and will be provided with staff to better help us all in our own work and to help solidify our movement. At the same time, we will also find an increasing coherence within the Assembly. We need one another's creative sparks, collegiality, strength, and friendship. We need collaborative efforts in all areas of Jewish communal life in order to benefit not only those whom we serve, but ourselves and our families. We need to bring rabbis and rabbinic families together for periods of study, for sabbatical periods of refreshment, and for programs of learning and exploration.

What an incredible one hundred years! The pages of this volume have wonderfully portrayed much of the development of the Rabbinical Assembly and the forces, both internal and external, which helped shape its direction and its impact upon the Conservative movement and world Jewish life. Yet the very soul of the Rabbinical Assembly, that essence which has enabled it to be such a force for good in Jewish life, has been, and is, derived from the collective hearts and minds of the individual rabbis who are its members. As our venerable teacher and friend Abraham Karp once observed:

> Conservative Judaism is not the product of the Jewish Theological Seminary, as is often asserted. It is the product of the products of the Seminary, the Conservative rabbinate. Its ideology was worked out in large measure at the annual conventions and within the committees of the Rabbinical Assembly. The RA conventions served as the workshops for the construction—ideological and practical—of the movement. The most enduring 'accomplishment,' of the Rabbinical Assembly is not its 'product'—the Conservative rabbinate, but the products of the product: the American synagogue, and even more so, the vast body of literature created by this rabbinate.[5]

We rabbis tend to shy away from the concept of the rabbinate as "a calling." We prefer to see ourselves fulfilling the *mitzvot* of study and following God's commandments. But we need to acknowledge that the absolute dedication of the rabbis of the Assembly has brought life and development to the Conservative movement, and has brought love of Torah and acceptance of *mitzvot* to millions of our people. This has been the propelling force in all Assembly activities and projects. To me, it always feels as though God is present, gently guiding us, reminding us that there is much to do and the day is short.

יהי רצון מלפניך ה׳ אלהינו ואלהי אבתינו
שתהא תורתך אומנותינו בעולם הזה ותהא עמנו
לעולם הבא.

NOTES

1. Report of the Strategic Planning Committee, April 1996.
2. Pamela Nadell, "Conservative Rabbis as Ethnic Leaders," *Judaism*, 39:3 (Summer 1990), p. 365.
3. Solomon Schechter, "The Charter of the Seminary," *Seminary Addresses and Other Papers* (New York: Burning Bush Press, 1959), pp. 22-24.
4. Morris Allen, unpublished document, 1998.
5. Abraham Karp, private memo to Joel Meyers, 1994.

Presidents of the Rabbinical Assembly

Seminary Alumni Association

1901–1904 Henry M. Speaker
1904–1907 Menahem Max Eichler
1907–1912 Charles Isaiah Hoffman

1912–1914 Jacob Kohn
1914–1916 Elias L. Solomon
1916–1918 Max D. Klein

The Rabbinical Assembly

1918–1922 Max D. Klein
1922–1925 Louis M. Epstein
1925–1928 Max Drob
1928–1930 Louis Finkelstein
1930–1932 Israel Levinthal
1932–1933 Mordecai M. Kaplan
1933–1935 Elias Margolis
1935–1937 Eugene Kohn
1937–1939 Simon Greenberg
1939–1940 Max Arzt
1940–1942 Leon Lang
1942–1944 Louis Levitsky
1944–1946 Robert Gordis
1946–1948 Israel Goldman
1948–1950 David Aaronson
1950–1952 Max D. Davidson
1952–1954 Ira Eisenstein
1954–1956 Harry Halpern
1956–1958 Aaron H. Blumenthal
1958–1960 Isaac Klein

1960–1962 Edward Sandrow
1962–1964 Theodore Friedman
1964–1966 Max J. Routtenberg
1966–1968 Eli A. Bohnen
1968–1970 Ralph Simon
1970–1972 S. Gershon Levi
1972–1974 Judah Nadich
1974–1976 Mordecai Waxman
1976–1978 Stanley Rabinowitz
1978–1980 Saul I. Teplitz
1980–1982 Seymour J. Cohen
1982–1984 Arnold M. Goodman
1984–1986 Alexander Shapiro
1986–1988 Kassel Abelson
1988–1990 Albert L. Lewis
1990–1992 Irwin Groner
1992–1994 Gerald Zelizer
1994–1996 Alan Silverstein
1996–1998 David Lieber
1998–   Seymour Essrog

Contributors

Robert E. Fierstien is rabbi of Temple Beth Or in Brick, New Jersey. A *summa cum laude* graduate of New York University, he received his M.A., rabbinical ordination, and doctorate from the Jewish Theological Seminary. As a cultural and religious historian, he has lectured widely on American Jewish history and is the author of *A Different Spirit: The Jewish Theological Seminary of America, 1886–1902*.

Joel H. Meyers has been executive vice president of the Rabbinical Assembly since 1989. Following ordination from JTS in 1966, he served as congregational rabbi in the Boston area for fifteen years and then as associate director of B'nai B'rith International in Washington, DC, directing many of the institution's worldwide operations. He holds graduate degrees from New York University and Andover Newton Theological School, and an honorary doctorate from JTS.

Pamela S. Nadell, professor and director of the Jewish Studies Program at American University, is the author of *Women Who Would Be Rabbis: A History of Women's Ordination, 1889–1985* and *Conservative Judaism in America: A Biographical Dictionary and Sourcebook*.

Michael Panitz was ordained at JTS in 1982 and received his Ph.D. in Modern Jewish History there in 1989. He has taught on the JTS faculty and served congregations in New Jersey and Virginia. He is currently the rabbi of Temple Israel, Norfolk, Virginia, and an adjunct professor of Religious Studies at the College of William and Mary.

Stanley Rabinowitz, ordained at JTS in 1943, served the Adas Israel Congregation in Washington, DC for twenty-six years before being named rabbi emeritus. Prior pulpits included Adath Jeshurun in Minneapolis, Minnesota, and B'nai Jacob in New Haven, Connecticut, as well as executive positions with the United Synagogue and the Jewish Theological Seminary. He is the author of *The Assembly*, a history of the congregation in Washington, DC.

Herbert Rosenblum was ordained at JTS in 1954 and has served congregations in Massachusetts and Pennsylvania. He completed a Ph.D. in American Jewish History at Brandeis University in 1970 and was professor of Jewish History at Hebrew College from 1971 to 1981. He has also been a visiting professor at Tel Aviv University, Clark University and New York University.

Theodore Steinberg retired to Jerusalem in 1992, after thirty-nine years of a satisfying career in the American rabbinate. His doctoral dissertation for New York University was on the life and valuational philosophy of the late professor Max Kadushin. In Jerusalem, he is an associate editor of the *Jewish Bible Quarterly* and an occasional writer for *Avar VeAtid*.

Shmuel Szteinhendler is a 1985 graduate of the Seminario Rabinico Latinoamericano and is currently rabbi of Congregation Or Shalom in Santiago, Chile. He is president of the Latin American Region of the Rabbinical Assembly and is the coordinator of Project Revival for Jewish Life in Cuba.

Index

N.B. Footnotes are not indexed.

A Time for Healing (Shapiro), 65
"A Union of Conservative Forces in America" (Rubenovitz), 11
Abelson, Kassel, 114, 121, 255, 256
Abelson, Alter, 6
Abramovitz, Herman, 23
Adler, Cyrus, background, 29–30; and Alumni Association, 13–14; concept of movement, 10–11, 23–24, 27, 31, 33, 46–47, 79; death of, 35, 80; death of Schechter, 24, 46; with Finkelstein, 33, 35–36; with Ginzberg and Marx, 30, 33, 58; and ideological issues, 30, 46–47, 79; opposition to liturgy, 79–80; possibilities with Orthodox, 24; and RA, 29–33; role at JTS, 9, 24, 28–29, 46, 58, 180, 194; role in rabbinic placement, 30, 32, 55–56, 184; in *Tradition and Change* (Waxman), 82; with United Synagogue, 10, 12, 30, 33; views on rabbis, 13–14, 30, 192
Adler, Morris, 50, 87, 88
After Life (Riemer), 257
Agunah (deserted wife) issue, 31, 42–43, 44, 45, 84, 94, 105; end of controversy, 92–93; temporary war measure for, 85

Agus, Jacob, 50, 82, 86, 88, 178
Allen, Morris, 270
Alumni Association (of JTS), and Adler, 13; becoming the Rabbinical Assembly, 1, 2, 16–17, 58; committees of, 15; early presidents of, 15; and education, 7, 8–9, 16; ideologies and origins, 4, 5, 6, 15, 45–46; last meeting as, 16; membership in, 7, 11, 15, 17; original resolutions of, 11, 16–17; relationship with United Synagogue, 10–11,13, 14–15, 16; role with JTS, 9, 17; social responsibility of, 9; topics of papers presented to, 7–8, 15, 16
American Hebrew (newspaper), 50
American Historical Society, 29
American Jewish Committee, 21, 29, 261
American Jewish community, *agunah* issue impact on, 93; within American society, 65, 118–119, 149–150, 174; and Conservative Judaism: 5, 11, 45–46, 111–112, 129; current dangers to structure of, 265; customs and practice in, 125–128, 129, 131–133 (*see also* Kashrut); demographics of, 1, 65, 156, 177, 269; denominations in,

American Jewish community *(cont.)* 2, 11, 23, 101, 126, 127,129; ethnicity of, 129–132, 174; holidays and ritual, 129, 178–179, 182; and National Jewish Population Survey, 157, 269; religious aspects of, 9–10, 21, 64, 127, 129, 178–179, 192; spirituality and tradition in, 129–133, 175

American Jewish Congress, 21

Anti-Defamation League, 21

Anti-Semitism, 7, 21, 41, 65

"Are You Considering Conversion to Judaism?" (Silverstein), 256

Aronson, David, 77, 84, 89,177, 178

Artson, Bradley Shavit, 119–120

Arzt, Max, 26, 37, 55, 56, 58, 82, 179; critique of *Judaism as a Civilization* (Kaplan), 48; own definition of Conservative Judaism, 48–49

Assembly of Masorti Synagogues, 266, 268

Assimilation, 100, 130

Association of Reform Zionists of America (ARZA), 262

Avar ve'Atid (journal), 203

Avni, Haim, 239

B'nai B'rith International, 184, 261

B'nai Mitzvah, 70, 91, 177

B'tsalmenu, 120

Baba Sali, 143

Baeck, Leo, 134

Bandel, Ehud, 218, 229

Baroway, Moses, 26

Bat Mitzvah, 103, 106, 182

Baumitz, Margit, 238

Bayme, Steven, 157

Benderly, Samson, Dr., 16

Beit din, 84, 90, 93, 110, 227, 228, 229, 262

Bet Midrash. *See* Machon Schechter

Berkun, Alvin, 259

Besofsky, Helen, 254

Bloom, Jack H, 181

Blue Ribbon Committee, 189

Blumenthal, Aaron, 50, 77, 90

Boesky, Ivan, 149

Bohnen, Eli A., 77

Bokser, Ben Zion, 50, 90

Bond of Life: A Book for Mourners, 135

Botnick, Annette Muffs, 254

"Bringing Up the Jewish Child"(Kaplan), 179

Brit Kodesh Program *(mohalim)*, 141, 220. S*ee also* RA, and continuing education for rabbis)

Brooks-Hislop, Lori, 254

Brown, Bobby, 263

Browne, Hoa, 254

Buber, Martin, 134, 135

Bulletin of the Rabbinical Assembly. See Publications Committee

Bullowa, Emilie, 25

Bureaus of Jewish Education, 21

Burnstein, Alexander, 55

CCAR Yearbook, 6

Cahan, Leonard, 256

Canada, 266

"Canons of Interpretation of Jewish Law" (Boaz Cohen), 45

Cantor, 174

Cantor, Debra, 138

Central Conference of American Rabbis (CCAR), 55, 65, 82, 112, 261, 264, 265; early years of, 1, 3, 4, 6, 10, 23

"Changing Forms of Jewish Spirituality" (Susannah Heschel), 148

Chaplaincy. *See* Israel; Rabbinic role; RA

Chaverah (newsletter), 155

Clements, Roy, 267, 268

Coffee, Rudolph, 8

Cohen, Armond, 41, 57, 74

Cohen, Boaz, 43, 44–45, 85, 86

Cohen, Gerson D., chancellor of JTS, 107, 115, 183; and Commission for the Study of Women in the Rabbinate, 108, 110, 112; and study of patrilineality and matrilineality issue, 117, 120

Cohen, Hermann, 134

Cohen, Jack, 203

Cohen, Moshe, 204, 209, 210

Cohen, Samuel M., 16, 28, 57

Cohen, Seymour, 152

Cohen, Shaar-Yashuv, 214

Commission for the Study of Women in the Rabbinate, 108, 109–110, 111

Commission on Human Sexuality, 122–123

Committee of Conservative Union, 10–14

Committee on Conservative Ideology, 115–116

Committee on Formulating the Attitude of the Rabbinical Assembly, 47

Committee on Jewish Law and Standards (CJLS), 120, 225, 250, 269–270; and *agunah* issue, 42–43, 44, 45, 84, 85, 88; CJLS and reorganization, 102–103, 109, 110; and Commission on Human Sexuality, 120, 122–123; and egalitarian issues, 106, 270–271 *(see also* Women*)*; as former Committee on Jewish Law, 41–45, 59, 64, 76, 84, 85–86, 92–93, 181; and homosexuality, 118–124; issues of halakhah, 90–94, 100, 105, 126, 133, 255; and JTS, 89–90; and *mara d'atra,* 88; on marriage and divorce, 89, 90, 93, 103, 105; new scope of CJLS, 255–256; and observance by rabbis, 183; responsa of, 88–92, 100, 119–120, 179, 237;

and *Siyum HaShas,* 78; and stance affirming matrilineal lineage, 116–117, 124; and synagogues, 119, 120, 121; *takkanot,* 90, 92, 105; and tension between ethics and halakhah, 105, 122; and *Tradition and Change,* 82, 83; and traditional views of halakhah, 71, 78, 83, 85–87, 179; *yom tov sheni shel galuyot* 77, 92, 126

"Community Center in its Relation to the Synagogue Center" (Glucksman), 57

Conference on Conservative Ideology, 115

Conference of Conservative Rabbis, 26, 27, 47

Conference of the Halachah and the Challenges of Modern Life, 86

Conference of Presidents of Major Jewish Organizations, 260–261

Conference of Science, Religion, and Philosophy, 37

Conference of Women and Change in Jewish Law", 106

Conference on Theology, 257

Confirmation. *See* Synagogues

Congregations. *See under* Placement Committee; Rabbinate, Conservative; Synagogues

Congregation Beth Simchat Torah, 119. *See* CJLS; Homosexuality

Conservative Judaism (journal). *See* Rabbinical Assembly

Conservative Judaism (Sklare), 83, 93

Conservative Judaism, analysis about in *Conservative Judaism,* 83; attitude of Cyrus Adler towards, 30; "Catholic Israel", 46, 193; conversion issues, 131–132, 226–228, 262, 263; creation of Chaplaincy Availability Board, 66; customs and practice, 125–128, 129, 146–148, 174, 220, 257;

Conservative Judaism *(cont.)*
definitions of, 111, 115–116, 133,
174, 181; demographics, 33, 72,
73, 100–101, 269; difference from
Orthodoxy, 13, 44–45, 101, 109,
133, 174, 181, 183, 188; difference from Reform, 105, 109, 112,
116, 133, 188; disparate views on
ideology of, 3, 24–26, 33, 47,
51–52, 83, 101–102, 109, 113,
124–125 *(see also Emet ve-Emunah)*; and homosexuality,
118–124; intermarriage issue,
157–158; relationship to Israel *(see
under Israel; Masorti movement)*;
and Jewish Law *(see under individual scholars; CJLS; Halakhah)*; in
Latin America *(see Latin America)*;
liturgy of, 79, 80–81, 124–125,
133–140; as a movement, 13,17,
23–24, 72, 156–157, 266–268;
and peoplehood, 174, 193; and
pluralism, 114, 115–116, 118,
270–271; sociology of, 79, 80–81,
87, 130–132; spirituality and tradition in, 129–133, 175; as "tradition and change", 116, 193; as
"unity and diversity", 193; and
women, 104–113, 114–115 *(see
also CJLS; Women)*
Conversion, 92, 131, 132, 219,
226–228, 256, 262, 263
Council of Jewish Federations (CJF),
262, 264
Creditor, Ruby Eisenberg, 155

Davidowitz, Harry, 201
Davidson, Charles, 182
Davidson, Max D., 68, 74, 77, 90
Davis, Moshe, 2, 50, 202–203, 216,
217
Dembitz, Louis M., 7
Depression, 29, 37, 40, 48, 56, 59,
65

Dietary laws. *See Kashrut*
Dobrzynski, Abram, 8
Dorff, Elliott, 120, 255
Doron, Eliahu Bakshi, 213–214
Dresner, Samuel, 78
Drob, Max, 23, 24, 28, 42, 51
Dropsie College, 11, 12, 29
Drucker, Aaron P., 6

Edery, Mordejai, 239
Education. *See* Jewish Education
"The Effect of the Jewish Immigrant
Population on the Public School in
New York City" *(*Margoshes), 16
Egalitarianism, 105. *See under indi-
vidual movements*; Women
Egelson, Louis, 9–10
Ehrenreich, Bernard, C., 4, 6
Eichler, Menahem M., 4, 7, 15
Eilberg, Amy, 113
Eisenstein, J.D., 2
Eisenstein , Ira, 77, 178
Eisenstein, Judith Kaplan, 178, 182
Eit Machar Seminar, 251
Elmaleh, Leon H., 4, 7, 8
Embracing Judaism (Kling), 157, 256
*Emet Ve-Emunah: Statement of Prin-
ciples of Conservative Judaism*,
83, 115, 116, 223
England, 145, 266, 267, 268
Epstein, Gilbert, 74, 151–153, 253,
254 retirement of, 152
Epstein, Jerome, 229, 239, 263
Epstein, Louis, 31, 34, 43–44, 56,
84, 85
Equal Rights Amendment, 103–104
Essrog, Seymour, 237
Et La'asot (journal), 143
"Eternal Light" (television program),
37
Ethiopian Jewry, 143
Europe, 142, 267
European Association of Masorti
Communities, 268

European Conservative Congregations, 268
Ezrat Nashim, 103

Fagan, Richard, 114
Feast of Freedom, 136–137
Federation Guidance Service, 250
Federation of Jewish Philanthropies, 21, 57, 176, 264
Federation of Men's Clubs, 91
Feinberg, Charles, 148
Feinberg, Louis, 178
Feld, Edward, 256
Feldman, David, 104
Felsenthal, Bernard, 7
Feminism. *See* Women
Fenster, Myron, 204–205
Fine, David, 255
Finkelstein, Louis, background, 35–36; with Adler, 33, 35–36; and beginnings of movement, 23–24, 33, 36, 47; as chancellor of JTS, 35, 37–38, 180; creation of programs at JTS, 37–38, 194; dates of, 35; differences with Kaplan, 36, 47; and Law Committee, 44–45, 89; and RA, 36–37, 47, 57, 58; with rabbinic placement, 36, 56, 185; Renascence Society, attendance at, 36
Fishman, Herzl, 203, 239
France, 266, 267
Fredman, Samuel, 26
Freedman, Jacob, 56
Freedman, Harry, 268
Freeman, Gordon, 256, 268
Freund, Richard, 239
Fried, Michael, 4
Friedlaender, Israel, 13,16
Friedman, Leslie, 155
Friedman, Theodore, 77, 86, 88, 89–90, 225, 236
Fundraising. *See under individual organizations*

Gamoran, Emanuel, 57
Gershfield, Edward, 91
Get (Jewish divorce), 84, 93; *hafka'at kiddushin*, 103, 105
Gillman, Neil, 148, 181, 183
Ginzberg, Eli, 34–35
Ginzberg, Louis, with Adler, 30, 31, 58; and *agunah* issue, 31, 43, 44, 84, 85; and Conservative ideology, 33, 86; halakhah, 7, 16, 25, 28, 33–34, 41, 51; and JTS, 28, 33–35; and RA, 31, 33, 34, 35, 58; retirement of, 35; in United Synagogue, 12, 24, 25, 28, 33, 34, 41; writings of, 7, 16, 33, 51, 86
Glucksman, Harry, 57
God, 135, 138, 245, 270
Goldberg, Abraham, 202
Golden, S. Herbert, 28
Goldin, Judah, 89–90
Goldman, Simchah, 131
Goldman, Solomon, 25, 37, 58, 77, 174, 187; in opposition to Adler, 31, 47; views on ideology, 39, 47
Goldstein, David, 56, 74
Goldstein, Israel, 22, 26, 40, 58, 174, 178; definition of Conservative Judaism, 51; in opposition to Adler, 31
Golinkin, David, 225, 256
Goodman, Arnold, 111, 117, 121, 152, 179
Gordis Robert, 40, 58, 76, 77, 80, 81, 187; discussions on Conservative ideology, 49–50, 76, 115; on patrilineal and matrilineal lineage, 117–118; in *Tradition and Change* (Waxman), 82
Gordon, Albert, 179
Goren, Shlomo, 213
Gottlieb, Amy, 254
Graetz, Michael, 142, 143, 211, 216, 220
Gratz College, 6, 11

Grayzel, Solomon, 26
Greenbaum, Michael, 37
Greenberg, Sidney, 203–204
Greenberg, Simon, 49, 57, 178; and RA, 54, 56, 72; relationship to Israel, 200–201, 203; on synagogues and federations, 57; in *Tradition and Change* (Waxman), 82; as vice chancellor of JTS, 83, 105
Greenfeld, William, 86
Greenstone, Julius H., 4, 8; with Alumni Association, 15; and Law Committee, 42, 44; symposium on Jewish education, 16; and United Synagogue, 14, 24
Grossman, Benjamin, 56
Grossman, Susan, 128
Gunther, Sara, 254

Habad Hasidim, 101
Hakohen, Shmuel Avigdor, 239
Hadas, Gershon, 82
"Halacha of the Book of Jubilees, Compared with the Corresponding Rabbinic Halacha" (Hirsch, Rabinowitz), 8
Halakhah, 46, 51, 71, 83, 84, 86–88, 89, 93–94,113. See also under *individual scholars and topics*; CJLS; and *agunah* issue, 45, 84–85, 88, 89; armed forces, 84–85; and *minyan*, 105; reforms in, 77, 92, 109, 126
Halpern, Harry, 77
"*Ha-Modi'a*" (Rabinowitz), 153, 156
Hammer, Reuven, 221, 226, 229, 230
Hammer, Zevulun, 221
Harlow, Jules, as assistant executive director, 74, 253; Conservative movement's chief liturgist, 82; director of publications, 134–136;

editor of *Conservative Judaism*, 78; editor of *mahzor*, 134, 135; redactor of new RA *humash*, 139, 256; and *Siddur Sim Shalom*, 137–138
Harris, Robert, 144
Hasidic masters, 134
Hasidism, 147
Hebrew Union College 2, 12,23, 104
Hebrew University, 201–203. See also Israel
Herberg, Will, 94, 134, 135
Hershman, Abraham, 15,16
Hertz, Joseph Herman, 3, 139, 172
Hertzberg, Arthur, 87, 186–187
Heschel, Abraham Joshua, 134, 147, 148, 176; and concept of depth theology, 135, 181
Heschel, Susannah, 148
Hevra Kadisha, 141–142, 179, 216, 220; and cemetery, 126–127
Higger, Michael, 86, 88, 91
Hirsch, Abel, 8
Hirsch, Ami, 263
Historical Judaism, 2, 34, 45–46, 51
Hoffman, Charles Isaiah, and Alumni Association, 7, 10, 14,15; and beginnings of movement, 10, 11, 12, 23; editor of *United Synagogue Recorder*, 24–25; and JTS, 8, 15; and United Synagogue, 14, 24
Hoffman, Isidor, 39, 40
Holocaust, 55, 82, 91, 134, 175
Homosexuality, 105, 118–124
Hyamson, Moses, 16

Institute for Converts (*Machon HaGiyur*), 219, 227–228
Institute for Religious and Social Studies, 37
Institute of Contemporary Jewry, 202
Institute of Traditional Judaism. See Union for Traditional Judaism

Interfaith, 56, 70
Intermarriage, 86, 90, 94, 101,
 131–132, 157; survey among
 Conservative Jews, 158
International Jewish Committee on
 Interreligious Consultations
 (IJCIC), 261–262
Israel, and *aliyah,* 67, 175, 176,
 200–202, 208–210, 216, 266;
 Conservative rabbinate in *(see*
 Masorti movement*)*; conversion
 issue, 226–229, 262–264; funding
 issue, 264; halakhah and, 91, 92,
 126; importance to movement, 66,
 67, 77, 176, 181, 201; and Law of
 Return, 109; and MERCAZ, 142,
 262; military service, 202, 203,
 207, 216–217; and Neeman Commission, 144–145, 213–214, 221,
 228–230, 264; and Orthodox rabbinate in 144, 204, 217, 226, 227,
 229–230, 264; RA in Israel,
 142–145 *(see also* Masorti movement*)*; TALI schools, 143, 210,
 218, 231
Israel Bonds, 176
Israeli Student Center, 38
Israeli, Phineas, 6, 16

Jacobs, Louis, 266, 268
Jastrow, Marcus, 2
Jerusalem Post, 213
Jewish Catalogue (Strassfeld), 136,
 148
Jewish Center. *See* Mordecai M.
 Kaplan
Jewish Community Council, 21, 41
Jewish Continuity, 122, 157
Jewish Education, 56–57, 59, 71, 78,
 104, 116, 141, 174. *See also*
 Junior Congregation; Religious
 School *Jewish Exponent,* 4, 5, 7,
 17, 50
Jewish Labor Committee, 21

Jewish Museum, 37
"Jewish Nationalism" (Greenberg), 49
Jewish Publication Society, 29
Jewish Theological Seminary, 1, 2, 4,
 6, 13, 17; Adler years, 24, 29–33;
 board members of, 15, 30, 37; as
 central institution, 47, 79, 239,
 242, 271; with Columbia University, 38; early curriculum and
 prize topics, 2–3, 8–9; early years
 restructuring, 3, 7, 46; *Emet Ve-
 Emunah,* study guide for, 116;
 enrollment, 7, 175, 179–181;
 Finkelstein era, 24, 35–38, 130;
 fundraising, 39, 51, 149; homosexuality issue at, 121, 122, 124;
 and Israel, 203–204 (*see also
 under Israel*; Masorti movement*)*;
 later education, 176; Louis
 Ginzberg and JTS, 33–35; merger
 with Yeshiva University, 39; ordination, 67, 140, 175; and the RA,
 75, 89–90; relationship with rabbis, 75, 191–192; "Schechter's
 Seminary", 9, 22, 46; synagogue
 of, 31–32; and women ordination,
 107–113, 111, 183–184; worship
 services, 114; and *Wissenschaft
 des Judentums* (Jewish science),
 148; and Ziegler School of Rabbinic Studies, 194, 257–258
Jewish Theological Seminary Library,
 8, 30
Joffe, Joshua, 3
Joint Retirement Board, 185–186
Joint Distribution Committee (JDC),
 55, 176
Joseph, Jacob, 39
JTS *Students' Annual,* 15
Judaism, *See American Jewish Community*
Judaism as a Civilization (Kaplan),
 39, 48, 49
Junior Congregation, 16, 56, 81

Kadushin, Max, 26, 39, 47, 200

Kaplan, Bernard M., 4, 6

Kaplan, Lena, 182

Kaplan, Mordecai M., alliance with colleagues, 39, 49; attitude towards synagogues and rabbinate, 40; in Alumni Association, 15; association with United Synagogue, 12, 14, 24, 38; and Congregation Kehilath Jeshurun, 172; and Conservative movement ideology, 15, 24, 26–27, 47, 49–50, 82, 135; and education, 179, 182; with the Jewish Center, 25, 38, 39, 40; *Judaism as a Civilization,* 39, 48, 49; *and Kehillah* (organic community), 39, 40–41; in opposition to Cyrus Adler, 30; and Reconstrucionist movement, 15, 26, 39; relationship with the RA, 38, 40, 181; and social justice, 40; Society for the Advancement of Judaism (SAJ), 26; Society of the Jewish Renascence *(see Tehiat Yisrael)* Karp, Abraham J., 2, 50, 69, 131, 271

Kashrut, 2, 213; halakhah on, 85, 90, 91, 92; *kashrut* supervisors program *(rav ha-makhshir),* 141, 220, 221, 250, 256; laity and, 70, 87, 94, 113, 130, 132, 178–179,182–183

Kaufman, Jan Caryl, 112, 254

Kauvar, Charles, 9, 15

Kehillah. See Mordecai M. Kaplan

Kelman, Wolfe, 68, 69, 92, 185, 253; as director of Joint Placement Commission, 73, 253; and ordination of women, 108, 110, 120; in relation to rabbis, 71, 73–74, 151, 209; retirement of, 152, 254

Kibbutz Hanaton, 201

Kibbutz Oranim, 201

Kippot, 131

King, Jr., Martin Luther, 77, 104, 176

Kirshblum, I. Usher, 109

Kishinev, 7

Klein, Isaac, 50, 86

Klein, Max, 15, 26

Kling, Simcha, 157, 205, 256

Knesset. See Masorti movement

Kohen, Leon, 25

Kohler, Kaufmann, 2

Kohn, Eugene, 37, 39, 41, discussions on ideology, 47, 49, 174; on Jewish education, 56–57

Kohn, Jacob, 7, 10, 11, 12, 39, 177; and Conservative movement ideology, 24, 26, 27; and education, 179; in opposition to Adler, 30, 32; and liturgy, 14, 31; in Society of the Jewish Renascence *(see Tehiat Yisrael)*; and United Synagogue, 14, 24

Kohut, Alexander, 2, 3

Kollin, Gilbert, 76

Konigsburg, Randall, 155

Kose, Elvin, 206

Kotkow, W. P., 25

Kreiman, Angel, 237

Kreitman, Benjamin, 92, 109, 267

Kushner, Harold, 129, 139, 187, 256

Lamport, Solomon, 25

Lang, Leon, 54–55, 57, 77, 78, 79

Languages, Hebrew, 8, 46, 53, 73, 125, 138, 140, 195, 236; Yiddish, 2, 16, 171

Latin America, 239–242; Conservative Judaism in, 142, 195, 235–236, 238, 266, 267; discussions of *hok hahamara,* 237–238; rabbinical school of *(see* Seminario Rabinico Latinamericano); and RA, 237; and RAVLAT, 237; relationship to Israel, 236, 241, 263; role of rabbi in, 236–237, 242–243; and statistics, 145, 237,

239, 240, 242; *Vaad Hakavod*, 237

Latin American Union of Rabbis (URAL), 237, 243

Leadership Training Fellowship (LTF). *See* Youth

Lederer, Ephraim, 12

Leeser, Isaac, 188, 192

Left-Right Split. *See under specific individual names;* Conservative Judaism, disparate views on

Lerner, Stephen, 146

Letofsy, Alan, 239

Levi, S. Gershon, 78, 102

Levin, Mordejai, 237

Levine, David, 4

Levine, Morris, 9

Levinthal, Israel, 56, 177, 179

Levitzky, Louis, 56, 58, 74, 77

Levy, Mordecai, 111

Lichter, Benjamin, 11

Lieber, David, 139, 158, 237, 256, 257, 258

Lieberman, Saul, 35; Lieberman clause (*takkanah*), 90, 92–93, 103, 139

Liknaitz, David, 6

Lissauer, Herman, 23

Lubow, Akiba, 152

Lupo, Rudolph, 26

Ma'ariv, 215

Machon Schechter, 143, 194, 243, 250, 251, 266, 268

Magidson, Beverly, 110–111, 112

Magnes, Judah, 10, 11, 24, 30, 201

Maimonides, 39

Mandel, Morris, 4

Mandelbaum, Bernard, 203

Mara d'atra, 88, 121

Marans, Arnold, 254

Margolis, Elias, 25

Margolis, Max, 25

Margoshes, Samuel, 16

Marshall, Louis, 23, 28

Marx, Alexander, 25, 30, 31, 58

Masorti movement, 142, 154, 199–203, 210–211, 214, 231, 267; conversion, 219, 226–228, 262–264; in *Emet Ve-Emunah*, 223; *Et La'asot* (journal), 143; and Institute for Converts, 219, 227–228; and Israeli politics, 144–145, 229, 230, 262–264; and military service, 216–217; rabbinic legitimacy issues of, 212–217, 218, 219–222, 226–231, 262–263; and RA International, 222–224, 250, 251, 266, 270 (*see also* Neeman Commission); statistics of, 208, 222, 231; *Va'ad Halakhah*, 143, 219, 224–226; *Vaadat HaGiyur*, 227

Meir, Gideon, 263

Melamed, R. H., 25

MERCAZ, 142, 262

Mercaz Olami, 267

Meyer, Marshall, 91, 145, 234, 239, 266; as founder of Seminario Rabinico Latinamericano, 235, 242, 243

Meyers, Joel, on behalf of the American Jewish community, 267; creating effective rabbinate, 251; on issues of homosexuality, 120; for Latin American rabbis, 237; as mediator in Israel, 223–224, 229, 263; as mediator with JTS and University of Judaism, 258–259; position of executive vice president of RA, 152, 153, 251, 254, 255

Midrashim, 148

Mikveh, 127–128, 129. *See also* Grossman, Susan; Women

Mikve Israel, 29, 192

"Modern Problems of Jewish Parents" (Kohn), 179

Minkin, Jacob S., 9
Moreh Derekh, 138–139
Morais, Sabato, 2, 3, 12
Mysticism, 148

Nadell, Pamela, 268
Nadich, Judah, 74, 106, 157
Nathan, Marvin, 11
National Council of Catholic Bishops, 261
National Council of Synagogues, 261
National Jewish Population Study, 157, 269
"Nationalism as a Religious Dogma" (Kaplan), 7
Nativ, Gil, 229
Nazism, 41, 48, 59, 174, 242
Neeman, Yaakov, 229
Neeman Commission. *See* Israel
Netanyahu, Benjamin, 229, 262
Neulander, Arthur, 26, 90
Neuman, Abraham, 9
Neumann, Emanuel, 25
Neve Schechter. *See* Machon Schechter
Novak, David, 111, 113

Orthodox Union (OU), 264
Orthodoxy, 1, 70, 87, 88, 131, 178, 261, 266. *See also* Israel; Latin America; and affiliated congregations, 6, 10, 33, 114; difference from Conservative interpretations, 9, 13, 34, 44–45, 51, 116, 129, 133, 74, 181; and intermarriage, 158; merging with United Synagogue, 46; resurgency of, 101, 129, 180, 188; structure of, 23; and women, 109
"Our Standpoint" (Ginzberg), 33

Palestine. *See* Israel
"Parallels and Contrasts in Roman and Jewish Law" (Hyamson), 16

Parzen, Herbert, 32, 39, 50, 55
Patrilineal and matrilineal lineage, 112, 116–117, 124
Pearlmutter, Fishel, 107
Peli, Pinhas, 239
Penimiah. See Schechter Institute of Jewish Studies
Pereira Mendes, Henry, 2, 24, 46
Perlman, Jonathan, 143
Perkins, Carl, 256
Petachim (journal), 203
Petuchowski, Jacob, 135, 137–138
Philipp, Alfred A., 209
Pittsburgh Conference of Reform Rabbis, 4
Pitzele, Peter, 155, 156
Placement Commission, in early years, 51, 55–56, 64–65, 68, 72–76, 78; change in emphases, 150–153, 249, 254; and congregations, 74, 190–193, 249–250, 255 (*see also* Rabbinate, Conservative; Rabbinic role); and early hardship pulpits, 175, 190; issues of homosexuality and, 119, 120, 123; and newly ordained, 251; non-pulpit positions, 140–142, 195, 245–247, 249–250; and pension fund, 74, 185–186; placement of women rabbis, 141, 248; Project RA, 151–152, 155; and United Synagogue, 255; winning trade union benefits, 71, 75–76, 184–186
Pluralism. *See under* Conservative Judaism
"Position paper on Women in the Synagogue" (Ginzberg), 16
"Position paper on use of unfermented wine for kiddush" (Ginzberg), 28, 51
Potok, Chaim, 139, 187, 256
Prayer book, early committee, 14, 25, 31, 52–54, 58. *See also* United

Synagogue; under Harlow, 134–137; Latin American siddur, 238; *Maḥzor for Rosh Hashanah and Yom Kippur,* 134, 135; *Sabbath and Festival Prayer book,* 79, 80–82, 134; *Siddur Sim Shalom,* 113, 137–138, 238, 256

Presidents of RA, list of. *See* Rabbinical Assembly

Price, Ronald, 113, 114

"Problems of the Jewish Ministry" (Goldstein), 22

Proceedings of the Rabbinical Assembly, 28, 50, 76, 78; book reviews in, 49; issues discussed in, 43, 70, 77

Project RA, 151–152, 155

Publications Committee, 134, 135, 136, 137, 256. *See also under individual names of editors;* and *Bulletin of the Rabbinical Assembly,* 57; and *Conservative Judaism,* 77–79, 82, 254, 256, 257; *Emet Ve-Emunah,* study guide of, 116; and haggadah, 136–137; and Hertz Ḥumash, 139–140, 256; issuance of first *luaḥ,* 139; and *maḥzor,* 134–135, 256; on mourning, 135–136, 257; prayer book and liturgy, 52–54, 64, 71, 79–82, 113, 133–140 *(see also* Prayer book; Harlow, Jules*);* and *Proceedings,* 28, 43, 49–50, 70, 76–77, 78; and *Rabbi's Manual,* 138–139; revision of, 139, 256; and *Tradition and Change,* 82–83; and weekday prayer book, 81–82, 256

Rabbi Isaac Elchanan Seminary. *See* Yeshiva University

Rabbinate, Conservative, 2; attitude towards Israel, 263–264 attitudinal divide between generations, 126, 155–156, 189, 196; and Blue Ribbon Committee, 189; as calling, 271; campaign of ordination of women, 106–113; as chaplains, 65–67, 85, 174, 175; Change of pulpit, 66, 72, 74–75,188, 190–193; change of congregational attitudes towards, 247; congregation-rabbi relationships, 67, 186–188, 189, 190, 191–192; dissatisfaction in position of, 70–71, 183, 188–190, 192–193, 195–196; early years of, 3, 9, 22, 172–174; feminism impact on, 154–156; impact on American Jewish community, 93–94, 126, 175, 177–178, 181–182, 253; and interview, 76; making *aliyah,* 175, 176, 200–202, 208–210, 216, 266; manpower, early years of, 66, 68, 140; ordination title of, 69, 188; personal observance, 126, 183; as professional career, 55, 71–72, 140–141, 172–174, 189; and ritual and liturgy, 182, 183, 186, 191; statistics on, 179–181, 189–190; status of, 65, 71, 75–76, 130; survey of rabbis, 155; as synonym to RA, 99, 199; training of, 180, 191; women rabbis in, 150 , 194, 248 *(see also* Rabbinical Assembly*)*

Rabbinate, Orthodox, 2, 43, 44, 66, 69–70, 227; as refugee rabbis, 55

Rabbinate, Reform, 55, 69–70, 93, 126, 173

"The Rabbinic and Prophetic Attitude towards Ceremonies" (Israeli), 16

Rabbinic Role, *See also* Rabbinate, Conservative; in community, 126, 145–146, 175–176, 177–178, 246–248; comparison to other denominations, 69–70; as

Rabbinic Role *(cont.)*
counselor, 176, 191–192; as exemplar and scholar, 22, 149, 150, 191, 250, 271–272; in Latin America, 235, 236; modern images of, 21–22, 57, 69, 172, 173, 174, 191; origins of, 171–172; priest vs. prophet in, 171, 176, 177, 191, 195; self-image in, 76, 153–154, 190, 196, 247–248; Sephardic terms for, 172; as sermonizer, 125, 174, 175, 194; views of Greenberg and Kelman on, 54, 69

Rabbinical Assembly, The. *See also individual committees, names, and topics*; administation of, 72–73, 74, 76, 108, 253–255; and behavior codes for, 73, 75, 78, 108; challenges of modernism, 181–182, 183; changes of name, 58, 64, 86; Conservative ideology and disparate views of, 47, 51, 59, 65, 100, 114, 124; congregation growth, 265–268; continuing education of rabbis, 78, 141–142, 220, 221, 250–252, 254; creation of relief fund, 56, 78; definition of, 27, 28; during the Adler era, 29–33, 192 (*see also* Alumni Association); early convention highlights, 48, 50–55; and establishment of National Council of Synagogues, 261; and Finkelstein, 47, 57, 58; formation of retired rabbis association, 153, 251; and *havurot*, 146–147, 148; honorary members in, 246; impact as national organization, 22–23, 28, 58, 260–262, 264–265 (*see also* American Jewish Community); impact as international organization, 68, 142–145, 248, 259–260, 268 , 270–271 (*see also under individual countries)*; and intermarriage, 157–158; and JTS, 51, 59, 76, 84, 116, 121, 250; as mediator, 77, 258–259, 268, 270–271; membership in, 57, 58, 64, 68, 99, 123–124, 175, 252–253, 259; mission statement of, 244–245; new challenges for, 252, 266–268, 269–270; and ordination, 67, 68, 75; ordination of women and, 183–184 (*see also* CJLS; RA, women rabbis and membership; Women); and paraprofessionals, 142; presidents, list of, 77, 273; and the rabbinic family, 153–155, 251, 252; recent statistics and demographics, 244, 245–246; and relations with United Synagogue , 24, 29, 58, 77, 193–194, 255; role in JTS and University of Judaism conflict, 258–259; separation from JTS, 45, 47, 85, 87, 103, 108, 110, 193; and Solomon Schechter, 23, 55, 58; in support of United Jewish Communities, 265; and technology, 254, 269–270; and Union for Conservative Judaism, 113–114; women rabbis and membership, 103, 108, 110–111, 112–113, 248

Rabbinical Council of America (RCA), 55, 65, 227, 264, 265

Rabinowitz, Elias M., 8

Rabinowitz, Stanley, 109, 117, 153, 156

Ramah, Camp, 104, 141, 159, 182, 239, 253

Rank, Perry, 256

Re'em, Moshe, 143

Reconstructionist movement, 15, 26, 77; and egalitarian changes, 104; and homosexuality, 118, 119; in Israel, 203; and liturgy, 80; Reconstrucionist Rabbinical Association (RRA), 265; and stance on patrilineal lineage, 117

Reform movement, 1, 3, 6, 23, 51, 66, 88, 109, 229; affiliated congregations, 33; first woman rabbi, 104; and homosexuality, 118; and intermarriage, 158; stance on patrilineal lineage, 112, 116–117

Reisinger, Dan, 136

Reisner, Avram, 256

Religious Action Center, 257

Religious school, 8, 16, 121

"Religious Text-books" (Coffee), 8

Responsa, *See under names of individual scholars;* CJLS; Halakhah

Riemer, Jack, 78, 257

Robison, Aaron, 25

Rosenblum, Herbert, 10, 11, 94

Rosenthal, Henry, 49

Rosoff, Jack, 108

Roth, Joel, 120

Roth, Joseph, 23

Routtenberg, Max, 32, 45, 47, 58, 83; as chair of CJLS, 90, 92; executive vice president, 70, 73, 74, 253; president of RA, 77

Rubenovitz, Herman, beginnings of movement, 10, 11–13; and Conservative movement ideology, 15, 26, 27, 39, 47; definition of Conservative Judaism, 13; formation of United Synagogue, 14–15, 24; with early RA involvement, 24, 32, 50; in opposition to Adler, 30, 32; and Society for the Jewish Renascence, 25 *(see Tehiat Yisrael)*

Russian Jewry, 7, 143, 227

Sabbath and Festival Prayer Book (Silverman), 80–81, 134, 137

Sabbath and holidays, halakhah on, 87, 88, 91, 94, 100, 183; *ḥavurot* and, 146; liturgy of, 27, 79–82,

124–126, 133–140; music on, 90, 130; observance of, 2, 70, 85, 87–89, 114, 132, 182, 213; Sabbath Revitalization Program, 88–89, 93; and suburban laity, 87–89, 113, 124,145–146

Sacks, Andrew, 219

Salit, Norman, 26, 51, 72

Sandrow, Edward, 39, 74, 77

Schechter, Solomon, beginnings of Conservative Judaism, 3, 10, 13, 14, 24; concept of "Catholic Israel", 46; death of, 24, 46; as founder of Rabbinical Assembly, 23, 58; and rabbis, 7, 13, 22, 55, 173, 194; role in JTS, 7, 268–269; in *Tradition and Change*, 82; and United Synagogue, 6

Schechter Insitute for Jewish (Judaic) Studies, 194, 203; first Conservative yeshiva, 218

Schiff, Jacob H., 252

Schoenberg, Elliott Salo, 153, 237, 249, 251, 254, 255

Schorsch, Ismar, against Orthodox rabbinate in Israel, 144; as chancellor of JTS, 114, 259, 262; decision regarding homosexuality, 121, 122; and Jewish continuity and inreach, 122, 158; and pluralism, 114; on ethnicity, 131; on Shabbat morning worship, 125

Schulweis, Harold, 122, 146, 187

Schwab, Laura, 255

Schwartz, Barry Dov, 119

Schwarz, Sidney, 93

Scouting. *See* Youth

Scult, Mel, 40

Segal, Bernard, 72, 73, 253

Seliḥot, 82

Seminario Rabinico Latinamericano, 194, 235, 236–237, 239, 242, 243, 259; *Bet Din le-Sidur Gittin,* 242; *Bet Din le-Giurim,* 242

Sephardim, 46, 172, 217, 234; Shas party, 218, 219
Shapiro, Alexander, 111, 113, 114, 115, 156
Shapiro, Edward, 65
Siddur Sim Shalom. *See* Publications Committee; Prayer book Committee; Cahan, Leonard; Harlow, Jules
Siegel, Charles, 208, 209, 210, 211, 212, 214, 216
Siegel, Seymour, 102, 103, 105, 118, 239
Sigal, Philip, 91
Silver, Abba Hillel, 174, 188
Silverman, Israel, 90, 181
Silverman, Joseph, 3
Silverman, Morris, 52, 54, 80
Silverstein, Alan, 125, 158, 237, 256, 258, 268
Simon, Charles, 267
Simon, Matthew, 117
Simon, Ralph, 77
Sklare, Marshall, 79, 80–81, 83, 93
Social Action Committee, 148–149. *See also* Social Justice Committee
Social justice, 7
Social Justice Committee, 40, 55, 59, 77, 78; publication of annual position papers, 257; shift away from, 148–149; *tikkun olam*, 147; Washington advocacy day, 257
Society for the Advancement of Judaism (SAJ), 26, 27, 203
Society of the Jewish Renascence. *See Tehiat Yisrael*
Solomon Schechter Day Schools, 122, 141, 159, 180, 253
Solomon, Elias, 14, 15, 16, 24
"Some Weeds of Orthodox Judaism" (Egelson), 9–10
Speaker, Henry M., 4, 6, 7, 12, 15
Spectre, Barbara, 207
Spectre, Philip, 142, 207, 208–210, 212, 213, 215; as chaplain,

216–217; as head of Masorti movement, 209
Spirituality, 129–133, 175
Steinberg, Milton, 31, 37, 39, 40, 49, 187, 188
Strassfeld, Michael, 136, 148
"Survey of Adult Education Through the Synagogues"(Lang), 54–55
Sussman, Gerald, 113
Synagogue-Center, 21, 41, 57
Synagogue Council of America, 21, 59, 261
Synagogues, and *aliyot*, 10; behavior in, 126; and bingo, 92; competition for affiliation with secular agencies, 65; confirmation in, 70, 178; construction on the Sabbath, 90; demographics, 67, 73, 159, 100–101; and development of, 87, 265–268; and education, 54, 59, 175; with federations, 57; *ḥavurot*, 146–147, 176; and homosexuality, 119, 122; innovations in worship, 2, 147, 182; liturgy, 2, 133–134; membership, 65, 67, 87, 100, 159; music in, 90, 130, 181; physical structure, 70, 175, 181, 186; and seating, 2, 16, 92; second day observance of festivals, 77, 92, 126; standards in, 91; statistics, 67, 73, 100,159; swimming pools as *mikveh* in, 92; *tallis* and *tefillin minyanim*, 178; worship services, 124–125, 146, 147, 186, 191
Szold, Benjamin, 2

Taharat ha-mishpahah, 113
TALI schools, 143, 210, 218, 231
T'nai b'kiddushin. *See* CJLS; *Get;* Lieberman, Saul
"Techinot in Jewish Literature" (Dobrzynski), 8
Tehiat Yisrael (Society for the Jewish Renascence), 25, 47

Teplitz, Saul, 109
"The Continuity of Jewish Tradition" (Rubenovitz), 13
"The Development of the Jewish Liturgy" (Solomon), 16
"The Future of Judaism in America" (Kohn), 49
"The Halacha as a Source of Jewish History" (Ginzberg), 16
"The Importance of the Halakha in the Study of Jewish Theology" *(Ginzberg)*, 7
'The Making of the Modern Jew" (Steinberg), 49
"The Purpose and Scope of the Jewish Religious School" (Greenstone), 8
"The Rabbi and the Center Movement" (Armond Cohen), 57
"The Second Book of Esdras" (Schechter), 7
"The Sunday School" (Ehrenreich), 8
"The Things that Unite Us" (Finkelstein), 37
"This Is My Beloved, This Is My Friend: A Rabbinic Letter on Intimate Relations" (Dorff), 257
Tikkun Olam. See Social Action Committee
Torah, reading of, 91, 125; carrying of *(hakafot)*, 106
"Towards a Philosophy of Conservative Judaism" (Friedman, Ginzberg, Greenfeld, Klein), 86
Tradition and Change (Waxman), 82, 83
"Tradition and the Bible" *(*Kaplan), 16
Tulin, Shaia, 31
Tutnauer, Moshe, 239

Union for Traditional Judaism, 113–114, 184
Union of American Hebrew Congregations, 23, 261, 262, 264

Union of Orthodox Jewish Congregations, 23, 46
Union of Orthodox Rabbis, 23, 264
United Hebrew Charities, 9
United Jewish Appeal, 176, 262; and creation of Unity Campaign, 264
United Jewish Communities, 264, 265
United Synagogue of America, in American Jewish community, 264; an "Agudath Jeshurun", 14; and Alumni Association, 16; beginning leadership of, 25, 28 committees of, 14, 25–28, 41, 59; constitution preamble, 46; early functions, 14, 27, 28; convention worship services, 125; development of synagogues, 266–268; and establishment of National Council of Synagogues, 261; ideological issues, 33, 46, 47, 59, 174; importance of education, 16, 46; and Israel, 204, 210, 229; liturgy and prayer book, 14, 31, 46, 58; and membership, 14; origins of, 6, 11–14, 22, 24; and ordination of women, 109; and Placement Commission, 55, 75, 255; relationship with RA, 24, 28, 58, 91, 255, 266; tensions between Rabbinical Assembly and, 29; usage of *Sabbath and Festival Prayer Book*, 80–81; and Wartime Emergency Commission, 72
United Synagogue Recorder, 25, 50, 51
United Synagogue Youth (USY), 91, 92, 101, 183
University of Judaism, 38, 73; Ziegler School of Rabbinic Studies, 141, 194, 257–259
Veghazi, Istvan, 239
Vietnam War, 77, 140, 176
"Vitalizing Public Worship" (Silverman), 54

Waldman, Morris, 4, 9
Waxman, Meyer, 9
Waxman, Mordecai, 78, 82, 83, 102, 261
Weilerstein, Reuben, 56
Weine, Max, 242
Weiss Halivni, David, 113
Wernik, Joseph, 267
Wertheimer, Jack, 9, 158; Ratner Center for the Study of Conservative Judaism survey, 158, 159
Wexler, Robert, 258, 259
Williamson, Arleigh, 180
Wilkes, Paul, 183
Winter, Bobbie, 155
Winter, Edward, 155
Wise, Isaac Mayer, 2, 12
Wise, Stephen, 174, 188
Wittenberg, David H., 4
Wohlberg, Jeffrey, 239
Wolkin, Carl, 267
Women. See also Agunah; and aliyot, 89, 103, 183; as bat mitzvah, 103, 182, 183; in Conservative Judaism, 104–113, 114–115; and feminist issue, 103–105; in Jewish law, 16, 84, 89, 90, 91, 103,104, 106; and mikveh, 127–128; in minyan, 105, 106, 183; and ordi-

nation of women rabbis, 106–113, 108, 183, 194, 248; and Orthodoxy, 109; wearing of tefillin, 104
Women's League, 91
Woocher, Jonathan, 149
World Council Newsletter, 211
World Council of Synagogues, 204, 210, 212, 239, 266, 267, 268
World Jewish Congress, 261
World War II, 22, 41, 84, 104; war years, 16, 65–67, 72, 175

Yearnings, 82
Yeshiva University, 23, 39, 46
Yoffie, Eric, 263
"You Shall Strengthen Them: A Rabbinic Letter on the Poor" (Dorff), 257
Youth, 78, 92, 104, 180, 183

Zangwill, Israel, 130
Zelizer, Gerald, 120–121, 123, 153, 239, 256
Zionism, 7, 21, Adler's attitude towards, 30, 33; and Conservative movement, 29, 77, 78, 83, 200, importance of, 174; in Latin America, 234, 241
"Zionism in the Pulpit" (Kohn), 79